TERRA AUSTRALIS

Praise for *Australia: A History*

'I have long respected Tony Abbott as a great wordsmith. His writing is lucid and direct. These talents are on display in his book on Australian history. It presents a balanced assessment of the contributions of those who have bulked large in our history such as Bob Menzies and John Curtin. It does not shrink from confronting controversial episodes involving Indigenous peoples and other early Australians. This is an immensely readable account of how – as I frequently call it – the "Australian Achievement" has been built' – Hon John Howard OM AC, former Prime Minister of Australia

'Scholarly researched, scrupulously fair-minded and very engagingly written, this is big narrative history at its best. It explains why Australia is such a wonderfully unique place, and why history is all the better when written by those who themselves helped make it' – Andrew Roberts, author of *Churchill: Walking with Destiny*

'Tony Abbott has written with reverence and richness, bringing our nation's past, although both painful and proud, to life with striking clarity. This is not a political text, it's a truthful account. It doesn't sugarcoat our past; it confronts it with courage, dignity and care. This book reminds us that we are all part of the story of this magnificent, ancient and richly modern Australia. It includes us, not erases us. This book deserves a place in every home and every school' – Nova Peris OAM OLY, first Aboriginal Australian Olympic gold medallist and former Labor senator

'Tony Abbott's book is inspired by love of country, yet he comes to grip with our flaws. This is a fresh, powerful, highly readable single-volume history of Australia that deserves a wide audience' – Paul Kelly, editor at large, *The Australian*

'Tony Abbott has been a devoted controversialist who wears his heart on his sleeve and is a good writer. These attributes come through in this book but [has] added massive research and an effort for balance. There is a fair bit with which I would have a different point of view. He stays firmly in the conservative camp. But if you have a serious interest in Australian history, the book will go on your shelves' – Hon Kim Beazley AC, former Deputy Prime Minister of Australia

'Australia's history is a tapestry of resilience and ingenuity. It is a story of disparate peoples pulling together against the odds to form a nation that is now the envy of the world. Tony Abbott provides an honest account of Australia's achievements, setbacks and enduring challenges, examining Australia's distant past and more contemporary events. This book is a compelling reminder of our inheritance, which gives us a reason to be proud of who we are and the country we've become' – Jacinta Nampijinpa Price, federal senator for Northern Territory

'*Australia: A History* is a masterfully told narrative that captures the spirit, struggle and triumph of a young nation shaped by an ancient land. With clarity, conviction and deep respect for the people and moments that forged modern Australia, Tony Abbott brings history to life in a way that is both enlightening and deeply engaging. His unique perspective, as both a scholar and a statesman, adds immense value to this work, offering readers a thoughtful, balanced and timely reflection on what makes Australia extraordinary. A remarkable contribution to our national story' – Brett Lee, former Australian international cricketer

'Tony Abbott's latest book is a powerful antidote to the poison of little and bad history. It reflects deep research, a commitment to the facts, a generosity of spirit and beautiful writing – and the more widely read it is, the more we will appreciate that while we can always learn from past mistakes, we have much to be thankful for and to build on' – Hon John Anderson AC, former Deputy Prime Minister and Leader of the National Party

'Tony Abbott brings a unique perspective to Australia's history – one which might make some feel vindicated for their beliefs, will encourage some to revisit what is accepted as the only angle on a past event, and will stir debate. By writing a history of Australia, Tony Abbott has channelled his inner Antipodean Winston Churchill, who famously wrote storied volumes about the history of the English-speaking people' – Bill Shorten, former Leader of the Opposition and Leader of the ALP

'As someone who came to this country as a refugee and now serves in the Australian Parliament, I see my family's journey as part of the broader Australian story – shaped by Indigenous culture, British settlement and waves of migration. Tony Abbott is a man who loves his country and its history. He doesn't shy away from its complexity – acknowledging the suffering of Indigenous peoples, the hardship of early settlers, and the contributions of migrants and refugees. This book helps us rediscover our past with honesty and respect, so we can better understand our present and shape a stronger, more inclusive future' – Dai Le MP, independent member for Fowler

'Not quite the "white armband" version of Australian history I was expecting in the first half, nor the "Liberal Party highlights package" I feared in the second half. I enjoyed reading it' – Peter FitzSimons, author, *Kokoda*

AUSTRALIA

A History

TONY ABBOTT

Foreword by Geoffrey Blainey

HarperCollinsPublishers

Aboriginal and Torres Strait Islander people are respectfully advised that this book contains descriptions, images and names of people now deceased.

HarperCollins*Publishers*

Australia • Brazil • Canada • France • Germany • India • Italy • Japan
Mexico • Netherlands • New Zealand • Poland • Spain • Sweden
Switzerland • United Kingdom • United States of America

First published in Australia in 2025
by HarperCollins*Publishers* Australia Pty Limited
ABN 36 009 913 517
harpercollins.com.au

HarperCollins*Publishers*
Macken House, 39/40 Mayor Street Upper
Dublin 1, D01 C9W8, Ireland

A catalogue record for this book is available from the National Library of Australia

ISBN 978 1 4607 6829 7 (hardback)
ISBN 978 1 4607 1899 5 (ebook)
ISBN 978 1 0381 0298 0 (international audiobook)

Cover design by Darren Holt, HarperCollins Design Studio
Jacket image: *Vaucluse, 1851* / painted by G. E. Peacock, courtesy Mitchell Library, State Library of New South Wales (ID: a128037)
Jacket flap: Tony Abbott by Jane Dempster Photography / Newspix
Endpapers: *A Complete Map of the Southern Continent*, Bowen, Emanuel, –1767, courtesy National Library of Australia
Typeset in Sabon LT Std by Kirby Jones

Printed and bound by CPI Group (UK) Ltd, Croydon, CR0 4YY

To my grandchildren,
Ernest, Romona and Angus,
and the new generation
that should take our country forward.

Contents

Foreword

by Geoffrey Blainey

Tony Abbott should be congratulated. For a prime minister to write a history of Australia, after his term of office was over, was an unlikely event – until this year. Even in the United Kingdom, with such a long succession of leaders, rarely has a top politician written a history of the country: Sir Winston Churchill is the brilliant exception.

This book not only evaluates facets of the political career of many other Australian leaders but tells the history of the nation. It begins with the First Fleet sailing into Sydney's harbour in January 1788 after completing one of the longest voyages of colonisation in the known history of the world, and it ends early this year. Tony Abbott is brave to become a historian, for he has to revisit his own time in Canberra and confront his admirers and critics.

Mostly a political history, Abbott provides a lucid outline of the steps by which Australia arose from a convict colony to a nation with a high range of political liberties. It is now recognised that Australia is one of the oldest *continuous* democracies in the world: Europe possibly has no equal. Tony's final verdict is that ours is a very successful nation, though scarred by failures.

In his reading list are many books written by authors who, being of another political colour to Abbott, will be surprised to find themselves quoted. Further, some political opponents at times are patted on the head rather than punched on the nose: Abbott when young was a boxer. For instance, high praise is offered to Kim Beazley, who happened to lead the Labor Party when Abbott was a political apprentice in Canberra. Paul Keating is praised as a strong debater, though less as a policymaker. Bob Hawke, if alive, would be delighted to read some pages of this book. Abbott writes that Australian voters in the 1930s depression 'had turned to Joseph Lyons; in the 1980s they turned to another healer and patriot'. Take a bow, Bob Hawke.

On the Liberal side, Abbott admires 'Bob' Menzies and John Howard, both of whom overcame a crucial failure or defeat then led their team and nation – between them for a total of nearly 30 years. Of his own achievements, Abbott is correct to point out – without boasting – that 'Australia is the only country in recent times to have stopped a wave of illegal immigration by boat'. Today, many European leaders, wishing they could cope with illegal immigration, would like to learn Abbott's secret.

This history offers a variety of observations and facts that are new to me and, I also assume, will be to other readers. One example is that 25 Australian nurses died on active service in the First World War. I was surprised, too, to read about Stanley Melbourne Bruce, prime minister from 1923 to 1929. The suicidal streak in Bruce's close relatives is eye-opening.

On crucial national events in wartime and peacetime, Abbott offers new insights and evidence. Sometimes I disagree, but that calls for no apology or explanation on my part. The hundred or more historians he mentions often disagree with one another. The study of the past thrives on debate.

He believes it is vital that we learn from our history. The high level of public ignorance is presumably one reason why he decided to climb over the fence and explore. He reports with dismay that, in a recent survey, 47 per cent of Australians believed that James Cook and his wooden ship *Endeavour* were in the first 'convict fleet' that sailed through Sydney Heads in 1788. In fact, Cook had been dead for years. Abbott also remarks, with clinching examples, how often the weather officials – or the people who misreport them – exaggerate the uniqueness of our recent floods, bushfires and other natural disasters.

This history of Australia is vivid, readable, provocative in some chapters, very tolerant in others, and usually patriotic without being flag-fluttering.

Geoffrey Blainey, AC, FAHA, FASSA, March 2025

Author's Note

This is the book that should never have been needed. Until quite recently it was taken for granted that Australia was a country that all its citizens could take pride in, even the Aboriginal people, for whom the 1967 referendum marked full, if belated, acceptance into the Australian community. But a generation of anxiety over Indigenous dispossession, and the academic triumph of what Geoffrey Blainey has called the 'black armband view' of Australian history, has left many Australians ambivalent about our past, even though it's far more good than bad.

I am not a professional historian and this is a personal account based on the existing sources. My hope is that a history by someone who has tried to shape it, however briefly and imperfectly, could have an appeal that a more academic exercise might lack. As well, I've had a passion for history, at least since my mother routinely brought home for the primary school-aged me the Ladybird 'adventures from history' books that were popular in the 1960s. Charles Moore accurately described their tenor: 'the overall picture is of great things done ... the Ladybird understanding that [history] is affected and dramatised by great men and women still convinces'.[1]

As a person whose adult life has been spent in the battle of ideas, I believe that individuals and their ideas matter;

hence this history attempts to illuminate the key individuals and the key ideas that have shaped our country. As will be plain to the reader, it's my conviction that Australia has been a fundamentally 'liberal' project. Even to Arthur Phillip, our first governor, the mission was not to establish a prison but to improve lives. There's been a consistent high-mindedness, a largeness of spirit or *liberality*, at least by the standards of their day, in almost all those who've sought to shape our country, from the early governors to more recent MPs. Overwhelmingly, they've seen their essential task, as Ben Chifley – prime minister from 1945 to 1949 – put it in his famous Light on the Hill speech, 'not as putting an extra sixpence in somebody's pocket, or making somebody prime minister or premier but ... bringing something better to the people ... working for the betterment of mankind, not only here but anywhere we may give a helping hand'.[2]

My perspective on the events of our past certainly won't be everyone's. I'm convinced, though, that on the objective facts as best we can know them, it's a story to be proud of: how outcasts among outcasts, in a hitherto timeless land, could create a country that millions have flocked to ever since. It's precisely because our national story is so well worth telling that I want it to be better known.

Just about all of us are endlessly curious about our parents and grandparents and also about our more distant ancestors, as the interest in family trees and social histories attests. 'How did they live and what did they do?' are the questions we typically ask and seek to answer. And most of us delight in telling and retelling the stories from our own past, sometimes understandably embellished to put ourselves in the best possible light. Indeed, most of us would regard individuals who know little of their personal past as not only somewhat strange but as unmoored, even adrift.

Yet there's not, currently, a comparable interest in our country's history, even though it's hard to understand the present or to plan effectively for the future without a sound knowledge of what's gone before. A 2019 survey reportedly found that 31 per cent of Australians thought that Captain Cook was the first European to land in Australia and that 47 per cent thought that his ship, the *Endeavour*, was part of the First Fleet that arrived in January 1788.[3]

It would hardly be surprising that a country in which ignorance or misconceptions about its history are widespread should be prone to believe the worst of itself. In 2023, a poll found that 56 per cent of Australians under 25 wanted January 26 to be known as 'Invasion Day', even though it marked the planting of a colony, albeit a penal one, and Governor Phillip had been instructed to 'live in amity' with the native inhabitants.[4]

This book is intended to give anyone interested – as every Australian should be – an account of our past that's positive, while not oblivious to our mistakes and imperfections as a nation. If, with all things considered, to be an Australian is still to have won the lottery of life, the history that's produced us is something to savour.

This book takes readers from British settlement through to a key recent decision point, the rejection of the proposed entrenchment in our nation's Constitution of a new body chosen by Indigenous people only and comprising Indigenous people only but with a significant say over the government of all of us. Its proponents saw this as a long overdue acknowledgment of the special place that Aboriginal people should always have had in modern Australia. To its critics, though, and I was one, the Voice to the parliament and to the executive government on matters 'relating' to Indigenous affairs would have given those whose ancestry in this country stretched back past 1788 a status and a say beyond that of everyone else. Far from being an exercise in negativity, to me, its rejection was the positive reassertion of an Australia in which none of its three elements of an Indigenous heritage, a British foundation or its immigrant character – a formulation first suggested to me by the work of Noel Pearson – took official priority over the others. In saying 'no' to race-based divisions, we actually said 'yes' to a society that's essentially colourblind, which is why I regard the referendum as a recent high point in our history.

Without claiming to be either definitive or comprehensive, this history of what was once called *Terra Australis Incognita*, the unknown south land, does aim to give the reader enough of our past story, the issues we've dealt with and the challenges we've met, to make more sense of our present – and, therefore, to spur more optimism and confidence for building our future together.

Introduction

When modern Australia began in 1788, it didn't emerge in a vacuum. Modern Australia involved the collision of two worlds: the ancient Aboriginal one and the modern British one. Over time, they would blend into what has become, arguably, the world's most successful immigrant nation.

This introduction is not an elaborate account of premodern Australia or of British history prior to the late 18th century. Still, these remain key elements in our story so need to be grasped if today's Australia is to be understood and appreciated.

§

In 1788, the modern world erupted into an ancient continent that had been substantially undisturbed for over 10,000 years – since the seas had risen after the last ice age, broken the land bridge from Southeast Asia and separated Tasmania from the mainland. Some 50,000 years before that, the first discoverers and pioneers had walked and paddled from the Asian landmass, through what's now Papua New Guinea (PNG) to northern Australia and thence throughout the continent, which they'd proceeded to occupy for many hundreds of generations. Since long before the beginning of recorded history, other than a bit of canoe traffic around northern Queensland and some trepang trading with Indonesian fishermen, the Aboriginal people of Australia, and the Aboriginal people of Tasmania, were entirely isolated from the changes slowly taking place elsewhere in the world.

Their story is now largely lost to us, glimpsed mainly through the surviving fragments found in archaeological sites; in such oral histories as have been recorded since 1788; and in what we can deduce from what we know of later lives. In 2016, the oldest axe fragment in the world was discovered in the Kimberley region of Western Australia, suggesting a sophistication to the lives of the first Australians at least equal to that of elsewhere at the time.[1] The voices of ancient Australia also survive in the rock art left behind. There are more than 100,000 rock art sites in Australia, some up to 30,000 years old.[2] The Gwion Gwion rock paintings of the northern Kimberley are particularly striking, depicting elaborately dressed figures quite unlike anything found by the first Europeans.

What the more acute Europeans did notice was a timelessness to Aboriginal being, described by the anthropologist W.E.H. Stanner as less a consciousness of past, present and possible future but of 'every-when' and a connectedness to country, almost a shared 'being-ness' with the land, which likewise almost defied description in English. Eventually, this 'one-ness' with time and place came to be described as the Dreaming.[3] And while the Aboriginal people did not practise agriculture as the settlers understood it, there was a form of cultivation – 'fire-stick farming', Tim Flannery called it – which created the park-like quality around Sydney that so struck the early settlers. Once this practice ceased, it led to the catastrophic bushfires that have plagued modern Australia.[4]

Because nothing was recorded, other than in paintings and in clan folklore, the latter told and retold down the generations, and now largely lost, we know little of specific people and events before 1788. What we do know, though, is that the Aboriginal peoples of Australia had survived, often ingeniously, on a harsh continent. Compared to most of Europe and the Americas, and much of Asia and Africa, this was no land of deep soils, vast rivers and teeming wildlife. Except in the far north of what would become Queensland and in the areas where fish were plentiful, such as the Murray–Darling Basin, there was little to sustain permanent occupation, so most Aboriginal people had a routine of movement governed by an intimate knowledge of the seasons and of the local flora and fauna.

As with comparable peoples elsewhere, it was a tough existence. A major drought could lead to famine. Women could be treated cruelly, and infanticide was common when food supplies were low. This is how Robert Hughes depicted it, and he was certainly no sentimentalist about British settlement:

> ... no property, no money ... no outside trade, no farming,
> no domestic animals ... no houses, clothes, pottery or
> metal; no division between leisure and labour, only a
> ceaseless grubbing and chasing for subsistence foods.
> Certainly the Iora [the Aboriginal people living in what
> became Sydney] failed most of the conventional tests
> of ... culture ... The Tahitians might live like prelapsarian
> beings, illiterate Athenians. Compared to them, the Iora
> were Spartans. They exemplified 'hard' primitivism and the
> name Phillip gave to a spot in Sydney Harbour alluded to
> this: 'Their confidence and manly behaviour ... made me
> give the name of Manly Cove to this place.'[5]

Even by 18th-century standards, the lives of Aboriginal people were largely ruled by natural events beyond their control. This must have bred the stoicism and the laconic approach to fortune – good and bad – that soon became characteristic of Australians, as the newcomers and the original inhabitants came to live among each other and to learn from each other.

* * *

In retrospect, it's surprising that it took European peoples so long to find Australia. The first known landing was by the Dutch East India Company mariner Willem Janszoon in 1606, on the western shore of what's now called Cape York. A few months later, a Spaniard, Luis de Torres, passed through the waters between Cape York and PNG that now bear his name; and it's likely that he saw some of the islands that are part of Australia. Similarly, it's possible that Portuguese navigators, who started going to East Timor in the 1500s, were occasionally blown too far and ended up on our inhospitable northwestern coast.

Then, in 1616, the Dutch captain Dirk Hartog, making for the trading settlement of Batavia on Java, got caught in the strong winds known as the Roaring Forties and eventually landed near what's now Shark Bay, north of Geraldton in Western Australia. He left behind a pewter plate that was discovered in 1697 by a subsequent off-course Dutch navigator, Willem de Vlamingh, and taken back to the Netherlands. Vlamingh left behind a new plate that incorporated Hartog's original inscription. In 1642, the celebrated Dutch adventurer Abel Tasman completely missed the Australian mainland, but sailed through the Great Australian Bight to reach what he called Van Diemen's Land, going ashore at North Bay and formally claiming possession for the Netherlands, before sailing east to make landfall in New Zealand. On a second voyage, two years later, he mapped much of western and northern Australia and named it 'New Holland'.

Other Dutch captains were blown onto our west coast. In 1629, a Dutch ship, the *Batavia*, ran aground and was wrecked on the Abrolhos Islands. The captain, Francisco Pelsaert, set off in a small boat for the Dutch East Indies in order to get help. Some of the remaining crew mutinied and killed over a hundred of their fellow survivors. When Pelsaert returned four months later, he executed seven of the mutineers. In 1727, another Dutch ship, the *Zeewijk*, was wrecked on the same islands. The survivors lived there for ten months before building a 59-foot (18-m) vessel that carried them and much of their cargo to Batavia.

The first Englishman to find Australia was William Dampier, who in 1688 spent two months near King Sound in northwest Western Australia while his ship was repaired. He was unimpressed by the local people, whom he described as the 'miserabilist' he'd ever seen.[6] In 1699, Dampier returned, this time to Shark Bay and points further up the western coast, along the way making the first written detailed account of Australian flora and fauna.

The east coast, though, was different: much better watered and with plenty of vegetation, as noted in 1770 by Captain James Cook, the first European to find it and sail its length. Cook first landed at what's now called Botany Bay, where he stayed for a week collecting botanical specimens and exploring the surrounding area. Much further north, at today's Cooktown, he spent seven weeks repairing his ship after the *Endeavour* hit the Great Barrier Reef and almost foundered. At what's now called Possession Island, in the Torres Strait, Cook claimed the entire coastline he'd just mapped as British territory.

At least twice, first at Botany Bay and then at Cooktown, Cook's crew fired on local Aboriginal people when he thought they were becoming dangerous, wounding one each time.

Cook's journal records the Aboriginal people of Botany Bay shouting 'warra warra wai', which he took to mean 'go away' but that may actually have meant 'they are all dead spirits'. But Cook's overall impression was by no means negative. In his journal, he wrote that while 'the Natives of New Holland ... may appear ... to be the most wretched People on Earth ... in reality they are far ... happier than we Europeans, being wholly unacquainted ... not only with the Superfluous but with the necessary conveniences ... They live in a Tranquility which is not disturbed by the Inequality of Condition.'[7]

Cook's expedition took on new meaning following Britain's defeat in the American Revolutionary War in 1783. The independent Americans would no longer receive the overflow from London's gaols (it's thought they had received some 100,000 convicts) so a new convict depository had to be found. Early sites of consideration included Senegal and Gambia, on Africa's west coast. The first alternative to be seriously entertained was Das Voltas Bay, Namibia, a coastal site of strategic importance that could be used to repair and refresh ships trading to India. But the idea was dropped after an expedition found the site fever-ridden, and attention turned to Botany Bay.

Both strategic and commercial motives guided the British government's choice of New South Wales as a convict colony. It would have been cheaper to send prisoners to the West Indies or Canada.[8] However, the east coast of Australia offered something grander and more ambitious: a new port of call in the East, far beyond the customary world, ushering in a new phase of British imperial endeavour. Cook's second expedition had identified that in Norfolk Island there was bounteous growth of a flax plant, whose fibrous stalks were thought to be a source of sailcloth and rope; and Joseph Banks, the brilliant botanist who had sailed on Cook's first expedition, had reported on the habitable terrain of Botany Bay. Another factor was Britain's intense geopolitical rivalry with France, then playing out across Europe, North America and the Pacific. Anxiety that the French had designs on New Holland prompted the administration of William Pitt the Younger to act quickly.[9]

When the First Fleet of convicts arrived in January 1788, Captain Arthur Phillip, observing Sydney Harbour, remarked, 'When this colony is the seat of empire, there is room for ships of all nations.'[10] This was to be no mere 'dumping ground'.

* * *

Despite the recent loss of its American colonies, the Britain of the 1780s had become the world's leading power and most enlightened country. The original inhabitants of southern and central England had been shaped first by Rome and then by Christianity, before suffering centuries of raids by the warlike seafarers of northern Europe and Scandinavia. After a final invasion, the Norman Conquest of 1066, England evolved slowly and organically into a unitary state with strong elements of local government (the shire-reeves, or sheriffs) and a legal system (the common law) based on precedent as well as statute and with strong elements of procedural justice.

After several centuries of mostly victorious warfare in France, as the Norman-descended English kings fought for their patrimony, and the social upheaval of the Reformation, which created the Protestant Church of England under Henry VIII, the offshore island became strong enough to defeat the 1588 Spanish Armada. This attempted invasion by the Latin American treasure-enriched strongest power in Europe aimed to restore Catholicism and avenge dynastic slights. Rallying the troops at Tilbury, the first Queen Elizabeth (Henry VIII's daughter) declared: 'I have always ... placed my chiefest safeguard in the loyal hearts and goodwill of my subjects, and therefore ...

resolved in the midst and heat of battle to live and die amongst you all ... I have the body of a weak and feeble woman but I have the heart and stomach of a king and of a king of England too ...'[11] In a somewhat similar vein, almost 400 years on, the second Elizabeth declared on her 21st birthday that her 'whole life, be it long or short, shall be devoted to your service and the service of our great imperial family to which we all belong'.[12]

From about the time of Alfred the Great (849–899), right down to our own King Charles III, monarchs have pledged in their coronation oath: first, to govern in accordance with the laws and customs of the people; second, to govern justly; and third, to uphold Christianity. At Runnymede, in 1215, the rapacious and duplicitous King John was forced by his mutinous nobles to agree to the Magna Carta, or great charter of freedoms, protecting rights, enshrining the courts and limiting royal prerogatives. Then, in 1258, the Provisions of Oxford were forced upon another weak monarch: thereafter, every king was required to govern according to law and regularly to summon parliament, a term first used in 1236 to describe the council of nobles and clergy. Under Edward I, in 1295, commoners – members of the emerging middle class – were summoned to parliament, because the reformist Edward believed that all those involved in paying taxes should have a say in their imposition. By the 14th century, parliament had taken on the form we see today, with elected representatives in the House of Commons and hereditary or appointed members in the House of Lords.

However imperfectly executed, thoughtful Britons continued groping towards a concept of authority at the service of the people, rather than as their master.

Despite the bloodletting among the nobility of the 15th-century Wars of the Roses, and the subsequent brutal royal dictatorship of Henry VIII, Elizabethan England had a well-developed system of justice administered by judges largely independent of the monarch; and of local control of local affairs. The feudal system, and notions of the 'divine right of kings', had never been as pervasive as on the continent, and had co-existed with the rights of prosperous towns and strong guilds of merchants and tradesmen.

In the famous speech from *Richard II* that Shakespeare puts into the mouth of John of Gaunt, he contrasts peaceable late-medieval normalcy with the tumult created by dynastic rivalry: 'this sceptred isle ... this other Eden, demi-paradise ... this happy breed of men ... this blessed plot, this earth, this realm, this England ... now leased out ... like to a tenement or pelting farm ... [that] hath made a shameful conquest of itself.'

By the time of the Stuarts (1603–1714) and the union of the crowns of England and Scotland, jurists such as Lord Justice Coke had started to articulate the notion, even to the king himself, that 'be you ever so high, the law is above you'.[13] It was to resolve this question of who was sovereign – the king or the parliament – that the English Civil War was fought.

After a brief republican experiment with Oliver Cromwell as Lord Protector (1649–1660), a restoration of the monarchy, and then a Glorious Revolution and a bill of rights to enshrine the supremacy of parliament, early 18th-century Britain – by then formally including Scotland and ruling Ireland – was the world's first constitutional monarchy. From the time of Sir Robert Walpole, regarded as the first prime minister (in office 1721–1742), the King reigned but did not rule. The monarch chose a first minister through whom to rule, who served at the king's pleasure, but was in practice collegial with other ministers (comprising the cabinet) and responsible to the parliament, which authorised the raising of money and made the laws of the country. The House of Commons had a very limited property-based franchise, and laws could be blocked by the House of Lords, so it was hardly a modern democracy, but the clear outline was there of government 'of the people, by the people, for the people' (in Abraham Lincoln's famous formulation).

These were some of the early milestones in the history of a country that the poet Tennyson described in the mid-1800s as:

A land of settled government,
A land of just and old renown,
Where Freedom slowly broadens down,
From precedent to precedent.[14]

Britain had also been developing militarily and economically. In the early 1700s, in the War of Spanish Succession, the British Army – commanded by Winston Churchill's great forebear the first Duke of Marlborough – became, for a time, the strongest in Europe. Then the Seven Years' War, culminating in the seizure of French Canada in 1763, established the Royal Navy as the world's most powerful and created what was to become the British Empire.

Unlike the subsequent French Revolution, which replaced an absolutist king with an absolutist state, the American one, starting in 1776 – brought about in part by resentment of the taxes on the American colonies to pay for the Seven Years' War – was to restore what the colonists saw as the traditional rights of Englishmen. These were freedom of speech, freedom of religion, freedom of association and, above all, the principle of responsible government: 'no taxation without representation'.

The Britain of the 1780s was that of the intellectuals David Hume, Adam Smith and Edmund Burke. It was at the forefront of the liberal enlightenment, of the development of private property rights, the growth of markets and the beginning of the anti-slavery crusade. As yet, it lacked tarmac roads, urban sanitation and universal education, but the seeds of all these were growing as the industrial and the scientific revolutions gathered pace. Here, more than anywhere else, the modern world at its best – free, humane and prosperous – was taking shape.

It was from here that the First Fleet set sail. This was the culture that animated the people on board. This was the underpinning of modern Australia: a country with an Indigenous heritage, a British foundation and an immigrant character, and, as we shall see in this, the story of us, a proud history all of our own.

1

An Enlightened Beginning

From the outset, Sydney could hardly have been less like a slave colony. The two most significant books the First Fleet brought with them were the Bible and Blackstone's *Commentaries on the Laws of England*. Governor Phillip's instinct for personal freedom and for convict reformation was in tension with his officer training and the British government's intention to create a small and well-ordered penal settlement. Because convicts in New South Wales had more legal rights than prisoners in England and because they were permitted to do their own thing once they finished work for the day, soon enough many were materially better off than their family members back home. The soldiers', ex-convicts' and free settlers' habits of self-advancement rapidly produced a lively and boisterous settlement quite at odds with the notion of a prison island and place of punishment. It's fitting that the text chosen for Australia's first Christian service was, 'What can I render unto the Lord for all his blessings to me'.[1] Harsh and strange though it could be, the new land was infused with faith and hope; and, in the first modern Australians, a spirit of can-do optimism.

§

As the first governor of the colony of New South Wales, Captain Arthur Phillip was the founder of modern Australia.

If not in command of a continental army, he was nonetheless commanding an unprecedented social experiment: a new settlement on the other side of the world, which turned out to be the world's greatest ever exercise in criminal rehabilitation. He was tasked with leading a flotilla comprising six convict transports, two armed vessels and three cargo ships 17,500 nautical miles (32,420 km) to Botany Bay, on the east coast of the vast southern land that Captain Cook had named New South Wales 18 years earlier.

Phillip well understood the magnitude of the venture. In the nine months prior to the fleet's departure, in preparation for the journey and the founding of a new colony, he penned hundreds of letters to Navy Board officials. Biographer Alan Frost has noted 'the touch of the visionary' in these writings: they reveal a leader determined to succeed.[2] From food supplies, to legal administration, to harmonious relations with the native population, Phillip's planning was wide-ranging and meticulous.

Once on board, Phillip treated crew and convicts alike with a fair-mindedness that struck some officers as indulgent. But that was the key to his success. A leader sets the standards.

Hardly a day after the *Sirius* weighed anchor on 13 May 1787, he invited an ailing midshipman, the fragile 23-year-old Daniel Southwell, to dine with him. 'Rest up,' the commander told the young man, 'take your time and eat well.'[3] Southwell was grateful to receive such attention, for Phillip was a charismatic figure, diminutive in size but gifted with a powerful presence. Through a combination of kindness and resolve, and a tough love that gave no quarter to ill-discipline, he won the loyalty and respect of his men.[4] 'The Governor is certainly one of a thousand,' Southwell wrote to his mother.[5]

Phillip was explicit that '[t]here can be no slavery in a free land and consequently no slaves'.[6] A 'free land' is an odd way to describe a prison settlement, but the new colony was unique from its very beginning. In America, the typical British convict had been taken ashore in chains and paraded through the streets in front of wealthy and often cruel buyers.[7] Owners of convict labour in America had total control over their purchase. They could prohibit convicts from making money outside their primary duties, which they often did. They could confiscate the money that was made. If the convict's legal status was greater than that of a slave, many who worked tirelessly in the plantations were made to feel little different. Not so in Sydney.

Sydney Cove was not a walled gaol but an open settlement – the continual guarding of convicts was impossible – and convicts were accorded a degree of freedom unheard of anywhere else. They worked in their own clothes and without leg chains. They lived in huts – many built their dwellings themselves – and provided the labour that kept the colony alive.[8] In what free time they had, they could trade or earn a wage and begin their second chance at life. They had legal rights and could own property. There was nothing like Sydney anywhere in the world.

The comparatively benign existence of convicts in Sydney was at odds with the prevailing view in London of a penitentiary where every aspect of the prisoner's life was observed and controlled by watchful authorities.[9] According to this perspective, convict 'freedom' risked descending into moral depravity. Although drunkenness was indeed a problem in New South Wales, and convicts could be lazy and dishonest, what these critics overlooked was the human capacity for self-improvement. Aspiration, it turned out, drove even convicts to ameliorate their own condition and to build social order.

Over time we have lost sight of how remarkable this was, but it was well understood, even if not widely accepted, back then. To a correspondent for the *St James Chronicle*, writing in January 1787, the despatch of the First Fleet was 'more than the mere Banishment of our felons; it is an Undertaking of Humanity'.[10] The Fleet looked much like a floating village, carrying almost 1500 people, including 775 convicts – 582 men and 193 women – with two years' worth of supplies.

Most of the officers on board were young, and some, like Watkin Tench, embarked in the 'spirit of intellectual adventure' that marked the age.[11] For others, the pain of separation from family was almost too much to bear. To the convicts below deck, suffering in the windowless gloom and hearing only the orders above that signalled departure, it must have felt as if they were leaving Earth altogether.[12]

The Fleet sailed from Portsmouth to the Canary Islands, then to Rio de Janeiro before a final stop and resupply at Cape Town, reaching Botany Bay on 18 January 1788. A few days later, Phillip moved his ships some miles north to Port Jackson, a more suitable deepwater harbour which, crucially, contained a creek of fresh water running down into the cove he named after his ministerial chief, Lord Sydney. Here, on 26 January, Phillip raised the Union Jack and toasted King George III.

* * *

The 47-year-old Phillip was a man who could be trusted to carry out difficult commissions in distant places. He'd risen on merit from his first years at a charity school for the poor sons of seamen; and, like Cook, served in the Seven Years' War against the French. In the 1770s, he'd served in the navy of Portugal, Britain's oldest ally, and was described as an 'officer of great truth and very brave, saying what he thinks but without temper or want of respect'.[13] He'd also witnessed Brazil's brutal system of enslaved labour and may well have transported Portuguese convicts to South America.[14] By the 1780s, he was well known to Britain's home secretary, Lord Sydney, whose under-secretary, Evan Nepean, was Phillip's close friend. As is so often the case, cometh the moment, cometh the man.

While Phillip was no modern-day 'bleeding heart liberal', it's abundantly clear that he did not want a colony of tyrannical gaolers and suffering convicts. He wanted the laws of Britain transplanted to New South Wales. He wanted to proceed with 'kindness' towards the Aboriginal people.[15] He said he abhored slavery. In Phillip's writings, we can see the origins of a free society.

Yet to govern effectively, Phillip was invested with extraordinary executive power. His commission gave him control of all appointments, finances, land grants and legal matters. With no legislative council to advise him, he was, in effect, to rule by direct proclamation. To the First Fleet naval surgeon, Arthur Bowes Smyth, this was 'a more unlimited [commission] than was ever before granted to any Governor under the British Crown'.[16] Another officer, Ralph Clark, had 'never heard of any one single person having So great a Power Vested in him as the Governor has'.[17]

Their fear of autocratic overreach was understandable. The contemporary English historian Edward Gibbon had reflected on the 'instability of a happiness which depended on the character of a single man'.[18] Who was to know when benevolent rule would give way to jealous tyranny? There were but two restraints on Phillip's power: his own decency and the civil law under which the colony was governed.

It was Lord Sydney who had opted to have the colony governed by civil law, not military.[19] This had surprised even some British officials. Lord Howe, the first lord of the Admiralty, wanted convicts 'punished according to the discretion and judgment of the Governor'.[20] But Sydney's under-secretary, Evan Nepean, argued that convicts sentenced under civil law in

Britain could not be governed by military law somewhere else; to do so 'would occasion infinite clamour at home'.[21]

When the issue went to the British cabinet in November 1786, it seems that the mundane questions of penal codes and imperial administration were considered in terms of the deeper philosophical questions posed by the Enlightenment. Could individuals be morally improved? Could the criminal be reformed? More and more, the answer was yes.

This decision to govern the colony under civil law was the key to the freer society that Australia was to become. Felons on British soil whose death sentence had been commuted typically forfeited their property and were subsequently disqualified from bringing civil actions in court. Yet the colony's civil court gave convicts, even those whose death sentence had been commuted, legal standing. Many important elements of English law were restricted, particularly in the early years of the colony, yet it remains remarkable how much of the rule of law, with fair trials and the presumption of innocence, would be applied in a settlement comprised almost entirely of convicted criminals.

* * *

Most of the convicts of the First Fleet had been sentenced for what we would now consider minor theft, often for stealing luxury items such as rolls of expensive fabric, like calico or linen. Half of the convicts were under 25. The youngest was John Hudson, an orphan, who had been sentenced for theft when he was nine years old. The youngest female, Elizabeth Hayward, was 13, while the oldest, Dorothy Handland, was 82.

At the last minute, the number of female convicts was substantially increased, which was to have tangible consequences. According to records, 14 were pregnant when the Fleet departed. The chief surgeon would report 28 births during the eight-month voyage, so the initial figure may not have been reliable. Although male and female convicts were separated on the Fleet, women were not separated from the crew and officers, and there were liaisons on board. Consequently, the first generation of Australian-born settlers appeared in the months immediately following the Fleet's arrival in New South Wales. Plainly, New South Wales was going to be 'something more than a jail'.[22]

The convicts were a cross-section of the British criminal class. They included a small number of French and American convicts and at least 12 of African descent, such as John Caesar, a runaway slave who'd fought alongside the British in the American War of Independence. About 300 of the convicts were Catholic and more than a dozen were Jewish. The male convicts who could specify an occupation were mostly labourers, while the female convicts were typically domestic servants. Robert Hughes described it as 'a Noah's Ark of small-time criminality'.[23]

* * *

A most startling event was the appearance of two French ships off Botany Bay on 24 January 1788. They were under the command of Captain Jean Laperouse, then undertaking a global naval expedition, ostensibly under the rubric of science and the advance of knowledge, but more likely a scouting expedition for future colonies. The coincidence of arrivals was a little too cute for the Fleet's officers. 'It seemed to us a pretty extraordinary circumstance that two ships should arrive in so little a time after us; where tis presumed no vessel ever was before, except Captain Cook's,' wrote the First Fleet naval surgeon Arthur Bowes Smyth.[24] If the French were trying to beat the British to Botany Bay, they lost by just five days. When Phillip raised the Union Jack at Sydney Cove on 26 January, he not only took possession of Britain's new colony but 'trumped any other European claim' in the region.[25]

We have reason to be thankful that the British reached the continent first. France, an absolute monarchy, would shortly plunge into revolution and descend into terror. Furthermore, British liberty – although far from perfect – was more substantial than anything on the European continent at that time. As well, the American experience had impressed on the British establishment the need for settler colonies to have a path to self-government: present freedom plus future self-government. No other coloniser would have offered such a prospect. Whichever European people had settled Australia first, almost certainly the Indigenous population would have suffered from disease and occasional violence. Indeed, settler violence would almost certainly have been worse under any other European power. Although sometimes more in theory than in practice, to the authorities in London, Aboriginal Australians were British subjects, under the protection of the Crown.

Despite the fierce Anglo–French rivalry, contacts between Laperouse's and Phillip's parties were friendly, and the French departed Botany Bay after six weeks. It was the last time they were seen alive; their ships later wrecked on the reefs in the Solomon Islands. There were no known survivors.

This surprising encounter between two global powers in the far corner of the world would have reminded Phillip of another crucial instruction signed by King George: the settlement of Norfolk Island, the small and, reportedly, flax-filled South Pacific island some thousand miles (1600 km) northeast of Sydney Harbour. Phillip asked his young lieutenant Philip Gidley King to settle the island with seven companions and

15 convicts, which King did in March 1788. Possibly this was 'the smallest ever party to establish a colony of the British Empire'.[26] What flax was found turned out to be unsuitable for naval purposes, though the soil proved fertile enough to support farming during Sydney's early lean years. In time it would take on a new role as another receptacle for convicts, and later as a 'secondary' penal site for serious offenders: a so-called hell in paradise. It remains settled to this day as an external territory of Australia.

* * *

How many Aboriginal Australians populated the continent at the end of the 18th century remains far from certain. The Australian archaeologist Josephine Flood regards 500,000 or, at most, 750,000 as a 'realistic estimate'.[27] There was an earlier and widely cited lower estimate of 250,000 to 300,000 by the anthropologist A.R. Radcliffe-Brown.[28]

Based on what the British government knew of the Aboriginal inhabitants, it did not substantively consider the question of sovereignty. Some historians have argued that, from the beginning, the British government relied on the doctrine of *terra nullius* – 'nobody's land' – which asserted full ownership of a vacant territory. Phillip, and Cook before him, had indeed claimed British sovereignty over half the continent, but as more recent scholarship has made clear, this did not imply that there were no Aboriginal rights.[29] Circumstance, more than doctrine, initially guided the relationship between the new arrivals and the Aboriginal locals. It is likely Phillip was prepared to negotiate with them; indeed, he had brought with him provisions for the very purpose of bartering.

Initial contact with the Aboriginal people was tense but mostly friendly. Phillip had been instructed to 'open an intercourse with the natives, and to conciliate their affection'.[30] Any British subject who felt moved to 'wantonly destroy them, or give them any unnecessary interruption in the exercise of their several occupations' was to be punished 'according to the degree of the offence'.[31]

Early interactions with the Eora, the Aboriginal inhabitants of the Sydney basin, did yield promising results. Marine and ships' officers built a good rapport with the Eora men. The two warrior cohorts exchanged gifts and emblems, taught each other their own dances and engaged in games of strength and dexterity. Captain Hunter recorded an encounter in which the two groups ran and threw spears alongside each other on the beach.[32]

Phillip's first approach to the Eora was an offer to exchange gifts. Musket fire was avoided and arms were outstretched in a display of amity and peace. Phillip soon recognised that Cook and Banks had underestimated the numbers and the capability of the Eora. They were not passive in their dealings with those they came to call the *Berewalgal*, meaning strangers from a distant land.[33] They, too, showed curiosity and good will. Both cultures were playing the role of discoverer, but the Eora were also prepared to defend their land from encroachment.

At the beginning, Phillip's objectives were narrowly confined to establishing a small settlement within Warrane country, the Aboriginal name for Sydney Cove. Although a few convict runaways were found dead with the barbs of spears lodged in their bodies, for the first year, the settlement was largely undisturbed. Possibly, the Eora expected the British to leave.

For the convicts, at least, the description of 'invader' would have struck them as bizarre: they were themselves prisoners. It was notable that between convicts and Aboriginal people there was more mutual suspicion and less respect than between the officers and the Eora. Phillip made a particular effort to punish convicts for assaulting or stealing from the locals. The future of the settlement was already subject to enough anxiety and uncertainty without the addition of conflict with the existing inhabitants.

The first documented Aboriginal protests came in October 1790, after settlement had reached Parramatta. A local elder, Maugaron, visited Phillip to complain about the impact of settlement. From the perspective of the local Burramattagal people, their gradual displacement may indeed have felt like an invasion. Phillip acknowledged Maugaron's concerns, but – for all Phillip's humanity – he was not deterred from his mission.[34]

* * *

The most potent symbol of Phillip's vision for an upright and self-sufficient society was the Government Store, or Commissariat: the repository of supplies that would feed the population upon a practicable basis without any need for market competition. '[T]here was a sort of sacredness about our store,' the governor's secretary wrote.[35] Surplus produce was to be public produce, sold only to the store at fixed prices.

In the early 'starvation' years, infertile soil and lack of know-how led to failed harvests and, consequently, strict rationing for the colony. As supplies dwindled, Phillip insisted on measuring out equal rations to convicts, soldiers and officers alike. After a formal trial, convicts caught stealing food from the Government Store were hanged; and when six marines committed the same crime, they too received the same punishment.

By April 1790, the Sydney settlement was reduced to less than half rations, which by Phillip's calculations gave the colony only several months until all the stock of pork, flour and rice was gone. Watkin Tench described the situation as an approaching famine, while John White wrote of 'new scenes of distress and misery'.[36] Fortunately, relief arrived in June when the first ship of the Second Fleet, the *Lady Juliana*, delivered enough food to hold off the prospect of starvation.

The Commissariat guaranteed that convicts would be fed; so, from the very beginning, people looked to the machinery of the state to provide a minimum standard of living. It is hard not to feel the lingering effects of this system: Australians, though distrustful of politicians, are very trusting of their institutions.

The Second Fleet seemed to prove the beneficence of government oversight. Initially organised to boost the supply of goods and labour, the Second Fleet delivered instead a full-blown humanitarian crisis. Private contractors operating the Fleet had been paid on a per-head basis, so had proceeded to cram the bulging hulks with convicts. They were kept heavily bound, in darkness, and received little food or medical treatment. The Fleet stopped at only one port, compared with three under Phillip. Almost a quarter of the convicts died en route, and more than half needed medical attention on reaching Port Jackson. Phillip was outraged and accused the ships' captains of murder.[37]

The British government took the lessons of the disaster seriously. They now faced a policy dilemma: the success of the First Fleet was widely acknowledged; but as far as London was concerned, such a large upfront cost could only be borne once. Eighteenth-century debates over government contracts reveal a tension between the emerging 'science' of public policy, which emphasised financial incentives, and more traditional and paternal views, which emphasised the values of public service, duty and honour.[38] Eventually, new measures were introduced to reduce mortality at sea, such as incentive payments for the safe arrival of convicts. By 1800, the mortality rate had halved and continued to decline over time. The solution was neither total government control nor total private self-interest.

The Second Fleet also delivered the first detachment of the NSW Corps (to replace the marines), around 500 men in total. Henceforth, these soldiers were to be the garrison for the new colony; they soon became the bane of future governors. Mostly of modest background, they saw the colony as a land of opportunity and quickly joined in the trade of spirits and other items. The new officers expected land grants, too. For his part, Phillip was hesitant to dole out benefits that would 'increase the number of those who do not labour for the public, and lessen those who are to furnish the colony with the necessaries of life'.[39]

* * *

Phillip was forced to make accommodations for the officer class, but even more for the convicts. He had to rely on them for important work: as builders, architects, hunters, fishermen, doctors, teachers, overseers, lawyers and even policemen. Using convicted thieves as police had a lurid, world-turned-upside-down ring to it when described in the street ballads of London, but Phillip made it work.

Equally crucial was the justice system, which Phillip largely left to run independently as the colony took shape. Initially, for both criminal and civil matters, the court comprised a judge-advocate, David Collins, with military officers serving as jurors. In the first month, a marine received 200 lashes for assaulting a convict woman.

The first civil case was brought by a married convict couple, Susannah and Henry Kable, who had met in an English prison. They had lost the contents of a parcel of goods that had been plundered aboard the *Alexander* on the First Fleet's journey to Australia. Outraged, they brought a successful action against the ship's captain and were awarded damages of £15. Having been condemned to death in England, common law should have precluded the Kables from bringing a civil suit. But in a colony composed mostly of convicts, whose labour was necessary for survival, it was imperative that everyone was equal before the law. Convicts were not slaves but subjects of the Crown with legal rights. Here, a convict could own property, give evidence and bring actions in court. A convict could be flogged, but only by order of the court – a more benign punishment regime than was then applicable to the sailors, soldiers and servants of Britain and Europe.

Convicts with a good record could even apply for their families to join them in the new colony. One example, albeit from a much later period, is George Brand, a Scottish labourer transported to Western Australia in 1855, who earned enough income on his ticket-of-leave to bring his wife and children over in 1859. They became successful farmers and active in politics. Brand's great-grandson Sir David Brand remains the longest-serving premier of Western Australia, having held the office from 1951 to 1972.

Soon enough, convicts were making the most of any skills and aptitude they had to better themselves. '[Y]ou [must] not think that I am made a Slave of, for I am not, it is quite the reverse of it,' one convict wrote home.[40]

* * *

In November 1789, two Eora men, Colebee and Bennelong, were captured and brought to the Sydney Cove settlement in furtherance of Phillip's quest to know better the local people. Colebee soon escaped. Over time, Bennelong learned the manners and language of his captors. According to Watkin Tench, he was 'of good stature, stoutly made',[41] lively, animated and full of character. He soon endeared himself to Phillip.[42] When he did escape some months later, he was found again at Manly Cove. After some casual talk with Phillip, Bennelong placed a spear on the ground that was then picked up by one of Bennelong's companions and thrust into Phillip's shoulder, possibly as an act of blood justice in retribution for Bennelong's earlier capture.

Phillip chose not to retaliate. He seems to have taken the incident as a misunderstanding, not aggression, and to have understood Bennelong's grievance at being captured and made to live at Government House. It showed, Phillip said, that 'nothing will make amends for the loss of their liberty'.[43]

Within a week, relations between the British and Eora improved. Gifts were once again exchanged and the Eora asked after Phillip's health. After some false starts, the Eora began to mingle among the settlers. Captain John Hunter expressed his view that '[t]he natives were becoming very familiar and intimate with every person in the settlement', and 'many of them took their rest every night in some of the gentlemen's houses'.[44]

In 1792, Bennelong sailed with Phillip to London to be presented to society. In British eyes, he was the most significant Aboriginal figure in early Sydney, at once a hopeful sign that the two cultures could find common ground but also a cautionary tale of the difficulties of assimilation.

If Bennelong stood as the reconciler of Aboriginal Australia, Pemulwuy was the symbol of resistance. In December 1790, the muscular warrior of the Bidjigal clan speared and killed Phillip's gamekeeper, John McIntyre. Among the settlers, Pemulwuy was feared but widely respected, because his attacks were invariably reprisals for misconduct. After he was finally declared an outlaw and shot dead in 1802, his head was removed and sent to Joseph Banks in London (and ultimately lost, perhaps due to bombing in the Second World War). 'Although a terrible pest to the colony,' Governor King wrote, 'he was a brave and independent character.'[45]

* * *

By 1792, Phillip was exhausted. He'd pushed himself to the limit, slept little and rested only when he could barely walk.[46] The colony had much to show for his efforts. When Major Francis Grose had arrived earlier in the year to become lieutenant-governor, he was stunned by the settlement's development. '[I]nstead of the rock I expected to see I find myself surrounded with gardens that flourish and produce fruit of every description. Vegetables are here in great abundance, and I live in as good a house as I wish for.'[47]

Meanwhile, in January 1793, the first free settlers arrived in response to a request from Governor Phillip: five men, two women and six children. Among them was a farmer named Thomas Rose and his family. Rose was granted 120 acres (48 ha) in an area named Liberty Plains, near today's Homebush.

Phillip's departure left a noticeable gap in the colony's government. For a time, New South Wales was governed by officers of the NSW Corps, which had taken over garrison duties from the marines in 1791.

Under two lieutenant-governors – Grose and Paterson – NSW Corps officers secured land grants and bought up land granted to those with little interest in farming. Private enterprise took hold as settlement spread. Ex-convicts, soldiers and free settlers applied themselves to farming with more gusto than when Phillip had tried to confine it to growing for the Government Store.[48]

Officers took advantage of convict labour to clear and work the land. Produce was reluctantly sold to the Government Store, which in turn fed the convicts working on private farms; it was enthusiastically on-sold in the private market. 'Not even the Russians after communism were so barefaced in transforming public goods into private profit,' the historian John Hirst wrote of the period.[49] The commercial initiative of the military officers drove the shift from a command to an open economy.

Convicts took advantage of their own considerable bargaining power as the only labour force in the settlement. Officially, convicts were to work for the government clearing land and felling trees from dawn to dusk, Monday to Friday, with a part day on Saturday. In practice, they insisted on 'task work' that, once completed, gave them time to do what they wished: fishing, hunting, gambling, drinking or taking paid work from other employers.

Meanwhile, Sydney was becoming a busy maritime port for ships from all over the region: India, China, Tahiti, the United States and South Africa were early partners in an expanding network of exchange. The trade in rum, sugar, tea and tobacco was initially dominated by the NSW Corps, hence the nickname 'Rum Corps'.

But the Rum Corp's quasi-monopoly was short-lived. The officers employed convicts as middlemen (and middlewomen) to sell the products they bought and sold from ships' captains. After all, officers and 'gentlemen' could hardly be seen engaging in something as grubby as mercantile exchange. This lasted about as long as it took for the convict middlemen to strike their own deals with ship captains. The maritime entrepôt continued its roaring trade, while the officers turned their attentions back to farming and grazing.[50]

Many freed convicts began to establish themselves on private farms along the Hawkesbury River, attracted by the rich soil. By mid-1795, some 400 settlers were living along the 'Nile of the colony'.[51] In their pursuit of private profit, the ex-convicts became the 'backbone of agriculture', growing most of the food to feed the population and doing so at a relative distance from authority.[52] Beyond the effective limits of the Port Jackson settlement, the ex-convict settlers happily declared 'they did not care for the Governor ... or the Orders of the colony – they were free men, and wou'd do as they pleas'd'.[53]

* * *

When Captain John Hunter was appointed governor in September 1795, the colony numbered just 3000, the majority of whom were convicts. This was as London had envisaged. Lord Sydney did not plan for a colony of any sophistication. There was no provision for currency because it was assumed there would be no trading, just basic, peasant-style subsistence farming by convicts and emancipists, the term for those who had served their time.

But governments, even potentially absolutist ones, can only control so much. Very quickly, the economy was evolving in a different direction. Governor Hunter was startled by the settlement's social mobility: 'Some of the very dregs of those who have been sent here [as] convicts are now in possession of their horses and chaise, servants and other symbols of wealth,' he wrote.[54]

By 1804, the colony had become largely self-sufficient in food. That year, only 37 per cent of the population was receiving government rations, down from 70 per cent in 1798.[55] '[Farming] certainly succeeds better with them than in the hands of the government,' wrote Governor Hunter.[56]

Hunter encouraged the exploration of the Australian coastline, with Matthew Flinders and George Bass charting much of southern and eastern Australia and circumnavigating Van Diemen's Land in 1798. These maps put to rest any speculation that New South Wales was part of some large island archipelago. After his circumnavigation of the continent from 1801 to 1803, now confirmed to be a single landmass, Flinders was the first to name it 'Australia'. Flinders had an Aboriginal companion, Bungaree, whom he described as a 'worthy and brave fellow' to act as a go-between in dealings with local people. After one such encounter, Flinders referred in his diaries to the Yolngu people of East Arnhem Land as 'Australians', and the place where it happened is now known as 'Australians Bay'.

Sealers were among the earliest to take advantage of Flinders' more accurate mapping by rapidly establishing seasonal camps around the continent's southern coasts.[57]

The next governor, Philip Gidley King, also a naval officer in the First Fleet, encouraged trade with the South Pacific in pork and sandalwood, fostered the whaling and sealing industries with subsidies, and energetically assisted local industries, including weaving, glassblowing and manufacturing. King permitted the building of large ships for trading purposes. He increased the market supply of goods by establishing public warehouses that sold cheap imported products. He expanded cultivated areas by providing land grants to farmers and boosted production on government farms, thus driving down the price of grain for ordinary settlers and ex-convict farmers.

Ideas as well as goods were among the early imports. By 1793, the French Revolution's radical doctrine of 'Liberty, Equality, Fraternity' had captivated the surgeon John Boston, a Birmingham radical who'd declared himself a Jacobin and drunk 'damnation to the King' on the voyage over to the colony as a free settler.[58]

The convict population were particularly receptive to radical ideas. News of a failed Irish Rebellion in Dublin reached New South Wales in early 1804, reigniting anti-British feeling among the Irish convicts. Three months later, 200 of them launched an uprising at Castle Hill. The plan was to attack Parramatta and Port Jackson, establish Irish rule, then sail home and continue the fight. It was promptly and decisively put down by the NSW Corps, led by Major George Johnston. Governor King declared martial law, 30 rebels were killed and the uprising's leaders executed, some without trial.

* * *

British fears over French designs on the unsettled parts of Australia were a nagging anxiety. After Matthew Flinders encountered a French expedition on the south coast during his circumnavigation of Australia in 1802, King despatched an expedition to secure Van Diemen's Land for the Crown.

On Van Diemen's Land, British settlements were established at Hobart on the Derwent River and Launceston on the Tamar. David Collins, another First Fleet veteran, became lieutenant-governor. For food, convicts were sent foraging into the bush, hunting kangaroo and emu. The Vandemonian hinterland had its own strong appeal as a place of freedom beyond the immediate purview of the governor, like the Hawkesbury and the Bass Strait sealing settlements. Hobart quickly became a hub for the whaling and sealing that became Australia's first significant export industries.

Meanwhile, the soldiers of the NSW Corps had mostly married convict women and started families, moving out of barracks and living alongside the general population in the town of Sydney itself.[59] The convicts were hardly meant to be their equals but that's how it mostly turned out, thanks to the need for convict labour and the public-spirited leadership of the colony's governors. Our colonial ethos was to see convicts more as people with a chance to make good than prisoners to be punished.

2

Rebellion and Restoration

The settlement was approaching a crossroads: was it to remain a convict colony with little more than the infrastructure needed to sustain a limited population or was it to develop into a new society, partly on the back of convict labour? Among much else, whichever decision was taken would determine the ongoing institutional arrangements: a small colony might be ruled by one man; a larger one would need government according to law, rather than the character of particular governors.

Only one of the early governors, William Bligh, turned out to be a natural despot, and the ultimate local reaction to his misrule had echoes of the American colonists' rebellion. While Bligh's successor, Governor Macquarie, was a military ruler, his vision was for the colony to become 'Australia Felix' – or 'blessed Australia' as the surveyor-general Thomas Mitchell was soon to christen it – a new country built by people who'd had a second chance at the good life. He was also the first governor to seek integration of the Aboriginal inhabitants into the life of the colony. Two centuries on, this is still a work in progress, but he was the first to see its necessity.

§

Captain William Bligh was a brilliant seaman, but a ferocious leader who inspired both reverence and fear in his subordinates.

He had already survived one mutiny when he became governor of New South Wales in 1806. In April 1789, an uprising aboard his ship, HMS *Bounty*, had forced him and his supporters to sail some 4040 miles (6500 km) aboard a small wooden boat – from the South Pacific to Kupang, in what's now Indonesia.

When news of the *Bounty* mutiny, and Bligh's subsequent journey, reached the shores of Sydney, it hit like a thunderbolt. For convicts looking to make an escape, Bligh's voyage was a revelation. 'After the escape of Captain Bligh,' Watkin Tench recorded, 'no length of passage, or hazard of navigation, seemed above human accomplishment.'[1] Most imitations were unsuccessful; although, in 1791, a Cornish convict, Mary Bryant, together with her husband, her children and other transportees, did manage to navigate their way up the coast to reach Timor. Perhaps it was the harsh treatment meted out to her husband, William, that motivated the escape: he'd been given 100 lashes for the crime of selling on-the-side fish that was supposed to go to the Government Store. The party was captured, and Bryant's husband and children died on the journey home to England for trial. James Boswell, the famed biographer of Samuel Johnson, took pity on Mary and represented her in court. After she was pardoned, he provided her with an annual allowance while she lived out her days in Cornwall.

The decision to appoint Bligh as governor of New South Wales, in 1806, was hardly uncontentious, but Sir Joseph Banks, a personal acquaintance, had convinced London that no one else could govern such a ragtag colony. What was needed, Banks said, was 'a mind ... firm in discipline, civil in deportment and not subject to whimper and whine when severity of discipline is wanted to meet emergencies'.[2]

Like the previous naval governors, Bligh was – albeit in his idiosyncratic way – a brilliant man who'd risen on merit. The

Royal Navy, a meritocratic institution in an age still ruled by privilege, was not just a superbly capable instrument of war but a force for enlightenment, an 18th-century version of the National Aeronautics and Space Agency (NASA).[3] It was a leader in scientific research, as well as in geographic and anthropological understanding. New South Wales had been a beneficiary of this comparatively enlightened leadership but it was not an easily governable society, as Bligh, even more so than his predecessors, would quickly discover.

* * *

London did not warn Bligh that Sydney was a colony full of the likes of Fletcher Christian, his rebellious lieutenant on the *Bounty*: skilled men and women who felt they deserved more than they got, who wanted dignity and a fair go and had the tenacity to fight for it. Any witness to colonial life in the early 1800s could see first-hand a bustling, raucous and largely unplanned port town, plugged into global trade networks.

By 1805, the NSW settlement comprised some 4100 free settlers (including emancipists), 2000 convicts and about 715 military personnel, plus their families: perhaps some 10,000 people all up. Already, the Sydney shoreline was quite a spectacle, with numerous impressive mansions. On shore, there was obvious prosperity. Even convicts liked to wear frilled shirts and waistcoats on their days off, paying good money for quality material if they had the means.[4]

Although there was no government treasury, nor a private bank until 1817, a sophisticated commercial system had evolved that combined bartering and credit. At first, the lack of a local currency favoured the officer class, who had access to London funds. They could buy goods directly from the incoming ships and sell them at inflated prices.

Unsurprisingly, given the circumstances, Sydney was awash with liquor. Phillip had tried, unsuccessfully, to regulate alcohol with a permit system. His successors mostly turned a blind eye to its manufacture and importation. When supply was limited, prices rose and illicit distilling increased.[5] Isolated on the other side of the world, and with limited capacity for enforcement, local authorities had little choice but to adapt to public demand.

This was much the story of the whole economy. To protect the British East India Company's monopoly on trade, each of the governors was instructed to prevent shipbuilding for private use. Nonetheless, from the days of Phillip there were private fishing vessels, while later governors, such as King, quietly permitted the construction of ships.[6] The first genuine export industry, sealing, relied on locally produced vessels. John Hunter ran into trouble of a different kind by moving convicts out of private farms and into public projects: the convicts responded by deserting their work.[7] The so-called invisible hand was the most potent force in early New South Wales – but not if William Bligh could help it.

* * *

Bligh rose early each day to get to know the town and noted many deficiencies. 'I found the Church standing with two sides and one end built,' he wrote. 'The principal store and granary were not watertight. The other places for receiving stores were in the same way.'[8] He thought the town's houses 'miserably neglected' and was aghast that even the fort – Fort Phillip on Observatory Hill, meant to defend the settlement – was only half built. 'All this will require a vast deal of attention on my part to remove,' he wrote.[9]

His instructions were to restore the subsistence economy that suited what London still saw as a penal colony. He viewed

Sydney's consumer culture as an expression of commercial greed and was repelled by the sprawling chaos of the town. He had much greater sympathy for the small farmers, who were still recovering from devastating Hawkesbury River floods. He called them the 'industrious settler farmers who feed us' and regarded them as the exploited victims of the trading class.

Bligh re-organised the Government Stores to buy local produce at fair prices and to provide much-needed lines of credit. With his own money, he purchased two farms on the Hawkesbury to establish a benchmark for how a properly cultivated and efficient farm should be run. The small farmers loved him for it. The trading class – aware that they now faced a formidable government competitor – did not.[10]

It was the lack of a proper currency that had been forcing farmers to accept rum for payment, and it was the trading of spirits that most offended Bligh.[11] In February 1807, the governor prohibited alcohol as a medium of exchange. Bligh thought the banning of bartering with spirits would provide farmers with proper compensation; but with less 'currency' in circulation, labour costs rose. No single act could have been better calculated to directly attack the economic life of the colony. Rum dominated economic exchange where 'any little piece of service' could be acquired for 'a glass of grog'.[12] The effect of the ban was to endanger every business 'at a stroke'.[13]

Land within the port township was chiefly held by what was termed 'naked possession', the most simple and elemental form of possessory title. Settlers had put up fences, built houses and shops, and assumed legal title purely by occupation. Some 85 per cent of land was held that way, and it had been customary and accepted until Bligh arrived.[14] Seeking to reinstate Arthur Phillip's original plan for the Sydney township, Bligh set about evicting 'illegal' occupants. Visiting the home of one senior officer, Bligh told the owner he'd 'have the house down by ten o'clock'.[15] He bawled out the ex-NSW Corps officer John Macarthur over his large land holdings, which Bligh believed had been improperly obtained. 'By God, you shan't keep it,' he yelled.[16] Those who had hitherto avoided the arbitrary exercise of the governor's power worried that they might be next. Bligh's language and demeanour made him, in the words of one close observer, 'hated by people who he never really [did] injury'.[17]

It was rather too much for people whose wealth and fortune relied on a dynamic trading economy. Bligh's predecessors had understood this and tacitly accepted practices that were not strictly within the law, like shipbuilding. But the new governor's approach was different, because what he saw was the future of the colony being stolen from government control. To put the most influential traders back in their place, he fined them for activities that previous governors had permitted. In at least one instance when his victims sought legal redress, Bligh directed the magistrates not to sit until he was present in Sydney and could handle matters himself. All this had the unintended effect of giving the colonists, for the first time, their own distinct political consciousness. All they lacked, as yet, was a leader of their own.

* * *

Of the alienated residents of the colony, it was John Macarthur with his wounded honour who would trigger rebellion. At the age of 40, Macarthur was already a dominant figure. To some, he was an extortionary rum trader; to others, a highly capable if combative man of business. He epitomised the thwarting of the efforts of early governors to contain Sydney's growth. In 1801, Governor King had Macarthur arrested and sent to

England for court martial following the latter's dual with a senior officer, only for Macarthur to return to the colony with yet more wealth and influence, including merino sheep and a promised grant of 5000 acres (2020 ha). During his time away, he'd established a network of patrons to rival the one he'd earlier created in New South Wales.

Macarthur's ambitions were limited by the colony's quasi-penal status. In his eyes, this was holding back the settlement's commercial potential. Others in the colony were fired up by the radical ideas in Thomas Paine's *Rights of Man*, published in 1791. In 1802, British philosopher, jurist and social reformer Jeremy Bentham had written a startling polemic, *A Plea for a Constitution*, claiming that the colony of New South Wales was a manifestation of 'the oppression of British subjects, innocent as well as guilty, in breach of Magna Carta, the Habeas Corpus Act, the Petition of Right, and the Bill of Rights'.

Under the circumstances, it's hardly surprising that Macarthur was plotting sedition. Neither were Sydney's traders, officers and townsfolk inclined to object. Previously resentful of Macarthur's domineering ways, in the shadow of Bligh, they saw him as an ally.

The trigger for rebellion came in January 1808. Despite failing to pay a bond on one of his ships, Macarthur refused to be summonsed before the judge-advocate, a refusal that led Bligh to order his arrest. On 25 January, Macarthur again refused to be tried by the judge-advocate, Richard Atkins, on the grounds that Atkins owed him money and – allegedly – harboured a personal grudge against him. Atkins was pressured to withdraw from the trial by the six military officers of the court, all of whom were sympathetic to Macarthur. In response, Bligh not only ordered the re-arrest of Macarthur but also summonsed Major George Johnston, the Corps commander, and the six officers to Government House.

The crisis of authority came to a head when Macarthur drafted a petition to depose Bligh. On 26 January, the 20th anniversary of the colony's founding, Johnston fronted at Government House with his soldiers to arrest the governor on the charges of endangering the colonists' right to life, liberty and property. After searching the house and grounds, they finally found and arrested Bligh, who spent 13 months under house arrest before being confined aboard the sloop *Porpoise*, first in Port Jackson and later on the Derwent River in Van Diemen's Land.

Those who orchestrated the Bligh coup likened it to a revolution. Macarthur thought it 'one of the most meritorious' things he had accomplished: he had restored good government to New South Wales.[18] This was the argument that his supporters excitedly scribbled in justification to London. His opponents, meanwhile, were scribbling the opposite. To them, it was the illegal overthrow of a legitimate government.

After a brief interregnum, with Major Johnston effectively in charge, another NSW Corps officer, Colonel Joseph Foveaux, arrived back from England in July 1808 with a commission as lieutenant governor. Given the circumstances, he assumed control, stating that he would favour neither Bligh nor the rebels, and sent both Johnston and Macarthur back to London for trial.

Back in England, in the course of Johnston's court martial, the bench seemed confused as to whether the colony was ruled under the military or the civil power. 'By what law is the colony governed; is it by military law or by civil law?' Judge-Advocate Charles Manners-Sutton asked Macarthur, a witness at Johnston's trial. 'Civil law,' Macarthur responded.[19] He had no doubt about his rights as an Englishman. Indeed, though Johnston was found guilty, and stripped of all ranks and cashiered out of the army, this was a relatively light sentence, and suggests the British government implicitly understood the motivations behind Bligh's overthrow.

There was more to the 1808 'Rum Rebellion' than Bligh's threat to the rum trade. Essentially, it was a conflict over the future of the colony: was it to be a government enterprise or was it to develop into a society of its own? Bligh's overthrow demonstrated that New South Wales could not be a government-run prison colony only. Officers, convicts, ex-convicts and free settlers wanted to be masters of their own destiny. As early as 1808, the colony had a vigorous public life. Consider a January 1808 petition from Hawkesbury residents in support of Bligh: of the 833 signatures, 19 came from women, including the convict midwife Margaret Catchpole. Though not a property owner herself, nor a free person, Catchpole and women like her had an unusual degree of independence in the new colony, to which the inclusion of her signature attests.

* * *

In a sign of the egalitarianism of the colony, the dignitary to officially greet the new governor, Lachlan Macquarie, on New Year's Day 1810 was Isaac Nichols, a convicted thief, who, as of March 1809, was assistant to the Naval Office.[20] Sentenced to transportation in 1790, he was a diligent worker who took every advantage the new land gave him. By the time of Macquarie's arrival, Nichols owned a shipyard and multiple buildings in lower George Street. In 1809, he was appointed Australia's first postmaster. And transportation was meant to be a punishment!

Macquarie had been expecting to meet Bligh, not Nichols. But the former governor, Nichols said, 'had not been heard of for some time'.[21] In fact, Bligh was still languishing on the

Porpoise on the Derwent River near Hobart, hoping in vain that the rebels might be brought to justice. Since his removal from office, there had followed two years of a surprisingly stable, if self-serving, military interregnum, led by the officers of the NSW Corps.

The sway of the NSW Corps ended instantly on Macquarie's arrival with the 73rd Infantry Regiment under his command. He had been sent to restore 'order and tranquillity'.[22] This he did and more, governing with the paternal hand of a Scottish clan chief.[23] At his most benign, he could display a liberal sentiment far ahead of his time. He raised the standing and treatment of emancipated convicts, in whom he saw the future of Australia.

While some retired officers and free settlers wanted to reproduce the social hierarchies of Britain in New South Wales, Macquarie quickly recognised that the intermingling of convicts, emancipists and free settlers had created an egalitarian free-for-all that drove out the old traditions of social deference. '[A] short experience showed me,' the governor later wrote, 'that some of the most meritorious men of the few to be found, and who were most capable and most willing to exert themselves in the public service, were men who had been convicts!' Writing in 1810 to Lord Castlereagh, the colonial secretary, he described a 'new line of conduct' that would characterise his government, bringing the emancipated convict 'back to that rank in society which he had forfeited'.[24] True to his word, he provided 366 pardons between 1810 and 1820, compared with only two under Bligh.[25]

While emancipated convicts were free to pursue work in any field, they had seldom been appointed to government posts before Macquarie's arrival, nor readily accepted into 'higher' colonial society. Macquarie defied the rigid British class system by appointing emancipists to key government positions and by including them in social events at Government House. 'This country,' Macquarie declared, 'should be made the home and a happy home to every emancipated convict who deserves it.'[26]

Why Macquarie acted so generously towards emancipists has been described as 'something of a mystery'.[27] It appears that, occasional autocratic tendencies notwithstanding, he was the product of an emerging liberal humanitarianism. For instance, he was an admirer of the anti-slavery campaigner William Wilberforce. When the two corresponded on the emancipist issue, Wilberforce was supportive of Macquarie's position.[28] Macquarie's wife, Elizabeth, a widely admired woman of 'excellent judgment and sound understanding', was likely an important influence, too.[29] Tellingly, Macquarie's close friend in the military was fellow Scot James Dunlop, whose mother was a patron of the great egalitarian poet of the age, Robert Burns.

Macquarie's mindset disconcerted the small band of wealthy landowners and government officials, with Macarthur as their leader, that came to be known as the 'exclusives'. Unlike the soldiers, convicts, ex-convicts and run-of-the-mill free settlers, who happily worked together, married each other and socialised with one another, the exclusives opposed integrating ex-convicts back into colonial society. They were horrified that former felons could be appointed to government roles without regard for their social origins or criminal past. Like most of British society at the time, they believed that criminality was an irredeemable moral failure that had to be marked by lasting social stigma. That was how it worked at home, so why should the settlement be any different? Macarthur and his faction felt that Macquarie's actions deranged the social order and challenged the dictates of English law.

* * *

In the early 19th century, the pejorative term for the growing population of native-born was 'currency lads and lasses', intended to imply an inferiority to British-born, just as paper currency was inferior to sterling coinage. In fact, the new Australians were distinguishable from their English counterparts by their good health and physical attributes. They were, on average, taller and slimmer, and better adapted to the warmer, drier climate that afforded greater space and a more nutritious diet. While the birth rate was not especially high in the colony, infant mortality was relatively low compared to urban Britain.

On arrival in the colony, Macquarie was dismayed by the trading activities and general military slovenliness of the NSW Corps. He initially characterised the settlement as marked by disorder and licentiousness.[30]

But what was degenerate to some was freedom to others. The public servant George Thomas Boyes wrote:

> You cannot imagine such a beautiful Race as the rising
> generation in this Colony ... There is a degree of Liberty
> here which you can hardly imagine at your side of the
> Equator ... They are in short as free as the Birds of
> the Air and the Natives of the Forests. They are also
> connoisseurs in horses, cattle, sheep, pigs, and wool ...
> and this they all understand before they can speak that
> two and two make four.[31]

One of the most striking success stories was Simeon Lord, the so-called merchant prince of Botany Bay. He was convicted in 1790 for stealing goods, yet within 17 years he could boast assets worth £30,000. Entrepreneurial individuals like Lord made Arthur Phillip's concept of an ordered, yeoman economy an impossibility. He was an auctioneer, a trader, a shopkeeper and a manufacturer; he helped break the monopoly of the officers over imports; and he secretly struck deals with foreign traders against the monopoly of the East India Company. In 1813, he was powerful enough to secretly meet with other merchants and discuss plans to stabilise the entire currency of Sydney. By then, the Government Store paled in comparison to the warehouses of the private traders.[32]

Once convicts had been assigned to a 'master', they had considerable freedom. They wore no chains or uniforms and were not kept in prisons. They were encouraged to work hard and were rewarded if they did. The term 'convict' was avoided – 'government men' or 'servants' were preferred. Under conditions like these, escape was easy. Convicts could simply walk off their job and go bush – live off the land, in other words – or, more likely, resort to bushranging. Even so, most convicts preferred a regular supply of bread, meat and rum, and the prospect of integrating into colonial society at the conclusion of their sentence. Female convicts could become the partners of officers, soldiers and emancipists. More than that, though, they had a right to property, backed by law, and many bettered themselves on their own account, with some becoming landholders. There were far fewer women than men, so they had a choice of partners and acquired a degree of social power as a result.[33]

* * *

Because almost two years had elapsed between Bligh's overthrow and the new governor's arrival, Macquarie's first and most important task was to re-establish legitimate government. Deposed government officials were restored, land grants and pardons revoked, and some legal trials invalidated.

Proclamations were issued in line with Lord Castlereagh's direction to discourage prostitution, Sunday work and excessive alcohol consumption. Naturally, marriage was fostered, so too education and regular church attendance. Constables – many of them ex-convicts – policed these orders, apprehending law breakers and bringing charges. Macquarie reduced the number of licensed houses from 75 to 20, but alcohol remained an economic as well as a social lubricant. To finance the construction of a general hospital, Macquarie gave its project leaders a monopoly over the importation of 45,000 gallons of spirits per annum for three years.

From his early days, Macquarie improved the planning of the colony. Seeking to impose some order on the haphazard growth of Sydney, he laid down new streets, regulated the city's layout and sponsored public works: among them hospitals, barracks, schools, orphanages and churches. He designated common land for the leisure of residents and instructed traffic to keep to the left side – a regulation in place to this day.

* * *

After the uprising at Castle Hill, the military focus of the colony shifted from policing the convicts to managing unrest on the fringes of settlement. On the Hawkesbury in the 1790s there were Aboriginal raids on crops and farmland. Unlucky travellers were ambushed, and isolated farm workers were easy targets. Occasionally, hundreds of warriors massed on the periphery of settlement to intimidate the newcomers.[34]

The governors were sensitive to the consequences of settlement. Philip Gidley King invited three 'Branch natives' – elders from around Portland Head – to Government House, to ask why the attacks on settlers continued. After listening to the elders, King promised that 'no more settlements would be made lower down the [Hawkesbury] river'.[35] There is no reason to think such a commitment was insincere, but it was hardly enforceable. The government could barely police its edicts in the heart of the settlement.

Just as London underestimated the ambition of convicts and ex-convicts to better themselves, it underestimated the original inhabitants' instinct to guard their country. This became a more pressing challenge in Macquarie's time, as colonist numbers multiplied and settlers began to move well beyond the Sydney basin. Macquarie hoped that friendly Aboriginal inhabitants could be absorbed into colonial society and become farmers, labourers and Christians. He believed it his duty to bring the best of European civilisation to the Aboriginal people.

A spate of encounters between 1814 and 1816 – likely exacerbated by drought – forced Macquarie's hand. For him, the worst possible outcome would be settlers responding to instances of speared animals and occasional violence by taking matters into their own hands. He understood that 'the first personal attacks were made by settlers and their servants'.[36] After a particularly savage revenge killing, he reminded the settlers that the Aboriginal people, 'in like manner with themselves', were 'entitled to the protection of British law'.[37]

Macquarie was a man of his time, a military officer governing a fledgling outpost in the dying days of the Napoleonic Wars. With some settlers abandoning their farms, after killings by Aboriginal warriors, Macquarie felt he had to act. Indeed, he may have ended up like Bligh had he not responded. He ordered three detachments of soldiers to sweep around the Cumberland Plains.

Near Appin, the detachment led by Captain James Wallis quietly approached an Aboriginal encampment around dawn and began firing. Whether or not they fired in response to resistance is unclear. It is not mentioned in the official report, though Macquarie made this claim in his letter to London. Overall, 14 people were killed, including women and children. The Appin Massacre was the most bloody incident of a campaign designed to control the Sydney hinterland once and for all.

* * *

Within Sydney itself, Aboriginal warriors like Tedbury, the son of Pemulwuy, came and went at will. John Macarthur liked Tedbury and the friendship was mutual. After Bligh's overthrow, the warrior visited Macarthur's farm and presented a spear as a gift.[38] Visitors to Sydney were often surprised to see so many Aboriginal 'natives' walking freely among the population.[39]

Across the two cultures, friendships were made and people learned from each other. One settler recalled 'learn[ing] all sorts of things from the blackfellows' as a child. 'I had many playmates amongst them, and I haven't forgotten the principal words of the tribes round here yet.'[40] The skills of Aboriginal labourers and guides were indispensable. In whaling and sealing – both crucial industries to Australia's early development and both less disruptive to the lives of the Indigenous people than agriculture – there were Aboriginal workers from the beginning.[41]

In the first 30 years of settlement, there was hardly a coherent 'Aboriginal policy'. Governors responded according to circumstance. Likewise, the Aboriginal population resisted or co-operated depending on the circumstance. In times of fierce resistance, they might be treated as enemies; in more tranquil times, as British subjects. In 1814, Macquarie instituted an annual 'grand feast' for local Aboriginal tribes – along the lines of a Scottish clan meeting. Its initial purpose was to promote the new Native Institution at Parramatta, established to educate Aboriginal children and marry them to partners who had been similarly 'civilised', after which land would be provided to both for farming.

One of the first Aboriginal children enrolled in the Institution was Maria, the daughter of the 'Chief of the Richmond Tribes', Yarramundi, a proud and well-known warrior who had developed good relations with men such as Watkin Tench, Arthur Phillip and Samuel Marsden. In 1819, after four years' education at the Native Institution, Maria won first prize in the public examinations, ahead of 100 white children. She lived a fruitful life. On 26 January 1824, she married Robert Lock, a convict carpenter, and received a land grant near Blacktown. As a convict, Robert was assigned to Maria. The Locks raised a large family and their descendants are thought to number in the thousands. At the time of her death, Maria was the owner of 60 acres (24 ha) in Blacktown and 40 acres (17 ha) in Liverpool.

Despite some successes like Maria, the Native Institution was closed in 1826. Its short life showed the difficulty of institutional integration.[42] Those who did attend gained lasting benefits, but shared endeavour, sought voluntarily, was usually more effective. Companionship could also go a long way in assisting mutual understanding. Often enough, shared humour brought out the common humanity that two very different cultures masked. Bungaree – Flinders' friend – was a legendary mimic. Bennelong was another noted humorist. These are the forgotten moments of early Sydney: two totally different peoples gathered around the campfire, laughing together over the absurd.

* * *

Thanks to Macquarie's 265 public works, the previously ramshackle town of Sydney soon boasted order and permanence. The best of these are still standing, including the Hyde Park Barracks (built to house convicts), the (Old) Supreme Court and St James Church. All three were designed by the convict architect Francis Greenway, who arrived in 1814 with a letter of recommendation from Arthur Phillip.

A visiting French couple, Louis and Rose de Freycinet, while initially impressed by Sydney were subsequently robbed, which they put down to the criminal proclivities of a penal colony. Mostly, though, the amenity of convict life exceeded that of most of the workers of urban England. The floor space per person of the new barracks was larger than that enjoyed by many of London's poor.[43] While the Napoleonic Wars (1803–1815) spelt austerity and high taxes for ordinary Britons and starved Sydney of transport ships and officers, Macquarie's public works program kept the local economy vibrant. When the war ended in 1815, crime in Britain soared and transportation resumed, doubling the population in six years in a colony that was much better organised to receive them.

Not everyone viewed Macquarie's regime favourably. Although the governor was a benign autocrat, he was still an autocrat. He wanted order imposed not only on Sydney, but on the people themselves. Some of the freedoms enjoyed by the convict population were eventually curtailed. Those working on government projects lost their 'extra time' to earn a private wage – they were now full-time government workers – and they were to be housed in the new barracks, not private lodgings. The non-convict population had their own grievances. John Macarthur could neither grasp nor approve of Macquarie's elevation of ex-convicts to positions of respectability; nor did he believe that public works' spending did much for the long-term prosperity of the colony. As an advocate for the wool trade, he wanted pastoral landholdings of good size, but he could only get them from large land grants, which Macquarie was not always willing to provide.[44]

Britain's colonial secretary, Lord Bathurst, was disturbed enough by such criticisms to conduct the first proper audit of the Australian colonies. Not unreasonably, Macquarie's spending habits struck many in London as extravagant and unnecessary. Moreover, Britain was more interested in solving its own crime problem than in the success of New South Wales. London wanted transportation to be a deterrent against crime, not a reward.

The British government sent John Bigge, a lawyer and capable administrator, to thoroughly investigate Macquarie's administration. His brief was clear: the Australian colonies had to 'render transportation an object of serious apprehension'.[45] That was the settlements' main purpose; 'their growth as colonies must be secondary consideration'.

Bigge set about tracing the colonial discord that had been hinted at in London. The public buildings in Sydney, he concluded, were indeed extravagant. He was troubled by convicts assimilating into the ordinary life of Sydney. This hardly made for a life of punishment. Aspects of the administration further troubled him, including the arbitrariness of the governor himself.

Though not heedless of Macquarie's strengths, Bigge was more naturally sympathetic to the free settlers than to the ex-convicts. Men like John Macarthur had persuaded him that the prosperity of New South Wales rested with the growth of enterprise, through large landholders employing convict labour. This made a great deal of sense in London, but invited the question: to whom did the settlement belong?

Macquarie had no doubt that it belonged in equal measure to all Australian-Britons, emancipated or free settlers, and their descendants. No previous governor, not even Phillip, was as preoccupied with the rehabilitation of convicts. In this regard, Macquarie's attitudes were remarkably modern.

Nonetheless, in three official reports published in the course of 1822 and 1823, Bigge elaborated on the governor's mistakes. According to Bigge, convicts should be denied the chance to earn an income, receive a land grant or be appointed to a government position. To put the deterrent back into transportation, Bigge advocated the development of secondary penal settlements, where severe punishment could be meted out to recalcitrants.

For all that, though, the colony was undeniably flourishing. A relatively high standard of living had emerged by the end of Macquarie's governorship. Large British subsidies – perhaps amounting to two-thirds of gross domestic product in New South Wales and Van Diemen's Land – spurred the fast development that would propel the settlements into a new phase of pastoral expansion.[46]

Lachlan and Elizabeth Macquarie departed Sydney in February 1822 to a grand farewell. Spectators lined the shores to pay their respects. The governor left his mark in the towns he established, and in much that he had named after himself. His most significant naming was of the continent itself – 'Australia' – making official Matthew Flinders' suggestion. His recommendation was formally adopted in 1824. Macquarie grasped the importance of identity and history. He initiated the official celebration of 26 January each year, calling it Anniversary Day. He fostered a sense of pride and place. But it was the embrace of the people themselves that gave these initiatives life and meaning. While Macquarie was the official builder, thousands were building their own lives and, in the process, starting to build what would become a nation.

A tally of Sydney shipowners from 1800 to 1821 reveals a startling fact: 100 of the 127 owners were either ex-convicts or related to ex-convicts.[47] When John Macarthur left for England in 1809, his wife, Elizabeth, managed his business affairs at home with astonishing acuity and energy. In her plain-spoken letters, written without complaint or favour-seeking, she was laying the economic foundations for the next Australian boom – wool. Here were the real founders of modern Australia.

3

'Not all the armies of England'

The period from Macquarie to the beginning of the gold rush, in 1851, was a time of expanding horizons in every sense. The southern half of the continent was effectively, if still sparsely, settled. The near absolute rule of appointed British governors started to give way to representative government. On the frontier of settlement, violence intensified as Aboriginal people asserted their right to hunt, and graziers often over-reacted. Still, the colonists saw themselves as a new and better type of Briton: smarter, richer, tougher, freer and often more humane, at least to their own kind. The extraordinary experiment of establishing a new society from a colony of convicts was becoming a remarkable success.

§

Modern Australia was never a grand design. It was the spontaneous product of all those individuals and families looking to make a home or to keep one – to strike it rich, to make fresh beginnings or to hold onto what they had. They were settlers and Indigenous Australians; poor emancipists and wealthy merchants; convicts and officers; single men and women; and family groups. Among them were humanitarians, pragmatists and the ruthlessly self-interested. There were as many opinions about what Australia could or should be as there were people – at least 34,000 settler inhabitants in 1820; 70,000 in 1830; 190,000 in 1840; and half a million by 1852, in the early days of the gold rush.

The story of the 1820s was the collapse of controlled expansion. In 1826, Governor Ralph Darling forbade settlement beyond the limits of what were to become 19 counties, stretching from present-day Taree in the north to Moruya in the south and Wellington in the west. The idea was to protect the colonists from the dangers of settling in the wilderness.

But even then, settlers were driving their flocks well beyond the permitted territory. Wool production increased rapidly because numerous settlers were pasturing flocks illegally on Crown land. About 175,000 pounds (about 80,000 kg) of wool was exported in 1823, exploding to 2.5 million pounds (1,130,000 kg) by 1831.[1] Perhaps a third of the colony's sheep were grazing west of the Blue Mountains by 1825, benefiting from its dry and accommodating climate. London needed the wool, and convicts needed the work. After the Napoleonic Wars, London was sending an unprecedented number of convicts to Sydney. In 1825, more than half of the workforce was convict labour.

In 1822, the Surveyors-General Department numbered only three people.[2] Law enforcement was barely adequate in Sydney itself. The Mounted Police, a force used against bushranging and, at times, Aboriginal unrest, only numbered around 100 in 1830. Troop strength fluctuated with transportation and other imperial commitments, reaching some 3000 in 1839, a tiny force for a territory so vast that most of it wouldn't be mapped for decades. 'Not all the armies of England,' one governor wrote in dismay, 'not a hundred thousand soldiers scattered through the bush, could drive back our herds within the limits of the Nineteen Counties.'[3]

* * *

By the 1820s, native-born British Australians were coming into their own. John Bigge's assistant, Hobbes Scott, found Australian adolescents 'conscious of their freedom', and 'tho' having daily the most horrid examples before their eyes [convicts], are rarely if ever infected by them'.[4]

The native-born were the products of their parents' ambition to start anew. From very early on in the life of the colony, 'dame schools' had begun operating, usually run by capable women. From the beginning, governors were keen to ensure that the children did not grow up too like their parents, and had fostered the education of those without home-schooling or whose parents could not send them to boarding schools back in England. Prior to the 1830s, schooling was an ad hoc mix of government-funded schools for the children of convicts and private venture schools for those of free settlers, but it was remarkably effective: four out of five native-born children were able to read, unlike most of their parents.

Thanks to plentiful land grants, particularly under Macquarie, the opportunity to become a landholder far surpassed that of their contemporaries in Britain. The relationship between private citizen and the state tended to be benign, with the early governors looked upon as benefactors rather than adversaries.[5] But as the colony continued to grow, both in size and complexity, different factions and interests vied for the governor's attention. The system of colonial autocracy became increasingly unstable.

One of the giants of Australia's early development was William Charles Wentworth. By the end of Macquarie's time, he was a law student in Britain and author of the first ever book by an Australian. Its title was as grandiose as its ambition: *A Statistical, Historical, and Political Description of the*

Colony of New South Wales and its Dependent Settlements in Van Diemen's Land: with a Particular Enumeration of the Advantages which these Colonies offer for Emigration, and their Superiority in many Respects over those Possessed by the United States of America.

Published in May 1819, it was a story Wentworth was eager to tell prospective British migrants. His objective was to illuminate the possibilities of British settlement in the Antipodes; to highlight for ignorant readers the gifts that God could bestow upon them in a land of abundance: rivers teeming with fish, timber of gigantic growth and coals of the best quality – he rhapsodised over this new world with the enthusiasm and embellishments of a young man in a hurry. His New South Wales was a land of beauty and plenty, of stupendous opportunity for those willing to seize it. As he put it poetically a few years later: 'May this, thy last born infant then arise, To glad thy heart and greet thy parent eyes, And Australasia float, with flag unfurl'd, A New Britannia in another world.'[6]

Of the Aboriginal population, young Wentworth had nothing positive to say; over time, his prejudices would pit him against the more humanitarian of the governors. For now, Wentworth wanted to advertise his native country while exposing the administrative rot he felt was holding it back. The rot was coming from within, he warned, from 'an aristocratic body, which would monopolize all situations of power, dignity and emolument, and put themselves in a posture to domineer alike over the governor and the people'.[7]

Wentworth hated the exclusives, that faction of free settlers that looked down upon the emancipated class – the ex-convicts – who vastly outnumbered them. In 1821, there were 7556 emancipists (plus 5859 of their children), compared with 1558 free settlers and their 878 children.[8] The convict and ex-convict classes dominated the physical and economic growth of the colony. Mostly, the emancipists were building entirely different lives to the ones they had left in the northern hemisphere. Among them were doctors, lawyers, teachers, landowners, shipowners and merchants – people frequently of equal or greater wealth than the free settlers. Their children could be as educated and finely dressed as anyone: receiving private tutoring, travelling to England and being taught the etiquette befitting people of high standing. Yet still they were considered a lower social caste. And post-Macquarie, they were again largely excluded from public office, from Government House and from 'proper' society.

Wentworth's father, D'Arcy, though not a convict himself, may as well have been one. He had been tried for highway robbery but was never convicted, choosing subsequently – prodded perhaps – voluntary exile in New South Wales. He was from the poor Irish branch of the eminent Wentworth family, which boasted a prime minister: Charles Watson-Wentworth, Marquis of Rockingham. For the best part of a generation, Rockingham had been the leader of the 'Whig' faction in the British Parliament, those less inclined than the 'Tories' to support Church, King and Empire. Rockingham (with Edmund Burke) was a supporter of American independence.

D'Arcy had fallen in with a bad crowd at home and had been determined to leave his troubles behind. He was charming and intelligent, rising up the professional ranks to become a leading doctor and a wealthy colonial public servant. On his way to the colony, he met the convict Catherine Crowley, who gave birth to their son, William Charles, in 1790. William was later schooled in England and introduced to his aristocratic and Whig heritage, meeting Lord Fitzwilliam, inheritor of Rockingham's grand estate.

Although D'Arcy was hardworking and prosperous, a perfect representation of success in the fledgling settlement, he was not accepted into the higher social class of the colony. That he remained an outsider grated on young William, who viewed himself in heroic terms and tried to live up to that self-image. Together with Gregory Blaxland and William Lawson, he pioneered a path across the Blue Mountains in 1813, paving the way for stockmen to follow and rapidly populate the fertile Bathurst plains with mobs of sheep. Three years earlier, aged just 21, he had been appointed provost-marshal, responsible for organising the courts. Upon receiving a land grant, he was well on his way to becoming an influential force in the colony.

Wentworth wanted an institutional order that would give successful, educated and property-owning emancipists and free settlers a say in the colony's governance. 'Every community,' he wrote, 'which has not a free government is devoid of that security of person and property which has been found to be the chief stimulus to individual exertion and the only basis on which social edifice can repose in a solid and durable tranquility.'[9] He proposed a popular Assembly with a restricted franchise, open to any emancipist or free settler who met certain qualifications.

While in London in the early 1820s, Wentworth expounded upon his arguments to Mary Reibey, the lively emancipist businesswoman who was emblematic of the reformed citizen. Convicted in 1791 at age 13 for horse stealing, Molly, as she was then known, was sentenced to transportation. When caught, she had been dressed as a boy – a disguise intended to blend her in with a crowd but also, likely, to keep her safe. She was high-spirited and street smart. At 17, she married an officer from the East India Company who purchased land in the Hawkesbury and became a successful trader. Widowed by 34, Mary was left with a business to run and seven children to raise. She would become the richest woman on the continent. Macquarie liked

Mary and invited her to Government House. In 1820, she went to England for a visit and stayed a year, and in the 1828 census, she marked herself down as an emigrant who had arrived as a free settler in 1821, thus hiding her convict history.[10] Mary was an archetype of the new Australian: hardworking, determined to succeed and benefiting from the opportunity to 'have a go'.

* * *

Commissioner John Bigge had returned to London with his luggage full of documents and a story quite different to Wentworth's. He did not approve of Governor Macquarie's effort to introduce the emancipated convicts into general society, regarding it as inexpedient and dangerous; although he did appreciate some of their grievances, because even ex-convicts deserved a political system not dependent on the whims of a governor. Still, his overall impression of Sydney was of vice and ill-discipline. He wanted the convicts sent out of town to the large-scale settlers as useful labour where they should expect no wages, no tickets of leave (parole) and no pardons.

Like the so-called exclusives whose side he mostly took, Bigge also wanted the colony to reflect the social hierarchies of Britain. By this time, the development of the lucrative wool industry had created a powerful commercial aristocracy comprising both exclusives and wealthy emancipists. While socially antagonistic, both groups were coming to agree on the need for a less autocratic system of government. Juries still exclusively comprised military officers and, above all, everyone was vulnerable to the autocratic rule of the governor and ultimately subject to London.

* * *

By the early 1820s, former convicts were not only advocating for political reform but were achieving remarkable success in doing so. Men like Edward Eagar, an ex-convict lawyer, were in constant communication with the Colonial Office over the civil disabilities suffered by emancipists. London, itself in the throes of debate over political reform, heeded the accusations of the 'pure and simple despotism' inherent in the governor's power. Eagar used his second chance at life to push for a Legislative Council and even an elected Assembly.

Largely thanks to the emancipist influence, the British Parliament passed the *New South Wales Act 1823*, which introduced a Legislative Council composed of a small number of locally appointed members to advise the governor and approve legislation. In addition, the military court was replaced by a Supreme Court with trial by jury for civil cases. For the first time, the governor no longer wielded absolute power in the colony.

The Act also provided for Van Diemen's Land to be administered as a separate colony from New South Wales, with its own Legislative Council and Supreme Court. It was the beginning, however modest, of a genuine constitutional government.

* * *

Macquarie's successor, Thomas Brisbane, like all previous governors, quickly learned that New South Wales could be managed, but not controlled. '[A]n angel from heaven could not get on' in the colony, he said, observing the bitter conflict between emancipists and exclusives. But it was the free settlers he found the most difficult: 'people who style themselves gentlemen, and the magistrates, who generally do all they can to thwart the government regulations, and the government measures'.[11]

One of the malcontents, John Dunmore Lang, who kept up a stream of criticism in letters to London, dismissed Brisbane as 'a man of the best intentions, but disinclined in business, and deficient in energy'.[12]

As best he could, Brisbane set about implementing Bigge's recommendations. Life for convicts was to be harder: tickets of leave were restricted, convict wages were abandoned and land grants to ex-convicts reduced in size. The new governor tasked John Oxley, a hardy explorer, with finding a suitable location for the reform and punishment of repeat offenders. Moreton Bay, to the north, was selected to be a place of exemplary punishment. Along with other such facilities, set up in sites such as Norfolk Island and Port Arthur, Moreton Bay quickly became notorious for its harsh treatment. There was a death rate of around one in ten for the recidivists sent there. But Brisbane also continued many of Macquarie's humane policies, regularly granting pardons to convicts and occasionally paying them as a reward for good work. He was sparing in floggings and executions, governing with a 'cautious liberalism' that favoured the emancipist class.[13]

* * *

Van Diemen's Land had a growing appeal for new arrivals. Droughts and floods were less a risk than in New South Wales, and the grasslands were rich and accessible.[14] The best pastoral estates were almost Edenic in their beauty, unspoiled by scrub or fern but perfectly shaded by wattle and eucalyptus trees and watered by a gentle network of streams. By 1830, almost half the land under cultivation was in Van Diemen's Land, and it was home to almost a third of Australia's settler population.

The first 20 years of settlement in Van Diemen's Land had been characterised by relative peace and co-operation with the original inhabitants. But as the pastoralists pushed forward into the interior, the Tasmanian Aboriginal people pushed back. Between 1824 and 1826, 24 Europeans were killed; between 1828 and 1830, over 50, often in farmhouse raids.[15] After discharging their weapons at Aboriginal assailants, settlers typically found themselves rushed before they could reload. The Aboriginal people could evade the clumsy redcoat with relative ease or abandon their spears to make a hasty escape, in full knowledge they could quickly manufacture more. On the other hand, press reports and settler memoirs suggest that some 260 Aboriginal people were killed in some 21 reprisal raids in the two years from 1828.[16]

In some ways, it was a one-sided extermination; in others, 'the most successful defense of the frontier in Australia'.[17] The British colonial secretary, Sir George Murray, blamed the settlers for the outbreak of violence and demanded that any settler responsible for killing Aboriginal people be tried for murder.[18] The lieutenant-governor of Van Diemen's Land, George Arthur, was inclined to agree with him but could not persuade his own Executive Council, which described restraining the settlers as 'extremely impolitic'.[19]

In September 1830, Arthur ordered an extraordinary military measure – the Black Line – consisting of 2200 men who advanced across the settled districts to push the Aboriginal population into the Forestier and Tasman peninsulas. It was a logistically impressive, if naïve, measure to 'protect' the original inhabitants. Unsurprisingly, given that there were, on average, only ten men per 1000 yards (1 km) of the line, and the Aboriginal people were skilled in bushcraft, only two were captured. Overall, though, hundreds of Aboriginal Tasmanians were killed during the expansion of settlement, a tally that deeply impacted Arthur. 'It was a fatal error in the first settlement of Van Diemen's Land,' he lamented, 'that a treaty

71

was not entered into with the natives.'[20] One of the participants in the Black Line was John Batman, a self-confessed killer of Aboriginal people, who would later venture into Port Phillip with a treaty of his own.

* * *

William Wentworth returned to Sydney in 1824 with a printing press and a desire to provoke. He had long been dissatisfied with the stiff and harmless *Sydney Gazette*, Australia's first newspaper, the proofs of which were submitted to the governor's office for approval. After all, what need had a convict colony for a free press?

A convict in Van Diemen's Land had been the first to challenge that assumption. Andrew Bent, convicted of burglary in 1810, had risen to establish his own newspaper, the *Hobart Town Gazette and Southern Reporter*. In June 1824, Bent decided his paper was good enough to print without government approval. This, of course, was unacceptable to Lieutenant-Governor Arthur, so Bent was fired from his job as government printer, fined, gaoled and subjected to numerous legal battles.

Wentworth had similar ambitions. Together with Robert Wardell, an Englishman who had previously owned *The Statesman* paper in London, he founded *The Australian* to promote a growing Australian identity.[21] On 14 October 1824, the first edition of New South Wales's first independent newspaper was published for one shilling. All 625 copies rapidly sold out. *The Australian* was filled with invective against the so-called exclusives. Wentworth and Wardell spoke of a divided society, of an aristocracy working against the interests of the people. They gave their readers a new lens for seeing New South Wales, importing the language of reform-minded Whig politics into the public conversation of the colony.

Remarkably, Governor Brisbane was prepared to tolerate this exercise in press freedom.[22] Indeed he went further, lifting censorship from the *Sydney Gazette*. And when his successor, Governor Ralph Darling, attempted to impose stamp duty on the colony's papers, the measure was invalidated by the newly instituted Chief Justice Francis Forbes. As London papers were still subject to tax, that made the Australian press, in a so-called penal colony, freer than in Britain.[23]

* * *

So much of modern Australia was initiated by convicts or ex-convicts. After a Royal Marines officer, James Stirling, surveyed the Swan River on the west coast of Australia, it was the ex-convict and merchant Solomon Levey who provided the capital for an investment syndicate in a new settlement there, in partnership with the Englishman Thomas Peel (cousin of future British prime minister Robert Peel). The first settler ships bound for the west coast left England in early 1829. Charles Fremantle officially declared the Swan River Colony for Britain on 2 May 1829, the first non-convict colony to be established in Australia. Three years later, it would be renamed the Colony of Western Australia.

Early accounts of the western colony were grim. Newspapers in the east informed readers of sandy soil, lack of grass and shortage of water for stock. Only 100 acres (40 ha) of land were under cultivation by 1832.[24] Peel and Levey's investment came to little, but more settlers and supplies were sent over in following years, even as the colony continued to struggle. With no workforce to perform the manual labour required, by 1846 the colonists were requesting convicts. Some 9000 were transported to Western Australia between 1850 and 1868, but the colony made little economic headway until gold was found in the 1890s.

* * *

In England, a new push for political reform had direct consequences for Australia. In 1828, the requirement for government officials to pledge allegiance and take communion in the Church of England was repealed. A year later, public office was opened to those outside the Church of England. These reforms 'exploded', said one Whig politician, the 'doctrine that Church and State are indivisible'.[25] In 1832, the British Parliament passed the *Reform Act*, expanding the franchise; and, in 1833, slavery was abolished throughout most of the British Empire. The 1833 Act was the culmination of the evangelical influence that was later to seal the fate of the 'white slavery' that was Australia's convict system.

A product of the time was the next NSW governor, Richard Bourke, a 54-year-old Irish Whig and imperial administrator whose appointment was greeted in the streets of Sydney with 'the most lively demonstrations of joy', according to the liberal *Monitor* newspaper.[26] A second appointment, in some ways no less significant, was the solicitor-general, John Hubert Plunkett, a 30-year-old Irish Catholic – another advocate for change and the first Catholic to be appointed to high office in the colony.

Plunkett had experienced first-hand the evils of religious discrimination. His most treasured possession was a silver chalice used by his ancestor Archbishop Oliver Plunkett, the Roman Catholic Archbishop of Armagh and Primate of Ireland, executed for high-treason in the late 17th century on the back of fabricated evidence.[27] Plunkett never forgot the many restrictions, official and informal, that stood in the way of talent and ambition for those who shared his religious convictions.

The first Catholic Mass in Australia had been conducted in 1803 by an emancipated convict priest, Father James Dixon, but his permission to minister was revoked after the 1804 Castle

Hill rebellion – even though he'd tried to persuade the rebels to lay down their arms. After volunteering to serve the Catholics in Australia, who by then were widely regarded as worthy of recognition, Father John Joseph Therry arrived from Ireland in 1820 and was accredited as a chaplain with a government salary. Governor Macquarie laid the foundation stone for what is today St Mary's Cathedral the following year.

After surveying Australian attitudes and institutions, Bourke declared it 'impossible to establish a dominant and endowed Church without much hostility'.[28] The *Church Act* of 1836 was Plunkett's and Bourke's most enduring measure, and one that had neither been demanded by the colonists nor insisted upon by London. It placed the largest Christian denominations – Anglican, Catholic, Presbyterian and eventually Methodist – on an equal basis, thereby ending the privileges accorded to the Church of England. Public money was made available on a non-denominational basis for the building of churches and schools, and to pay clergy. It was actually three Irishmen that drove this Act: Bourke, Plunkett and Plunkett's old Trinity friend Richard Therry, a judge and barrister in the colony.

Bourke's church reforms were unprecedented in the British Empire. Not yet half a century old, and still with a settler population of just 125,000 in 1836, Australia was already a leader in liberal reform. A genial Anglican, Bourke felt duty-bound to expand the moral and religious education of the colony. As settlement expanded and Aboriginal dispossession accelerated, evangelical Christians pondered what might comprise a good and godly government.

* * *

Whatever natural riches Australia was endowed with, the evangelicals feared it would come to nought if the Christian faith did not follow the pioneers into the vast interior of the continent. A convict society must necessarily be morally compromised, it was believed, so the advocates for social improvement were anxious about the convict-fuelled rapid expansion of settlement. The official insistence on the 'limits of location' meant that men or women could choose to live within the limits as lawful British subjects, or beyond them as effective outlaws. Within the 19 counties, they could expect proper administration: law enforcement, schooling, decent roads and other government benefits.[29] Outside the boundaries, their lives were their own business.[30]

Notwithstanding numerous official expeditions, the 'discovery' of the interior was decentralised to countless adventurers driven largely by self-interest. Within several years, the sprawling Bathurst Plains had been populated, and land further to the west, which explorer John Oxley had described in 1820 as inhospitable, was soon teeming with settlers. Expansion continued north to the Liverpool Plains and to New England, and south along the Murrumbidgee River. As the Australian sheep population exploded from 75,000 in 1816 to 16 million in 1850, Australian farmers captured an increasing share of the British wool market – one-tenth in 1830 and half of it by 1850.[31]

In New South Wales and Van Diemen's Land, newcomers could get rich 'running sheep' thanks to abundant land, a benign climate and readily available convict labour. The so-called squatters – the term for individuals who helped themselves to land to establish pastoral enterprises – were a diverse bunch, not the 'landed aristocracy' of later caricature, but often middle-class, young, aspirational and hardworking.

With the advent of assisted migration – British-government-funded no-cost passages for suitable settlers – free-migrant ships began to outnumber convict transports. Those selected were often chosen by British officials based on what was needed in the colonies: young, fit, skilled workers – plus women. To correct the female-to-male imbalance, British officials went to considerable effort to find women of marriageable age. On arrival, assisted migrants were fed, housed and often helped to find jobs by government. Of the one and a half million British migrants to Australia between 1831 and 1900, half were subsidised.[32]

* * *

Small bands of sealers and whalers had been in and around Port Phillip since the early 1800s. The Henty family had settled in Portland Bay in 1834, and their presence had startled the explorer Major Thomas Mitchell – who was, like many government officials, often a step behind the squatters.

One of the most noteworthy settlers was the Vandemonian landowner John Batman, who aspired to expand his wealth beyond the Bass Strait into the fine country near Port Phillip, on the central coast of what is now Victoria. Batman's father had been a convict who became a devout Wesleyan and ran a Wesleyan Sunday School at Parramatta, where young John met many Aboriginal children. Eventually, he recruited Sydney Aboriginal men for the roving parties he led against Aboriginal groups. Although he could be an effective conciliator between white and black, and took into his home Aboriginal orphans, by his own shockingly blunt account of an operation in the Ben Lomond District, he shot in cold blood two wounded Aboriginal captives, unable to walk.[33]

In 1835, Batman formed the Port Phillip Association, an alliance of property speculators and would-be graziers who subsequently took their sheep and cattle across the Bass Strait. They brought with them a treaty drafted by Joseph Tice

Gellibrand, a former attorney-general of Van Diemen's Land. According to Batman's account of events, an agreement was struck by the settlers and representatives of the Kulin people, transferring 600,000 acres (243,000 ha) – including what's now Melbourne – to the Association in exchange for an annual tribute of goods, including clothes, flour, blankets, knives and tomahawks.

Batman's thinking was that the treaty might legitimise his claim against likely pushback from the NSW government – at that time, the land he was developing was still part of New South Wales.[34] Anti-slavery activism in Britain had been extending to more humanitarian concern for the treatment of Australia's Aboriginal population, through the efforts of humanitarians such as Thomas Fowell Buxton, a disciple of abolitionist William Wilberforce. The Port Phillip Association knew that in lobbying London for possession, they needed to acknowledge the rights of the local Aboriginal people.

In the event, Governor Bourke swiftly voided the treaty as 'against the rights of the Crown'.[35] Any private treaty was an obvious affront to the government's authority and would open the door to countless similar land grabs. Nevertheless, even a voided treaty testified to the notion that Aboriginal people could have inherent rights in land, independent of anything that was granted by the Crown. The colonial secretary, Lord Glenelg, wrote to Bourke, concerned that Aboriginal people could be conned should they be able to alienate land to 'private adventurers'.[36] Counterintuitively, but quite reasonably, the bureaucrats in London thought private treaties might lead to even more violent dispossession if they were backed by some semblance of legality.

In 1836, Bourke sent Captain William Lonsdale to establish a civil administration in the settlement that he named Melbourne, after the British prime minister. It was 'a beautiful site for a

Town', said Bourke, who conferred upon it the street names that, for the most part, have survived. Ever the liberal, he could proudly boast that 'I have had the pleasure of affixing Whig names in the bush.'[37] As the supply port for the pastoral expansion, Melbourne grew quickly: from 500 inhabitants in 1837 to 12,000 in 1841. Rapid growth meant it did not take long for the settlers to agitate for separation from New South Wales as an independent colony. That Sydney was the main beneficiary of Port Phillip's productivity was unacceptable to the local settlers and their new superintendent, Charles Joseph La Trobe.

The fast-expanding pastoral frontier raised anxieties about the moral welfare of squatters living in isolation. Philanthropists such as Caroline Chisholm sought to create Christian families on the edge of settlements. She was raised as an evangelical but converted to Catholicism when she married. Chisholm saw the family as the foundation for the colony's prosperity and she worked to support young single women to find a job and a husband. In 1841, she established a female immigrants' home in Sydney. Subsequently, she travelled throughout New South Wales to place young migrant women in the homes of decent families. The settlers on the frontier appreciated her efforts. Pubs offered a meal and free lodging; the women travelled by coach and, though they would have been easy pickings, no bushranger harassed Chisholm's parties. The image of Caroline Chisholm on horseback, leading at times hundreds of young female immigrants on journeys into the interior – 'a second Moses in bonnet and shawl' – resonated strongly in the colonies, as well as back in Britain.[38] Respectable, but with little money or social standing, Chisholm settled some 11,000 women in security, dignity and independence.

* * *

Some in Britain believed that Australia's growth had been stunted by scattering the settlers away from the urban growth centres while encouraging immorality and barbarism. At much the same time, a new theory of colonisation was also developing. Devised by Edward Gibbon Wakefield, an eccentric whose outsized ambitions had landed him in British prison for the abduction of a 15-year-old heiress, the plan was elegant, if simplistic. Australia had land with few people; England had people with little land. Emigration to Australia could help both if it could be funded by the sale of Australian land at 'sufficient price': not so high as to prevent settlement altogether, but high enough to prevent large numbers becoming landowners and dispersing as independent farmers across the country. This was the essence of the program of 'systematic colonisation'.

'Wakefieldism' focused on South Australia, which had previously been seen as a land of little promise. From the sea, naval explorers had recorded a coastline that suggested infertile soil and scant fresh water. None had noticed the mouth of the Murray River, where Australia's largest river system meets the ocean. That discovery was made in 1830 by Charles Sturt, a Cambridge-educated soldier who had arrived in Sydney in 1827 and made a name for himself by charting the upper Darling River in northern New South Wales in 1829.

Wakefield's proposals generated enormous interest, and in 1833 the South Australian Association was founded to promote the idea. Among its members was the young John Stuart Mill, who at one point considered emigrating to Australia. A year later, the *South Australian Constitution Act* was passed by the British Parliament. South Australia was established as a convict-free society, 'a civilized country from the very commencement', Mill proclaimed.[39] It was to be the best of the old world, a community that protected civil and religious freedoms. Over the course of the next century, South Australia would prove itself a leader in liberal reform.

On 28 December 1836, the first governor of South Australia, Sir John Hindmarsh, who had earlier served on Lord Nelson's *Victory* at the Battle of Trafalgar, stood next to an arched gum tree at Glenelg and proclaimed South Australia a British colony. Two days later he chose the site of the capital, which he named Adelaide, after the wife of King William IV.

With a skilled, high-minded and educated populace, plus favourable geography, Adelaide did not take long to prosper. The population had reached 60,000 by 1850. Arable land was located close to the coast, which allowed the settlers to sow more wheat than any other colony. In 1838, Charles Bonney and Joseph Hawdon, at the head of 300 cattle and a flock of sheep, established a droving route from Victoria to Adelaide. They were greatly assisted by Aboriginal guides they met along the way.

The founding of Adelaide as a British settlement, according to Geoffrey Blainey, 'was one of the far-reaching events in the history of Australia'.[40] No longer was it possible for another European power to establish a colony in Australia. Britain, for the first time in history, was in possession of an entire continent.

4

Towards Self-government

As sheep and wool became the economic foundation of Australia, free settlers poured in and soon outnumbered the emancipists. Pressure grew for political reform and an end to transportation. The first elected members entered legislative councils. The nationwide campaign against convict transportation encouraged the colonists to think of themselves as Australians with a common interest. On the frontiers of settlement, there was much mistreatment of Aboriginal people, even as elsewhere humanitarian concern for their wellbeing grew.

§

If the British conscience of the 19th century had a name, it was William Wilberforce. Through dint of personality and pursuit of the great cause of the eradication of slavery, the evangelical Yorkshireman amassed a devout and reverential following that extended to Australia. He nominated chaplains and missionaries; he corresponded with at least one governor; and was fervently admired by Lachlan and Elizabeth Macquarie. On their journey to New South Wales in 1809, they had witnessed first-hand a Portuguese ship throwing overboard fever-ridden slaves to prevent the spread of an infection that had already killed many. 'We all thought on Mr Wilberforce,' Elizabeth wrote.[1]

Wilberforce died in 1833; his political heir was Thomas Fowell Buxton, a physically imposing man known as 'the elephant' and chair of the Select Committee on Aborigines, which published its grim report in 1837: 'Too often, their territory has been usurped,' the Committee said of Australia's Aboriginal population, 'their property seized; their numbers diminished; their character debased; the spread of civilization impeded.'[2]

The more distance there was from Sydney, the more the laws of England gave way to the laws of survival and retribution. The frontiersmen wanted physical protection from hostile tribes and fair compensation for stolen livestock but could hardly sue the Aboriginal perpetrators. William Wentworth railed against the hand of 'Exeter Hall', the London meeting place for the evangelicals and humanitarians who looked upon frontier killings with disgust and demanded protection for Aboriginal people.[3] Other settlers speculated that the 'blacks' were acting so aggressively in the belief that the Crown was actually on their side.[4]

In 1838, another select committee, this time on transportation, applied the moral fervour of the abolitionist cause to transportation, finding it little more than a form of white slavery. Ignoring the relatively benign treatment of most convicts, the committee focused on the brutality of the punishment centres: Port Arthur, Moreton Bay, Port Macquarie and Norfolk Island. The committee's chair, the radical William Molesworth, recommended the phasing out of transportation altogether. Molesworth felt strongly that the whole system morally compromised NSW society: not just the convicts, but the settlers, too.

Molesworth's indignation masked the report's obvious flaws. Had the committee travelled to New South Wales, it would have seen that most convicts worked for settlers more humane than those depicted in their report. This is clear from the convicts' own accounts: in letters to relatives, they wrote of good food and leisure, the likes of which they never would have had in Britain. Some even encouraged extended family to emigrate.

Since the arrival of the First Fleet, convict masters and colonial authorities had learned that rewards rather than severity were more conducive to prisoner reform and productivity. As John Macarthur's son, James, put it, 'where a man behaves well ... [we] make him forget, if possible, that he is a convict'.[5] The 'Fatal Shore' caricature of officially sanctioned brutality is far from the whole story. In fact, military officers generally had no involvement in the punishment of assigned convicts, who were no more likely to be flogged for indiscretions than were the soldiers and sailors of the Empire.[6]

No country had a system of punishment that so upended social hierarchy as early New South Wales. An emancipist landowner might send a badly behaving convict to a magistrate – also an ex-convict – who would perhaps order a flogging, overseen by an ex-convict policeman and carried out by a convict.[7] The Australian aversion to 'tall poppies' possibly begins from this 'unique social formation'.[8] No one in this system was deemed inherently superior. There is a strong case to be made that it was the most successful penal experiment in human history.

Perhaps influenced by the Molesworth inquiry, the British government decided to suspend transportation to New South Wales; an announcement that Bourke's successor as governor, George Gipps, made in 1840. The common designation of the colony as a 'den of thieves' had upset all the local factions – emancipists and exclusives alike. By the 1830s, they were already re-aligning off the back of Australia's fast-developing pastoral industry. Macarthur and Wentworth recognised their common interests as landowners and squatters. It had dawned on them, as on their supporters, that the real political divide was not between emancipist and exclusive, but increasingly between Australians and London.

* * *

Arriving in large numbers, the free migrants changed the temper of the colony. Convicts could be fatalistic or cynical about institutional structures, while the settlers tended to be grateful for the freedom and opportunity that life in New South Wales offered. After all, they had chosen to come. The free migrants, young and industrious, were highly literate and carried with them the reforming temper of British politics.[9] The Launceston preacher John West found many of them to be 'distrustful of the rich, jealous of rank, and fond of the equality of human rights'.[10]

Between 1831 and 1845, 59,275 assisted migrants arrived in New South Wales. For most immigrants, their fare was paid, their food provided and their children schooled. In South Australia, the colonial government was required to provide public employment to assisted migrants if the private sector could not do so.[11] Here was another glimpse of the 'vast public utility' of the Australian state.[12]

Henry Parkes, a future premier of New South Wales and 'Father of Federation', arrived in 1839 as an assisted migrant, with no more than two or three shillings to his name, a wife and a newborn infant to look after. Parkes spent his first two weeks searching for work until a labouring job presented itself 36 miles (58 km) north of Sydney. The family spent their first four months in miserable conditions: sleeping on a bed made of tree bark and an old door covered with clothes, nestled in a rickety little hut. It was a modest beginning for one of Australia's greatest statesmen.

Many working men of Parkes' generation had experienced a political awakening. The Chartist movement – the most spectacular product of years of economic discontent in Britain – generated monster rallies, at some of which upwards of 100,000 people gathered demanding political reform. The Chartists sought universal manhood suffrage, annual parliaments, payment of members, no property qualification for members, the secret ballot and constituencies of equal size. Parkes had attended these rallies and marched in the torchlit processions. In March 1839, he announced his departure for Sydney in a Chartist journal: 'as one of the many who cannot now obtain the means of living in their native country. In a fortnight's time I shall be gone to seek a better home in the wilderness of Australia.'[13] By the late 1840s, he was a shopkeeper in Sydney, and his store became a hub for Sydney's Chartists, radicals and democrats – the 'toyshop mob' as they were known – all agitating for political change.

These New Australians were already imbued with 'the popular principles of government', increasingly pushed by the champions of an impatient and propertyless working class.[14] In challenging the older generation of Whig reformers, like Wentworth, they ushered in a new phase in modern Australia's political development.

* * *

During the 1830s the area of settlement in Australia expanded every year by the size of Ireland.[15] Indigenous Australians' hunting grounds were invaded and their sacred sites trampled. In the pastoral plains and beyond, two alternative conceptions of humanity played out: the Hobbesian view of life as 'solitary, poor, nasty, brutish and short', driven by survival of the fittest, and the Lockian alternative of man as free, instinctually just and naturally inclined to co-operation and harmony.

Trouble usually followed a pattern. Pastoralists grazed their sheep and cattle on new land, killed the kangaroos and monopolised the waterholes. When Aboriginal people killed livestock and sometimes shepherds and drovers too, punitive raids quickly ensued. It was not uncommon for a raiding party to kill the first Aboriginal person they spotted. Colonial officials were aware of the conflict and humanitarians were appalled by it. One Gippsland squatter found himself 'familiarized with scenes of horror – from having murder made a topic of everyday conversation'.[16]

Quantifying the numbers killed in frontier conflict has been highly contentious. The Colonial Frontier Massacre Map, managed by academics at the University of Newcastle, claims 421 sites with 11,257 Aboriginal deaths between 1788 and 1930.[17] Because eye-witness accounts and reliable contemporary records are often not available, these numbers should be regarded as guesstimates. What can't be denied is that frontier life was brutal and dangerous, and that Aboriginal people suffered grievously.

Yet to see the expansion of settlement as only a series of 'frontier wars' is hardly accurate either. Settlers relied on Aboriginal workers for their local knowledge of the country and for their skills in working it. Aboriginal people were not just useful, but indispensable.

In the opinion of one settler at Wimmera, his Aboriginal employees were 'the best shepherds in the district', and he believed they outperformed the average stockman by dint of 'better nerve' and 'better sight'.[18] The most valuable resource on any expedition was the Aboriginal guide, whose ancestors knew what British Australians were only just 'discovering'.

These skilled native bushmen helped explorers find their way through inhospitable terrain, hunt for food and negotiate safe passage through hostile country.

Aboriginal workers outnumbered white stockmen five to one in some areas. Landowners accepted their cultural habits as part of business.[19] Some of the workers simply downed their tools and 'went walkabout' once they had accumulated enough food or supplies. Others demanded decent housing and clothes in exchange for the changes they'd endured, not just for themselves but for their kin, including the old and sick.

With their parents busy, settlers' children could be left in the company of nearby Aboriginal tribes. Often enough, they revelled in exploring country or experiencing the previously hidden delicacies of the bush. 'I spent most of the time with the blacks,' William Ross Munro recalled of his younger days on the mid-north coast of New South Wales in the 1850s. Parents, he said, 'let their children wander about with them at will. But that faith was not misplaced. The blacks were marvellous in the attention they gave to children – the care they took of us, and the affection in which they held us.'[20]

* * *

The evangelical solution to settler–native conflict was to appoint 'protectors' throughout Australia. Protectors were to master the local languages, act as a liaison between the Aboriginal peoples and the government, encourage the education of Aboriginal children, ensure religious instruction and ease the native population into a thoroughly European way of living. The colonial secretary, Lord Glenelg, bluntly told the new NSW governor, George Gipps, that the colonists should have no problem funding these roles. Glenelg was happy for the inevitable resentment to be over-ridden.[21]

In the Port Phillip District, a chief protector and four full-time assistant protectors had the unenviable task of trying to reconcile the local Aboriginal people with a drastically changed existence. With few resources, their success was limited, though some – such as Assistant Protector William Thomas – made genuine achievements in mediating tensions and saving lives in the process. 'I could not but feel for the poor blacks,' wrote Thomas in March 1841. 'They had till this visit an undisturbed range among the lagoons ... now ... the Yarra is forever closed to them.' Thomas, it's said, was 'more successful than any other first-generation settler in attempting to comprehend and sustain Aboriginal society. His charges knew him as Marminata [Good Father].'[22]

Similarly, the establishment of Aboriginal missions throughout remote Australia – perhaps 200 of them, starting from 1837 when George Langhorne established one on the banks of the Yarra up until the 1960s – provided occupation and sustenance to people who had been displaced. Some, such as the Hermannsburg Mission in the Northern Territory – run by German Lutherans – and the Presbyterian-run Kunmunya Mission in Western Australia, preserved Aboriginal culture that otherwise would have vanished.[23]

More often, though, the experience resembled the Langhorne mission where attendance was irregular and the demand for land for settlement soon saw the mission closed.

The absence of an Australian version of the New Zealand Treaty of Waitangi, signed in 1840 – a week after Captain William Hobson arrived in the country as the lieutenant governor of New Zealand, responsible to the governor of New South Wales – is sometimes cited as evidence of the racism and discrimination on this side of the Tasman. In reality, the circumstances were quite different.[24] There was the issue of possible competing legal claims over New Zealand from France and the United States.[25] As well, compared with the Māori, Aboriginal Australians were more diverse, with a profusion of different languages, more divided, more nomadic and spread across a much larger country. The Māori resistance to colonisation was fiercer, better organised and more effective, and they had a hierarchy of authority that the newcomers could readily deal with.[26] There were Māori chiefs, who could consult with one another and sign such a treaty.

By today's standards, the Aboriginal protectorates seem like a ludicrously inadequate response to the extreme disruption, trauma and despair inflicted on Aboriginal lives. Even so, many settlers thought colonial authorities were doing too much. '[W]e can no longer move with confidence,' one correspondent declared in the *Sydney Herald*. 'It is true we have a Sergeant of Mounted Police with six or seven Troopers ... but tied as their hands are, and strict as their instruction are against the use of their weapons upon these savages, what protection are they to our lives and property?'[27] Any spike in frontier violence tended to worsen settler relations with the government. In June 1838, Governor Gipps refused a request to send an armed force to suppress 'the blacks', on the grounds they were British subjects and had to be dealt with according to the law. 'The fact is that it will come to this,' one correspondent threatened, 'that the settlers, unless they witness a disposition to protect them ... against the aggression of black British subjects, will take the matter into their own hands ...'[28] This happened, in horrific circumstances, at Myall Creek, near the Gwydir River in northern New South Wales, on 10 June 1838.

* * *

The Myall Creek massacre was shocking and controversial, not simply because it occurred, but because the perpetrators were caught and brought to trial. This was almost unheard of in colonial society. The details were particularly gruesome: a party of 11 stockmen wantonly murdered in cold blood up to 30 men, women and children; the victims' bodies were subsequently hacked apart and burned. Word of the murders reached the governor only thanks to an eyewitness, an Aboriginal boy named Davy, and a station manager, William Hobbs. Because of their courage, we know more about the Myall Creek massacre than of any other.

Despite public pressure not to prosecute (led by the *Sydney Morning Herald*, which has in more recent years apologised), and despite the difficulties of the case, Governor Gipps and Solicitor-General Plunkett were determined to set an example. The law prevented the only eyewitness to the event, Davy, from giving evidence because Aboriginal people, as non-Christians, were then regarded as being incapable of giving sworn testimony. To make matters more difficult, the defendants had enough public donations to use the best lawyers, and had most of the colonial press on their side.

At the first trial, the jury returned a verdict of not guilty, which Plunkett interpreted as 'they're guilty but we won't convict'. Plunkett sought a second trial, reducing the accused from 11 to seven and focusing his case on the murder of a small boy. Justice Burton, the judge at the second trial, was visibly moved and delivered an emotional speech to the jury. '[T]he blood of the victims cries for vengeance,' he said.[29] The accused were found guilty and sentenced to death. Gipps ignored petitions to spare their lives.

In this instance, the British principle of equality before the law prevailed against intense social pressure. However, so vehement was the public reaction that later investigations were not always pursued with the same vigour. In one case, Gipps informed Lord Glenelg that it was 'deemed inexpedient to hold an investigation while the Public Mind remained in a very excited state in respect to the Blacks'.[30]

Some settlers took their violence 'underground', using devious methods like the poisoning of food or water sources. In one such instance, in November 1847, a settler from the Clarence River in northern New South Wales, Thomas Coutts, gave poisoned flour to a group of 23 Aboriginal workers. After rumours of this swept the district, he was arrested and put on trial for wilful murder. Coutts was unpopular, and one local wrote to his father of the 'atrocious murder of Blacks', stating 'everybody hopes [Coutts] will be hung'.[31] However, Plunkett discontinued the case despite concluding that 'the suspicion is very strong that the prisoner is not guiltless of the dreadful deed charged against him'. What frustrated the prosecution, according to Plunkett, was 'the defect of the present law [in] excluding altogether the evidence of the Aboriginal natives'. A charge against local Aboriginal people for the murder of one of Coutts's hut-keepers was also dropped for the same reason. In 1849, Plunkett sought to have the law changed, citing the poisoning as a case where 'justice was entirely evaded because native testimony could not be admitted'. His Bill was narrowly defeated in the Legislative Council, and it was not until 1860 that the then attorney-general declared that 'being an aboriginal is no ground to reject his testimony'.[32]

* * *

The great land boom continued apace, and the NSW governor was under pressure to retain control in an era of constant change and soaring expectations. In 1836, the Legislative Council gave a regulatory basis to those pastoralists squatting illegally on Crown land. Outside of the 19 counties, land was carved into districts overseen by a commissioner of Crown lands. For a yearly payment, squatters could rent as much land as their capacity would allow. Bourke established a border police force, funded by a levy on squatters' herds.[33] This was a bare-bones regime that neither satisfied the squatters nor stopped them: Bourke had given them recognition but not security of tenure, nor any preemptive rights to purchase the land.

The most dramatic display of grazier intransigence came in February 1840, when William Wentworth and John Jones 'purchased' from Māori chiefs the whole of the South Island of New Zealand. Bourke's successor, Governor Gipps, was furious, declaring in a ferocious speech to the Legislative Council that Wentworth 'will never get one acre, one foot, one shilling for the land'; and that his behaviour was corrupt. The Council duly invalidated the purchase.[34]

But both the wealthy emancipists and the free settlers saw their future in the expansion of settlement. 'No one would be so silly as to contend, that henceforth the Colony of New South Wales should be confined to the narrow limit of the nineteen counties,' John Macarthur's son James argued.[35]

Meanwhile, between the boom in assisted migration and the cessation of transportation, the fear of ex-convicts dominating an elected legislature eased and the prejudice against emancipists began to disappear. These new conditions suited the liberal inclinations of the British Whigs, whose subsequent *New South Wales Constitution Act 1842* gave ex-convicts the right to vote and stand for the Legislative Council, a big further step towards responsible government. So, too, was the increase in the Council's membership from seven to 36, of whom 24 were to be elected. Property qualifications – in other words, the requirement to own a certain quantum of property – limited the franchise: this somewhat mirrored the situation in Britain, following the 1832 *Reform Act*. Effectively, about one in five men in New South Wales could vote.

Wentworth, together with his running mate William Bland, an emancipist doctor, was the most high-profile candidate to stand for this new-look Council. Their supporters flew white banners containing a star and a Union Jack – probably the earliest precursor to something resembling the Australian national flag. The pair topped the poll. On 1 August 1843, Wentworth, now 53, entered Australia's first elected parliament dressed in the rough squatter clothes he wore on his sheep stations. The large landholders and squatters, with Wentworth as their leader, dominated the elected membership of the Legislative Council.

Land policy took up most of the Council's deliberations. Pastoralists, seeing themselves as the true developers of the country, demanded a pathway to freehold title. By 1845, they were exporting 24 million pounds (10,800,000 kg) of wool, up from only four million (1,814,000 kg) ten years earlier. So busy was the London to Sydney wool trade that transport costs were less than the route from London to the south of Germany.[36]

Governor Gipps was not prepared to gift freehold to the 700 station holders: between them, they were managing some three million acres (1,214,000 ha). 'The lands are the unquestionable property of the Crown,' he wrote, 'and they are held in trust by the government for the benefit of the people of the whole British Empire.'[37] If the squatters understood the economic significance of land title, Gipps, wary of creating a country of plutocrats, understood its political significance no less well. Nonetheless, he had a powerful opponent in Wentworth, whose political skill was in associating the financial interests of the squatters to a more popular program of responsible government.

The Council, though reformed, was neither fully representative nor responsible. It could not impose fines or levies and had to consider legislation proposed by the governor.[38] The exclusives, emancipists and the new free settlers all wanted different reforms: many landholders wanted transportation restored as a source of free labour, while the townspeople of Sydney mostly felt that ending transportation had boosted wages, reduced crime and improved the colony's standing.

Under the Gipps-sponsored *Waste Lands Occupation Act 1846* and the subsequent Orders-In-Council, squatters were given much better security of tenure: no longer would they be subject to annual licences, but instead could be granted leases for up to 14 years, plus they were provided with priority rights of purchase for a minimum price of £1 an acre. Still, they did not gain outright freehold and London remained the landlord.

* * *

While New South Wales forged ahead, the colony of Van Diemen's Land struggled. Convict transportation, far from ending, had increased fourfold in two years: from 1267 in 1840 to 5334 in 1842. By 1853, some 35,000 convicts had arrived and London was reluctant to give a colony so full of convicts and emancipists the same reformed Legislative Council that New South Wales had achieved in 1842.

To many, this only proved that transportation had to end. An Australia-wide anti-transportation movement began in Launceston, in particular via the Congregationalist minister John West and his paper, the *Launceston Examiner*. West was a captivating speaker, a skill he used to full effect in advocating political and religious freedom. He did not despise convicts as others did; rather, he despised a system that did not sufficiently care for them or their future. He drew on the moral arguments against slavery to formulate his demand that convict transportation be abolished for good.

In 1845, the Launceston politician Richard Dry stood in the Legislative Council in Hobart and called for a committee to inquire into all the costs of transportation. In October, Dry and five others – the 'Patriotic Six' – resigned from Council, refusing to pass a supply Bill unless convict transportation was ended.

In 1846, the British government temporarily suspended transportation to Van Diemen's Land, only to reintroduce it in modified form in 1849, this time sending only convicts who were halfway through their sentence – the so-called exiles. Still reeling from the 'Hungry Forties' – the period of economic depression and famine linked to the failure of the potato crop in Europe – Britain needed a solution for overcrowded gaols. Then, to the shock of Australian abolitionists, the British government also resumed transportation to New South Wales.

London had not anticipated the marked change in Sydney's political culture since the original cessation of transportation in 1840. Protests erupted immediately upon the arrival of the convict ship *Hashemy* on 9 June 1849. It was one of the largest public meetings ever held in the city up to that point. The most striking speaker was Robert Lowe, an Oxford-educated lawyer who could deploy a poisonous tongue in his advocacy of popular causes: he described the pro-transportationists of the Legislative Council as '[t]raitors, trimmers, rosewater liberals and political tidewaiters'. Lowe worked within the moral universe of English liberty, calling on the crowd to 'exercise that right that every subject has – to assert his freedom'. Ominously, he added that, 'as in America, oppression was the parent of independence, so will it be in this colony'.[39]

Antipathy to convict transportation was no less vigorous in the Port Phillip District. Its residents had no intention of living with the taint of convictism. Upon hearing that an approaching convict ship, the *Randolph*, might be rushed by an angry and unruly crowd, Superintendent Charles La Trobe wisely ordered its diversion to Sydney.

By the late 1840s, Melbourne was a city on the rise, with a population almost level with Hobart's at 23,000. Its surrounding sheep population had increased fourfold to 6.6 million between 1843 and 1851, effectively equal to that of New South Wales (in its modern boundaries).[40] No other area in Australia was experiencing so rapid a rise in prosperity.

Melburnians were independent and ambitious for their own political autonomy. This made their status as a 'dependency within a dependency' – still formally part of New South Wales, with representatives sitting in the NSW Legislative Council – utterly intolerable. Separation festivals, banquets and bonfires became regular features of the late 1840s. In a show of defiance, all six candidates for the Port Phillip District withdrew their candidacy for the Legislative Council at the last minute, leaving but one nominee – the London-based secretary of state for the colonies, Earl Grey. Angered by this impertinence, the NSW governor held another election, this time in Geelong, to fill the vacancies. So politically conscious was the Victorian populace that by 1850, three of the five daily papers in Australia were in Melbourne, another was in Geelong, and there was just one in Sydney.[41]

* * *

While convict transportation was the founding purpose of British settlement, its abolition helped define modern Australia. Increasingly, transportation came to be seen as the ultimate barrier to fuller measures of self-government. Henry Parkes thought transportation 'incompatible with our existence as a free colony, desiring self-government'. The transportation question forced the colonists to reckon with their identity as Australians and to ponder the nature of their political system. As a continent-wide problem, it required a continent-wide solution. The democratic argument against transportation, Parkes said, was that it was 'in violation of the will of the majority of the colonists'.[42]

By the end of 1851, the Australasian Anti-Transportation League established in Launceston had branches in New South Wales, South Australia, Victoria (whose boundaries would soon be formalised) and New Zealand. A notable feature of the League was the presence of women, whose influence was a key to its success. The League's banner had earlier been unfurled in Launceston: a blue ensign with the Union Jack next to the stars of the Southern Cross, each star representing a member colony – another forerunner to the Australian national flag. John West was reportedly its designer.

The elder statesman William Wentworth, then in his 60s, speaking for the old Australia, feared the kind of democracy that some of the abolitionists like Henry Parkes celebrated. 'Wherever the principle of universal suffrage has prevailed,' he boomed, 'it has been the signal for rapine, massacre and bloodshed.' To a big-time pastoralist, a steady flow of convicts was no bad thing; but Wentworth's view was not informed purely by self-interest. He had seen Australia rise from a dumping ground to a place of respectability and prosperity. Convicts had helped with that. In the Legislative Council he quoted from a recent Australian poem: 'A convict nation from whose tainted root/Sprang goodly stems, and cultivated fruit'.[43] That, he declared, was the story and the miracle of Australia.

In 1850, the NSW Legislative Council debated a call to the British government to end convict transportation once and for all. The speeches were long, eloquent and emotional. No other debate had taken up so much time. By its end, it was plain where opinion was. Outnumbered, Wentworth and his faction staged a walk-out. The resolution to cease transportation to New South Wales passed unanimously.

* * *

Reform continued by way of the *Australian Colonies Government Act 1850*, which provided for more elected representatives in the NSW Legislative Council and, significantly, separated the Port Phillip District from New South Wales to create the colony of Victoria, complete with its own Legislative Council. South Australia and Van Diemen's Land were also granted representative Legislative Councils. Further, the new Act gave the WA Legislative Council the power to grant itself a two-thirds elected body, provided certain political and economic conditions were met. It empowered the colonies to alter and revise their constitutions in the future, subject to consent from London. This was Grey's answer to the swashbuckling of Lowe and those who warmed to his threat that 'oppression was the parent of independence'. London's message was there would be no oppression in Australia.

Nor, yet, would there be full self-government. Territorial revenue remained in the hands of the Crown. The British government could veto any legislation that displeased it. Even to William Wentworth, and to all those more radical, this was a constitution on training wheels, a condescending exercise in British supremacy that displayed little faith in the Australian project.

Wentworth formalised his objections in a Declaration and Remonstrance against the *Australian Colonies Government Act*. Biographer Andrew Tink has called this document 'as close as Australia ever got to a Declaration of Independence'.[44] It laid out the grievances of the colonies with the Bill: that the Imperial Parliament 'has not, nor of right ought to have any power to tax the people of this Colony'; 'That the revenue arising from public lands derived ... by the labour and capital of the people of this Colony is ... their property'; 'That ... all Departments should be subject to the direct control ... of the Colonial Legislature which should [appropriate] ... the revenues of the colony.'[45] There was no clearer statement of Australia's right to govern itself. Henry Parkes, some years later, described it as 'one of the foundation-stones of the fabric of our constitutional liberties'.[46] Just as Wentworth had done in the 1820s, he harnessed the rhetoric of the English liberal tradition and asserted the right of his countrymen, as Britons, to enjoy the same political liberties as those in the Mother Country.

As the Australian Colonies Bill was being considered in London, Lowe successfully lobbied the British government to halve the franchise qualification to £10. This was the same level as in Britain. His argument was that too high a qualification would favour the wealthy ex-convict at the expense of the honest but poorer free settler. As one historian put it: '[T]heir lordships – for the first and last time in their history – made an electoral measure *more* radical.'[47]

On 2 May 1851, just a fortnight after the NSW Legislative Council had adopted Wentworth's Declaration and Remonstrance, the *Sydney Morning Herald* finally broke news of contagious excitement: gold had been discovered in Australia.

5

Gold!

The discovery of gold brought a vast influx of immigrants from all over the world, plus untold wealth to the new colonies. But far from heralding the collapse of the established order, the gold rush merely accelerated the move to responsible self-government. The protesting miners who took part in the Eureka rebellion turned out to be more interested in lower taxes and greater freedom than revolutionary change.

§

The discovery of gold was transformational. Within two years, more migrants had arrived than the total number of convicts transported over 80 years. The gold rushes killed off convict transportation in eastern Australia for good, and by 1858, the settler population reached one million. The rapid influx of migrants and wealth upended old hierarchies and shaped a new political culture. Looking back on the gold rush, Australia's second prime minister, Alfred Deakin, felt 'it gave us a large proportion of the best of our population, men with a far wider and more advanced liberalism'.[1]

* * *

There had been rumours of gold before its much-ballyhooed discovery in February 1851. Particles of it had been seen as early as the 1820s. Colonial authorities were aware of such claims, and even more aware of their potential consequences in what was still a penal colony. Governor Gipps reportedly told one discoverer to 'put it away ... or we shall all have our throats cut'.[2]

In reality, once the awareness of gold had taken hold, government had as much chance of stopping the gold rush as it had of stopping the earlier land rush. When the publicity-hungry Englishman Edward Hargraves found five specks of gold in a creek bed near Bathurst in New South Wales, the rush was on. In June 1851, more gold was found on the Turon River. A few weeks later, at nearby Meroo Creek, an Aboriginal stockman discovered a nugget yielding 88 pounds (40 kg) of gold, larger than anything seen in the earlier California rush. Within days, people from all over Victoria and New South Wales were flocking to the Ophir goldfield near Orange; months later, ships from every corner of the Earth were headed for Australian ports bringing gold prospectors.

The biggest discoveries occurred in the south. In Victoria, at places like Ballarat, Buninyong, Castlemaine, Bendigo and Ararat, rich veins of gold were found close to the surface. Unlike in New South Wales, where gold was buried deeper underground, diggers in Victoria could easily pluck nuggets from the soil, creeks and rivers with pick, shovel and pan. Following the Ballarat discovery, *The Argus* reported, 'The whole town of Geelong is in hysterics ... Gentleman [are] foaming at the mouth, ladies fainting, [and] children throwing somersaults.'[3] Charles La Trobe reported to the Colonial Office that men from all walks of life had left Melbourne for the diggings: 'Cottages are deserted, houses to let, business is at a standstill, and even the schools are closed. In some of the suburbs not a man is left.'[4]

As soon as a new find was unearthed, word spread like wildfire. Men in their thousands stampeded to the site and protected their digs zealously. Accompanying them were the blacksmiths, publicans, butchers, bakers, servants and grocers who were among the first to make their fortunes. Shantytowns sprang up wherever a fortune might be made. When news came of a fresh discovery, these temporary towns were often hastily abandoned, leaving the country pockmarked with holes.

Much of the countryside around the goldfields was physically transformed. Tents carpeted an increasingly desolate landscape, typified by felled trees and muddy waters, and swarmed by desperate gold seekers. The digger William Howitt likened the phenomenon to a 'flight of locusts'; and another was struck by the colour of the men – a deep, earthy yellow – 'yellow clothes – yellow hands – yellow faces – yellow everything, and working in closely compacted pieces of ground as thick as possible over the whole surface of a hill or mountain'.[5]

In the vast incoming human tide were individuals of future significance who would reshape colonial life. David Syme, later the owner of *The Age*, arrived on 29 September 1852, 'with very little money in my pocket'.[6] On his first night he slept under a table at a Bourke Street hotel. Graham Berry, a largely self-educated cockney draper who would go on to become premier of Victoria, arrived the same year. He set up a general store in South Yarra before moving to Collingwood.

As the gold seekers flooded in, La Trobe worried that the government was losing control. He feared that the prospect of riches was attracting young, excitable men touched by the afterglow of the 1848 revolutions in Europe. 'There is a spirit abroad,' he wrote, 'partly induced by that of the times in which we live.'[7]

La Trobe adopted the administrative rules used in New South Wales to regulate gold mining. The first step was to assert the

Crown's right to the land and to exclude unauthorised diggers.[8] The second was to introduce a licence fee to permit authorised mining at 30 shillings a month. A licence gave miners the right to peg out a claim of eight square feet (0.74 m²). The idea of this tax was to discourage the less successful and force the shepherds, drovers and clerks back to their old jobs. In fact, as Geoffrey Blainey has described it, La Trobe's decision democratised the goldfields by offering one of the country's richest resources equally to everyone.[9]

At the peak of the rush, hundreds of ships crammed into Port Phillip Bay, and carts, carriages and pedestrians jammed the roads to the goldfields. Provisions from around the world flowed into Melbourne. 'All down, near the wharves, it is a scene of dust, drays and carts, hurrying to and fro, and heaps of boxes, trunks, bundles and digging tools,' wrote Howitt.[10] Imports increased fivefold in two years. The value of imported alcohol and tobacco alone in 1852 exceeded all the imports from the United Kingdom in 1850.[11]

The global impact of the Californian gold rush (1848–1855) and the Australian was to double world gold production, kickstarting European and North American trade and industry out of the prolonged 'Hungry 1840s' depression – much to the consternation of would-be revolutionaries Karl Marx and Friedrich Engels. 'It is to be hoped that the Australian gold-shit will not hold up the commercial crisis,' Engels wrote to his *Communist Manifesto* co-author.[12] Concerned for the suddenly diminishing prospects of the imminent collapse of Western capitalism, they began noting instead the plethora of new international trading routes springing into existence.[13]

By the mid-1850s, Victoria had supplanted New South Wales as the most populous colony. By 1861, it was home to 500,000 people, compared with fewer than 80,000 a decade earlier. Even the British military headquarters moved from Sydney to Melbourne. Possibly it had the highest average income of anywhere in the world. Melbourne became the financial centre of Australia; and goldfield camps like Ballarat and Bendigo swiftly transformed into bustling rural cities that ranked among Australia's five most populous for the next quarter-century.

* * *

For those arriving from the stratified societies of Britain and Europe, the gold diggings were extraordinary. A 'boisterous egalitarianism' was tearing down social barriers as the diggers 'enjoy[ed] a new liberty, of which they never dreamed before'.[14] One visiting British aristocrat, Lord Robert Cecil – the future Lord Salisbury and British prime minister – attracted taunts for his white top hat. He was dismayed by the diggers' vulgarity but surprised by the relative lawfulness of the goldfields, estimating that 'there is not half as much crime or insubordination as there would be in an English town of the same wealth and population'.[15]

On some goldfields, miners developed their own informal rules in the absence of a well-established police presence.[16] Often enough, a measure of civil society – and the free associations that sustain it – emerged spontaneously among a population imbued with a pre-existing sense of what was right and proper. There were places where all work stopped on Sundays for the diggers to attend religious services. In Ballarat, a theatre was opened, a horse racing club was formed and cricket was played in the warmer months.

Still, the diggings were rough places. At Fryer's Creek, just south of Castlemaine, it was recorded that 'quarrels, dissensions, bloodshed and danger of the direst description reign supreme'.[17] Summary justice could be meted out, sometimes brutally. Crime was checked 'by an occasional pistol-shot'; word was passed from tent to tent relaying the consequences of a bad decision.[18] Authorities in Melbourne feared that 'lynch law' would rule the fields, as vigilante justice had become known during the California gold rush; only one instance of a lynching is recorded in Victoria, however.[19]

Convict and master, rich and poor, labourer and lawyer, man and woman, black and white – all became diggers. Suddenly they could afford 'meat, grog, horses, dogs and revolvers'.[20] There was little in the way of social deference. 'How different,' exclaimed Howitt, 'to the state of the silk-stocking, crimson-plushed livery-servants at home, who stand touching their hats at every word of their employers.' Others considered this 'plebeianism of the rankest, and, in many instances, of the lowest kind ... Although your father might have been my Lord of England all-over, it goes for nothing in this equalizing colony of gold and beef and mutton.'[21]

In 1853, the government further regulated the goldfields, introducing uniform claims – 144 square feet (13.3 m²) for individuals and 576 square feet (53.5 m²) for groups – to ensure everyone was given a fair go. A 'fair go', however, did nothing to reduce the inherent randomness of success on the goldfields.

The lottery of the rush normalised risk-taking in a society already used to the booms of 'bonanza' industries like whaling, sealing and woolgrowing. Migrants were more than willing to 'have a go' and pay the cost of the journey in the hope of striking it rich. Even the unsuccessful remained enterprising, speculative and adventurous. If politicians were initially aghast at the thought of so much wealth falling into the hands of the 'uneducated, unreflecting, and sensual portion of the community', in time they would be surprised by the moderating influence of aspiration, and the dreams of every person to rise above his or her station and seek security from the vicissitudes of life.[22]

* * *

The Chinese started to arrive in January 1853. Their numbers peaked at 40,000 in 1858 – equivalent to almost the entire population of the Port Phillip District in the late 1840s. Initial reactions to their arrival were marked by curiosity and confusion over their habits and dress; but as the number of Chinese increased, indignation and prejudice grew.

Discrimination notwithstanding, there were noticeable differences from the Chinese experience on the Californian goldfields. In Victoria, despite the chaotic flood of migration, the colonial government had a better grip than in California, which had only recently been seized from Mexico. Legal institutions were better established and more liberal. A judge at Castlemaine declared, 'All men here are equal; they come here from all parts of the world in equality, and you have no right to attempt to drive any away because they do not work as you please.'[23]

In practice, language and cultural barriers hurt the Chinese newcomers, and European migrants were made more welcome. Still, unlike in California, Chinese migrants could give evidence in court. Commercially, too, Chinese migrants generally found it easier to trade and also to achieve social mobility than in California. According to the historian Mae Ngai, Chinese capitalists 'believed their status as British subjects entitled them to equal political and economic rights (even if these were not always forthcoming)'.[24] Lowe Kong Meng arrived in Victoria in 1853 and carried on a significant trading business as well as becoming a founding board member of the Commercial Bank of Australasia, which issued bilingual notes to assist Chinese customers. By contrast, 'no American corporation welcomed Chinese capital'.[25]

In 1856, when the Victorian government imposed a large tax on each Chinese newcomer, the Chinese ingeniously thwarted it by landing at Robe in South Australia and walking, in large parties, roughly 250 miles (400 km) to the Victorian goldfields. This route was closed when South Australia passed similar anti-Chinese immigration restrictions a year later.

Using modern liberal arguments, in 1879, Lowe, together with Louis Ah Mouy and Cheok Hong Cheong, published a pamphlet titled *The Chinese Question*, rebutting the claim that Chinese migrants were innately different to the average European wage-earner:

> Human nature is human nature all the world over; and the Chinaman is just as fond of money, and just as eager to earn as much as he can, as the most grasping of his competitors ... And so it will be, after a very little time, with our own countrymen here ... [T]he expenditure of the Asiatic will soon rise to the European level, because his mode of living will approximate to those of his neighbours.[26]

It was an early instance of the universalism, and sense of a common humanity, that later came to characterise Australia.

* * *

The republican John Dunmore Lang thought that the discovery of gold was 'tantamount to an authoritative proclamation ... that Australia henceforth shall be free', while William Wentworth thought that '[gold] must in a very few years precipitate us from a colony into a nation'.[27] The *Australian Colonies Government Act 1850*, which applied to all four colonies as the rush began, had conceded many of the colonists' demands, apart from the one they wanted most – self-government.

Throughout 1852, the NSW Legislative Council agitated for the right to draft it. Colonial Secretary Earl Grey had long resisted such a measure, viewing the Australian colonies as an imperial project whose resources were to be held on trust for the benefit of future citizens of the British Empire. He was not prepared to grant a premature autonomy.

His successor, Sir John Pakington, took a different view, writing to Governor Fitzroy in New South Wales about 'the extreme difficulty of ... keeping our fellow subjects in Australia on a different political footing from those to whom those rights have been fully conceded in America'.[28] New South Wales, South Australia, Victoria and Tasmania were now invited to draft their own constitutions. Pakington's advice was to fashion them after the British system, with elected lower houses and appointed upper houses, and for London to retain a significant say in the colonies' governance.

The question for the colonists was how to follow the 'spirit' of the British Constitution rather than its specific form.[29] Generally, it was agreed that London should retain a say in Empire-wide matters, such as external affairs, but that local issues, including the control of Crown land, should be a matter for the elected assemblies. All agreed on an elected lower house, while debating the extent of the franchise. Opinion differed sharply over whether the upper houses ought to be elected or appointed. Elected upper houses were almost unknown at the time (the Province of Canada gained a partially elected one in 1856 and the US states' upper houses were then invariably appointed); yet again Australia was at the forefront of liberalising reform.

Throughout his public life, William Wentworth had fought for a meritocratic society where the most deserving could rise to the highest positions; but he'd also resisted enfranchising those who had demonstrated less enterprise – the propertyless workingman. He feared that democracy could easily degenerate into tyranny, even while invoking liberty, equality and fraternity. 'The history of Europe,' he said, 'had served to teach ... the unvarying truth that this universal suffrage was a curse wherever it prevailed.'[30]

Wentworth wanted a hereditary upper house akin to the House of Lords, dedicated to preserving the prosperity of the colony and balancing the excesses of democracy in the lower house. It would protect the individual from the arbitrary power of the mob and give citizens the freedom to live their own lives. Wentworth's belief was that stability required a balance of monarchy, aristocracy and democracy.

Many of the rich squatters supported Wentworth's proposal. They saw themselves as the pioneering founders of the colony's wealth. They demanded a constitution that would protect their private property. Anything that imperilled their individual enterprise, they thought, was an attack on colonial prosperity, even though they numbered less than a thousand.

The knockout blow to Wentworth's proposal came from the young colonial-born Daniel Deniehy. Although the son of two convicts, Deniehy had enjoyed an ample education and emerged as the voice for those who detested the hereditary politics and class prejudices of the old world. At a public meeting in Sydney's Victoria Theatre, he savaged Wentworth and his allies, referring to them as 'those harlequin aristocrats – these Botany Bay magnificos – these Australian mandarins' who wanted to replicate the 'worn-out grandees of continental Europe'. Deniehy continued, 'In some distant emulation of this degeneracy, I suppose we are to be favoured with a bunyip aristocracy.'[31] To rapturous applause, Deniehy evoked the picture of English, Irish, Scottish and European migrants flocking to Australia: 'Wherever man's skill is eminent, wherever glorious manhood asserts its elevation, there is an aristocracy that confers honour on the land that possesses it. That is God's aristocracy. That is an aristocracy that will grow and expand under free institutions, and bless the land where it flourishes.'[32]

Both Deniehy and Wentworth wanted stability and prosperity, but the elder statesman saw this as better protected by 'the great interests of the country' than by 'mere population' alone.[33] He advocated a British constitution over a 'Yankee' one. The American experience, he reasoned, offered a warning against the mediocrity of full democracy, in which the likes of Washington and Jefferson were supplanted by lesser men.

Wentworth accused his opponents, such as Parkes, of wanting to sever ties with Britain. Some democrats, like Deniehy and Lang, were indeed advocates of an Australian republic. But few wanted complete separation. Indeed, Parkes declared, 'I do not want a "Yankee Constitution" any more than Mr. Wentworth.'[34]

While democratic sentiment forced Wentworth to abandon his hopes of a hereditary upper house, his next favoured model – a nominated one, with appointments made by the governor – was accepted. South Australia, Victoria and Tasmania all settled on elected upper houses, albeit with high property requirements. Ironically, history would show that nominated upper houses were generally more co-operative with governments than elected chambers with a limited franchise. In 1854, the draft constitutions were sent to London for parliamentary and royal assent.

* * *

Meanwhile, mining was now subject to diminishing returns. Once surface deposits were exhausted, mining shafts had to be dug deeper and deeper, requiring more capital and long lead times. Many unsuccessful miners, after spending much money just to get to the goldfields, struggled to pay the monthly licence fee. Some refused, arguing that it was a tax on labour rather than production.[35] Fierce protests were directed towards a 'juggernaut tax' designed 'to crush the poor'.[36]

As the draft constitutions were being debated in the British Parliament, tensions rose on the Victorian goldfields. To fund the cost of policing the goldfields, La Trobe's replacement, Governor Hotham, ordered more stringent collection of licence fees. Licence searches were conducted twice a week and a lost or destroyed licence could attract a fine or gaol time.

In November 1854, the new Ballarat Reform League demanded the abolition of the licence fee. The League declared that 'taxation without representation is tyranny', and that 'the people are the only legitimate sources of political power'.[37] A new flag was adopted – the flag of the Southern Cross, today referred to as the Eureka flag. A crowd of 10,000 at Bakery Hill adopted the League's principles with their strong echoes of Chartism.

By December, some of the diggers had built a stockade near the Eureka diggings, where they could retreat when the police launched a licence hunt. They also began gathering firearms and training in quasi-military formations. There, under the Southern Cross flag at Bakery Hill – and, according to one widely circulated newspaper report, the Union Jack, too – they swore to 'stand truly by each other and fight to defend our rights and liberties'.[38]

There was British Chartism, Irish rebelliousness and the American political tradition in the Eureka movement. Yet for all its anti-authoritarian trappings, it largely occurred within an idiom of the rights and liberties granted by the British Constitution. Many of the diggers saw themselves as fighting for their rights as freeborn Englishmen, just as the American colonists had, and Robert Lowe and Henry Parkes did. As the historian Clare Wright described it:

The miners were not disloyal to their sovereign, but rather had lost any shred of respect for the minions who served her. They did not want to change the system of government; they wanted to be included in it. At no time did they riot against or launch an assault on authorities. They were not insurgents. They were not revolutionaries. For the most part, they were British subjects denied the basic civilities of British justice ... They rebelled against an unpopular and viciously policed poll tax when all peaceful means of protest had been rebuffed. They fought back when attacked ...[39]

An autonomous stockade in the heart of the Ballarat goldfields was clearly untenable. At sunrise on Sunday 3 December 1854, soldiers and police – on horse and foot – stormed the barricade. Not expecting an immediate attack, most of the diggers had either left the stockade or were asleep; consequently, the melee was short. Some 30 miners and five soldiers were killed in the space of 15 minutes. Some of the diggers were killed by police after they had surrendered.

As the details of the decisive defeat of the rebel diggers emerged, fear of mob violence soon turned into sympathy for the miners. The radical *Age* newspaper editorialised, 'Let the Government be undeceived. There are not a dozen respectable citizens in Melbourne who do not entertain an indignant feeling against its weakness, its folly and its last crowning error ... they do not sympathise with injustice and coercion.'[40] John Dunmore Lang went further: 'There had not been a more incapable, a more extravagant, a more unprincipled or a more unjust and oppressive government in Christendom.'[41] In Melbourne, crowds vowed never to swear loyalty to the Union Jack over the Southern Cross and denounced the government for not preventing the massacre.

It was that feature of British justice, trial by jury, that resolved the crisis. When 13 of the rebellion's leaders were arraigned before the courts, the juries refused to convict, knowing that any conviction would validate an arbitrary and authoritarian administration of the goldfields. The acquittals galvanised the cause of the diggers and, more broadly, the democracy movement in Victoria. Paradoxically, it demonstrated the value of the British Constitution in securing a free and open society and strengthened the case for Victoria as 'Eureka Britannia'.[42]

Governor Hotham set up a commission of inquiry that subsequently recommended the abolition of the licence fee. The voting franchise was extended and new seats established to give diggers immediate representation in parliament. Tellingly, within a year, one of the leaders of the rebellion, Peter Lalor, who had lost an arm in the conflict but evaded capture, was elected to parliament.

The Eureka Rebellion was the high watermark of the protest movement on the goldfields, and symbolic of the wider push for democracy and self-government. The US humorist and literary sensation Mark Twain, author of *Huckleberry Finn*, pronounced the rebellion, 'The finest thing in Australian history' when he visited Ballarat in 1895. 'It was a strike for liberty, a struggle for principle, a stand against injustice and oppression ... It is another instance of a victory won by a lost battle.'[43] The lost battle helped Victorians win the right to both 'control their own local affairs and to be joined to the mother country'.[44] This was the best of both worlds, mirroring the original demand of the American colonists in the previous century.

While Eureka was a historical watershed, other parts of Australia were advancing just as rapidly down the road of democracy, only without a rebellion. South Australia proved itself 'an early citadel of democracy', without the political violence of the Ballarat goldfields.[45] Later in the century, Australian federation was achieved without any civil unrest. This peaceful transition from autocracy to democracy is almost unparalleled anywhere in the world.

6

Colonial Liberalism

The newly self-governing colonies' political development was no less dramatic than the economic development driven by gold and ongoing pastoral expansion. In Victoria, an acute struggle between the lower and upper houses of parliament, elected on very different franchises, eventually produced a new and much more interventionist version of liberalism. In New South Wales, by contrast, where an appointed upper house was less inclined to be difficult, the more English style of laissez-faire liberalism continued to be dominant. As the two largest colonies diverged in interests, Australia developed two liberal political traditions, which are still relevant today.

§

Mid-19th-century Australia was 'that rare thing in the history of mankind' – said the historian Geoffrey Serle – 'a social democracy in which gentility and education carried with them neither respect nor reward'.[1] Visitors expecting the same social deference as in Britain were often disappointed. Those inclined to be critical observed that 'selfishness', or money-making, was a leading feature of Australians.[2] Few succeeded on the scale of the merchant John Frazer, an assisted immigrant who arrived as a carpenter and joiner and died with a personal estate valued at over £400,000 (worth perhaps $100 million in today's money), but that was the colonial dream. The English novelist Charles Dickens sent two of his ten children to New South Wales, having regularly preached to them the benefits of an honest life in the antipodes. His younger son, Edward Dickens, known as 'Plorn', was a member of the NSW Parliament from 1889 to 1894.

A British lord on the goldfields had no title but 'mate'.[3] The son of a gentleman sent out to a sheep station could find himself 'tyrannised' by a mere 'common shepherd' for the simple crime of acting a gentleman.[4] Australians told themselves that old-world distinctions had no place in their new country. Sometimes the colonial parliaments even legislated this claim, as in 1846, by banning commemorative processions relating to religious or political divisions; this was in the aftermath of a particularly fierce clash between Catholics and Protestants.

Education was another crucial means of achieving social mobility. The colonial policy of 'free, compulsory and secular' schooling – that over the final quarter of the 19th century replaced Bourke's policy of funding the different denominational schools – sought, in Parkes' words, 'no distinction of faith, asking no question where the child has been born, what may be his condition of life, or the position of his parents, but inviting all to sit side by side ...'[5]

Whatever taint it might still have had elsewhere, democracy in Australia produced exemplars of aspiration and order. Emancipists, after all, had not set about to destroy the system they were born into but to become accepted into it. George Storefield, the honest farmer in Rolf Boldrewood's bushranging adventure, *Robbery Under Arms* (1888), had a simple creed: 'A man must work and save when he's young if he don't want to be a beggar or slave when he's old.' His wants in life were not complicated: to 'have a good farm, well stocked and paid for, by and by, and then to take it easy ...'. In time, Boldrewood's character accumulates enough wealth to build a mansion and run for parliament. Australian egalitarianism was fundamentally about equality of opportunity and a fair set of rules that gave ordinary people a reasonable chance to get ahead and to prove that they, too, could win in the game of life.

* * *

By this time, responsible government was emerging in all of Britain's settler colonies. Powerful currents were reshaping British constitutionalism, not only in its colonies but at Westminster. Outbreaks of rebellion in Upper and Lower Canada in the late 1830s led to the Durham Report of 1839, authored by the Whig John Lambton – 'Radical Jack' to his contemporaries because of his liberal politics – which recommended the introduction of responsible government there. The British government concluded that 'it is neither possible nor desirable to carry on the government of any of the British provinces in North America in opposition to the opinion of the inhabitants'.[6] Self-government in Canada was deemed an impossibility in 1840, but a necessity by 1846.[7]

London's changing views of what was right for Australia were not simply a product of the liberalism of the times. When considering self-government for the Australian colonies, the new secretary of state for the colonies, the Duke of Newcastle, felt obliged to respond to a range of voices urging more freedom, not less. Robert Lowe was now a colleague of his in the Aberdeen Ministry and strongly in favour of self-government. John Dunmore Lang, then in England, had no qualms about pushing his democratic preferences. Perhaps the most telling admission came from the permanent under-secretary for the colonies, Herman Merivale, a former professor at Oxford

University, who spoke of the success of Australia in absorbing the demographic and economic tsunami of the gold rush. How could one honestly say Australians were not ready to govern themselves?[8]

Having received royal assent, the new constitutions arrived back in 1855 and 1856: Victoria, New South Wales, South Australia and Tasmania were now self-governing. Queensland would have to wait until 1859, following its separation from New South Wales.

Henceforth, the new parliaments could legislate for all domestic matters, including land policy and taxation. The government was to be elected by the people. The British Westminster model was the template. Responsible ministers served the Crown and were accountable to parliaments comprising two houses: a Legislative Assembly, the 'people's house' in which the government was formed; and a Legislative Council, intended as a house of review like Britain's House of Lords, although not comprising hereditary peers.

In Australia, full adult male suffrage came two generations before Britain. In 1850, a New South Welshman who owned a small property or paid £10 annual rent qualified to vote. When prices and rents soared after the discovery of gold, almost all men living in town could vote. For city dwellers, this was manhood suffrage in all but name. By 1856, 95 per cent of Sydney men were entitled to cast a vote.[9] In Victoria, after the Eureka Rebellion, diggers holding a licence – which now cost a mere pound – could also vote. In 1856, South Australia created one of the world's most democratic constitutions: all men, including Aboriginal men, had the right to vote for the Legislative Assembly.

By contrast, in mid-century Britain, only one in five men could vote, and property qualifications remained in place until 1918.[10] Most Britons fighting and dying on the battlefields of the First World War had no right to vote; nor did the female nurses, orderlies and ambulance drivers who cared for them.

For some time, what we now know as the secret ballot was called the Australian ballot. To vote anonymously, the Chartists had said, was to vote independently, free from undue influence.[11] The Australian who gave practical shape to the idea was Henry Chapman, a member of the Victorian Legislative Council and lawyer: he had successfully defended the African–American Eureka rebel John Joseph against a charge of treason. Chapman's concept was that voters would arrive at the booth empty-handed: all the necessary materials would be provided. They would take their ballot paper from a clerk, who would mark their names off on a roll. After completing their vote in private, the voter would fold the ballot before placing it in a secure box, to be tallied later. This was the system adopted for the Victorian elections of 1856. Though the secret ballot already existed in France, Belgium, Switzerland and the United States, the combination of secret ballots, government-printed ballot papers and no property qualifications was uniquely advanced for the time. The other colonies soon copied the Victorian system, transforming the election process from a sometimes riotous and drunken affair into a 'well-mannered civic ritual'.[12]

* * *

To enter a colonial parliament in 1860 was to arrive at a carnival of personalities, where the currency of politics was the magnetic individual – the small breed of 'superior men', as Henry Parkes called them, who could command alliances. This was a system of personal followings, not of parties, where loyalties and factions were fluid. In the first 25 years of self-government, 19 premiers took the oath of office in New South Wales.

Gold was running out, towns were overpopulated and unemployment was growing. Land reform was the great struggle of the mid to late 19th century. From southern Queensland to the fertile Western District of Victoria, over 160 million acres (65,000,000 ha) were in the hands of just a few thousand squatters, mostly held on leasehold.[13] In the three decades after 1860, via a series of land Acts in the colonial parliaments, most of this land was converted to freehold and, in the process, much of the squatters' vast holdings passed into the hands of tens of thousands of small selectors.

'Unlock the Land!' was the popular cry; selling small lots at a fixed price was the preferred reform, underwritten by an appeal to the near biblical righteousness of agrarian life. David Syme, editor of the new and radical newspaper *The Age*, thought land reform 'the most momentous of all political questions'.[14]

On the evening of 28 August 1860, the land debate reached a boisterous climax when several hundred rioters, many wearing red ribbons – as the miners did during the goldfield protests – broke through the entrance to Melbourne's Parliament House. Stones were thrown, injuring overwhelmed police. Premier William Nicholson ordered troops to break up the crowd. It was a 'scene without parallel in the history of this colony', wrote another Victorian newspaper, *The Argus*.[15]

Standing between the Victorian protestors and the land reform they wanted were the crimson velvet ropes of Victoria's Legislative Council. Unlike the Council in New South Wales, Victoria's Upper House was elected on a heavily restricted franchise: an elector required freehold of at least £1000; a member, a freehold of at least £5000. The Council rejected the first major land Bill in 1857 and made no less than 250 amendments to the 1859 Bill – the tepid *Nicholson Act* of 1860. Amending Bills in 1863 and 1864 were also rejected.[16]

Another showdown between the people's house, the Victorian Legislative Assembly, and the Legislative Council arrived in 1865 over the issue of tariff protection. A parliamentary deadlock over a supply Bill threatened a full-blown government shutdown. Charles Dilke, the English radical and staunch imperialist, was visiting Victoria at the time, and expressed shock at the intense partisanship infecting all aspects of society. 'Class animosity and political feud runs much higher, and drives its roots far deeper into private life in Victoria than in any other English-speaking country I have seen.'[17]

Parliament was dissolved. Across two weeks, a general election was held that was more intensely fought than any previous contest. The incumbent premier, James McCulloch, and his supporters achieved an astounding victory: 58 members out of 78 were returned. With considerable difficulty, and with further crises yet to unfold – including a second deadlock – the first protectionist measures were passed. But with the powers of the Council left entirely intact, the door was open for future conflict.

* * *

To make a living on the land was no simple thing. Many new settlers had no idea how to be farmers. Perhaps half of the selectors failed on their first farm.[18] Those who persevered survived rather than flourished, far short of the yeoman ideal. Land had to be cleared, fenced, ploughed, sowed and harvested. After Thomas Austin released breeding rabbits into the wild near Geelong in 1859, the grass-gobbling invaders joined drought as a menace to be overcome. Women and children generally worked long hours on their farms, while husbands and fathers often took an off-farm job with a wage to supplement a poor income.

When Queensland separated from New South Wales in 1859, the race was on for yet more land. The new government wanted speedy development. Railways were built, and between 1860 and 1866 about 51,000 assisted immigrants arrived in the northern colony.[19]

Inevitably, expansion triggered resistance from Aboriginal clans. Parts of Queensland became conflict zones, but local Aboriginal people had little chance when pitted against units of the Native Mounted Police. Typically these consisted of three to eight Aboriginal troopers headed by a European officer.[20] Recruiting some natives – to use the terminology of the period – to fight against other natives was a practice that went back to Roman times.[21] Britain had employed similar methods in India and South Africa. In Queensland, Aboriginal troopers were often brought in from country far distant to the area they patrolled in order to minimise chances of desertion. Some troopers were press-ganged – effectively kidnapped – while others were prisoners given the option of enlistment. But most volunteered, probably because it was a job, with a uniform and regular food.

The Native Mounted Police operated from remote camps spread across the vast colony, where distance made central supervision almost impossible. Going from pastoral station to pastoral station, they 'dispersed' local Aboriginal people impinging on newly settled land. 'Dispersal' was a cryptic word in this context: sometimes it meant scaring away and sometimes encouraging people to come in to take work on the new pastoral stations; but sometimes it meant shooting.

The worst of it happened in Queensland; the death toll is unknown but is likely to be well into the thousands.[22] Often, episodes of bloodshed began with the killing of settlers. In 1861, 19 settlers were killed in the Cullin-la-ringo massacre with some 300 Aboriginal people killed in retaliation, according to contemporary historians. About 14 settlers were killed after a shipwreck in 1872. Invariably, the settler responses were grossly disproportionate, unconnected with any real attempt to identify perpetrators, and almost completely undocumented. 'I know you have no conception of how things are carried on here,' one northerner wrote to the commissioner of police, David Seymour, then nominally in charge of the Native Police.[23] Even a premier, Sir Samuel Griffith, later grumbled that the 'doings of the Native Police were like a sealed book to the Department'.[24]

A growing number of citizens viewed frontier violence as an appalling moral failure. 'This in plain language is how we deal with the Aborigines: On occupying new territory the Aboriginal inhabitants are treated exactly in the same way as the wild beasts or birds the settlers may find there,' the Brisbane journalist Carl Feilberg wrote. 'The least show of resistance is answered by a rifle bullet.'[25]

Only one officer of the Queensland Native Mounted Police was ever put on trial for murder, but he skipped bail and fled the colony.

The stark evidence of this indifference to 'British justice' convinced many that there had to be a better way.[26] What stymied authorities was the 'silence of the bush', an unspoken code that made witnesses to killings extremely unlikely to come forward.

Eventually the system began to adapt.[27] Courts widened their jurisdictions to cover crimes committed by Aboriginal people against Aboriginal people, and Indigenous customs and beliefs found their way into the courtroom. An analysis of 160 Queensland coronial inquiries into Aboriginal deaths between 1860 and 1897 found 'a general reluctance to prosecute Aborigines for deaths arising within their own communities', taking into account their culture and ignorance of colonial law.[28]

Intertribal conflicts were a notable feature of the 19th century, exacerbated by Europeans pushing Aboriginal people into enemy territory. There were at least 250 documented Aboriginal deaths in the Port Phillip District between 1835 and 1850 that resulted from intertribal violence. The escaped convict William Buckley, who spent decades with Kulin tribes west of Melbourne, claimed to have witnessed dozens of such violent deaths.[29]

In the hundred years following the First Fleet's arrival, the Aboriginal population suffered a steep decline, falling by some hundreds of thousands, and settling to somewhere between 60,000 and 80,000 by the late 1800s. But the biggest existential threat was lack of immunity: disease was the pernicious killer. Epidemics of smallpox, influenza or tuberculosis could devastate communities, and new venereal diseases spread infertility.

* * *

Co-operation and adaptation are the less talked about stories of the frontier. Port Phillip's Native Police Corps, formed in 1837, was a different outfit to its counterpart in Queensland.[30] The original 22 troopers, all clan leaders around Melbourne, used their newfound status to build relationships between local tribes and even develop an early form of an Aboriginal Australian identity. They had powers of policing not extended to the force in Queensland, including the ability to arrest settlers. Their role included patrolling for bushrangers and, later, acting as law enforcement on the goldfields. Their activities were better supervised and less prone to unsanctioned violence. One former trooper, William Barak, later became the Aboriginal leader most associated with the settlement of Coranderrk, near Healesville, specially set up for displaced Aboriginal people.

As the century stretched on, liberal humanitarianism was infiltrating even the frontier. Queensland was the final colony to allow testimony by Aboriginal people in courts – in 1876. By the 1880s, the Queensland Native Police was steadily replaced with standard police units. Similarly, Aboriginal missions and reserves were gazetted, and these were increasingly supported by the government.[31] These changes were consequences of popular anxieties about the mistreatment of Aboriginal people and a desire 'to do the right thing'. In the coming century, a new generation of Aboriginal activists would draw on these decent instincts to achieve genuine legal and political equality.

* * *

To the gold miners, covered in dirt, tired and poor, the sight of the uniformed Aboriginal troopers guarding and escorting large quantities of gold must have been unexpected. What strange new land had they entered? There was so much about Australia they did not know. Even by 1860, large swathes of the continent were as yet unseen by British Australian eyes. Explorers became pioneering heroes. The streets of Melbourne were packed at the departure of Robert O'Hara Burke and William Wills, whose expedition to cross Australia south to north and back again beguiled the confident and democratic populace. Here, distilled into a team of 19 men, 26 camels, 23 horses, and six wagons and drays, was the progress and hubris of the age.

The expedition reached Cooper's Creek, near the border of Queensland and South Australia, by late 1860. There, the party split. Burke and Wills, along with two others, left their companions and any unnecessary supplies to make a dash for the Gulf of Carpentaria. A supply party was supposed to receive them on their return. But after waiting for months, the team left; unbeknown to them, their erstwhile companions were only a few miles away. When Burke and Wills reached base camp that afternoon, the exhausted explorers lacked the supplies to keep them alive – although their remaining companion, John King, survived thanks to help from the local Aboriginal people. There were 50,000 mourners at a state funeral in Melbourne.

What drove such transcontinental expeditions was the prospect of an overland telegraph line connecting Australia to Europe. The new technology offered a rapid mode of communication, which would strike a heavy blow to the tyranny of distance.

South Australia had its own hero for the task: John McDouall Stuart, a short, gaunt binge drinker, whose alienation from urban life pulled him towards the bush. As Burke and Wills lay dying, Stuart and his team were themselves in the middle of an expedition to cross the continent from South Australia. They had reached the oasis of Newcastle Waters, a little more than halfway between Alice Springs and Darwin, before thick scrub and a lack of food saw them turn home. A further expedition began in late 1861. This time they were successful, but Stuart returned to Adelaide physically wrecked and almost blind. Still, he had the answers to some burning questions: there was no inland sea, as legend had it, but there was a workable route for a telegraph line. Construction began in 1870. The Overland Telegraph Line was a government project of monumental scope, some 2000 miles (3200 km) long and completed in 1872.

Stuart described the Australian bush as deceptive. What was so familiar to the Aboriginal people was inscrutable to the early pioneers. Where water might be expected, there was aridity; yet, near impenetrable scrub, there were waterholes. Good weather might suddenly become an unwelcoming storm of heat and dust. A drought might ease, then quickly return. Nevertheless, these were costs the pioneers were willing to endure to become 'kings in grass castles', as Mary Durack titled her classic book on the pastoral expansion.

Often assisted by Aboriginal guides, drovers pushed their herds forward, and by the late 1880s most of the suitable outback land – the Barkly Tablelands, the Channel Country, the area near the Gulf of Carpentaria and even the remote Kimberley – was under hoof. Skilled drovers became famous for their exploits. In the late 1870s, Nat Buchanan, at the head of thousands of cattle, pioneered a stock route through the Barkly, linking Queensland and New South Wales with the Northern Territory. His overlanding exploits may have seen him traverse more country than any other drover and helped a generation of graziers to settle new lands in western Queensland and the Northern Territory. In 1871, Harry Redford drove 1000 stolen cattle from Queensland to South Australia, pioneering the Strzelecki Track. In 1882, Patrick Durack organised 8000 breeders to be driven from his station in southwest Queensland almost 3000 miles (5000 km) to the Ord River in the Kimberley. It took well over two years, and half the cattle and several stockmen perished, but they made it. It remains the longest overland trek ever undertaken by Australian drovers.

For future novelists and mythmakers, this was the 'real' Australia. The contribution of pioneering women was central to this success, working as shepherds, station managers, nurses, housekeepers and conciliators. Emma Withnell of the Pilbara region, in Western Australia, known as the 'Mother of the northwest', delivered babies, tended to the sick and mediated relations with the Aboriginal population, including by vaccinating the local children. A member of the pioneering Hancock family, Emma encouraged her husband to set out for the northwest, and the two endured many hardships along the way to establish the first real cattle station in the area. Her son, Jimmy, was the first to come upon gold-bearing rock in the Pilbara, later to become the Pilbara goldfields.[32]

* * *

By letters patent, the Northern Territory was annexed to South Australia in 1863 and another round of land speculation began. But the deceptions of the bush did not abate. Drought impeded early development and devastated sheep and cattle populations, while frontier conflict flared as land was claimed and cleared and food sources for Aboriginal people diminished. After a series of false starts, Port Darwin was chosen as the main settlement by the South Australian surveyor-general George Goyder, in 1869.[33]

* * *

The visiting novelist Anthony Trollope, arriving in Adelaide in 1871, concluded that 'no city, not even Philadelphia, has been laid out with stronger purpose of regularity and order'.[34] As well as being the first colony to extend the franchise to everyone, including women and Aboriginal people, it was the first to exclude churches from receiving taxpayers' money – thus dissolving 'the last remaining vestiges of the traditional connection between church and state'. Adelaide turned out to be a 'city of churches' but with no established church. It also pioneered three-year electoral terms. The first Australian state secondary school for girls was in Adelaide, and in 1876 South Australia was the first colony to give workers the right to strike. As well, in 1858, there was another innovation, one that was subsequently adopted throughout Australia and then much of the 'British' world: this was Torrens title, a system of land title where registration alone – rather than the old common-law chain of title from original Crown grant – conclusively determined the ownership of land.

Most of the various colonies' Catholics were Irish and were typically of modest education and wealth: 'all plain working people', Bishop Francis Murphy, the first Catholic bishop of Adelaide, called them in 1847.[35] Because state aid to religion was so unpopular, especially in South Australia, the Catholics relied largely on their own communities and networks to preserve their faith. Mary MacKillop – the daughter of Scottish immigrants – who dressed in simple black and embraced a life of poverty, showed that extraordinary outcomes could be achieved. In 1866, she co-founded with Julian Woods – a priest from the Adelaide diocese – the Institute of St Joseph, a religious order devoted to teaching and to creating schools where the students were 'constantly breathing the atmosphere of their religion'.[36] At her death in 1908, Mary left behind 750 sisters then educating more than 12,000 students across Australia; she had also established a network of schools in New Zealand.[37] She was canonised on 17 October 2010.

Anti-Catholic prejudice was a curious feature of colonial liberalism, and was noticeably more prevalent in Australia than among British liberals.[38] Editorials against 'popery' regularly featured in *The Age*, particularly after the 1864 papal encyclical *Quanta Cura* declared against modernity and liberal reform.

Meanwhile, Victoria's *Education Act 1872* was among the first in the world to provide a system of state education, 'free, compulsory and secular'. Between 1871 and 1876, the number of state schools trebled. The other colonies shortly followed suit. Few governments in the world devoted the resources to education as Australia did. But it was not without a social cost. As it turned out, the 'secular' system was also largely Anglo-Protestant. This fed into sectarian tensions that persisted until

Robert Menzies' Liberal government revived the policy of state aid to non-government schools in the 1960s.

* * *

Australians had high expectations of government, especially on transport infrastructure. Between 1860 and 1900, some 40 per cent of public investment went to rail. Governments also developed ports, took over the wharves and created the big public utility services of water, sewerage and urban transit.

Western Australia continued to rely on convict labour for much of its public construction. At a cost of approximately £2 million, the British government transported 9668 male convicts to the state between 1850 and 1868,[39] who built Government House, the Perth Town Hall and the Colonial Hospital, among many other public buildings. Their labour sustained an otherwise tepid economy – so much so that when transportation ended in 1868, the colony fell into recession.[40] Desperate to reboot growth, the colonial government offered a prize of £5000 for the discovery of gold deposits within 110 miles (180 km) of a port and capable of producing at least 10,000 ounces (283 kg).[41] In 1882, alluvial gold was discovered in the far north, but the great rush really arrived a decade later in Kalgoorlie, propelling Western Australia to a new level of development.

After years of political conflict, the Victorian protectionists began to win successive battles, and the average tariff increased 11 times in the 14 years after 1865.[42] Manufacturing employment began to swell, from around 10,000 in 1865–66 to more than 33,000 by the end of the 1870s.[43] Visitors had long observed the eagerness with which Victorians advocated protection as a symbol of economic independence and colonial identity.

Victorian liberalism distinguished itself from its New South Wales counterpart by its readiness to use state power to improve individuals' lives. It was a Victorian politician, Graham Berry, who founded the first proper political party in modern Australian politics. The National Reform and Protection League was an amalgam of protectionist and progressive leagues that united manufacturers, miners, artisans, small farmers and trade unionists. Berry toured the state and stumped for candidates. His speeches were angry and highly charged, savaging the elites and the wealth-takers. More than 150 branches were formed, and thousands joined. This 'astounding innovation', barked one opponent, seemed designed to 'degrade politics and political men', but it actually gave birth to modern mass democratic politics in Australia.[44]

Berry's innovative approach paid off. At the 1877 election, his liberal (Protectionst) party claimed 62 of 86 lower-house seats – 'the most complete partisan triumph of the nineteenth century'.[45] The new MPs included grocers, drapers, printers, booksellers, publicans and journalists. It was a ministry of radicals – including the 'determined and masterful autocrat' Peter Lalor, hero of Eureka; the minister for justice, James Grant, who had defended the Eureka rebels in court; and John Woods, the commissioner of railways, who had led protests against the dreaded licence fees at the Goulburn River diggings.[46]

Here lies the genesis of what journalist and historian Paul Kelly terms the Australian Settlement of the early 20th century – an unspoken pact that entailed a large role for government. Forged in the fires of partisan conflict in the 1860s and 1870s, the radical liberal leaders did not trust the old liberalism, with its emphasis on individualism and laissez-faire. They believed the laws of economics were undemocratic in their consequences, favouring the propertied class at the expense of the majority.

Northwards across the Murray River, a different liberal strand was developing. The NSW premier, Henry Parkes, had flitted between radicalism and moderation before settling into a natural state of pragmatism. He prided himself on his capacity to draw broad support. 'This was not a time when we could cry "down with the merchants" or "down with the cabinet makers",' he told a large 1863 meeting in Sydney to protest tax increases. 'We were all here men of one community, and the interests of one could not suffer without entangling the interests of others.'[47] Parkes disliked protectionism, and with generous Crown land revenue in New South Wales, he had no need for it. With a Legislative Council populated with nominated members, the fear of a catastrophic deadlock was less acute. As far as he was concerned, the central tenets of British liberalism had served the colony well. But as Australia began to form its own national identity, the interests and ideals of the two largest colonies increasingly diverged. An accommodation would be necessary for federation to be achieved.

7

Empire and Federation

The formal achievement of Australian nationhood was a triumph of politics at its best. A remarkably talented group of leaders managed to turn a noble ideal into practical reality via a decade-long process of vigorous public debate, sensible compromise and ultimately a people's vote showing that this really was an idea whose time had come. There was no 'war of independence' or even a 'glorious revolution'; our constitutional founders were generally only too happy to acknowledge that the new commonwealth was firmly part of a great empire and unambiguously proud of its history and heritage. Still, a new nation largely the product of peaceful evolution has very few parallels.

§

Like the colonies' previous political achievements, federation was a liberal project. What's most striking about the federal movement is its key leaders' deep and abiding faith in the destiny of Australia as a free society where everyone would get 'a fair go', especially if prepared to 'have a go', too. Its support came from the 'moral middle class', who thought that the collection of British colonies on one continent would be stronger together, and who were positive 'a nation for a continent and a continent for a nation' would maximise freedom and opportunity. As well, the long Pax Britannica – the relatively stable 19th-century world secured by British commercial and naval supremacy – was coming under challenge from rising imperial powers. France and Germany had established colonies in the Pacific and Germany was trying to outbuild Britain in battleships. Australian security was less assured, hence the desirability of a united Australia that could speak with one voice and act with a united strength.

* * *

In January 1883, at the age of 67, Henry Parkes resigned as premier of New South Wales, terminating his third – and at four years longest – administration. Temporarily wearied from politics, he set off for England, his second visit in two years. In 1881, British audiences had embraced him as 'one of the social lions of the season'.[1] Parkes had been feted with banquet after banquet and mingled with Queen Victoria and the British prime minister, William Gladstone. He had spoken to large and distinguished audiences, telling them excitedly of the 'experiment' of Australia, of trialling British institutions 'removed from all possible hostility from other nations' and 'free from all the errors of the older civilised states of the world'.[2] On his second visit, he arrived as a commercial agent keen to speak with prospective clients; he found they were not so much interested in Australian patriotic sentiment as in financial opportunity. '[I]n commercial and monetary circles,' he wrote, 'the question is what profitable thing can be done in Australia.' Beyond that subject matter, he noted, there was 'utter indifference'.[3]

The experience left Parkes thinking about Australia's place in the world. He thought of the 'Englishness' of white Australians – 'more English than Old England herself', prosperous, educated and ambitious.[4] Were they to remain a 'convenient appendage' to the British Empire, a second class of British citizens? 'If we are not reckoned as English people, and yet not as foreign people, what kind of status must we occupy in the British-Isles-limited English mind?'[5]

Britain's politicians were asking much the same question, and one possible response was thrilling educated circles. The Cambridge historian John Seeley declared in his bestselling *The Expansion of England* (1883) that imperial policy had to take the settler colonies, like Australia, far more seriously.[6] Seeley was worried about the state of England, its rising radicalism and its imperial adventurism in Afghanistan, Egypt and Southern Africa. All of this was exposing elements of imperial overstretch. Britain, Seeley wrote, had to consolidate into a 'Greater Britain', encompassing the white self-governing colonies so that migrants might flow unimpeded between them, freeing up colonial resources and, most audaciously, establishing a liberal global polity across continents, bound by a common nationality. Australia and Canada, Seeley argued, should 'be to us as Kent or Cornwall'.[7]

Seeley's book excited Parkes. He thought its vision of a monumental Anglosphere that could propagate the 'principles of justice, freedom, and peace' was an 'amazing destiny'.[8] But it could only work, he reasoned, if Australia's interests were elevated in imperial considerations. His own experiences revealed that was not so. '[W]e are seldom thought of by any class of the English at home as forming an integral part of the Empire,' he wrote.[9]

Australia would soon be at a crossroads, Parkes warned: having to choose between Empire or separation – the latter 'not out of the range of possibilities within the next generation'.[10]

Already, there was a growing restiveness in the colonies. In April 1883, the British government swiftly disallowed the

Queensland government's annexation of New Guinea, even though Queensland Premier Thomas McIlwraith claimed he had moved in response to rumours of German designs over the same territory. When whispers of French activity in the New Hebrides (now Vanuatu) raised anew the demand for annexation, again Westminster stalled. In October 1884, Thomas McIlwraith – then no longer premier – said, 'It is only within the last twelve months that I have seen it really considered whether the Australian Colonies would be better off as part of the British Empire or as a federated nation by themselves.'[11] A year earlier, in the first serious move towards better colonial co-operation, a rudimentary federal council had been established at an intercolonial conference, but it was little more than an occasional talking shop that New South Wales refused to join after Parkes described it as a 'mere sham' without authority or power.

* * *

Australians were thinking about their future and whether it was safer with – or without – the British connection. 'England would give us no protection in regard to the New Hebrides, and yet we would share in the disasters if she plunged into war with any other country,' said one speaker at a meeting of the newly established Australian Republican Union in 1887.[12] The union was founded in a year marked in England by angry protests against Queen Victoria's golden jubilee celebrations. Henry Lawson had his first poem, 'A Song of the Republic', appear in *The Bulletin*, a publication whose own bellicose anti-imperialism stirred the emerging national sentiment. 'Australia for the Australians' was its cry.

The British government responded with a Colonial Conference, the first of its kind, held in conjunction with Queen

Victoria's golden jubilee. It brought together representatives from across the self-governing colonies – Australia, New Zealand, Canada and parts of South Africa – to consult on matters of imperial communication, trade and defence.

Of the 15 delegates representing Australia at the conference, it was Alfred Deakin, the 30-year-old leader of the Victorian Liberals, who made the deepest impact. He told the conference that Australia's interests were being ignored, even though colonial interests were the Empire's interests. His genial nature and charisma made his criticisms more palatable to British ears, and he displayed an intellectual depth and philosophical understanding that impressed London society. He represented the best of Australia: a prototype of the independent Australian–Briton. The conference was successful in securing tangible benefits for Australia, including an agreement that the colonies would part-finance a new Royal Navy squadron in Australian waters.

Deakin returned with clear views about Australia's future. The Imperial Conference, he said at an 1887 banquet held in his honour, 'marked a great change in the policy and politics of this colony'.[13] Australians were no longer to be regarded as dependants, but as respected self-governing polities. The conference came at a crucial moment in world affairs, he continued. 'Never was there a time when nations measured their strength and standing less by their civilisation than by their men and guns.'[14] Militarism in Europe was rampant, and 'the weight which each colony holds in the council of the mother country is very largely affected by the degree to which that colony is prepared to defend itself when the inevitable hour of need shall come'.[15]

In an age of consolidation, Deakin saw the destiny of Australia in national federation at home and a kind of imperial federation abroad, even if informal. In London, he had witnessed how intercolonial disunity worked against Australian interests. His was a dual nationalism combining 'the sovereignty of our own parliaments' – ever attuned to the Australian tradition of popular democracy – while keeping the door open 'for the larger and more important step ... to combine in one the dominions of the British race all the world over'.[16] Only then, he believed, would Australians reach 'the highest political organisation which it is possible for us to have, and so found an empire the like of which has never been seen in the world before'.[17]

* * *

There was a new rush in Australia in the last quarter of the 19th century: one of ideas rather than gold. It was the age of -isms: imperialism, nationalism, socialism, spiritualism, secularism, social Darwinism, 'new' liberalism and (Henry) George-ism. The revolution in transport and communications lowered the cost of acquiring ideas. Sail was giving way to steam by the end of the 1870s, opening up new possibilities for travel. Rail was rapidly being laid across Australia. Most towns in Victoria became a day's train ride from their capital. By 1883, direct rail had connected Sydney and Melbourne – but not without the changeover at Albury to account for different railway gauges. Between 1881 and 1891, Australia's colonial government-owned railways extended from 4011 miles (6456 km) to 9500 miles (15,290 km). The number of registered letters passing through NSW post offices exploded from 13.7 million in 1875 to 63 million by 1890. Australia was a country of letters, with a post office for every 600 people, compared with 2000 in Britain.[18]

Cobb & Co. horsedrawn coaches delivering mail, supplies and people were the other key transport link. In the more isolated towns, the arrival of a Cobb coach attracted much of the town's excitable population to the post office. Cobb & Co. had been established on the Victorian goldfields. At the end of the century, James Nicholas and Sidney Kidman seized the opportunity presented by a new gold rush in Western Australia and quickly expanded Cobb services in the west. Like many 19th-century innovations, the mail coach and its world are unknown to us. In its day, it was looked upon as a symbol of adventure, and driving a stagecoach was 'a man's job', according to Nicholas. Coach drivers had typically endured all manner of hazards, from floods to bushrangers, so in small towns enjoyed some celebrity.[19] When, early in the 20th century, Nicholas spotted his first motor vehicle, he knew at once the age of the coach was ending and went about the conversion of Cobb & Co. into an engine-driven enterprise. The roads, byways and rail lines we use today often follow the trails of these early drivers whose feats of endurance still benefit Australians.

Rail and road were in high demand to meet a new mineral boom in the final decades of the 19th century. In the semi-desert of Broken Hill, in far western New South Wales, the discovery of silver transformed the town into one of the great mining cities of Australia. In 1885, Broken Hill Proprietary was incorporated; today, its successor, BHP Group, is the largest mining company in the world.

After a period of relative quiet, metal mining output almost doubled between 1886 and 1896. In the first years of the 1900s, metals were Australia's leading export, not wool.[20] Money markets, more sophisticated and willing to invest in far places, turned to Australian mining as a good bet in a decade otherwise plagued by financial failure.

The lesson of the boom was not to underestimate even the driest and least hospitable parts of the continent. In the span of 20 years, Western Australia evolved from a small and relatively quiet colony to one of the major world producers of gold. The discovery of 554 ounces (15.7 kg) of gold near Coolgardie in 1892 had sparked a new rush and flood of migrants; by the early 1900s, Australian gold production surpassed the peak years of the 1850s.[21] In the 50 years between 1839 and 1890, about 26,000 people arrived in the colony, exploding to 430,000 arrivals in the 30 years after 1898.[22] Kalgoorlie–Boulder became one of the largest inland towns in all of Australia.

Equally striking was the political engagement: in the 1890s, some 43 newspapers were published in the goldfield towns alone.[23] Among the new educated populace was a young American and future president of the United States, Herbert Hoover, who worked in Western Australia as a mining engineer for two years. In his memoirs he would recall the 'Australian attachments' of the new towns: 'Government was more rigid, violence was absent, but petty crime, immorality, and good cheer were as generally abundant as in the California [gold rush] of '49.'[24]

* * *

Meanwhile, Australia was changing from a destination to a home. By 1888, 70 per cent of its population were native-born. To the settlers and their descendants, 'native' described the connection to the land that they had come to feel. They were increasingly urbanised – less than half lived outside the towns and cities by the end of the century – but that didn't stop Australians from idealising the hardy pioneers taming a harsh land. The 'bush poetry' of the late 19th century, together with the emergence of Australian impressionism – the Heidelberg School – gave artistic expression to a growing national identity suffused with the spirit of mateship, egalitarianism and pioneering adventure. In 1871 in Victoria, the Australian

Natives Association (ANA), a mutual society exclusive to the native-born, was formed. The ANA encouraged its members to lift their gaze beyond parochial attachments and towards some higher, national aim. They were to become a critical constituency in Victoria's push for Australian federation.

In New South Wales, the old system of factional politics had given way to something more identifiable as a modern party system. At the 1887 election, Henry Parkes returned to government as the leader of the Free Trade grouping. He found himself surrounded by 'young men of much promise', displaying 'zeal, ability and political firmness'.[25] 'New' liberals, like the Oxford-educated Bernhard Wise, associated free trade with a larger program of reform, more interventionist in scope, and aimed at improving the living and working conditions of the poor. 'Classical' liberals, like Bruce Smith, were suspicious of interventionism of any kind, adopting an individualist doctrine that prioritised freedom and small government.

Australia was a global leader in political rights for women because of its advanced democratic political tradition, with South Australia the pioneering state. As early as 1885, its parliament passed a resolution supporting the principle of female suffrage. Nine years later, it was the first Australian colony to give women the right to vote and stand for parliament. South Australia's suffrage movement included the writer and reformer Catherine Helen Spence, the first woman to stand for elected office, albeit unsuccessfully, when she stood as a candidate for one of the conventions to consider federation.

Spence had become something of an expert on electoral reform, as a champion of proportional representation in parliament – 'the hope of the world', she called it. A version of her Hare-Spence system of voting (known as Hare-Clark) has been used in Tasmania since 1896. Inspired by the writings of John Stuart Mill, Spence was the product of a particularly liberal culture. As the *Express and Telegraph* wrote in 1885: 'The old ideas concerning the limited rights of women in the home and in relation to society as a whole … have experienced of late years a modification so vast as to be perfectly astonishing.'[26]

* * *

This was the intellectual climate in which Henry Parkes boldly told the NSW governor, Lord Carrington, that he 'could confederate these colonies in twelve months'. Carrington was surprised, but enthusiastic. 'Then why don't you do it?' he responded. 'It would be a glorious finish to your life.'[27] Carrington observed that Canada, since achieving dominion status (full internal self-government within the British Empire) in 1867, had spoken with one voice, unlike Australia's multiple, disunited voices. 'That must be so until we federate,' Parkes replied.[28]

Parkes' first great oration on the federal cause was not given at Tenterfield, as commonly believed, but delivered months earlier, in parliament, on 7 August 1889. Speaking about Western Australia's demand for full self-government, then under consideration by the imperial parliament, Parkes used the moment to consider the future of Australia. '[T]he day is now come when we may safely act upon the maxim of Australia for the Australians,' he said. That did not mean severing the ties to Britain – 'I have no dream of separation,' he told his colleagues – nor did he dream 'of a different form of government from the parent state', which was his way of referring to the republican model. What it did mean, said Parkes, was that 'the future of this whole continent ought, beyond question, to be purely Australian', bound by common interest and attachment.[29]

... because the earth spaces of the globe have been so far
taken up that nothing like Australia can again arise ...
[o]ur path, I say, is broad, and it is distinct ... and it is that
we, the free people of this land, shall to the best of our
power avoid the errors of our ancestors, shall free ourselves
from their prejudices and trammels: shall as far as possible
assimilate to ourselves the wealth of their intelligence, the
wealth of their inventive genius; and while we inherit all
their glory in the past, try to acquire for ourselves a new
and purer glory founded upon the everlasting basis of
good-will and peace.[30]

Parkes was so pleased with the speech that he sent a copy to his
friend James Froude, the British historian and novelist. 'I never
witnessed such enthusiastic unanimity as marked the adoption
of this Address to the Queen,' Parkes wrote. 'If you can find
time to read my own speech you will see that I foreshadow –
very imperfectly, of course – what I regard as to the only basis
for a lasting union of the Empire.'[31]

An independent nationalism that retained the British
connection – that was Parkes' model. Even back then,
Australians had the choice of a republic or a constitutional
monarchy. Overwhelmingly, they preferred the British
connection.

Parkes was naturally concerned about how Victoria might
react. He had written to its premier, Duncan Gillies, after his
initial discussion with Carrington on 15 June 1889, raising
the possibility of convening a 'Parliamentary Convention of
Australasia' to consider a draft federal constitution. Gillies
responded cautiously. Gillies and Deakin's preferred approach
was to use the Federal Council as basis for any further
action but Parkes was too impatient for that. After a visit to
Queensland in late October, he exploited a recent report on

Australia's defences by Major-General James Edwards – which had recommended the federation of the colonies – to make a bold move.

Parkes formally announced his campaign for federation at the Tenterfield School of Arts on 24 October 1889. Australia had to federate, he said. It was 'absolutely necessary … to have one central authority, which could bring all of the forces of the different colonies into one army'. Drawing comparisons with America, he noted that Australia's population of three and a half million was similar to that of the United States in 1789, when it ratified its own constitution. '[W]hat the Americans had done by war,' Parkes said, 'the Australians could bring about in peace.'[32]

If some were sceptical, others were inspired to act, among them the NSW attorney-general, Edmund Barton, then 40 years old. As a recent convert to protectionism, Barton was a political opponent of Parkes, but he was prepared to put that aside for the greater cause of national union.

For Parkes, Barton's support was the bridge to the new generation of leadership then emerging in Sydney. It was quickly agreed that Parkes and another representative from New South Wales should convene with the members of the Federal Council in Melbourne. They met during one of the hottest summers in living memory. On 6 February 1890, with temperatures nearing 40°C (104° Fahrenheit), Parkes gave notice of his intention to proceed with Australian federation immediately. Despite continuing scepticism, there was much good cheer at the banquet held in the evening. It was there that Parkes spoke of the 'crimson thread of kinship [that] runs through us all'. In the first speech of the evening, the former Victorian premier, James Service – who thought that free trade produced greater wealth but protection ensured fairer distribution – had warned of the 'lion in the way' of federation: the tariffs on trade between the colonies. '[T]he conference must either kill the lion,' Service said, 'or the lion will kill it.'[33]

* * *

Everyone agreed that federation had to remove the nuisance of internal customs barriers. It had long confused visitors to Australia that people 'who speak the same language, are engaged in the same occupations, and are subjects of the same sovereign' should treat each other as foreigners.[34] Stories abounded of creative attempts to dodge the customs officer. In the NSW–Victoria border town of Moama, Victorians could be seen purchasing bundles of clothing then dressing themselves in them – adding layer after layer – before crossing the Murray River bridge into the neighbouring Victorian town of Echuca, duty free.[35] Echuca bakers, to avoid tax on imported flour and bread, established dough-houses in Moama.[36] Children were trained as professional smugglers and taught how to lie to border officials.[37] More debilitating to residents was the tax on livestock. Farmers just north of the Murray, whose natural market was Melbourne, had instead to look to the far more distant Sydney.

The Melbourne conference revealed quickly that any federal scheme had to manage pronounced differences among the colonies. Victorians viewed internal free trade as a benefit; South Australia, anxious of competition, did not. Western Australia relied on its customs revenue. The conference sat for seven days and agreed to an 'early union' of Australia under 'one legislative and executive Government'.[38] The next step was a national convention, drawing seven delegates from each colony to design a federal scheme. Observing Parkes up close for the first time, Deakin saw 'a born leader of men', battle-hardened, vain, 'a doughty parliamentary warrior neither giving nor asking quarter'.[39]

* * *

It was a golden age that did not bypass organised labour. In New South Wales alone, union and unionists' numbers doubled in the six years after 1885.[40] By then, about 20 per cent of the Australian workforce was unionised, far more than in Britain or the United States.

In 1890, maritime workers in Melbourne – both ships' officers and wharf labourers – inspired by radical class politics, joined in striking for five consecutive months over pay, conditions and security. Across Australia, coal miners, shearers, station hands and transport workers held strikes of their own in solidarity. In 1891, shearer unions – angered at the pastoralists' refusal to adopt the terms of the union contract and resenting lower wages with the end of the wool boom – stopped work, coalesced in outback camps, collected rifles and ammunition, attacked private property and intimidated non-union shearers.

The strikes were eventually broken but not the strikers' ideas of class conflict. Realising that unions could not control the labour market in opposition to the legislature, labour pivoted to democratic politics. In 1890 and 1891, political labour parties emerged in New South Wales, Queensland, South Australia and, to a lesser degree, in Victoria.

Notwithstanding the rhetoric of the radical socialists, there was really never an entrenched class divide in Australia. Social mobility was relatively high. Many employers were self made. When, in 1889, the London dock strikers received the extraordinary sum of £30,000 in Australian contributions – more than three-fifths of their entire strike fund – it mostly came from individuals of all classes.[41] Most donations came from Victoria, the heartbeat of colonial liberalism, where labour and capital got along fairly well. This was the distinctive character of Australian democracy.

* * *

The weather was grey and wet as the convention delegates made their way to Parliament House, Sydney, on 2 March 1891, to draft and approve a federal constitution. Parkes, still reeling from a carriage accident that had badly injured his leg, presided over the event. He was the undisputed leader of the convention. Keeping his contributions to a minimum, his interest was in its spirit rather than its detail. He did, however, make a case for the name to be 'Commonwealth of Australia', the term he had regularly used for years. 'Let us set before ourselves one common object – the common welfare of this rising commonwealth,' he had said in 1887.[42] Australia was not to be a 'dominion', like Canada. Federation was a 'national' project: 'One People, One Destiny' was how Parkes put it.[43]

Across several weeks, the convention debated principles and voted on resolutions, with committees working closely on a draft Bill (which would ultimately have to be presented to the British Parliament). One of the delegates, the 43-year-old Tasmanian Andrew Inglis Clark, had drafted a constitution of his own and privately distributed copies to colleagues. His draft achieved an important objective discussed at the Melbourne conference a year earlier: reconciling the British 'Westminster' model of responsible government with an American federal system. In Clark's proposal, there was to be a house of representatives and a senate. The government would be formed in the lower house and be responsible to it. There would be equal state representation in the senate. Much of Australia's so-called 'Wash-minster' system is in Clark's draft.[44]

During the Easter break, the drafting committee were invited by the vice-president of the convention, Sir Samuel Griffith, then the Queensland premier, aboard the steamship *Lucinda*.

Travelling up the Hawkesbury River, they worked closely on an official draft largely drawing upon Clark's document.

Two clauses on Indigenous Australians were included. One concerned the Commonwealth power to make 'special laws' for people of any race, excluding Aboriginal people (and, in the 1891 draft, also excluding the Māori population of New Zealand). A second concerned the exclusion of Aboriginal Australians 'in reckoning the numbers of the people of the Commonwealth'.

The genesis of the 'race power', later to become section 51 (xxvi) of the Constitution, lay in Griffith's own experience in Queensland with the importation of Pacific Islanders, known as 'Kanakas', to work on sugar cane and cotton farms.[45] Since the 1860s, tens of thousands had been brought over, often against their will. Griffith hated the practice – 'as bad as the African slave trade at its very worst,' he said, 'where nearly every man was procured by force or fraud.'[46] His opposition aroused the planters, some of whom pushed for their own separate colony. In 1891, Griffith expected that this would become a Commonwealth issue and that the federal parliament would require the power to exclude such workers and to regulate their trade. 'The Dutch and English governments in the east do not allow their people to emigrate to serve in any foreign country unless there is a special law made by the people of that country protecting them, and affording special facilities for their going and coming,' he said during the Convention debates, suggesting the race power could be used beneficially.[47] 'Aboriginal natives', though, were excluded from this 'race' provision because they were Australians; therefore, Griffith thought, the states would enact any legislation that might be needed for them.

Griffith also added the exclusionary provision of not counting Aboriginal people for constitutional purposes. This later became section 127. A candid statement Griffith made to a Melbourne journalist provides an insight into its rationale: 'We do not know how many blacks there are in Queensland ... there are miles and miles of wild country into which the white man scarcely penetrates.'[48] As a recent study of section 127 has shown, this was the logistical issue that the Constitution sought to avoid, that is, 'counting itinerant or even unknown Aboriginal peoples'.[49] Nonetheless, it was easy to read the negative symbolism behind it. By the mid-20th century, the provision had clearly run its course, even discouraging efforts by census officials to 'count' the Aboriginal population.

Overall, what is remarkable about the Australian Constitution – as it was finally settled in 1900 – was not its racialism, but its liberalism. Its minimalist and utilitarian language masks a generous and democratic flexibility. Deakin later spoke of being 'awed by the thought of the constituency which is not visible, but which awaits the results of our labours – we are the trustees for posterity, for the unborn millions, unknown and unnumbered – whose aspirations we may help them to fulfil and whose destinies we may assist to determine'.[50] Australia has subsequently developed politically and economically with very little need for constitutional amendment. Whatever its defects as a mission statement, the Australian Constitution has been a remarkably effective rule book for a nation.

* * *

Parkes finally had the document that he had been dreaming about for years: a national constitution. Yet he faced more immediate problems. By the end of 1891, southeastern Australia was engulfed in an economic crisis. Highly indebted to London for national development projects, about 40 per cent of export income was devoted to paying off foreign debt.[51] Then there was the local debt created by a property bubble. When the music stopped – as it did after the near collapse of London's Barings bank – Australia's financial intermediaries fell like dominoes, with some 54 banks closing their doors over two years.[52] By 1895, the economy had contracted by 30 per cent.[53] In many respects it was worse than the Great Depression of the 1930s, especially for Victoria, the epicentre of the crisis.

The economic slump helped to energise a new force in politics. Born out of the humiliating disaster of the 1890 maritime strike, workers and unionists pledged themselves to the creation of an organised and influential parliamentary machine. At the 1891 NSW general election, the newly formed Labour Electoral League secured 35 out of 141 seats and, more importantly, held the balance of power. Parkes had had enough. He resigned the premiership and the leadership of the Free Trade Party.

George Reid was elected the new leader of the Free Trade Party. A committed liberal and streetwise politician who could entertain crowds with his humour and repartee, Reid was a critic of the draft federal constitution. Grossly overweight, balding and sporting a walrus-like moustache, it was often remarked that Reid was a cartoonist's dream. He could also offer what few of his colleagues could: political survival as a free trade–supporting pragmatist that a working-class party could support.

Reid led his party to electoral victory in 1894 against a protectionist government drowning in a tide of depression, strikes and natural disasters. Meanwhile, the Labour Electoral League had reconstituted itself as the Labor Party, with unprecedented internal discipline, including the 'pledge' that all its MPs vote together in favour of party policy. Reid's centrepiece reform, a radical reduction in the colony's tariffs, appealed to the commercial classes and fellow liberals. A land tax and income tax were intended to make up the forgone revenue. In Reid, both the urban voters and labouring classes had a champion. He proposed reform of the Legislative Council, 'those dynasties of royal mummies' as he called them, leading the *Australian Workman* to dub him the 'prince of radicals'.[54] Reid established himself as the outstanding political strategist of the decade. Elected somewhat reluctantly by his colleagues in 1891, within five years he would carry through the most wide-ranging fiscal reform in generations.

* * *

The term 'White Australia', used consciously as a political slogan, can be traced to New South Wales's 1896 extension of its *Chinese Restriction and Regulation Act 1888*.[55] The new Bill expanded restrictions to persons of 'any coloured race', regardless of their status as British subjects. This was a harsh Bill, but Labor wanted it, and Reid wanted Labor's support. It came after Britain's 1894 Treaty of Commerce and Navigation with Japan, the reciprocal residency provisions of which unsettled the Australian colonies.[56] The NSW Bill, replicated by other colonies, upset the British government. Colonial Secretary Joseph Chamberlain issued a plea to Australian legislators to:

> bear in mind the traditions of the Empire, which makes
> no distinction in favour of, or against race or colour; and
> to exclude by reason of their colour, or by reason of their
> race, all Her Majesty's Indian subjects, or even all Asiatics,
> would be an act so offensive to those peoples that it would
> be most painful, I am quite certain, to Her Majesty to have
> to sanction it.[57]

British liberal imperialism of the late 19th century was in many respects more humane than Australia's home-grown nationalism.

* * *

Meanwhile, a revived federal movement was brewing in the Riverina District. New federal leagues were established with farmers, traders and small business owners, all suffering the daily inconveniences of colonial borders – tariffs, the stock tax and different laws governing water use and rail freight. A conference in Corowa endorsed the proposal of John Quick, a lawyer and former Victorian MP, for the direct election of a national convention that would draft a federal constitution, which would then be put to a people's vote. When the premiers met in Hobart in 1895 to consider the future, Reid successfully championed Quick's proposal, and enabling legislation was passed by a majority of the colonies, setting the course for the 'popular phase' of the federal movement.

Three constitutional conventions were held between 1897 and 1898 – in Adelaide, Sydney and Melbourne – and attended by ten delegates from each colony except Queensland. Most of the 50 delegates were Protestant, liberal and middle-class. A third were lawyers. Labor delegates were largely absent, sceptical as they were of a federal project that gave no consideration to class division.

Protectionists argued with free traders; secularists debated advocates of constitutional religious recognition; supporters of women's suffrage fought against those satisfied by manhood suffrage alone. On the core issue of federalism there was a familiar pattern. The less-populous states demanded a strong Senate – the states' house – to protect their interests against the popular lower house dominated by representatives from the larger states. The South Australian delegates, who Deakin recognised as the most able, played something of a go-between for the two groups. Reid, by contrast, wanted a 'democratic' constitution, which meant a weaker Senate, less capable of stalling the will of majority opinion. As the premier of the most populous colony, this argument killed two birds with one stone: he could invoke principle while protecting the interests of New South Wales.

These conventions were Edmund Barton's greatest moment. An eminent lawyer, who had contributed to the earlier 1891 draft, and a tireless advocate of federation, he was, in Deakin's words, 'loved by most and respected by all', despite a reputation for languor.[58] Federation was his moment to make a difference, so he threw himself into it, attending every session, studying and working on every clause into the late hours of the evening, and chairing and directing discussion. Under his leadership, the convention drafted one of the most democratic constitutions of its time.

There were big differences from the 1891 draft. The Senate was to be popularly elected. Ministers of the Crown had to be members of parliament. The federal franchise was to be determined by the Commonwealth, but could not exclude anyone on a colonial electoral register.

The Womanhood Suffrage League of New South Wales had presented the first petition to the Adelaide Convention. It called for true democracy, 'resting upon the will of the whole people, not half the people'.[59] The Victorian suffragist Vida Goldstein argued that the Commonwealth franchise should be copied from the widest one available – that of South Australia.[60] Eventually, the compromise clause of South Australian Treasurer Frederick Holder won the day, providing that 'no elector possessing the right to vote shall be deprived of that right'. George Reid knew the consequences immediately: 'It will compel female suffrage.'[61] This was South Australia's great contribution to federation.

The final draft resolved many of the controversies that had plagued colonial parliaments for generations. The new constitution forbade anyone having more than one vote, required no property qualification for voting or for standing for the Senate, ensured payment of members, and provided for a deadlock remedy, a wide franchise and a referendum process for constitutional amendments. What we take for granted today were great breakthroughs then.

* * *

The draft constitution was put to the people. Switzerland routinely used referenda, as did some American states. While the referendum mechanism was a novelty within Westminster systems, it appealed to Australians' sense of popular sovereignty.

In the lead-up to the first federal plebiscite, all eyes were on George Reid. 'We ought to have,' he said, 'a more democratic constitution,' asking voters to make up their own mind, even if he, as a delegate, felt obliged to vote for it.[62] The opinion of their 'yes–no' premier mattered in New South Wales, which had inserted a requirement that at least 80,000 voters (out of the 260,000 thought to be eligible), and not just a majority of those voting, had to approve the Bill.

If there were any doubts about Reid's influence, it arrived in humiliating fashion on 4 June 1898, the day of the vote. A narrow majority voted in favour, but less than the required 80,000. Despite the overwhelming success of the referenda in Victoria, South Australia and Tasmania – voting in Queensland and Western Australia would come later – New South Wales was not yet ready to say yes.

At a premiers' conference in Melbourne, further amendments to the draft were agreed upon. Federal financial relations were a sticking point, so a provision guaranteeing a portion of Commonwealth customs duty to the states was limited to ten years, while the provision for resolving parliamentary deadlocks between the two houses of parliament now only required a simple majority in a joint sitting of parliament – not a three-fifths majority. It was further guaranteed that the federal capital would be located in New South Wales.

These were amendments Reid could take to his party, and to his colony, as a best and final offer. The compromise worked. The 1899 referendum campaign was better organised, more vigorously fought and with a much higher voter turnout than the previous one. Most importantly, Reid had the authority to campaign for a Yes vote; it received 107,420 votes, defeating No's 82,741. Every other colony also achieved substantially higher turnouts and majorities. Victorians voted yes with a whopping 94 per cent approval. After some minor wrangling, which ended up authorising appeals from Australian courts to the judicial committee of the Privy Council, the British Parliament passed the *Commonwealth of Australia Constitution Act 1900*, which received royal assent on 9 July 1900. The new nation was born.

8

A Bold Experiment

Australia's first decade as a nation was marked by three major developments: the consolidation of White Australia, 'protection all round' via tariffs and wage arbitration, and the creation of a two-party system pitting a union-dominated Labor Party against the first incarnation of a more market-friendly but still 'statist' Liberal Party. This was the 'Australian Settlement' that persisted until well into the 20th century. It may not have maximised economic development, but it preserved social cohesion for the tumultuous times ahead.

§

Australia is a young nation but an old democracy: young because modern Australia only began in the late 18th century; old because Australia was a democratic pioneer.

On 1 January 1901, the Commonwealth of Australia's Constitution was more democratic than that of Great Britain, Canada and the United States of America; even Switzerland, the citadel of direct democracy, had an unelected upper house. Not so in Australia. Both houses were to be chosen by the people, based on a franchise that by 1902 was wider than almost anywhere else in the world: most women could vote; and no state law prohibited Aboriginal people from voting due to their race, although Queensland and Western Australia had tough eligibility requirements.[1]

As a then unique political and social laboratory, Australia drew from far and wide politicians, activists and intellectuals curious to experience this advanced new polity and learn from it. Some things, then almost unheard of elsewhere, were becoming within reach here: such as equal pay for women and men working as telegraphists under the 1902 *Commonwealth Public Service Act* – a battle won by the unionist Louisa Dunkley.

The Irish republican and labour leader Michael Davitt, born into the wrenching poverty of the Great Famine, had visited the colonies in 1895 and concluded 'unhesitatingly' that they 'give better all-round conditions of existence to the average man than any of the European countries I am acquainted with'.[2] Even in the aftermath of the catastrophic 1890s depression, Australians were still better nourished than their British kin, consuming twice as much meat per week, and a more varied diet of fruit and vegetables.[3] Materially, it was a more equal society than most European countries. The British intellectuals Beatrice and Sidney Webb found Australia 'a most promising experiment': democratic with durable institutions, a politically engaged middle and working class, a professional press corps and no domineering upper class comparable to that in Britain.[4] A visiting Mark Twain encountered a people 'so jealous of [their] independence that [they grow] restive if even the Imperial Government at home proposes to help'.[5]

If the founders of this democratic experiment are mentioned at all today, it is often to condemn them. They were people of their time, carrying – most of them – the prejudices of those days. The Australian Parliament's first major legislative action, and the law it is most remembered for, is the *Immigration Restriction Act 1901*, otherwise known as the White Australia policy. It consolidated and built upon existing colonial laws restricting non-white immigrants from residing in Australia, in addition to removing South Sea Islanders from the sugar plantations of Queensland. Understandably, it's regarded as a blot on our history that's hard to reconcile with our preferred image of Australia as the land of the fair go.

We should judge our founders by the standards of their time, not ours, and extend to them the understanding that we would seek for ourselves in wrestling with our own issues. The world they lived in was quite different from our own. General economic advancement on the scale we are used to today only began after 1870 and wrought enormous economic and political changes.[6] These transformations smashed against long-cherished cultures and traditions, delivering unprecedented wealth but also a bewildering sense of flux and anxiety. Parochial attachment fed into crude generalisations of racial difference. Australians were concerned to protect their newfound wealth and to guard it as best they could. That explains why the debates of those days are characterised less by a condescending superiority than by a desperate appeal to national survival.

Australia's federal leaders were probably more humane in their attitudes than the majority of Australians. Federation, after all, was a profoundly liberal project, and the early political contests of federation were between competing versions of liberalism. The two main political groupings of the first parliament were the Protectionists and the Free Traders – the former dominated by Victorians, the latter by the New South Welsh. Each considered themselves a truly 'liberal party'. The most important political development of the new Commonwealth's first decade was the decline of free-trade liberalism (and the subsequent consolidation of both liberal groupings) and the rise of the Australian Labor Party as a major political force.

To a liberal or a conservative of today, these early years were hardly satisfactory. The long boom of the late 19th century was over. Australia was no longer the richest country in the world, measured by wealth per person. The economic story from 1900 to 1914 is one of relative decline. Prior to 1890, Australia was roughly 40 per cent richer per person than the United States. By the First World War, per capita income was broadly equal with that of the USA. Depression and drought had not helped; nor had the turn inwards. Industrial regulation, tariff protection and White Australia had all become central pillars of government policy and all were productivity killers. Thus began a long period – well over half a century – of liberalism under challenge.

* * *

Few people expected the size and responsibilities of the Commonwealth government to grow so quickly. One delegate at the federal convention thought that the federal parliament would sit for no more than two months in the year.[7] John Downer, the former premier of South Australia, asked 'where, in this Constitution, any great expenditure can come in, either in the first five, seven, or eight years, or at any subsequent time, except, possibly, it may be in regard to defence ...?'[8] In the early years of the Commonwealth, Victoria's public service in Melbourne was larger than the federal government's.

Yet if the first decade challenged Downer's widely shared assumption, the remainder of the century made a mockery of it. Constitutional conservatives have since bemoaned the expansion of federal power, the growth of which proved steady after the first generation of High Court justices retired, and which exploded after both world wars. Yet Australian sentiment has always been to trust their governments. They were creations of the burgeoning democratic era and were never regarded as either hostile to the public or the embodiment of ancient privileges. Australians expected their institutions to be helpful in their daily lives and to focus on the business of nation building. They were prepared to equip them with the means to do so, as their collective common sense thought best.

Because customs revenue was the federal government's main source of funding, the tariff question was central to the first federal election. Alfred Deakin in Victoria and Edmund Barton in New South Wales organised their supporters to advocate a moderately protective tariff, while George Reid continued his tireless advocacy for what could loosely be called a 'revenue' tariff – large enough to fund the essential functions of government but no more.

On the surface, this was a dry contest devoid of drama. But the so-called 'fiscal issue' – how 'protective' the federal tariff was to be – can be understood as a contest about the size and scope of government. This was how many of the politicians saw it at the time. 'The question of the Tariff is far more than one of fiscal policy,' the NSW Free Trader Edward Pulsford wrote. '[I]t lies at the bottom of sound finance, honest government and true democracy, and it affects the friendly relations of our country with every other.'[9] The actual names of the political organisations are revealing: Deakin had established the Victorian National Liberal Organisation in November 1900, and Barton had founded the Australian Liberal Association, in New South Wales, the following year. Both groups rivalled the NSW-based Australian Free Trade and Liberal Association, led by George Reid. All were 'liberal' in the sense of mistrusting the control that the growing Labor Party exercised over its members and sought to exercise over society at large. But they differed in the extent to which they thought government could or should ameliorate human suffering or facilitate human flourishing.

Even then, *The Worker* newspaper could not help but ask whether the Protectionists or the Free Traders would 'be as liberal were there no Labor Party in the field. The answer must be no.'[10] Liberalism, broadly speaking, was the defining political principle of the age, although it meant different things to people who called themselves 'liberals', just as there are many different types of 'democrat' today.

Australians went to the polls in March 1901. Liberal Protectionists claimed 31 seats in the House of Representatives; Free Traders, 28; and Labor, 14; with two independents. These political groupings were much more fluid than modern political parties, with personal friendships and ideological preferences sometimes overriding any sense of party loyalty. George Turner, for instance, served as federal treasurer under both Edmund Barton and, later, George Reid. With the tacit support of Labor, Barton became Australia's first prime minister as the leader of the Liberal Protectionists.

* * *

White Australia became the first major law passed by the federal parliament because it was bipartisan policy and overwhelmingly supported by the public. Embodied in two Acts – the *Pacific Island Labourers Act 1901* and the *Immigration Restriction Act 1901* – the debate took up some 600 pages of Hansard. Prior to federation, each colony had already restricted non-European immigration, so White Australia was already in effect. Nonetheless, a federated Australia held the promise of strong uniform legislation, plus the power to speak with one united voice on a matter regarded as central to social cohesion and economic prosperity.

The most uncompromising supporters of White Australia were the Labor Party, with their trade union base. Initially,

Labor leaders' concern was non-white workers out-competing white Australians for jobs, working for lower wages and in worse conditions. Over time, this economic justification became increasingly racialised. The federal Labor leader, John Watson, said his main objection to Asian immigration was 'the probability of racial contamination'.[11]

Deakin thought such arguments exhibited the 'unreasoning hostility to strangers and foreigners for which no justification can be offered'.[12] Even though he was repulsed by the rank racial prejudice on display in parliament, Deakin remained committed to the policy of White Australia, which he regarded as crucial to ensuring cultural homogeneity. He was convinced that Australia had the most liberal and democratic culture in the world and wanted to avoid the racial disharmony exhibited elsewhere, including in America. He was at pains to recognise the 'high abilities' of the Japanese. Nonetheless, he was also convinced that a multi-ethnic state would be divided and unstable. Other Liberal Protectionists, including Edmund Barton, were more explicit in their racial preferences.

The most sensitive and humane contributions to the debate came from a small number of liberal Free Traders. Senator Edward Pulsford declared, 'I look upon the whole of the inhabitants of Asia as my friends.'[13] The NSW Free Trade MP Bruce Smith felt 'the foundation of the Bill is racial prejudice', adding 'it is a humiliating confession that the principal reason for shutting out the Japanese race is, not that they are a low type of humanity or a degraded people, but they are too thrifty. They work too hard, and they are too provident, and they possess so many of those old-fashioned virtues that we Britishers cannot compete with.'[14]

As a brash assertion of nationhood, White Australia sat awkwardly with the British government. Britain prided herself on outlawing slavery before any other world power and contrasted the colour-blind nature of its legal traditions with the overt racial discrimination practised in the United States and elsewhere. This position infuriated Labor. One young MP, Billy Hughes, even suggested Australian independence would be preferable to any British veto of the immigration Bill: an instance of the illiberalism of early Australian republicanism.[15]

The Act was designed with British law in mind. In preference to outright exclusion based on race, and following other colonial governments, the Commonwealth proposed a dictation test that would determine eligibility to come to Australia. Immigration officials could test immigrants in an unfamiliar European language. Four weeks after the Act was legislated, two Indians arrived on a Japanese ship. Despite being subjects of the King, who had served in the British Indian Army, they were unable to pass a dictation test and were refused entry at Townsville, Brisbane and Sydney. The dictation test was still in use in the late 1930s, when the Lyons government used a dictation test in Gaelic to refuse admission to the communist intellectual Egon Kisch.

Despite the Act, exceptions were made for some Chinese, Japanese and Indian traders and students, who were allowed to settle as temporary or essential workers. As well, a considerable number of non-British European migrants – Italians, Greeks, Maltese and Jewish Russians – landed in Australia and established thriving communities.

The Pacific Island Labourers Bill, to phase out the use of indentured Pacific Islanders in the North Queensland cane fields, was even less contentious. By the time of federation, Australia's tropical north was home to Islanders, Japanese, Afghan cameleers, Malays, Indians and Chinese. In towns like Townsville, Darwin, Broome and Cooktown, non-whites were often the majority and a mainstay of the economy. The *Pacific Island Labourers Act* saw most of the so-called Kanakas deported back to their original islands, even though many planters and employers feared that white men could not work and survive in the same conditions. They were compensated with high tariff walls for their products. Of the 10,000 Islanders in Queensland in 1901, more than 7500 had left by 1908. Only those who had been living and working in Australia for over 20 years could stay.

* * *

Australians of the federation era wanted nationhood but not separation from Britain. They generally viewed themselves as independent Australian–Britons, entitled to self-government behind the protective shield of the Pax Britannica. This dual identity was mostly taken for granted then in a way that has few echoes now. Perhaps an approximate contemporary parallel is the state identity that can readily co-exist with a national one. It's not a perfect parallel, though, as Australia in 1901 was far less subjected to London on domestic matters than an Australian state was or is to the Commonwealth. Even on foreign policy, which generally reflected that of Britain, there were differences of opinion between London and Melbourne (the temporary capital of Australia until the site could be chosen and the first Commonwealth Parliament House opened in Canberra in 1927).

Australia's leaders did not regard themselves as subservient to Britain. Indeed, they thought of themselves as leaders of the British global community in the Pacific. Hence, they championed and advocated for imperial interests as much as London did. Australia gained its own colonial possession, British New Guinea, in March 1902. It had originally passed into British hands after Australian pressure to forestall German expansion in the Pacific. But only in 1906 was the *Papua Act* proclaimed, and only in November 1908 was a lieutenant-governor appointed: Sir Hubert Murray, who stayed in the post for 31 years.

The new Commonwealth's military history began with participation in the Boer War. Rich gold discoveries in the territory of the Boer Republics had drawn in thousands of English-speaking migrants, known as Uitlanders, demanding equal political rights with their Boer counterparts. After war broke out late in 1899, all the settler colonies rushed to make a military contribution. Eventually, some 16,000 Australians served in this conflict, initially in separate colonial contingents but eventually as part of the Australian Army. About 600 Australians died overseas: half from combat casualties, half from disease.

By the time the conflict officially ended on 31 May 1902, the world had been given its first proper glimpse of the Australian soldier. A young Banjo Paterson – whose best-selling poetry collection *The Man From Snowy River and Other Verses*, had vividly depicted bush life and rugged individualism – was sent overseas as a war correspondent for the *Sydney Morning Herald* and *The Age*. On returning home, he spoke of the 'mobility, dash, and intelligence' of the Australian and New Zealand regiments. 'It must never be forgotten,' he told a crowd, 'that the Australians were accustomed all their lives to finding their way in the open, to noticing what was taking place around them, and to relying on themselves at a pinch; the English "Tommies" were drilled and trained to obey orders, and there their ideas stopped.'[16]

* * *

Another achievement of the first federal parliament was to guarantee federal voting rights for women. Female voters in South Australia and Western Australia, who already had the right to vote in their colonies, had voted in the first federal election. The *Commonwealth Franchise Act 1902*, which extended this right across all other states, was globally significant. One newspaper in the US (which didn't get women's suffrage until 1920) declared it to be 'the greatest victory ever won for woman and ensures the establishment of woman's complete equality in the near future throughout the Southern Hemisphere'.[17]

But the *Franchise Act* was far less benign for Aboriginal Australians. Prior to 1901, no colony prohibited Aboriginal people from voting, although Queensland and Western Australia came close to doing so through complex restrictions. Section 41 of the Constitution should have ensured that all those who could vote in colonial elections could vote federally. The original Bill did not mention race at all.[18] Introducing it, Richard O'Connor, the government leader in the Senate, declared: 'It would be a monstrous thing, an unheard of piece of savagery on our part, to treat the aboriginals, whose land we were occupying, in such a manner as to deprive them absolutely of any right to vote in their own country, simply on the ground of their colour and because they were aboriginals.'[19]

But as the federal parliament debated the matter, it became clear that most MPs wanted a very narrow interpretation of section 41. Labor's leadership worried that Aboriginal workers in the north would vote according to their squatter employers and against the interests of white workers. Ultimately, the Act disqualified Aboriginal Australians from voting unless they were already enfranchised in the states at the time of federation. What this meant in practice, according to a 1961 federal parliamentary inquiry into the 'voting rights of Aborigines', was that Aboriginal people would normally only go on the rolls and vote if they were well integrated into the wider community. In Queensland and Western Australia, there was a specific presumption that Aboriginal people would be excluded from voting. For at least half a century, there were no voting facilities in Aboriginal settlements.

* * *

The first decade of the Commonwealth was the Age of Deakin. To a later prime minister, Robert Menzies, Deakin was Australia's greatest leader, who set the foundations of Australia's national policies on immigration, tariffs, defence and industrial arbitration. He was the spirit behind Barton's prime ministership and the ghost that haunted Chris Watson's Labor government and George Reid's Free Trade government. He was the biggest presence in a fluid and sometimes chaotic parliament: in the first decade, Australia went through seven different administrations. Despite this, Deakin's leadership – both in office and out of it – created a distinct antipodean vision of the good society, with an active role for the state, and with a local and imperial patriotism.

Deakin was the pre-eminent figure who gave Australians a national consciousness that had not existed before 1901. His economic record is more mixed. He did not trust human nature to sort out its problems in the absence of a strong and beneficent government and wanted to protect Australians from themselves and from the outside world.

At federation, the main symbol of this tradition was compulsory arbitration. The shock of the 1890 maritime strike had elicited not only a new phase of politics – the emergence of the modern Labor Party – but a new policy, compulsory arbitration: the idea that a judicial solution could be found to industrial conflict. In 1894, New Zealand was the first country to try, establishing a national Court of Arbitration to settle disputes and make binding awards. Western Australia and

New South Wales followed, in 1900 and 1901 respectively. For some Liberals, and for a growing constituency of Labor parliamentarians, this was a deeply felt political project. For Deakin, the Compulsory Arbitration Bill was the great challenge of his first term in government.

Like all idealistic projects, the devil was in the detail. Deakin was adamant in limiting its scope. Labor wanted the Bill to extend to state public servants. A stalemate followed, Deakin resigned, and Labor's Chris Watson formed the world's first national labour government. Vladimir Lenin's remark that the Labor Party in Australia was, in fact, 'a liberal-bourgeois' party, was telling. Class in Australia – if it ever really existed – was vastly different to that in Britain. Federal Labor pitched itself as a party for the whole nation, and would, in time, succeed in broadening its appeal to Australians outside its traditional blue-collar union base. Still, Labor's insistence on covering state employees under federal industrial law killed Watson's government within months. As well, neither Deakin nor Reid could support the new government's proposal to give the Arbitration Court power to preference union workers over non-union workers. So, Labor fell, and George Reid succeeded Watson in August 1904.

The merry-go-round of prime ministerships in this first decade was a product of a divided liberalism. Reid governed with the precarious support of Alfred Deakin, but such an alliance required the federal tariff to be left alone. It was an ineffective government, but its very ineffectiveness encouraged a redrawing of the political battle lines, away from the rivalries of competing liberalisms, towards a clearer demarcation between socialism and anti-socialism. With a combination of Liberal Protectionist and Liberal Free Trade ministers, Reid successfully passed the Conciliation and Arbitration Bill in December 1904. He then turned his attention to uniting the two liberal strands of the parliament, establishing the Australian Liberal League to mount a campaign of anti-socialism under the banner of 'Liberty, Loyalty, Progress, and Enterprise'.[20]

Reid's ministry lasted less than 11 months, collapsing in July 1905 following Deakin's withdrawal of support. Speaking at Ballarat on 24 June, Deakin scolded Reid's anti-socialism rhetoric as too vague to be meaningful and accused him of re-opening the tariff debate. In parliament, Deakin gathered enough support to return as prime minister, holding office for a further three years.

* * *

Deakin did not trust private enterprise as a means of economic development; but neither did he favour its abolition. The extent to which markets are deemed to have failed, and state intervention becomes justified, is a line that all governments must draw – but Deakin's default position was for a more interventionist state. An honest question arose: what, exactly, were the fundamental differences of principle in economic policy between Deakin's Protectionists and a moderate Labor Party? This became acute with Deakin's policy of 'New Protection', which sought both to suspend tariff protection for manufacturers who did not pay 'fair and reasonable' wages, and impose excise duty on manufacturers who underpaid their staff.[21]

But what was fair and reasonable? In a case brought by unions against the owner of the Sunshine Harvester Works, claiming that the business should not get excise exemption because it had failed to pay 'fair and reasonable wages', the Commonwealth Arbitration Court, then headed by Henry Higgins, settled on seven shillings a day. Higgins' benchmark was the minimum needed to live as a 'human being in a civilised community'.[22] He wanted enough for a husband and wife with three children to live comfortably and with dignity. Under this framework, supply and demand were irrelevant.

The direct impact of the Harvester judgment was short-lived because, on appeal, the High Court declared that excise legislation could not be used as a back-door means to set wages. The judgment became 'educational rather than practical'. It was not until the early 1920s that wages reached a level compatible with the Harvester case's ambitions.[23] But the Harvester judgment remained symbolically important, as a rejection of the invisible hand of the market as the best means for promoting growth and distributing wealth. That government needed to protect both employees and employers from adverse market forces became the accepted political wisdom for decades. For radical liberals and the labour movement, the High Court's rejection of the Harvester decision also revealed the limits of the federal Constitution. Attention soon turned to expanding its scope.

* * *

Although state paternalism was held to be a liberating force for white workers at the turn of the century, that's not how it worked out for Aboriginal communities. As mission-run settlements slowly came under government management, efforts to encourage economic initiative were increasingly stifled. Farms turned into ration depots. Working-aged men and women were pushed off the reserves in the expectation that they should find work elsewhere. As a mission, Cummeragunja, on the NSW side of the Murray River, had successfully cultivated 346 acres (140 ha) of farmland, and provided primary education to children and a stable community for its residents. But in 1907, after it had become a reserve, its 20 individual smallholdings were revoked by the NSW Protection Board. In the early 20th century, Aboriginal Protection Acts in the various states gave officials a large measure of control over Aboriginal people's lives, including the removal of children from their mothers if it was thought to be in the child's best interests – often because the child was of mixed race.[24]

Mission-controlled settlements were, of course, hardly idyllic communities. Nonetheless, prior to the various Protection Acts, Aboriginal Australians had a degree of autonomy that was gradually stripped away. Prior to the *Commonwealth Act* of 1902 they were not generally excluded from voting – at least not in theory.[25] This crushing of human dignity in the name of 'protection' only began to change with the liberal revival after the Second World War.

* * *

To our generation, perhaps the least familiar features of the Commonwealth Day procession, on 1 January 1901, were the grand masters and grand secretaries draped in Masonic-style regalia and insignia, representing organisations such as Oddfellows, Royal Foresters and the Ancient Order of the Druids. These were the friendly societies that then provided income protection and health insurance to around 260,000 Australians, plus their dependants.

Perhaps 30 per cent of the population were covered by friendly society benefits. In coal mining towns, where accident and injury could spell destitution, membership could reach half of the working adult population. With their rituals and fraternal ethos, they were central to communal identity and informal networks of support. Membership was seen as the responsible alternative to charity, encouraging thrift and a culture of 'self-help'. They instilled in Australians a sense of civic duty. The advent of universal welfare was to replace the friendly societies and to extend such benefits to the least well-off. But it came at the cost of substantially reducing voluntarism and reducing the notions of civic duty that were so palpable in the early 20th century.

But if some social movements were starting to decline, others were beginning to flourish. Surf bathing had long been discouraged to avoid offending public sensibilities and was often banned. In 1902, journalist William Gocher announced that he would challenge a local ban and bathed in daylight on Manly Beach. Manly council and others soon lifted their bans but usually with the condition that bathers wore neck-to-knee costumes. The first informal beach protection group (suggesting that sea bathing was already common) had been formed at Manly in 1899 and the first official 'surf bathers life saving club' was established at Bondi in 1907. By the end of that year, the New South Wales Surf Bathing Association had nine affiliated clubs and 'the beach' was on its way to becoming a key element in the Australian way of life.

* * *

The final pillar of the Deakinite Settlement was the encouragement of national pride within an imperial tradition. Foreign policy was shaped by two considerations: Australia's place in the Pacific, and its participation in the British Empire. Under previous arrangements, colonial governments had contributed support to a local squadron of the Royal Navy. Britain's domination of the sea was Australia's greatest security asset but, as Germany and Japan emerged as significant naval powers, something more was demanded.

Deakin was convinced that an Australian navy was essential to national security, especially after the Japanese Navy had pulverised a Russian fleet at Tsushima in 1905. With cautious agreement from London in 1907, the Australian government announced plans to acquire a flotilla of submarines and destroyers for local defence. In times of war, Australian ships would be transferred to the British admiralty's command – a compromise aimed at securing the support of the British government.

While Deakin was developing his naval strategy, the United States was busy flexing its own muscle on the global stage. Sixteen battleships with, in total, 14,000 sailors were sent by President Theodore Roosevelt on a circumnavigation of the globe. To strengthen support for an Australian navy, and to bring America closer to the Empire, Deakin requested the US Navy visit Australia on the Pacific leg of its tour. The arrival of the 'Great White Fleet' in Sydney Harbour, with subsequent stops in Melbourne and Albany, was a national event that brought out hundreds of thousands of sightseers. The effect was to galvanise momentum for Australia's own military forces. When Deakin lost government, plans for a local naval force continued under Andrew Fisher's Labor government, but it took Germany's increasing naval capabilities to finally persuade the British Admiralty to accept the utility of an Australian fleet. As well, in 1911, with bipartisan support, a form of compulsory military training was introduced, with men under 26 required to participate in 16 days of drill every year.

* * *

The resignation of George Reid as leader of the Opposition, in November 1908, cleared the path for a 'fusion' between the two Liberal camps. Reid had never succeeded in federal parliament as he had as premier of New South Wales. He represented a strand of liberalism that was out of tune with early 20th-century politics. His departure did more to influence events than anything he could have done in office or on the Opposition benches. In April

1909, a draft liberal platform sought 'the union of all Liberal men and women throughout Australia in one Party to secure in the Federal parliament Liberal Legislation for the development of the Australian Nation on a democratic basis'.[26] In May, Deakin and the new Free Trade leader, Joseph Cook, agreed to unify, on the basis of New Protection and a strong defence.

This merger of the two strands of liberalism in Australia joined the traditional British liberalism that emphasised individual rights and private enterprise with the Victorian liberal tradition that advocated a higher level of state interference. The new Liberal Party won support from businesses, pastoralists, bankers, merchants and the urban middle class: clerks, shopkeepers, teachers, civil servants and women, recently enfranchised. Unlike Labor, which tended to appeal in male-dominated occupations, Liberals more often emphasised the concerns of households, reflecting their support from homemakers and middle-class professional women. The two-party system of Australian democracy was taking shape.

The first united Liberal government was short-lived, convincingly defeated at the 1910 federal election. Under the leadership of Andrew Fisher, Labor won a majority in both houses of parliament. This was an extraordinary achievement, a world first: a working-class party winning government at a national election. Labor cast itself as the embodiment of Australia, seeking 'the cultivation of an Australian national sentiment based upon the maintenance of racial purity, and the development in Australia of an enlightened and self-reliant community'.[27] Its success indicated how loose a hold class distinction had on Australians.[28]

Deakin believed Labor's electoral success was due to its advanced extra-parliamentary organisation. Union supporters could mobilise and proselytise in a way that the liberal middle-class base could not. Compulsory arbitration further incentivised union membership. 'We are all socialists now,' Fisher said. His government made significant policy changes, introducing a Commonwealth Bank, which monopolised the issuing of bank notes. Labor introduced a maternity allowance, as well as a Commonwealth land tax. The irony, of course, is that Deakin had prepared Australians for the interventionist state.[29]

* * *

The Commonwealth entered its second decade with deep divisions over the perceived limitations of the Australian Constitution. Labor activists and radicals, late converts to the idea of Australian federation, were convinced that only a strong, centralised state could counteract economic inequality. The more militant trade unionists were disillusioned at the failure of compulsory arbitration and wage regulation to deliver the workers' paradise they had hoped for. The High Court stubbornly held fast in limiting the powers of the federal government to comprehensively regulate trade and commerce. Under Fisher's leadership, and masterminded by his energetic attorney-general, Billy Hughes, Labor embarked on a campaign for greater centralisation of Commonwealth power, which was to dominate the public debate up to the First World War.

In April 1911, a referendum was proposed to expand the Commonwealth's authority over trade, commerce and labour. Heavily defeated, this was the first of a continuing series of missteps by Labor in overestimating Australians' appetite for bigger government. Perhaps the most influential of the liberal bodies mobilising against change was the Australian Women's National League, which feared that any change would disrupt the social order. By 1912, the AWNL had some 50,000 members – one of the largest partisan women's organisations in the world. Operating at a grassroots level in cities, suburbs and country areas, the League canvassed and persuaded neighbours and acquaintances over teacups in the back parlours and sitting rooms of households throughout Australia. They were the first liberal group to commit to Reid's anti-socialism – indeed they encouraged and influenced his campaign. They remained suspicious of Deakin's more social democratic leanings, even after he became leader of the fusion Liberal Party in 1908. Deakin, for his part, found them 'fierce and unceasing'. Nonetheless, the AWNL were instrumental in the slim Liberal Party victory at the 1913 election, campaigning actively in the rural Victorian seats that the Liberals gained.

Despite the 1911 referendum loss, Fisher and Hughes were not prepared to abandon the cause of constitutional change, holding another referendum in conjunction with the 1913 election. Liberals mobilised once more, and Joseph Cook attacked the referendum's sectional objectives. 'The Constitution was framed for the benefit of all the people, and not for a particular class.'[30] Liberals of all stripes united around a shared citizenship that was meant to cross class and social boundaries. Cook succinctly summarised the new Liberal Party's ethos of pragmatism based on values:

Liberalism is more than a theory of government, or even a program, no matter how admirable its planks may be. It is a state of mind, an attitude, an outlook which is as wide and comprehensive as the needs of the community. It determines its principles of action not with reference to the program of a party, but with regard to the actual facts of life.[31]

The referendum was rejected for a second time, but Cook's bare majority in the lower house, together with his minority position in the Senate, led him to plan for a double dissolution in the following year, the first one to be granted since federation.

Labor won convincingly, achieving its highest ever primary vote at 50.89 per cent. The election, held on 5 September 1914, was just six weeks after the outbreak of the Great War.

In 1914, almost five million Australians populated the continent. Intense political debate and industrial unrest did not detract from the reality that Australia was relatively prosperous and growing. That year, the first Coles variety store opened; Australia's first military aircraft was flown in March and the first delivery of airmail arrived in July. Australians were well educated: around 96 per cent of those over five years old were literate (a figure about the same as in Britain and a little higher than in the United States). The future of agriculture and manufacturing looked promising. Loyalty to the British Empire was undisputed. As Britain embarked on war, 'Australia will stand by the mother country to our last man and our last shilling,' declared then Opposition leader Andrew Fisher.[32] In a matter of weeks, he would again lead the country.

9

The Great War

For Australia, the Great War was a dreadful watershed, announcing our arrival to the wider world but at stupendous cost. From a population of under five million, over 400,000 volunteered to fight; 330,000 went overseas; 155,000 were wounded and 60,000 never came home. At Gallipoli, Australia sustained a glorious defeat, but on the Western Front was instrumental in a terrible victory. As the official historian, Charles Bean, said of the men of the First Australian Imperial Force: their example 'rises, as it always will rise, above the mists of time, a monument to great-hearted men; and for their nation, a possession forever'.[1] The battles on the home front were hardly less significant. Alone of the major combatants, Australia put the question of conscription to a popular vote. The issue split the Labor Party and left it markedly less enthusiastic for alliances and for the armed forces – something that arguably echoes to this day.

§

John Simpson Kirkpatrick was a British merchant mariner who'd jumped ship in Australia in 1910 and took on various odd jobs before signing on to the Australian Army immediately after the outbreak of war in August 1914. He landed at Gallipoli on 25 April 1915 as part of the 3rd Field Ambulance and soon started using donkeys to help carry wounded soldiers to relative safety. Colonel (later General) John Monash wrote:

> Private Simpson and his little beast earned the admiration of everyone ... They worked all day and night ... and the help rendered to the wounded was invaluable. Simpson knew no fear and moved unconcernedly amid shrapnel and rifle fire, steadily carrying out his self-imposed task day by day and he frequently earned the applause of the personnel for his many fearless rescues of wounded men ...[2]

After scarcely three weeks at Gallipoli, Simpson was killed by enemy machine gunfire but his fame grew and grew, helped by the conflation of his deeds with those of other stretcher bearers using donkeys. The legend of Simpson and his donkey as the epitome of selflessness under fire took hold, memorialised by the 1977 addition of a donkey to the Australian Army Medical Corps under the name of 'Jeremy Simpson' and the donkey's subsequent adoption as the corps' official mascot.

For several subsequent generations of Australian school students, Simpson and his donkey became synonymous with courage and selflessness and seemed to typify the chivalrousness of Australian soldiers, who were thought to be no less dedicated to their mates as they were to fighting the enemy. After a war in which over 60,000 Australians had perished, signifying one of the highest death rates of any of the combatants in the First World War, the story of Simpson became one of the sustaining myths persuading a grieving people that it had not been all in vain.

Simpson and his comrades left Australia for a global conflagration of unprecedented destruction and consequence. As The Argus put it, Australia 'stepped into a worldwide arena in the full stature of great manhood'.[3] In our collective consciousness, the Great War marked a coming of age both for individuals and for the nation itself. And while Gallipoli has dominated our imagination, it was on the Western Front that Australia made its greatest contribution. Not only were Australians often the spearhead of the battles that determined the outcome of the war, but they exerted an outsized influence that no one had foreseen in 1914. Hence the assertion of Charles Bean, the official war correspondent, that 'the consciousness of Australian nationhood was born'.[4]

* * *

The German statesman and master diplomat Otto von Bismarck is said to have predicted the Great War in an off-hand remark: 'One day the great European War will come out of some damned foolish thing in the Balkans.'[5] We might credit, too, the Australian who, during a meeting of the Republican Union in 1887, expressed concern that 'in a little place like Bulgaria we were liable to be thrown into wars which would prove disastrous to trade and commerce'.[6] Had he only shifted his gaze 250 miles (400 km) northwest to Sarajevo, he would have anticipated the most momentous event of the 20th century.

By 1910, an entanglement of alliances had set the stage for a gargantuan European conflict. Two blocs of great powers had emerged – the Triple Entente of Russia, France and the United Kingdom; and the Triple Alliance of Germany, Austria–Hungary and Italy. The economic and political backdrop was the 'tinderbox of Europe', imperially restless, industrialising, militarising and beset with democratic and nationalist pressures.

The catalyst was the assassination of the Austrian Archduke Franz Ferdinand by a young Serbian nationalist on 28 June 1914. A succession of demands followed, first by Austria against Serbia, then by Russia against Austria, and finally by Germany against Russia, culminating in Germany's invasion of Belgium – the first element of its two-front plan to annihilate France before opening an eastern front against Russia. With Germany's refusal to withdraw, on 4 August 1914, Britain and her dominions entered the war.

Australia was not 'dragged' into the conflict, as Paul Keating has claimed. Enthusiasm for the fight was immediate. Spontaneous patriotic demonstrations erupted across the continent. A crowd of 30,000 in Adelaide was thought to be 'without parallel in the history of the State'.[7] Australians instinctively knew that Great Britain had to win. Australia's long-term freedom depended on the global order that British power sustained. Australia's leaders knew that if Britain entered the war, it would be a conflict of global reach. That is why Australia's first engagement was not Gallipoli but Rabaul, in German New Guinea. The first Australian gun to be fired was at Fort Nepean on Port Phillip Bay – a warning shot against the German commercial vessel SS *Pfalz*.

Australians needed little prompting to enlist. They participated in the same history and myths as the Mother Country. Australians could regard the British government with a respectful but independent mind, while embracing Britain's 'long island story' as central to their own heritage: in language, political traditions and institutions, culture, food, sport and way of life. Australians saw themselves as part of the 'British race', which meant more than an ethnic affiliation: it was an intimate association, with parliamentary democracy, political liberalism, religious freedom and the rule of law. Despite the war's complex causation, British and Australian leaders would rightly reduce its consequences to a future of British freedom or German militarism. It was axiomatic that when Britain declared war, Australia would be at war, too.

* * *

Australia's initial offer of 20,000 soldiers swiftly expanded to 50,000 by the end of the year. It could have been more. The initial conditions for enlistment in what became the Australian Imperial Force (or AIF) were peculiarly strict: only men between the ages of 18 and 35, more than five feet six inches (168 cm) tall, possessing a minimum chest measurement of 34 inches (86 cm) who could pass a strict medical examination. Recruitment officers had the privilege of selecting the best and refusing many on minor grounds. Within three months, in October 1914, 38 transports carrying the first convoy of 30,000 Australian and New Zealand volunteers left King George Sound off Albany, Western Australia.

Ivor Warne-Smith was 17 years old when he fooled enlisting officers about his age and joined the AIF in May 1915. He was not going to stay at home after his two older brothers had enlisted. He served at Gallipoli before joining the 15th Machine-Gun Company on the Western Front. Both his brothers were killed, while Ivor himself was gassed and wounded in the head and leg. Returning to Melbourne and civilian life in July 1919, he went on to become the first man to win the Brownlow Medal twice in the Victorian Football League, in 1926 and 1928. After the conclusion of his celebrated sporting career, Warne-Smith again answered his nation's call – 'retreads' was the colloquialism applied to men like him – to serve in the Middle East and Borneo during the Second World War.

The rules did not allow Aboriginal and non-European recruitment but many found a way around them. Private Richard Martin, from Stradbroke Island, Queensland, claimed on his papers that he was from New Zealand and had previously fought in the Australian Light Horse. Corporal Harry Thorpe, from the Lake Tyers Mission Station near Lakes Entrance,

Victoria, won the Military Medal for 'conspicuous courage and leadership' near Ypres in Belgium in 1917. More than a thousand Indigenous Australians fought in the Great War, including around 70 at Gallipoli. Men of Asian, Mediterranean and Northern European ancestry could also be found in the AIF. Trooper Billy Sing, the son of a Chinese father and English mother, was the most successful sniper in the Australian Army, with at least 150 confirmed 'kills', and won the Distinguished Conduct Medal. At Gallipoli, his 'spotter' was the author Ion Idriess. Caleb Shang enlisted at Townsville and would later serve in Belgium at Messines Ridge. He was awarded the DCM and welcomed home a hero – the local paper called him 'the greatest of Cairns soldiers'.[8]

Of the 400,000 plus Australians who enlisted over the course of the war, very few had actual military experience.[9] The Royal Military College at Duntroon's first class of potential officers did not graduate until August 1915. In the rush to assemble the AIF, many officers in the 1st Division were appointed to posts they were ill-equipped to handle. Some would have to be relieved of operational command. These early misjudgments forced the AIF to embrace a highly meritocratic approach. It was a steep learning curve; however, by the war's end, the AIF were, in the words of Britain's official war historian, Sir James Edwards, 'finished artists, not only in fighting but in staff work'.[10]

Australia's first Great War task was to occupy German territories in the Pacific and destroy the wireless radio stations, whose signals the German East Asia naval squadron relied upon. On 9 September 1914, Australian forces occupied Nauru. Two days later, the newly formed Australian Naval and Military Expeditionary Force landed at Rabaul, New Guinea. After 24 hours of skirmishing, the Australians took control of the town and the territory, suffering six deaths.[11]

The commander of that operation was William Holmes, who went on to serve at Gallipoli and on the Western Front, where, as a major-general, he commanded the 4th Division in its successful action at Messines in Belgium. Shortly afterwards, while showing the NSW premier William Holman around the battlefront, Holmes was killed by a stray shell burst, the most senior Australian to die on the Western Front. Even at the time, reports focused on the minor injuries to the premier; and one of our most successful generals is today remembered only through the often clogged Sydney traffic artery, General Holmes Drive, near Sydney Airport. Charles Bean said of Holmes: he was 'famed for his courage and enforced his standards by daily visiting its most dangerous sectors'. These visits, Bean said, 'helped keep the officers and men at a high pitch of performance'.[12]

On 9 November 1914, while escorting the initial convoy of 36 troopships from Albany, in Western Australia, to the Middle East, HMAS *Sydney* received a distress call from soldiers stationed in the Cocos Islands – a British territory roughly halfway between Australia and Ceylon. The islands had been captured by a German landing party that had disembarked from the light cruiser *Emden*. Leaving the allied Japanese cruiser *Ibuki* to help guard the convoy, the *Sydney* engaged the *Emden* and, with its heavier and more powerful guns, destroyed it in only 25 minutes. The Battle of Cocos resulted in 134 of *Emden*'s crew killed, but only four aboard *Sydney*.[13] Banjo Paterson, accompanying the Australian troops as a war correspondent, registered a feeling of surprise at the battle, 'for our people are not seagoing people and our navy – which some of us used to call a pannikin navy – was never taken seriously ... and now we have actually sunk a German ship!'[14] Sinking the *Emden* vindicated the foresight of Deakin and Fisher in constructing and expanding the Royal Australian Navy before others saw the need.

* * *

The AIF was landed in Egypt, where its 1st Division joined with New Zealand forces to form the Australian and New Zealand Army Corps (ANZAC), led by the British lieutenant general Sir William Birdwood. The Anzacs trained on the basis that they would go to the Western Front, but the War Council in London had other ideas. The first lord of the Admiralty, Winston Churchill, had long wanted to force open the Dardanelles, the waterway linking the Aegean Sea to the Sea of Marmara and the Ottoman capital of Constantinople. The stalemate on the Western Front had made an 'eastern solution' all the more appealing. 'Knocking Turkey out of the war' (which was Churchill's objective) by taking Constantinople was proposed as a pathway to opening a new front and diverting German resources from the west.

Popular memory, in Britain as well as in Australia, has blamed the legendary British statesman for the failed Gallipoli campaign. In the years after the war, he regularly would face the taunt in parliament, 'What about the Dardanelles?' Undoubtedly, Churchill underestimated the strength and quality of the Turkish opposition. His plan for a new front looked much better on paper than on the hilly peninsula of Gallipoli. But this was a War Council decision – not just Churchill's, who was its most junior member. More recently, it has been shown that the British prime minister Hebert Asquith was most persuaded by the urgent economics of the mission: Britain's dire need for Russian and Romanian wheat, which could no longer come via sea or land, to hold off a catastrophic price rise that might sabotage the war effort.[15]

An unsuccessful attempt in March to force open the Dardanelles by destroying the shore batteries with naval gunfire merely alerted the Turks to the coming land campaign, which opened on 25 April 1915. Approaching the shore in small boats, the Anzacs were exposed to rifle fire from Turkish soldiers perched above the coastal cliffs. The campaign was to last eight months, but it was the first day and the final evacuation that are most embedded in Australian lore. Storming the narrow beach only to find steep cliffs before them, the troops repeatedly climbed and charged. 'How they got up fully armed and equipped over the rough, scrub clad hillsides one can hardly imagine,' an Allied staff officer observed.[16] Australian readers at home received the first accounts from the British journalist Ellis Ashmead-Bartlett: 'The Australians rose to the occasion. They did not wait for orders or for the boats to reach the beach, but sprang into the sea, formed a sort of rough line, and rushed the enemy's trenches.'[17]

But courage alone was not going to capture the peninsula. The Gallipoli campaign was also characterised by mistakes, poor leadership and a lack of experience and training. After the first day, the campaign degenerated into trench warfare, with little ground gained for great losses. This was exactly the kind of fighting that the decision makers had hoped to avoid. Faced with the horrors of the stalemate – the many dead and wounded, the disease, the shock and suddenness of the violence – Australians at home looked to what the conflict revealed about the Australian character.

Bean was struck by the devotion individual soldiers had to their comrades and their determination to see the job done. '[T]o live the rest of his life haunted by the knowledge that he had set his hand to a soldier's task and had lacked the grit to carry it through – that was the prospect these men could not face.'[18] Even in Egypt, British officers had noted the peculiarly democratic character of the Anzac, some surprised to find privates and officers so casually mingling with one another. Birdwood had little choice but to take his new nickname of

'Birdie' in good humour. Later in the war, General Sir Douglas Haig, the commander-in-chief of the British Army on the Western Front, would complain of the 'revolutionary ideas' the Australians placed in the minds of his own troops.[19]

The wounded and the sick were treated in overcrowded hospital ships anchored offshore. One of the wounded was Major-General Sir William Bridges, the 1st Division's commander. Twenty days after the initial landing, on one of his regular inspections of the front line, he was shot in the leg by a Turkish sniper and evacuated; only subsequently to die of infection at sea. Until the burial of the unknown solider at the Australian War Memorial in 1992, Bridges was the only Great War casualty whose body was returned to Australia for burial at Duntroon, where he'd been the first commandant. Likewise, his horse, Sandy, was the only one of the tens of thousands of Walers sent abroad to be repatriated at the war's end.

Makeshift hospital tents and shelters were constructed on the nearby Greek island of Lemnos, 50 miles (80 km) from Gallipoli. It was there that more than a hundred nurses of the Australian Army Nursing Service cared for thousands of wounded Australians, plus the casualties of other Allied nations. In cramped tents and with limited medical supplies, the nurses saved many lives. After Gallipoli, they moved to France and Belgium, serving in first aid dugouts and hospitals, often within range of the enemy artillery. More than 2000 Australian nurses served overseas and 25 lost their lives.[20]

As casualties mounted, doubts grew about the wisdom of the Gallipoli campaign. The British secretary of state for war, Field Marshal Lord Kitchener, inspected Gallipoli in mid-November and recommended evacuation, with soldiers re-tasked to the Western Front. The withdrawal of troops from the peninsula was the most successful and ingenious element of the campaign. With remarkable efficiency and movement, all

Australian soldiers were off the beaches by 20 December. Not a single Anzac soldier was lost in the two-day retreat.

The figure of 87,000 Turkish dead dwarfs the 8700 Australian losses and the 57,000 Allied troops who were killed in action or who died from wounds and disease.[21] Still, the first major Australian military engagement of the war had ended in failure.

* * *

As the infantry moved on from Gallipoli to France, the Australian Light Horse remained in the Middle East, fighting in Allied campaigns throughout Sinai, Palestine, Lebanon and Syria. The Light Horse was a formidable unit, mostly made up of Australians from the bush and rural towns, some of whom had served in the Boer War. At the Battle of Romani in August 1916, the 1st and 2nd Light Horse Brigades, together with other forces of the British Empire, withstood the Turkish attempt to capture the Suez Canal. Initially heavily outnumbered, the Australians held on long enough for reinforcements to arrive. Among many feats, the legendary Australian war horse 'Bill the Bastard' carried four injured Tasmanian troopers to safety.

Ultimately commanding four Australian Light Horse Brigades, four British, one New Zealand and a Camel Brigade, Harry Chauvel was the first Australian to command an army corps and the first to attain the rank of lieutenant-general. Chauvel's greatest victory was the Battle of Beersheba on 31 October 1917. As mounted infantry, the Australian 4th Light Horse Brigade charged the Turkish defenders, swiftly taking the town and crushing the Turkish 8th Army. Beersheba was one of the few successful mounted attacks of the First World War and one of the last cavalry charges in history. It altered the course of the Middle Eastern campaign by enabling the

British capture of Gaza after repeated attempts. The Mounted Corps then helped capture Jerusalem in December 1917, and took Syria and Lebanon in October 1918, forcing the Turkish capitulation.[22] In the aftermath of the victory at Beersheba, the British government made the Balfour Declaration: the commitment to support a 'national home for the Jewish people' in Palestine.

On the Western Front old tactics met new weaponry – massed heavy artillery, machine guns and mustard gas – creating vast human sacrifice for relatively small territorial gains. By the time the Australian soldiers arrived in early 1916, the stalemate had been in place for over a year and would not end until 1918 when technological advances, such as aircraft and tanks, plus the better co-ordination of infantry, armour and artillery, finally paved the way for genuine forward movement.[23] During the Battle of the Somme in July 1916, the Australian 5th Division was tasked with a diversionary attack on the town of Fromelles. In their first major engagement in France, the Australians suffered 5533 casualties in little more than a day.[24] Later in the offensive, the Australian 1st, 2nd and 4th Divisions were tasked with capturing the village of Pozières and holding it against German counterattacks and constant bombardment. Over seven weeks from late July to early September 1916, the Australians attacked the German positions 19 times, eventually capturing the village at the cost of 7000 lives.[25] Of Pozières, Charles Bean wrote that it 'is more densely sown with Australian sacrifice than any place on earth'.[26]

* * *

Worn out by the burden of war, Andrew Fisher resigned in favour of his attorney-general, Billy Hughes, in October 1915. A diminutive figure with severe hearing problems, Hughes was hardworking, fiery, combative, demanding and autocratic. He once said of the British prime minister, Asquith, that 'he looked upon action as a kind of disease ... life terrified him'.[27] By contrast, Hughes was energised by life and knew only action. These were priceless qualities in a wartime prime minister.

As Australian enlistments began to decline in 1916, Hughes considered the possibility of extending conscription to overseas service. The *Defence Act 1903*, which had passed with general support, already provided for compulsory military service but only within Australia. While conscription was common in continental Europe, the English-speaking countries had been much slower to adopt it. By the summer of 1916, though, Britain and New Zealand had introduced conscription and Canada would follow in 1917. Hughes was in favour, but his party was not. Here was another barrier to be overcome. Pleading strategic necessity, the prime minister convinced a slim majority of his cabinet and caucus to support a plebiscite.

The conscription plebiscites are a landmark of Australian democracy. A plebiscite has no legal consequence but enormous political significance. Hughes, the only Empire leader to call for a popular vote on compulsory military service, believed it would bind his own party to a popular mandate. It has been suggested that High Court judges Samuel Griffith and Edmund Barton gave Hughes the idea.[28] If true, a direct line can be drawn from the federation plebiscites of 1898 and 1899 to the conscription debate.

Hughes believed that the nation itself was at risk. He did not want Australia to lose the war or for the global order to be re-organised on the basis of what he called 'Prussian militarism'. Agreeing with Hughes, the Liberal opposition, and many business and church leaders, often rallying under the banner of the United Services League, looked at the scale of destruction on the Somme and the fact that a higher proportion of Britain's population had enlisted and wondered whether compulsion at home was their best hope of victory abroad.

On 28 October 1916, the first plebiscite was narrowly defeated by just 72,476 votes from the 2.5 million votes cast. For a voluntary vote, the turnout was very high: 82.8 per cent. The first plebiscite came just after the bloodbath of the Somme and after Britain and New Zealand had already settled their own policy.

Politically, the first plebiscite result was disastrous for Labor. At a special meeting of caucus on 14 November 1916, a motion was immediately put to oust the prime minister. A line of speakers rose one by one to attack him, some with immense, often justified, bitterness. Hughes had been savage towards his opponents and was unapologetic for his use of wartime powers to censor dissent.

A supportive colleague, Defence Minister George Pearce marvelled at 'the sight of that small figure, wearied almost to the point of exhaustion, sitting there at the head of the table giving verbal blow for blow to his now triumphant and exulting opponents'.[29] After a lunch break the attacks continued, until Hughes raised his hand and silenced the room. 'Enough of this,' he said, grabbing his papers and inviting his supporters to follow him. Taking up space in the Senate party room, Hughes and 23 former Labor MPs became a new grouping, the National Labor Party. In the following month they merged with the Liberal Opposition to form the Nationalists. Campaigning with the slogan 'Win the War', the new government won a resounding victory at the May 1917 federal election, taking control of both houses of parliament.[30]

Hughes called a second conscription plebiscite in late 1917. Australian casualties had continued to mount in the Western Front with no sign of significant military progress. The United States had introduced conscription shortly after entering the war in April 1917. Yet in Australia, the question only further divided communities and families. Demonstrations occasionally became violent. Queensland police reported an unusual build-up of privately owned arms, increasingly carried at public rallies. After Hughes was hit by an egg at a rally in Warwick, Queensland, he rushed into the crowd and reached for his own gun – which, fortunately, he did not have.[31] Believing that the Queensland government (led by the anti-conscriptionist T.J. Ryan) was not doing enough to protect him, Hughes set up the first Commonwealth police force.

Using the *War Precautions Act*, Hughes not only censored opponents, but also tried to censor Hansard when the Queensland premier used parliamentary privilege to read censored material in the Legislative Assembly. The tragedy of Hughes' leadership was that his undoubted patriotism and relentlessness could be so tainted by an illiberal streak. When Robert Menzies took the nation into war in 1939 and dismissed what he called the crude 'stump oratory and excited denunciation' of the past, it was most likely Hughes he had in mind.[32]

Sectarianism became an issue in the second plebiscite. The Easter Uprising in Dublin the previous year had left many Irish Australians aggrieved. Melbourne's charismatic Archbishop Daniel Mannix, a former rector of Ireland's Maynooth seminary, gave powerful expression to Irish-Catholic dissent. He drew large crowds at public rallies, including 20,000 at Melbourne's Royal Exhibition Building.[33] Meanwhile, letters arrived from the front line with horrific descriptions of the conflict. Nathaniel Jacka, father of two sons who had served in the war – one of whom, Albert, was Australia's first Victoria Cross recipient for his service at Gallipoli – opposed conscription on the grounds that 'We should keep free the land [for] which my sons went out freely to fight.'[34] A union organiser and future Australian prime minister, John Curtin had been arrested and gaoled the previous year for failing to report for his compulsory military training. On the question of conscription, however – compulsory military service overseas rather than for local defence – Australia would not budge. Thanks to the defeat of the second plebiscite, in December 1917, by a slightly larger margin than the first, the AIF remained a volunteer force.

* * *

Meanwhile, as the war was reaching its decisive moments, it was an Australian general, John Monash, whose innovative use of co-ordinated and mechanised warfare helped transform tactics. The British prime minister, David Lloyd George, declared Monash to be 'the most resourceful general in the whole of the British Army'.[35] An engineer by trade, Monash was not a professional soldier, and yet, according to the historian A.J.P. Taylor, he was 'the only general of creative originality produced by the First World War'.[36] The Anzacs did not normally take to authority figures but warmed to Monash. The Anzac myth was originally built on the defeat and endurance of Gallipoli, a planning disaster. In contrast, Monash's fame rests on victory and his reputation as the ultimate planner. He had an encyclopaedic understanding of the mechanics of warfare and had memorised every major battle since the late 18th century.[37]

A veteran of Gallipoli, Monash saw first-hand the fatal consequences of exposing infantry to merciless fire. 'Our men are being put into the hottest fighting and are being sacrificed in hair-brained schemes,' he wrote.[38] The year 1917 was described by the historian Ross McMullin as 'the worst year in Australian history since European settlement'.[39] In one fatal week in September, there were some 11,000 Australian casualties in the battles at Menin Road and Polygon Wood near Ypres in Belgium. A new type of fighting was needed, one that reconciled men with technology.

By this time the Australians had a new nickname – 'diggers' – a term originating in the gold rush but which took on a more resonant association with trench digging; at Gallipoli, General Sir Ian Hamilton's instructions at the end of the first day were to 'dig, dig, dig until you are safe'.[40]

At home, Hughes pushed for an Australian Corps, led by an Australian and staffed by Australian officers. Initially sceptical, Haig eventually accepted this proposal. The Corps was established on 1 November 1917 but Monash did not take command until May 1918. With just over 100,000 troops, it was nearly double the size of Wellington's army at the Battle of Waterloo.

Monash felt that the war's turning point occurred at the small French town of Villers-Bretonneux, in April 1918. On 24 April, the town fell to the Germans at the last gasp of their 'big push'. The Australian 13th and 15th Brigades, commanded by Brigadier-General Harold 'Pompey' Elliott, counterattacked. Fighting through the night and into the dawn, they secured the village despite heavy fire from German machine guns. To this day, an Australian flag flies in Villers-Bretonneux; on the school classroom walls, the words 'N'oublions jamais l'Australie' (Never forget Australia) can be found.[41]

By the time he took command of the Australian Corps, Monash had developed a clear sense of the new way of fighting.

[T]he true role of infantry was not to expend itself upon heroic physical effort, not to wither away under merciless machine-gun fire, not to impale itself on hostile bayonets, but on the contrary, to advance under the maximum possible protection of the maximum possible array of mechanical resources, in the form of guns, machine-guns,

tanks, mortars and aeroplanes; to advance with as little
impediment as possible; to be relieved as far as possible of
the obligation to fight their way forward.[42]

Monash first comprehensively deployed this 'all arms' tactic at
the Battle of Le Hamel, on 4 July, by co-ordinating infantry
advances with tanks, artillery and aircraft swiftly to crush an
enemy's position, building on a combination that the British
had begun to trial at the end of 1917.[43] At Hamel, Monash's
set-piece battle strategy prevailed in 93 minutes with relatively
light casualties and only three of 60 tanks disabled. To give
them fighting experience, platoons of Americans were attached
to some of the Australian companies. On their national day,
the Americans had their first combat of the Great War under
Australian command.

Monash's 'all arms warfare' was deployed on a much
larger scale in the Battle of Amiens, on 8 August 1918, later
described as the 'black day of the German Army'. Australian
and Canadian infantry spearheaded an Allied attack that
overran the enemy's front line, capturing 29,000 prisoners and
advancing almost eight miles (12.8 km). It was the first time all
five Australian divisions were engaged in the same operation.

Monash repeated his success at Mont St Quentin on
31 August 1918. Three divisions attacked early in the morning
and held the summit and neighbouring village by breakfast.
Withstanding a three-day German barrage, Monash forced
the enemy out of the neighbouring town of Peronne by
3 September. With only eight tanks at his disposal, Monash
had created 'dummy tanks' to give the illusion of possessing
a larger force. The success of the action was instrumental in
helping the Australians to break the German Hindenburg
line, in the process taking 4300 prisoners.[44] The final battle
for the Australians took place on 5 October, when they

captured the village of Montbrehain, with heavy casualties. On 11 November, the armistice took effect.

The Australian contribution to the Western Front remains a stellar achievement. Australian forces made up less than 10 per cent of the British Expeditionary Force, but in the decisive final months won 22 per cent of ground gained and captured 23 per cent of prisoners and 24 per cent of artillery.[45] These victories should rank with Gallipoli in the Australian story of the Great War. It was a nightmarish struggle for the future of Europe and the world, but the worst of times brought out the best in us.

10

A Funereal Decade

The 1920s were a difficult decade, not so much roaring as stuttering. While proud of their wartime record, Australians were haunted by its human and financial cost. Habituated by war to take an even bigger role in economic and social life, governments over-borrowed to fund ambitious schemes that often failed. In some ways, it was an economic re-run of the 1890s, only with a much worse national mood. Still, while countless families wrestled with unimaginable grief, advancements in science and technology started to make people's daily lives considerably easier, with cars and radios becoming common and domestic appliances like fridges and washing machines starting to make an appearance.

§

In January 1917, Captain Stanley Bruce returned to Melbourne. Handsome, intelligent, tall but stooped, and relying on crutches, the Australian government thought him a perfect candidate to speak at AIF recruitment meetings around the country. At a gathering in Martin Place, Sydney, he rose to address the crowd: 'I am wounded. I want a man to take my place. Who will volunteer?' Almost immediately a man stepped forward. 'I have been wounded twice,' Bruce continued, indicating the two wound stripes on his sleeve, 'I want another volunteer.' Another man stepped forward. 'Thank you,' said Bruce, 'I've got two. I ought to be satisfied, but I'm sure I am worth more.'[1]

From an early age, Bruce carried himself with a self-assuredness that served him well in business and in life. At the age of 23, he was chairman of his late father's importing firm, Paterson, Laing and Bruce. He had been school captain of Melbourne Grammar in 1901; indeed, captain of most things he put his hand to, including football and boats. Athletic and charming, he took his talents to Trinity Hall, Cambridge. Spending much of his time in England, he enlisted in the British Army and distinguished himself in the Gallipoli campaign. A bullet to the knee sent him home with a Military Cross.

If success appeared to follow Bruce wherever he went, tragedy stalked closely behind. In 1899, his brother William suicided, and two years later, his father took his own life on an overseas business trip. His sister and mother both died before the outbreak of war and, in 1919, another brother Ernest, debilitated from his experiences on the Western Front, shot himself. Depression and death lingered over the Bruce family, as it did for many of the returning soldiers. Although opponents would caricature his wealth, his expensive tastes and his aloofness, his most obvious characteristic was his limp and the slow and painful dragging of his foot. Bruce exemplified Australia in the 1920s: a scarred nation hoping to return to some sense of normalcy and dignity.

These were the pressure years, beginning with the influenza pandemic that globally killed far more than the Great War, including 14,000 Australians, many of them young. Then came the Great Depression, the most prolonged economic catastrophe to afflict modern Australia and the world. These years further challenged the liberal-democratic national project. Australia jettisoned much of its best colonial tradition – its broad and generous liberalism – while doubling down on its worse aspects: higher tariffs, state socialism and a more pronounced and aggressive racialism.

Even within this morass, there were streaks of hope. A certain relief followed the end of the war. A modern consumer economy began. Australians drove cars in larger numbers, went to the movies, listened to the radio, dressed better and built new and more modern houses. Charles Kingsford Smith piloted the first transpacific flight together with Charles Ulm. David Unaipon became the first Aboriginal author to be published, introducing new readers to the Dreaming stories. And in 1925, work began on a great steel arch bridge in Sydney, the largest and most magnificent of its kind, spanning from the tip of the city at Dawes Point, to the harbour's northern shores.

* * *

'Repatriation' was the Australian term for the resettlement of returning soldiers. Other countries spoke of 'reconstruction', 'rehabilitation' or 're-establishment'. Repatriation suggested something different: a return to what was now truly a nation.[2] Australians felt recognised in the community of nations. In 1921, an Act of Parliament was passed to protect the term 'Anzac' from commercial use. In 1927, the date of 25 April – 'Anzac Day' – was declared a statutory national holiday in honour of the dawn landing at Gallipoli. Large public donations provided for the construction of the Shrine of Remembrance in Melbourne, a grand monument resembling a Greek temple. Its opening in 1934 attracted 300,000 people, one of the largest crowds ever to assemble on the continent up to that point, almost a third of Melbourne's population.[3]

The returning soldiers had to adjust 'with no more protection than the naked framework of their character', said Charles

Bean.[4] An estimated 10 per cent suffered from shell shock.[5] Night terrors, speechlessness, depression and anxiety were widespread. Many turned to drink, which was the driver for the continuation of the wartime measure of six o'clock closing that was supposed to counter drunkenness.

Stanley Bruce, after being appointed as Australia's first representative to the newly established League of Nations, asked the Assembly 'to think for a moment of what it means to be a soldier':

> If you had seen men mutilated and dying without the possibility of being helped, if you had ever heard the cry of a wounded man out between the lines with no possibility of assistance being given him, and with a likelihood that he may lie dying there for days, if you had seen men gasping their lives out, their faces discoloured because of some hideous and frightful gas, then, I venture to say that you would look on this question with a different eye.[6]

The post-war suffering did not discriminate. Harold 'Pompey' Elliott, a former brigadier-general, was no less tormented than any other, notwithstanding being a fine motivator and leader and forging a political career through his election to the Senate in 1919 as a Nationalist, and again in 1925. In parliament, he spoke up for the soldiers and their families; he called on the government to fulfil its promises to employ returned servicemen. But in the evenings, he had his share of nightmares, fits and insomnia. In 1931, he took his own life. A scan of any metropolitan newspaper in the immediate post-war years reveals many such stories.

Inevitably, repatriation policy struggled to adapt general rules to complex personal circumstances, and was made no less difficult by its expense to a struggling economy. A Repatriation

Commission and a Department of Repatriation, together with state repatriation boards and local bodies were established to deal with the array of benefits and schemes introduced to resettle soldiers back into civilian life. By 1924, 237,000 Australians were on the war pension, including disabled veterans, dependants, widows and mothers.[7] These benefits, together with health, education and home subsidies, designed to assist the families of both fallen and returning soldiers, amounted to a 'second welfare state' that sat alongside civilian welfare provision.[8]

The challenge of managing this vast new interest group altered the dynamics of Australian politics, exacerbated by unemployment that peaked at 11 per cent in 1921 and remained stubbornly high throughout most of the 1920s.[9] In January 1919, 200 of Victoria's returned servicemen marched into government offices in Melbourne demanding the jobs of 'ineligibles' – people who due to age, sex or disability had not served in the war.[10] In July 1919, after rioting soldiers were arrested in Melbourne, a mob stormed government offices demanding their release. When the Victorian premier, Harry Lawson, refused to give in to the soldiers' demands, he was assaulted with an inkstand.[11]

Old soldiers crying out for a voice found one in the Returned Soldiers and Sailors Imperial League (now the Returned and Services League of Australia), established in 1916 as the Returned Soldiers' Association. The League had tens of thousands of members and the ear of all governments in seeking practical resolutions to soldier discontent. Although many former soldiers joined political parties, the League acted as a 'union' that could negotiate with officialdom. With one in three returned soldiers as members – a much greater proportion than in other dominions – it was a stabilising force through a time of heightened social tension.[12]

* * *

John Monash returned home 'in the most real sense, the leader of Australia', according to John Latham, a future chief justice.[13] The great question was: what would he do with that authority? The Melbourne *Age* thought him 'very much of a civilian and a democrat in his views' but there was pressure to exercise his leadership more forcefully.[14] In 1920, he became general manager of the State Electricity Commission of Victoria. Utilising the vast seams of brown coal in Gippsland, the SEC was tasked with constructing a state-wide power grid and merging smaller distribution networks. Monash's leadership lent the project a heroic air. '[He] was not only a distinguished soldier and a powerful administrator,' wrote the former Victorian MP Sir Frederic Eggleston, 'but as a politician was head and shoulders above those he came into contact.'[15]

Monash received letter after letter from returned soldiers looking for work or in need of financial aid. For one veteran injured at Messines, Monash paid all his outstanding debts.[16] Unable to quell a riot in November 1923 – due to a Victorian police strike – the Melbourne City Council called on Monash for help. Along with several of his former officer comrades, Monash put together a private militia of several thousand, many of whom were returned soldiers. Within four days, order was restored and his special force disbanded.

Events like these were symptomatic of a society under strain. Anti-communist riots in Brisbane had earlier led to looting and destruction of private property. A meat-worker strike in Townsville encouraged the siege of a police station. The writer and former politician J.K. McDougall was kidnapped, tarred and feathered by returned soldiers for a pacifist poem he had written in 1902. Whispers of clandestine paramilitary groups and communist plots fuelled a culture of political paranoia.

A visit to Australia by the author D.H. Lawrence in 1922 inspired his novel *Kangaroo* (1923), peering into the ecosystem of Sydney's fringe politics and secret organisations. Even the influenza pandemic – known as the 'Spanish flu' – seemed to confirm 'the growing paranoia about the need to safeguard Australia from external dangers'.[17]

Industrial unrest worsened. In 1919, 6.3 million days' work were lost to disputes.[18] A burst of economic activity following the end of the war was followed immediately by long-delayed demands from impatient trade unions. A strike at Broken Hill lasting a year and a half eventually secured a 35-hour week while a three-month seamen's strike challenged the very existence of arbitration itself, which increasingly looked to radical socialists as an instrument of oppression. Justice Henry Higgins, reaching 70, looked around with dismay at a system in peril – a system he had spent much of his life championing. He found the practice of sympathy strikes, which extended disputes across jurisdictions, at odds with the liberal purpose of the law: '[I]f men in unions could be brought to see that their duty to the public, to humankind, is higher than their duty to other unions, the problem of sympathy strikes would be nearly solved,' he wrote.[19]

The optimistic liberals of the federation era were fading away. Australia's first former prime minister to die was George Reid – in London, months before the end of the war. His final year was dogged by poor health, exacerbated by a gruelling speaking tour in the United States in support of the war effort. Alfred Deakin followed in October 1919, afflicted by years of cognitive decline. Barton died only three months later and, shortly after that, so did his colleague and friend Samuel Griffith.

* * *

As a motivating political idea, the light of liberalism was flickering, whether of the laissez-faire or statist variety. Hughes' Nationalists had earlier absorbed most of the Liberal leagues around the country, thereby subordinating any philosophical predilections to the war effort.

The Nationalist moniker certainly suited Hughes better. He was a patriot but one who took the aggressively political style of the Labor machine and used it to advance the national interest as he saw it. At the Paris Peace Conference, he successfully demanded that Australia have its own seat at the table. He met with Woodrow Wilson at the White House in May 1918 and made plain his appetite for Germany's Pacific islands south of the equator. Wilson did not like the impertinence of the Little Digger but at Paris found his domineering style hard to resist. Although an agreement was reached allowing Australia to administer New Guinea under a League of Nations mandate, Wilson and Hughes continued to butt heads: 'Am I to understand that if the whole civilised world asks Australia to agree to a mandate in respect of these islands, Australia is prepared to still defy the appeal of the whole civilised world?' Wilson asked. 'That's about the size of it, President Wilson,' the prime minister replied.[20]

Hughes' biographer, F.C. Browne, once observed that '[t]o the average Australian citizen of 1918, the State and the Prime Minister were one and the same thing'.[21] This was as Hughes wanted it. The war had centralised the administrative state in a way that few could have foreseen. The government borrowed £265 million to fund the war effort, which cost £311 million in total. The scale of spending can be seen against the Commonwealth's total tax revenue of £16.5 million in 1914–15.[22] A Commonwealth income tax was introduced in 1915 and a tax on 'wartime' profits in 1917. Australia's agricultural industry had changed overnight as the Commonwealth took over the sale of primary produce to world markets. This was unthinkable in 1913 but almost unquestionable as the war progressed.

The rise of wartime marketing schemes meant farmers had a direct and urgent interest in government policy. The open market had been replaced by an Australian Wheat Board, whose membership comprised the prime minister and a minister from a wheat state. There was a Central Wool Committee, meat boards, price-fixing for dairy products and controls on the export of sugar, all underpinned by an array of state-based commissions and regulation. These were reasonable wartime measures at a time of total mobilisation, but had a curious tendency to survive long afterwards. At least in the short term, marketing boards seemed to offer higher prices and greater security to an industry too often at the whims of external uncertainties.

In this environment, the Country Party emerged. Rural interests had long felt squeezed by the fusion of the early Free Trade and Protectionist parties. The average Australian farmer was for free trade and smaller government – at least for others – while the essence of the Australian character was supposed to be found in the bush, where the pioneering spirit still flourished. A Country Party emerged in Western Australia in 1914, Queensland in 1917, Victoria in 1918 and New South Wales in 1920. Federally, the Australian Country Party was established in 1920.

The key founder of the federal Country Party was Earle Page, a rural doctor from Grafton, New South Wales. Living closer to Brisbane than Sydney, he came to resent the 'Sydney octopus', whose regulatory tentacles were said to wrap around rural communities when they least wanted it, while ignoring rural voices when help was needed most.[23] The great scourge of Australian politics, as he saw it, was centralisation. In the early stages of the war, he launched the Northern New South Wales Separation League before enlisting as a doctor in the AIF. Entering parliament in 1919, he became Country Party leader in 1921. The job of his party, he said, was 'to switch on the lights when the burglar is about'.[24]

Page did not like 'the thinly disguised socialism and the theatrical posturing and extravagance of the Prime Minister'.[25] He sensed anti-Hughes hostility within the government, too. His party's strong performance at the 1922 election provided an opportunity to dictate terms. As a condition of a coalition agreement, Page wanted ministerial portfolios and a new Nationalist leader. Hughes was out and Stanley Bruce – only recently appointed treasurer – was in. The federal cabinet of 11 included five Country MPs. This new conservative partnership began 'one of the longest and most influential coalitions in the history of modern democracy'.[26]

* * *

Australia had become a nation of interests to be reconciled. There were returned soldiers and 'ineligibles', labour and capital, white and non-white, rural and town, Catholic and Protestant. The immense effort of the federation-era liberals to foster a sense of common identity, which had made possible Australia's stupendous wartime effort, gave way to the autocratic and divisive style of Hughes, which was not the calming antidote the country needed. His solution to most problems was to accrue still more Commonwealth power, while ferociously attacking his enemies in parliament.

Old liberals were unhappy and fought back. In 1922, the Nationalist member for Kooyong, Robert Best, was ousted by a liberal independent, John Latham, running on the slogan 'Get rid of Hughes'. The new prime minister, Stanley Bruce, was attuned enough to national sentiment to make the 'one great object underlying [his] administration' the determination 'to see whether they could not again generate that spirit which everybody remembered'.[27]

The war had left deep scars. Population growth between 1914 and 1918 was half the pre-war rate.[28] Per capita income declined by 16 per cent.[29] Even by 1922, half of Commonwealth expenditure was war-related and included interest on loans, pensions and repatriation costs.[30] To return to normalcy – as conservative a promise as could be made – required change. Hence Bruce's policy of 'Men, Money, Markets': designed to populate the nation with immigrants, to increase foreign investment to fund development projects and to build up Australia's manufacturing base.

Targeting British migrants, particularly former British soldiers struggling to find work at home, the Australian and British governments jointly agreed to the Empire Settlement Scheme. Under this arrangement, Britain covered half the transport and settlement costs, while migrants were granted land in undeveloped areas, with the object of boosting food production for export. The scheme brought in over 200,000 people that decade.

In April 1925, Bruce secured the 'money' to fund his immigration and land settlement scheme with a £34 million loan from Britain. This helped Australia to its longest period of sustained immigration since the 1880s: the population grew from 5.46 million in 1921 to 6.53 million by 1931.

The next step was to expand Australian markets. Using British loans, Commonwealth and state governments commissioned irrigation systems, railways, roads, sewerage systems and public buildings. Australia's housing market exploded, with around 20,000 houses built annually in Sydney and Melbourne.[31] Larger investments included the Hydro-Electric Commission of Tasmania, which began the construction of its first hydro-power station in 1929. The most iconic project was the Sydney Harbour Bridge. The term 'Australia Unlimited', the title of a 1918 book by the journalist E.J. Brady, captured the hope that the best times were still to come.

Bruce governed with the inclinations of a businessman. He avoided the polarising politics of radicals and reactionaries, but he made the classic technocrat's mistake of assuming that good sense and expertise could solve any problem by taking the politics out of policy. A case in point was the newly established Tariff Board, introduced in 1921 as an independent statutory authority intended to make scientifically respectable recommendations on tariff levels. Science, it turned out, was strongly protectionist. Of the 180 cases brought before the Board between 1924 and 1930, only 19 recommended a reduction in protective tariffs.[32] Union agitation encouraged favourable wage board rulings, which increased labour costs; that, in turn, encouraged the Tariff Board to recommend still higher tariffs, fully institutionalising the merry-go-round of interest-group politics.

The resettlement of returned soldiers on rural land was also plagued by poor decision-making: the promise of a golden future in agriculture was often thwarted by poor soil and lack of rainfall. Insufficient thought had been given to the viability of soldier-settler blocks, including the upfront costs of clearing and levelling the land and the likely overseas demand for their product. In large part, the project was an act of political faith, a determination to find 'homes for heroes' and to take a gamble on the long term. 'The whole thing was, of course, ludicrous,' remarked one soldier-settler – the future Country Party leader John McEwen.[33] Though he himself remained on the land, more than 27 per cent of the soldiers who settled across Australia did not, including Albert Facey, whose struggles with bad harvests, falling market prices and a plague of rabbits were described in harsh detail in his autobiography, *A Fortunate Life*.[34] Plans to settle 8000 British farming families in New South Wales and Victoria were whittled down to only 730.[35] By 1929, the assisted migration scheme was abandoned.

* * *

To put the trauma of war behind them, Australians' inclination was to make the most of new opportunities. Over the decade to 1929, the number of private motor cars quadrupled to 474,000. In 1924, the first radio station 2FC began broadcasting the news and, by 1925, Melbourne and Sydney had their own stations with hundreds of thousands of licensed listeners. Record crowds flowed into sporting events. In 1926, more than 118,000 attended the Melbourne Cup, a number that would not be surpassed until the year 2000. For the first time, annual cricket attendance surpassed a million in 1924–25, and set a record of 1.4 million four years later. In 1928, a 20-year-old Don Bradman made his cricket Test debut, and in 1930 he set the world record, still unbeaten, for most runs made in a Test series: 974.

It was a decade of creation. In 1920, the Queensland and Northern Territory Aerial Service (QANTAS) was founded, operating two open-cabin planes. Starting with joy flights, Qantas – the all-capitals version of the name was dropped – soon secured government contracts to fly mail services. Today, it is the second oldest airline in the world.[36] Dr Mark Lidwill – who had studied medicine at Melbourne University – alongside physicist and returned soldier Edgar Booth engineered the first electronic pacemaker.[37] In 1928, the pair successfully used their apparatus on a stillborn baby, whose heart began beating independently after ten minutes of 'pacing'.[38] In 1923, the first jars of Vegemite appeared on grocery store shelves.

Modernity began to knock at the doors of parliament, too. In 1921, Edith Cowan became the first female parliamentarian in Australia when she was elected to the Legislative Assembly of Western Australia as a Nationalist. Millicent Preston-Stanley followed in the NSW Legislative Assembly, elected in 1925 as a Nationalist. Irene Longman, a Progressive Nationalist, was elected to the Queensland Legislative Assembly in 1929. While parliaments remained mostly male preserves, middle- and upper-class women exerted significant influence in civil society, organising and attending meetings, advocating causes and campaigning for candidates. In homes and in meeting halls, political conversations shaped minds and set agendas. The voluntary nature of this work contrasted with the compulsory element of militant trade unionism and was seen by liberals as essential to the civic health of the nation.

Aboriginal Australians ramped up their agitation for fairer treatment. With the advent of the state-based Aboriginal Protection Acts in the late 19th and early 20th centuries, Indigenous people had been stripped of some of the basic freedoms enjoyed by other Australians. The last documented massacre of Aboriginal people occurred remarkably late, in August 1928, at Coniston Station, Northern Territory. A punitive raiding party led by police, initially responding to the death of a white dingo-trapper, killed dozens of Aboriginal people over the course of several weeks. Public outcry led to a board of inquiry, which controversially exonerated the responsible constable on the grounds of self-defence. The failure to prosecute indicated there was still much work to be done in applying the rule of law to all Australians on a fair and equal basis.

The former Northern Territory parliamentarian Bess Price has written about her father who, when he was aged about 14, 'had to run far to the west with other refugees to avoid the killing that began on Coniston Station'. 'When the respected and trusted Lutheran missionary Friedrich Albrecht caught up with the refugees,' she said, 'they told him that they would have handed over the killer if they'd been asked to.' Her father, she said, was happy to work for the kardiya (white men) on the stations once the killing had stopped. Once the war came to Australia, he and others were arrested, 'chained and walked naked and barefoot behind camels' before being trucked to Alice Springs where they were paid five shillings a week to labour for the Army. Subsequently, he worked for a Baptist minister who, Price said, 'didn't set out to destroy our culture [but] to add to it'. Tom Fleming, who learned Warlpiri, and had the church built at Yuendumu in the Northern Territory, 'risked his life to stop violence, striding between groups of armed Warlpiri men and shaming them into putting down their weapons and walking away'. According to Price, missionaries like Fleming 'believed that we could be both Christian and Warlpiri, loyal to our traditions, the ones worth keeping, but replacing those not worth keeping with the teachings of Christ'.[39]

Across the interwar period, Aboriginal Australians were starting to organise. In response to the NSW soldier-settlement scheme that stripped farming lands from some Indigenous communities, Aboriginal leaders Bill Ferguson and Fred Maynard established the Sydney-based Australian Aboriginal Progressive Association, which advocated Aboriginal rights over land as well as rights to full citizenship. It campaigned against the removal of Aboriginal children from their homes, and organised protests, rallies and petitions to parliament. Its membership grew quickly to 600 Aboriginal Australians in 13 branches. At a 1925 conference, Maynard articulated the purpose of the APA: 'As it is a proud boast of Australia that every person born beneath the Southern Cross is born free, irrespective of origin, race, colour, creed, religion or other impediment we, the representatives of the original people, in conference assembled, demand that we shall be accorded the same full right and privileges of citizenship as are enjoyed by all other sections of the community.'[40]

* * *

Compulsory voting was introduced federally in 1924 and tested for the first time in 1925. This has become an Australian tradition. Although some 19 other democracies have some form of compulsion, fewer enforce it and even fewer are of a comparable population size. Compulsory voting is not practised by any other English-speaking country.

The idea of compulsory voting was first raised as early as 1861 by a South Australian newspaper and initially included in an 1888 Victorian Bill but later removed. Early arguments against compulsion focused not on the curtailment of individual rights but the impracticality of its enforcement. In the United States, where similar debates had played out, the idea of compulsion seemed more threatening and illiberal. Americans, it seems, tended to see themselves as the creators of their government, rather than a product of it.

The Queensland Liberal government had first introduced compulsory voting in 1914 as a measure to counteract the capacity of trade unionists to mobilise and get out the vote. The 1915 state election delivered an expected high turnout of 88.14 per cent, but not the expected result. Labor won a majority with a swing of more than 5 per cent. As a consequence, Labor parties around the country were more inclined to give compulsory voting a sympathetic hearing. A 1915 Royal Commission on Commonwealth Electoral Law recommended compulsory voting 'as a natural corollary of compulsory registration', which had been introduced in 1911.[41]

With the distraction of the war over, and a poor turnout at the 1922 federal election, a successful private member's Bill introduced compulsory voting for federal elections in 1924. Victoria followed in 1926, New South Wales and Tasmania in 1928, Western Australia in 1936 and South Australia in 1942.

Likewise, the Hughes government had introduced preferential voting (as opposed to 'first past the post') at the federal level in 1918, in time for the following year's election, in order to prevent Labor taking advantage of a divided conservative vote.

* * *

The Communist Party of Australia (CPA) was founded in 1920. Within two years, it was recognised by the Comintern in Moscow as part of the Third (Communist) International. A numerically small group committed to the destruction of democracy, this was an unwelcome presence in a liberal society, in which conflict was resolved democratically. Among the CPA's founders was John 'Jock' Garden, secretary of the NSW Labour Council, 'the peak council of the trade union movement'.[42] 'The business of the Communist Party,' Garden said, 'is to get Communists in control of all positions, and to do anything, and everything, to get them there.'[43] In 1922, he met Lenin in Moscow and outlined his plan for communist infiltration of labour councils and for eventual revolution in Australia.

In 1923, the CPA became an affiliated organisation of the NSW Labor Party. This was revoked a year later: 160 votes to 104. Leftist historians tend either to dismiss the communist presence as a 'bogey' or, alternatively, to devote much effort to documenting its importance.[44] While communism clearly never had mass appeal in Australia, communists certainly punched well above their weight inside unions and, therefore, inside the political party that the unions sustained and largely controlled.

This Gwion Gwion rock art from the northern Kimberley is one example of Australia's vast array of Aboriginal rock art, with some sites estimated to be up to 30,000 years old. (Wikimedia Commons)

A Complete Map of the Southern Continent: Survey'd by Capt. Abel Tasman & Depicted by Order of the East India Company in Halland [sic] in the Stadt House at Amsterdam by Emanuel Bowen: one of the earliest known European maps of Australia, created 1744, was derived from the voyages of Dutch explorers Willem Janszoon and Abel Tasman. (National Library of Australia)

Landing of Captain Cook at Botany Bay, 1770, by E. Phillips Fox, 1902, is the most famous depiction of Captain James Cook's arrival. Although there was some hostility with the Aboriginal people, Cook observed that they had a degree of happiness that far exceeded that of the Europeans. (National Gallery of Victoria)

A depiction of Bennelong, who was captured and learned the ways of the British before escaping. His abduction resulted in the spearing of the governor, Captain Arthur Phillip, on 7 September 1790. Phillip used the moment to show restraint, choosing not to retaliate, which improved relations between the Eora and the British. Bennelong's story reflects both the limits of assimilation and the good intentions of Phillip. (National Library of Australia)

Captain Arthur Phillip raising the flag and toasting King George III at Sydney Cove on 26 January 1788 – the moment that marks the beginning of modern Australia, the great experiment: a prison colony destined for freedom. *The Founding of Australia. By Capt. Arthur Phillip R.N. Sydney Cove, Jan. 26th 1788*, by Algernon Talmage, 1937. (Mitchell Library, State Library of NSW, FL3141725)

The only known engraving of Pemulwuy, a Bidjigal warrior who was both feared and respected. Ultimately he was declared an outlaw and shot dead; his head was sent to naturalist and botanist Joseph Banks in London. (State Library of NSW, Q80/18)

William Bligh, an exceptional seaman, was governor of New South Wales from 1806 to 1808. His despotic tendencies were seen to stifle the colony's growth, leading to his arrest by the NSW Corps, as depicted in the painting *The Arrest of Governor Bligh, 1808*. (Mitchell Library, State Library of NSW)

At Myall Creek on 10 June 1838, 11 stockmen wantonly murdered at least 28 unarmed Aboriginal men, women and children. The perpetrators were caught and brought to trial, and seven of them were hanged. The memorial is a powerful tribute to the victims and a reminder of the need for justice. (Alex Garipoli)

During the Eureka Rebellion, Ballarat miners fought for what they believed were the natural rights of Englishmen. In the space of just 15 minutes, some 30 gold miners and five soldiers were killed, as depicted in this watercolour painting *Eureka Stockade Riot, Ballarat, 1854*, by John Black Henderson. (State Library of NSW, SSV2B/Ball/7)

A wood engraving titled *Rebels in the Dock* depicts the participants in the Eureka Rebellion on trial, whom a jury refused to convict. This moment served to galvanise the democratic movement in Victoria and the country at large. (Published in *The Age*, 10 March 1855)

In 1813, Gregory Blaxland, William Lawson and William Charles Wentworth successfully crossed the Blue Mountains in New South Wales. The expedition opened access to the Bathurst Plains, which proved to be ideal for wool production. (State Library of NSW, SPF/1396)

Australia – a land of drought and floods. In 1867, the Hawkesbury-Nepean River in New South Wales reached an all-time peak level of 19.7 metres at Windsor. The *Sydney Morning Herald* illustrated this flooding at the Nepean, west of Sydney, on 24 June 1867 (left). The image below shows the extent of flooding at Windsor in 1961. (SMH)

BRIDGE COVERED BY FLOOD

ROAD FROM SYDNEY

The landscape around Broken Hill in far western New South Wales was transformed in the late 19th century by the discovery of one of the world's richest deposits of silver, zinc and lead. The Broken Hill Proprietary Company, formed in 1885, would grow into the world's largest mining company, BHP Group. (Top: State Library of NSW, 446151; below: BHP)

Given wool's foundational role in the 19th–century Australian economy, the shearing shed became a byword for Australian culture. Tom Roberts' 1894 depiction of the shearing shed in *The Golden Fleece* has become iconic. (Art Gallery of NSW)

Members of the Australasian Federation Conference in 1890, including the 'Father of Federation' Henry Parkes (standing fourth from left) and future prime minister Alfred Deakin (standing sixth from left). (National Library of Australia)

State-based suffrage leagues, such as the Womanhood Suffrage League of New South Wales, pictured in 1902, fought for equality at the ballot box and representation in parliament. (Mitchell Library, State Library of NSW, ON 219 96)

Australian soldiers crowding Anzac Beach, Gallipoli, in 1915. The defeat shaped our national identity arguably more than any other moment in our history. (AWM H03574)

Private John Simpson Kirkpatrick and his donkey repeatedly rescued wounded soldiers during the Gallipoli campaign. Killed after just three weeks, Simpson is still revered as an exemplar of selflessness and courage. (AWM J06392)

French children tending the graves of Australians killed in battle on the Western Front, 1919. (AWM E05925)

Dubbed 'the most resourceful general in the whole British Army' by British Prime Minister David Lloyd George, Sir John Monash was knighted in 1918. His crowning innovation in the Great War was 'all arms warfare' – a co-ordinated strategy integrating infantry, artillery, tanks and aircraft – which gave Australia an outsized impact on the Western Front and was later adopted by other Allied forces. (AWM E02964)

A team of horses working on landscape development around the newly built Parliament House. Canberra was a completely new city, born of a political compromise between Australia's two largest states. (NAA A3560, 863)

Edith Cowan was Australia's first female parliamentarian, elected as a Nationalist to the Legislative Assembly of Western Australia in 1921. (Wikimedia Commons)

The arrival of the first air mail flight, from Charleville to Brisbane in 1929, by the Queensland and Northern Territory Aerial Services – now Qantas, the world's second-oldest airline. (Cliff Postle, National Library of Australia)

Completed in 1932, the Sydney Harbour Bridge was the world's largest steel-arch bridge, and remained so for much of the 20th century. It was an extraordinary undertaking in the depths of the Great Depression. (National Museum of Australia)

One hundred and fifty years after the arrival of the First Fleet, a group of Aboriginal Australians organised a Day of Mourning to advocate for 'raising our people to full citizenship status and equality within the community'. (State Library of NSW, Q059/9)

A solemn Prime Minister Robert Menzies declares war in 1939: 'Fellow Australians, it is my melancholy duty to inform you officially that, in consequence of the persistence by Germany in her invasion of Poland, Great Britain has declared war upon her. Consequently, Australia is also at war.' (National Library of Australia)

In the Second World War, local Papuans allied with the Australians against the Japanese; they played a vital role carrying the wounded and assisting troops through the notoriously harsh terrain of the Kokoda Track and the jungles of Papua and New Guinea. (AWM 014028)

John Curtin (seated right) took only one overseas trip as prime minister, to London in May 1944 where he met with Winston Churchill (seated left). The trip was aimed at strengthening Australia–UK relations. Far from 'looking to America', by the war's final months Curtin was looking back to the motherland for post-war defence. (PNA Rota/ Getty Images)

The single biggest attack on Australian soil, the Japanese bombing of Darwin in February 1942 saw twice the number of bombs dropped than at Pearl Harbor. (NAA C3298, 161)

The wreckage of one of three Japanese midget submarines that entered Sydney Harbour in 1942, sinking the HMAS *Kuttabul* and killing 21 sailors. (Anzac Memorial)

Australia's non-British migrants following the Second World War – the 'Beautiful Balts' – initially arrived in Melbourne in 1947 on board HMAS *Kanimbla*. (NAA A12111, 1/1947/3/6)

The Snowy Hydro Scheme was Australia's greatest engineering project. This 1960 photo (right) shows German and Swiss immigrants working in one of the tunnels, a typical representation of its diverse workforce. (NAA A12111, 1/1960/16/60)

Evdokia Petrov, wife of the third secretary of the Soviet Embassy who defected in April 1954, was escorted against her will onto a plane at Sydney airport by Soviet guards. The plane was intercepted while refuelling in Darwin and Evdokia was taken off, on Prime Minister Menzies' orders, and given the opportunity to defect. (NAA A6201, 62)

The support of Prime Minister Harold Holt (standing) for the Vietnam War was unwavering. After famously declaring that Australia was 'all the way with LBJ', he met US President Lyndon B. Johnson (sitting) during his 1966 tour of Australia. (Alamy/KEYSTONE Pictures USA)

Neville Bonner (right), the first Aboriginal member of the Commonwealth Parliament, catches a boomerang he handmade for his company, Bonnerang, shortly after delivering his maiden speech in 1971. Bonner switched his support from the Labor Party to the Liberal Party because he resented the expectation that his skin colour would determine party allegiance. (News Ltd/Newspix)

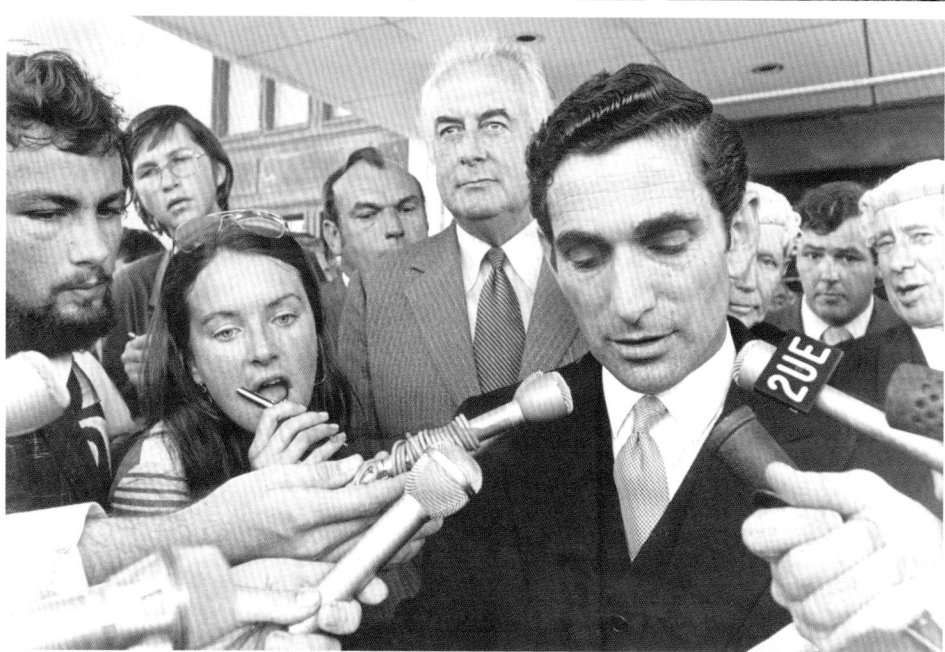

David Smith, the governor-general's official secretary, announced the dismissal of the Whitlam Government on the steps of Old Parliament House, 11 November 1975. Moments later, Gough Whitlam (centre) famously declared: 'Well may we say God save the Queen because nothing will save the governor-general.' (Guy Wilmott/Newspix)

Tycoon Alan Bond and the crew of *Australia II* celebrate winning the 1983 America's Cup – one of the greatest moments in Australia's sporting history. Prime Minister Bob Hawke quipped, 'Any boss who sacks anyone for not turning up today is a bum!' (Jean Guichard/Sygma via Getty Images)

Prince Charles joined Prime Minister Bob Hawke for Australia's 1988 Bicentennial Day celebrations in Sydney. It was the largest public gathering in the nation's history. (Above left: Tim Graham/Getty Images; above right: Alamy/David Cooper)

Prime Minister John Howard's policy of gun restrictions following the 1996 Port Arthur massacre was hugely contentious, particularly among country people. Senior ministers often faced hostile crowds, such as at this rally in Victoria, where Howard wore a bulletproof vest on police advice. (Ray Strange/Newspix)

Australia's victory over France at the 1999 Rugby World Cup, captained by the legendary John Eales, was a major sporting success at a time of many triumphs. It was held the same day as the republic referendum, in which Australians voted to remain a constitutional monarchy. (Sportsfile/Corbis/Sportsfile via Getty Images)

The 2000 Sydney Olympics was a high point for Australia, with an outstanding opening ceremony watched by 3.7 billion viewers worldwide. But it was Cathy Freeman (above) winning gold in the 400 metres that most united the country. (AAP Image/ Dean Lewins)

A visit to a school in northeast Arnhem Land, 2014 – part of my annual tradition as prime minister to spend a week in an Aboriginal community. (Alex Ellinghausen/ SMH)

Police officers capsicum-spray a woman in her seventies at an anti-lockdown protest in Melbourne in 2021, just one of the many examples of excessive force used during the COVID pandemic. With residents under virtual house arrest for 262 days, Melbourne was the most locked-down city outside of China. (Jason Edwards/Newspix)

At the Snow Goose Hotel in Adaminaby, while on a fire brigade deployment in January 2020. The 2019–20 Black Summer bushfires were not Australia's worst, but they were the most extensive in New South Wales since settlement. (Snow Goose Hotel)

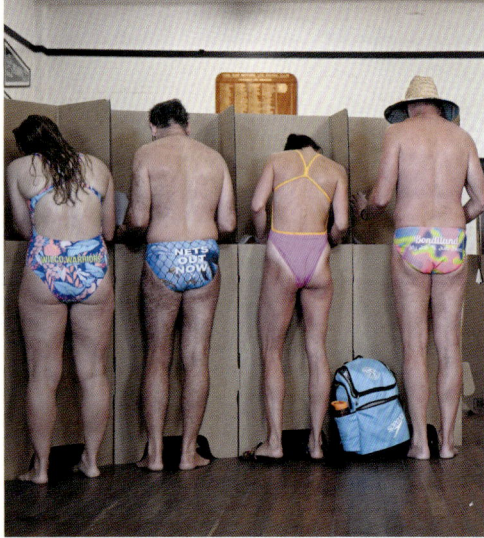

On 3 May 2025 Labor was returned to government in a landslide under Anthony Albanese. While it was a disappointing day for a former Liberal prime minister, it was nice to see that some fashions were finally catching on.(AAP Image/Bianca De Marchi)

Communists did not need to win a majority in an election to undermine Australia's institutions. As long as they followed the Bolshevik playbook, as their leaders intended, it was necessary only to take control of the workers' 'soviets', or unions, which operated the vital choke points of daily life – the waterfront, power stations, train lines and large factories. With enough chaos and civic turmoil, committed unionists could seize power just as Lenin's Bolsheviks had. 'Revolution has stepped upon the stage,' Jock Garden asserted in the Labour Council's 1924 Annual Report.[45] The situation was threatening enough for one young Labor MP, H.V. Evatt (a future federal Labor leader), to pose the following question: 'whether the labour movement is to remain Australian in spirit and ideals, or whether it is to be secretly controlled by a Communist minority who are out to degrade, disintegrate, and destroy the labour movement of Australia'.[46]

Labor was badly tainted by these machinations and its parliamentary leaders knew it. In New South Wales, the Labor leader John Thomas 'Jack' Lang attacked Garden as 'having sat at the feet of his master, Lenin'.[47] In 1924, the Queensland Labor premier, Ted Theodore, submitted to the ALP Federal Conference that 'no member of the Communist Party shall be eligible to become a member of the Australian Labor Party'.[48] Yet both these anti-communist Labor leaders had to accommodate a growing radical wing. 'Capitalism must go,' Lang himself had declared; and already by 1921 Labor had adopted its 'socialist objective', aspiring to the 'socialisation of industry, production, distribution, and exchange',[49] which survives to this day. In its 2023 National Platform, the ALP committed to: 'the democratic socialisation of industry, production, distribution and exchange to the extent necessary to eliminate exploitation'. In Queensland, Theodore abolished the Legislative Council, took on London's money markets and established an array of state-owned businesses, from bakeries, to pubs, to sawmills, to farms and mines.

At its best, Labor practised a more thorough-going version of Deakin's liberalism. Theodore introduced unemployment insurance, abolished the property franchise for local government, encouraged agricultural development and improved workplace safety. Lang passed a range of progressive reforms: a widow's pension, an expanded franchise for local government, a family endowment scheme and compulsory insurance for workers.

But these popular policies were too often spoilt by a degraded political culture. Theodore and Lang were political bulldozers who lacked some of the most important civic virtues. Theodore was a surly, broad-shouldered radical who could be physically threatening if he thought circumstances required it.[50] Lang's authoritarian inclinations meant he governed with an 'air of menace'.[51] His premiership lasted two years before his own cabinet disintegrated under his overbearing manner. Lang had the NSW Labor Party rules changed to consolidate his power and sideline his enemies. In 1927, after he'd sacked half his cabinet, Evatt compared him to Mussolini and Lenin.[52] The public had had enough. At the 1927 state election, Lang's government was thrown out of office.

* * *

Amid such tumult, the opening of the new federal Parliament House in Canberra on 9 May 1927 must have been a serene contrast. In 1909, Canberra had been selected as the future seat of government; by 1913, the foundation stones were laid. 'What are we going to do at Canberra?' one senator had asked. 'It is just a windswept, cold, miserable place in poor country that would not keep a bandicoot.'[53] It was a 'dry' town, under federal ordnances in the 'temperance' era, so getting a drink required driving nine miles (14.4 km) to Queanbeyan on the NSW border on roads that were half made and muddy on bad days.[54]

Canberra had been a compromise choice, equally acceptable and equally unsatisfactory. Public servants were initially holed up in hostel accommodation until they could be allocated better housing. As prime minister, Stanley Bruce was more fortunate, moving into a specially built 40-room residence: The Lodge. Bruce wanted to expand the federal government's powers. He'd already established a Loan Council to co-ordinate state and federal public debt, ratified in 1928 by one of our few successful referenda. It might have been dry policy but was very important to the nation's ability to raise money and service its ballooning debt.

London financiers were concerned about Australia's high tariffs and heavy labour market regulation. Industrial unrest was proving intractable, even though it remained largely a state issue, with federal arbitration still limited. Tired of what he called 'industrial warfare' – the strikes, the defiance of the Arbitration Court, the increasing bitterness and radical politics – Bruce submitted two proposals for constitutional amendment, both aimed at securing industrial peace: the first to create authorities 'to control the terms and conditions of industrial employment', the second 'to allow the Commonwealth to take measures to protect the public against interruption of essential services'. The referendum was held on 26 July 1926 and both proposals were defeated.

In 1928, Bruce's Nationalists were returned with a reduced majority only to face more industrial disputes. Bruce had promised to be 'guided not by ideological motives but by strict business principles'.[55] Against the advice of his attorney-general, he sought penalties against a striking timber union, while withdrawing a prosecution against a mining proprietor, John Brown, accused of illegally locking out his men. Critics attacked Bruce for double standards.

Writing to his colleague Richard Casey, Bruce declared he was 'going over the top' and added that 'the present system of dual control in industrial matters is impossible ... the Commonwealth or the States must be the sole authority'.[56] The government introduced a Maritime Industries Bill to establish a new authority that would regulate the entire maritime industry under the Constitution's commerce power. Paradoxically, it also repealed the *Conciliation and Arbitration Act*, leaving other industrial matters largely to the states. This was 'going over the top' in a particularly audacious way, as it reversed the whole political and legal trend since federation. Hughes was aghast at the Bill and moved to delay its effect until a referendum or election had taken place. His amendment was carried.

Parliament was dissolved and an election was set for 12 October 1929. Bruce had made industrial relations the defining issue but was ill-suited to the challenge. He had told the electorate in 1926 that their problems would be solved with increased Commonwealth industrial power. In 1929, he told the electorate their problems would be solved by the Commonwealth abandoning its industrial power. This was not the politics of principle but of desperation. The Nationalist government was defeated, and Stanley Bruce, who had risen to the highest office in history-making speed, crashed out of it with equal swiftness. He was defeated in his own electorate of Flinders.

Less than two weeks after the Labor landslide of 1929, the New York Stock Exchange suffered the largest share sell-off in history.

11

The Economic Crisis

The Great Depression was an economic earthquake for most who lived through it. After a world war and a decade of political restiveness, radical voices grew louder. The Labor Party split again; the Nationalists fell apart before reconstructing themselves; and New South Wales experienced its worst civic crisis since the Rum Rebellion, culminating in the dismissal of a Labor premier. All of this occurred against the backdrop of economic collapse: per capita GDP fell by 20 per cent; trade union unemployment reached almost 30 per cent; and there were more bankruptcy proceedings in 1929 to 1930 than in the previous six years combined. In the midst of this crisis, one man, Joe Lyons, rallied the country to accept short-term pain all-round. Australia's economically orthodox response to the Depression meant that its recovery was quicker than that of the United States, despite the latter's much-vaunted New Deal.

§

To the extent there was a 'Roaring Twenties' at all, the Wall Street Crash of October 1929 heralded its abrupt end. In any event, such economic exuberance as there was had largely bypassed Australia. By the late 1920s, prices of its primary staples – wool and wheat – had begun to fall. This was bad news for a highly indebted nation whose capacity to service its debt depended on selling commodities. Profits and incomes fell and unemployment soared.[1] A balance-of-payments crisis was emerging in Australia well before the Depression started to make its mark.

Between 1925 and 1928, Australia had borrowed more than twice as much as Africa and the Middle East combined.[2] It accounted for 43 per cent of British lending via overseas government bonds between 1925 and 1929. Interest and dividend remittance costs rose considerably, from 16 per cent of exports in 1919–20, to 28 per cent in 1928–29.[3] On the other side of the ledger, between 1929 and 1932 export prices of primary products fell by 40 per cent. With almost £119 million due for redemption in 1930, governments scrambled to find the means to pay.[4] At the end of the decade, the economist James Brigden lamented how 'the present generation of wage earners in Australia has been brought up on the idea that its standard of living is a creation of Parliament'.[5]

Possibly James Scullin was Australia's unluckiest prime minister. He was the first Labor prime minister to win an election since Andrew Fisher and both had the misfortune of winning elections on the brink of world crises. Scullin's thick crop of hair told the story: it turned from a sandy colour at the start of his prime ministership to a ghostly white only two years later.

The new prime minister did not drink or smoke. Only hours after selecting his ministry, he announced that he and his wife would not live in the Prime Minister's Lodge but in a small apartment in the Hotel Canberra. He liked to read and play the violin. He was a skilled public speaker, which he credited to the Catholic Young Men's Society and the Australian Natives' Association. He was Australia's first Catholic prime minister, intelligent and likable, and had been an effective Opposition leader. 'I'd place my life in Jim Scullin's hands' was the testimony of one Labor MP after the election.[6]

The government he led had little room to move. The world was still hurting from the war, its economic institutions had yet to fully recover and Australia was uniquely constrained by the spending spree of the 1920s and the accumulation of foreign debt that followed. Unless it could service the debt, it could not further borrow. Yet without further borrowing, it could not maintain its standard of living.

Scullin did his best to carry out a Labor program. He suspended the licences under Bruce's controversial 'Dog Collar Act', which required waterfront employees to obtain a government licence to work. He abolished compulsory military training, increased tariffs to favour local manufacturing and imposed additional taxes on individuals and companies. But to the frustration of Labor's radical wing, Scullin was a pragmatist on macroeconomic management and accepted economic orthodoxy. He had, at first, an able treasurer in Ted Theodore, the former Queensland premier who had recently entered federal parliament, but in June 1930 Theodore was forced to resign after a financial scandal.

* * *

The severity of the Great Depression varied with occupation, region and wealth. Australia's agricultural and manufacturing industries were hit particularly hard. BHP Newcastle received so few orders for steel products, it dismissed half its workforce and could not pay a dividend for three years.[7] Employment in manufacturing dropped by 40 per cent; farm income fell by 65 per cent.[8] Employers tended to reduce costs by letting go of workers, rather than keeping them on at reduced wages. Private indebtedness dramatically increased and those unable to support existing mortgages lost their homes. In the Sydney working-class suburb of Bankstown, 60 per cent of males were unemployed and 40 per cent of homes were empty at the peak of the Depression.[9] Many families were forced to live in tents under bridges or on the banks of rivers where makeshift homes were constructed from available scraps.

In Western Australia, a booming gold industry softened the downturn for people in Kalgoorlie, Norsemen, Wiluna and Coolgardie. In 1933, these towns were more prosperous than any capital city on the continent.[10] For Western Australians, the national policy of high tariffs, which spiked in the early 1930s, appeared little more than a protection racket for the eastern industries. In July 1930, the Dominion League was established to advocate WA secession. It quickly grew to 10,000 members. A state plebiscite on secession was held on the same day as the state election, on 8 April 1933, and carried two to one. The message was clear but the legal consequence negligible, given that Australia was declared in its constitution to be 'one indissoluble Federal Commonwealth'. Paradoxically, the voters who supported secession had, on the same day, elected an anti-secessionist Labor government and the issue fizzled out as the economic crisis eased.

To a degree, the Depression was moderated by the extent of home ownership. At about 53 per cent, Australia had relatively high home ownership, compared with 48 per cent in the United States, 45 per cent in Canada and less than a third in the United Kingdom.[11] With a house and a garden (especially one that was mortgage-free), a family had some reprieve from the income loss that attended unemployment. A good-sized backyard could yield home production of fruit, vegetables and eggs. The professional middle class, or at least those of them with capital in hand, could take advantage of falling asset prices. Their experience of a decade in which thrift and self-help thrived was often quite different from those who were dependent on landlords, banks and a welfare system then in its infancy.

* * *

As the Depression deepened, radicals inside the parliament, and activists outside, saw a broken system in need of replacement. Communists blamed capitalism and offered revolution. To one unemployed printer, 'the Labor Party was doing nothing' while at least the Reds were 'doing something'.[12] The Communist Party of Australia expressed unconditional loyalty to Stalin and embraced the 'Third Period' doctrine, which regarded the broader labour movement and Labor Party as little more than 'social fascists'. By 1931, its membership had increased fourfold to more than 2000, still numerically small but large enough to exert an uncomfortable influence over Labor politics.[13] It pushed the Labor mainstream leftward and injected the language of violence into an already febrile public debate.[14] Regarding parliamentary democracy as another form of capitalistic oppression, the CPA established a number of front organisations like the Labour Defence Army, which enlisted thousands of members from the coalfields of South Maitland, and the Unemployed Workers Movement, which grew to 30,000 members, organising marches, clashing with police and conducting 'sit-ins' to prevent evictions.[15]

Young ideologues preaching 'socialism in our time' challenged the hegemony of Labor Premier Jack Lang and his 'Inner Group' in New South Wales by establishing Socialisation Units, effectively quasi-branches within Labor but open to non-party members.[16] Their greatest success came in May 1931 when the Labor Conference adopted a three-year plan to transition New South Wales to socialism.[17] After an intense 24-hour period of lobbying, Lang had this motion reversed.

Lang's comparative moderation showed the extent to which radicalism had taken root inside Labor. Lang was a political brawler of the fiercest kind: a hater who divided his world into allies and enemies, and who didn't see a political problem that conflict could not solve. He snarled at London financiers, at his conservative opponents and at the communists. There was an element of anti-semitism in his tirades, especially when the nebulous 'money power' was the target. In 1931, he submitted his 'Lang Plan' to beat the crisis, a drastic shift in policy at odds with Prime Minister Scullin's more orthodox approach of settling debts and tightening budgets. Lang wanted the suspension of interest payments to British bondholders, a reduction in interest rates for government borrowings in Australia and an abandonment of the gold standard. This was labelled 'repudiation' by his opponents, after the Bolshevik 'repudiation' of debts that Russia had incurred under the Tsar.

In Europe, the crisis was throwing up dictators. In 1930, the German Nazi Party secured 18 per cent of the vote and 107 seats in the Reichstag. Mussolini's slightly milder version of authoritarianism in Italy found adherents here. At a conference of the Young Nationalists in 1933, the Victorian attorney-general, Robert Menzies, then 39, watched Wilfrid Kent Hughes advocate a corporate state, where political power lies more in the hands of key organisations and institutions than in those of individual voters. To his credit, Menzies contradicted his friend, declaring that '[f]ascism is inconsistent with parliamentary government' and that while '[w]e may not produce 100 per cent efficiency under our parliamentary system ... we do produce a very high percentage of liberty, and as a British people we are not inclined to exchange that freedom for some form of dictatorial control'.[18]

In March 1931, a demonstration of 60,000 in the Sydney Domain organised by the Sydney Metropolitan Labor

Conference inaugurated an anti-capitalist 'Labour Army'. Across the country, paramilitary groups formed in anticipation of communist-inspired violence, pledging to forestall any upheaval to the existing order. The Old Guard in Sydney, whose leaders were former army officers, organised clandestine branches of volunteers, numbering in the thousands by 1932. There was a similar White Army in Melbourne, possibly led in secret by Thomas Blamey, a returned former brigadier who was then chief commissioner of police. The New Guard, a Sydney-based conservative paramilitary organisation established to defend the Constitution, gained notoriety when Captain Francis de Groot, on horseback, pre-empted Premier Lang in cutting the ceremonial ribbon with his own sword to open the Sydney Harbour Bridge. The New Guard had over 50,000 members and was the largest such group to exist in Australia.

Still, the nation's democratic ethos proved resistant to authoritarianism. The stand-out candidate for dictator would have been Monash (before he died in October 1931), who had himself once admitted that he 'had only to put up his little finger to call the A.I.F. back to life'.[19] Monash was bombarded with appeals from ordinary citizens, ex-soldiers and prominent businessmen to 'assume dictatorship'. But these requests misjudged the man. 'Depend upon it, the only hope for Australia is the ballot box and an educated electorate,' he wrote to one concerned citizen.[20] In countless conversations and correspondence, Monash would repeat this argument. He would not countenance anything less than a democratic resolution to the crisis.

* * *

The Depression amplified the political character of every affected nation. So while continental Europe – Germany, Italy and Spain – descended into various forms of fascism; Stalin consolidated his grip on Russia; the United States yielded to the empathetic patrician in Franklin Delano Roosevelt; and Britain lumbered forward with the ageing anti-war icon and Labour turncoat Ramsay MacDonald; Australia produced a new political movement under Joe Lyons.

Joseph Aloysius Lyons was neither a brawler nor an intellectual. He had served, very successfully, as Tasmania's premier from 1923 to 1928 and was noted for his moderation, calling his Nationalist rival, John McPhee, 'my greatest friend', and declaring that there was 'no enmity between the Government and the Opposition'.[21] He had restored state finances and saved enough for investment in new industry and development.

Lyons was a Labor man, but of the kind that an ordinary Australian, less attuned to politics, could readily warm to. From his parents he had inherited a genial Irishness, more sceptical than threatening, and had learned from an early age the rigours of working life, especially through the bankruptcy of his father after gambling destroyed the family finances. Perhaps this informed his future political principles because no Labor leader before or since has championed financial propriety and stability quite so fervently.

He had a natural gift for politics, enjoying the company of his constituents and always speaking at the level of his audience. Cartoonists liked to caricature Lyons as a koala because of his round face, his unruly curls of greying hair and his friendly disposition.[22] As a young Tasmanian teacher involved in Labor politics, he rode for miles on his bicycle along the dirt tracks of the north of the island, addressing meetings, supportive and hostile. On his way he would visit his future wife, Enid Muriel Burnell, a woman of intelligence and insight, who was to become his indispensable confidante and partner, and ultimately a pioneering female leader; an outstanding Australian in her own right.

Lyons entered federal parliament in 1929 and was 50 years old when he was appointed acting treasurer following Theodore's resignation. Tensions in Labor ranks had been exacerbated by the visit to Australia of Otto Niemeyer, a Bank of England advisor who had become a lightning rod for radical discontent. Niemeyer recommended drastic fiscal discipline. Only through improved balance sheets, he told the nation's leaders, could Australia retain the confidence of London's money markets and fund its debt. The 'Melbourne Agreement' followed, a commitment from most state premiers and the Commonwealth to cut government spending. Many in Labor hated the deal. In New South Wales, Jack Lang positioned himself in direct opposition to it, but Scullin saw little choice but to accept Niemeyer's prescription. When, in August 1930, Scullin left Australia to attend the Imperial Conference in London, the rancour only grew.

Caucus reached breaking point over the matter of a £28 million loan that fell due in December. The fiery anti-semite Frank Anstey, who could trace all of modern civilisation's woes to the perfidy of private finance, proposed that parliament postpone its redemption – an idea that amounted to repudiation. Theodore thought the idea too extreme, while a distraught Lyons exclaimed that 'I will go out of public life first!' and immediately left for home.[23] Caucus approved the resolution 22 votes to 16. Lyons' colleague Albert Green, sensing the acting treasurer's pending resignation, ran after the departing train shouting, 'For God's sake, Joe, don't do it!'[24] The incident caused a political sensation and magnified Lyons as the 'honest finance' leader of the caucus.

From afar, Scullin did everything he could to stop the political bleeding and convinced caucus to delay the matter until his return. Lyons had grander plans. He instead embarked on a public campaign to raise subscriptions for the £28 million loan conversion. This was a risky undertaking with only a month to spare. But Lyons' advocacy swayed the nation. He spoke at public events, on radio and in cinemas, appealing to the best instincts of Australians to back their national obligations, drawing on the same sentiments that propelled the success of the war bond campaigns – loans that the public were invited to subscribe to on the basis of patriotic duty rather than simply financial gain. 'Let the world know that the heart of Australia is sound,' Lyons said in his final appeal, 'that her fighting people possess the same fighting spirit in peace as they showed in war, and that they will not repudiate their obligations.'[25]

Most of the nearly 100,000 subscribers were individuals and families determined to play their part.[26] Some businesses allowed employees to deduct an amount of their salary for the loan while others co-contributed. Not only was the loan conversion oversubscribed, but, more importantly, Lyons was exposed to a groundswell of grassroots support that both major parties had previously been unable to harness. He had become a national figure. Central also to the campaign's success was the support of the Nationalist Opposition leader, John Latham, and the Young Nationalists in Victoria, led by Robert Menzies. With Melbourne's non-Labor forces co-ordinating aspects of the campaign, a door had opened on new political possibilities.

* * *

When Scullin returned in January 1931, caucus was as divided as ever. The left treated Lyons with the greatest suspicion, while Theodore was eager to return to the Treasury bench. On 26 January, Lyons called for every cabinet position to be spilled. A lengthy debate followed and, perhaps sensing he did not have the numbers, Lyons withdrew the motion. Theodore was reinstated as treasurer, and Lyons resigned from the ministry.

By early 1931, the Melbourne Agreement was unravelling. The Commonwealth Bank chair, Robert Gibson, an avowed champion of economic orthodoxy, pleaded for fiscal discipline, while Lang and his supporters urged the repudiation of burdensome interest payments. Theodore suggested a program of monetary and fiscal expansion to encourage economic activity, a proposal that had the appearance of Keynesianism before Keynes, whose *General Theory* would not be published until 1936.

Lang's debt repudiation would have irrevocably harmed Australia's credit standing. Theodore's proposal was problematic, too, as its inflationary potential worried a sceptical Senate whose support Theodore needed. The greatest economic constraint was Australia's balance-of-payments crisis, which any boost to Australia's aggregate demand in 1931 would have worsened.[27] Only fiscal restraint was within the government's control.

Few recognised this more clearly than Joe Lyons. '[W]e are marking time,' he said, 'while so many of our people are tramping the country bare-footed, hungry and shelterless.'[28] He had come to believe that his Labor colleagues were unwilling to accept political reality and take the kind of action that was needed. On 13 March 1931, he rose in parliament to attack the government and support a no-confidence motion against it. This amounted to resigning from the Labor Party. Members sat 'spell-bound', the Melbourne *Herald* observed, as he attacked the inflationary policy of Theodore, the leadership of Scullin and the general political paralysis. He spoke of the 'women and kiddies' who were 'suffering and starving while we draw our salaries'.[29]

The arguments struck a chord because Lyons was saying what multitudes of Australians were thinking. He appealed to 'honest' and practical government, of doing things 'the right way'. He focused on sound finance and the fear of inflation, but his deeper point was that machine politics was failing Australians. It was an appeal to patriotic duty to solve what was, at its heart, a deep political problem.

Australians were already mobilising into new political associations – citizens movements that preached the virtues of anti-party politics and patriotic leadership. The Citizens League of South Australia, the All for Australia League and the Australian Citizens' League were the largest of such movements. A reporter attending one meeting was reminded of 'the camps and enlistment depots of 1914 and 1915. Clerks, bank managers, labourers, small shopkeepers, accountants, barristers, a mixed audience but all inspired by a wave of patriotic ardour.'[30] Altogether, these leagues probably recruited up to 300,000 members across Australia. As one historian has described it, they aimed for 'nothing less than the awakening of the civic spirit of the citizenry and the transformation of the nation's moribund political apparatus'.[31] Nothing like it has been seen before or since.

Because they are without direct political descendants, neither in Labor nor in the modern Liberal Party, these citizens' movements are largely forgotten. Yet they demonstrated that Australians can be persuaded to mobilise politically on a mass level if the times seem to call for it. The political idealism of the citizens leagues, with their appeals to patriotic duty, lingered into the 1940s and was tapped into by the founders of the Liberal Party. Importantly, they proved the critics of parliamentary democracy wrong and Monash right. The 'system' ultimately worked to resolve the nation's issues.

The failure of the political class was not hard to see. The lurch to radical populism in New South Wales culminated with defaults on interest obligations in February and March 1931, leading to a rush of withdrawals from the Government Savings Bank of New South Wales. In April, the bank suspended payments, which invited another run on the Commonwealth Savings Bank. Only through the intervention of Robert Gibson, who assured the public that 'the Bank will never close its doors, so long as the nation itself stands', was a greater financial crisis averted.[32]

As Lyons toured the country, he drew huge crowds. Speaking from the doorstep of a carriage in Adelaide, he assured his supporters that 'we will strike a match tonight which will start a blaze throughout Australia'.[33] Meeting with the Nationalist Leadership, he co-authored a Seven Points program that championed honouring all financial obligations, balanced budgets, rural assistance, imperial tariff preference and pragmatic industrial policy. By 7 May 1931, the United Australia Party had emerged, led by Lyons, including both the old Nationalist Party and Labor defectors, and backed by the United Australia Movement of citizens leagues around the country.

Something had to be done to steer the country back on course. The opportunity came at a premiers conference held across May and June 1931. A principle of 'equality of sacrifice' governed the proceedings: the belief that concessions on Australia's interest obligations had to be balanced by reduced government expenditure. A sub-committee of four economists recommended that interest payments be reduced by 22.5 per cent; and that adjustable government expenditure be reduced by a similar amount – except for old age pensions which were to be cut by only 12.5 per cent. These measures revived the loan market and restored confidence, even winning approval from John Maynard Keynes himself (although they were hardly 'Keynesian'), who wrote in 1933: 'I am sure that the Premiers' Plan ... saved the economic structure of Australia.'[34]

The Premiers' Plan was Scullin's last great achievement. It was his own side that brought him down in the end, falling to a parliamentary no-confidence motion in which a small pro-Lang group, fronted by Jack Beasley, switched their support to the United Australia Party.

An election was called for December 1931. Lyons, having already toured the country stumping for his new brand of politics, was in prime position. His message was simple: that Australia had to restore confidence in itself and in its markets, an objective that was beyond party or sectional antagonisms. His wife, Enid, was an essential component of the campaign. In a speech organised by an Adelaide Citizens' League, it was reported that Enid 'carried a doubtful audience off its feet'; 'the little mother of the family,' she said, was 'the best financier'.[35] '[T]ogether on the platform,' Enid recalled, 'Joe and I worked like partners in a game of bridge.'[36] Lyons led the UAP to a resounding victory.

In New South Wales, the political situation had become desperate. The Labor government's policy of defaulting on interest payments had so deepened divisions that civil unrest threatened. Lang defied a Commonwealth law to extract the NSW government's interest obligations from state banks. He even had the locks changed on the doors of the State Tax Department. By instructing the public service not to comply with federal law, Lang gave Governor Philip Game grounds to dismiss him, which he did on 13 May 1932. Lang was shocked but did not hesitate to accept the decision. 'Well, I must be going. I am no longer Premier, but a free man,' he told a reporter in his office. It was an out-of-character acquiescence but probably his finest moment as premier.[37]

* * *

Relative political calm followed. Key decisions, such as the Premiers' Plan, had already been taken. Australia had effectively left the gold standard in September 1931 (when the British pound, for which the Australian pound could be exchanged, could no longer be exchanged for a fixed weight of gold); as well, the Australian pound was devalued against the pound sterling meaning exports were more attractive. Improved international conditions further pushed Australia along the path to recovery.

Even in the worst of national crises, life goes on. Modernity continued its inexorable march with new innovations changing ordinary living. In 1932, a South Australian chemist, H.A. Milton Blake, sold the first commercially available sunscreen in the world – Hamilton Sun and Skin – after years of experimenting in his kitchen. Communications technology expanded rapidly. By the end of the 1930s, around two-thirds of households had a radio and those without them could visit a 'wireless house', a listening space open to the public. Scullin thought the new medium meant long election campaigns were no longer justified.[38] The first successful Australian 'talkie' film, *The Diggers*, released in 1931, was a story of two veterans reminiscing at their 12-year reunion. Two years later, a handsome 24-year-old Tasmanian, Errol Flynn, was cast in his first movie, *In the Wake of the Bounty*. Qantas completed its first million air miles (1,610,000 km) in 1930 and launched its first international flight – from Brisbane to Singapore – on 17 April 1935. Lyons was the first prime minister to take advantage of air travel in his campaigns and made a point of notifying reporters of his schedule so the press could be there when he arrived.

Aboriginal Australians challenged prevailing orthodoxies in more visible public campaigns. Far from 'dying out', as was once thought inevitable, Aboriginal Australians had actually increased in number from about 71,000 in 1921 to 80,000 in 1933.[39] A new phase of Aboriginal activism began, with William Cooper, a Yorta Yorta elder who moved to Melbourne in his early 70s. Cooper spoke in the language of the missionaries that had educated him but he remained deeply connected to the traditions of his kin, and to what he termed 'thinking black', the value-system of Indigenous communities.[40] He co-founded the Australian Aborigines' League (AAL) in 1933, which drafted a petition to King George V asking for Aboriginal Australians to be represented in parliament. The petition received almost 2000 signatures, or nearly 3 per cent of the then Aboriginal population. Cooper called for 'no differentiation between the full blood and those of mixed blood' (effectively a call for all Aboriginal people to be treated identically with other Australians, as lighter-skinned Aboriginal people mostly were) and frequently pressed for Aboriginal 'emancipation', recalling both the great anti-slavery campaign of Wilberforce as well as the ex-convict emancipists who were the first builders of modern Australia.

A Day of Mourning was held on 26 January 1938, 150 years after the First Fleet arrived in New South Wales. Led by Cooper, Bill Ferguson and Jack Patten, a group of Aboriginal Australians urged the government to 'raise our people to full citizenship status and equality within the community'.[41] A pamphlet was distributed titled 'Aborigines Claim Citizens Rights!' forcefully arguing that 'the cards have been stacked against us and we ask you to play the game like decent Australians'.[42] Five days after the Day of Mourning, Cooper and other Aboriginal people formed a deputation that met with Joe and Enid Lyons (the first formal meeting of an Aboriginal delegation and a prime minister) and made the case for the government to address the issues of land rights, citizenship and state protection boards.

* * *

Meanwhile, the UAP became increasingly directionless as time went on and the crisis that had given it birth eased. Lacking a federal organisational structure, its anti-party origins, perhaps predictably, prevented it from developing the kind of party machinery necessary to consolidate its power and provide a coherent, principled basis on which to govern. Its animating force remained Joe Lyons, who held it together against the factionalism and divisions that invariably befall multi-term governments. As the decade progressed, the gap between its animating idealism and its transparent disorganisation encouraged murmurings of revitalising liberal politics in some other way.

For some time, Lyons' capable treasurer, Richard Casey, had been working on a National Insurance Scheme, an ambitious attempt to redesign Australia's welfare policy on a contributory basis. Australian wage and salary earners with an annual income less than £365 (the Commonwealth basic wage was about £200) would be required to register for compulsory insurance, which covered 'sickness benefits, disability support, an aged pension, and a pension for the widows of insured men'.[43] Employers and workers alike would make equal contributions; government funds would be contributed only for the pension scheme.

Its contributory element, Casey thought, would encourage thrift and individual initiative without straining the public purse. Although the scheme was successfully legislated, negotiations over its administration and cost broke down comprehensively. Defence spending put pressure on the program, and business and medical groups feared its impact on their own pockets, while the Country Party wanted rural industries excluded altogether. Labor did not like the contributory principle and believed such benefits should be paid out of consolidated revenue. Under such intense pressure, the government backed down.

Behind closed doors, Lyons was upfront about his weariness in office. 'I am absolutely beat,' he told Stanley Bruce, then the high commissioner to the United Kingdom, in January 1939.[44] An abortive attempt to bring back Bruce as his successor only underscored the need for a transition plan.

Less than a month later, Enid received a call from a friend that Joe had taken ill in Sydney. He suggested she come immediately from Canberra. Enid took the express train – there were no night landings for flights then, even in major cities – and arrived at the hospital to see two nurses standing beside her husband. He 'was holding his own', they told her.[45] The deputy prime minister, Earle Page, soon arrived, as did other members of the cabinet, but Lyons' condition worsened. On 7 April 1939, with Enid by his side, Australia's prime minister died, the first to do so while in office.

12

Australia Threatened

Although in 1939 Australia was lamentably unprepared for war, the country fully mobilised under prime ministers Menzies and then Curtin. Almost a million men and women wore uniform in the Second World War, and some 550,000 of them – one in 12 Australians – served overseas. To meet the demands of the 'home front', there was a 31 per cent increase in women in the paid workforce. Some 40,000 Australians lost their lives – fewer than in the Great War – but our sovereignty was directly threatened for the first and, so far, only time.

An unlikely source testifies to the extent of our fighting spirit: 'If the invasion [of Australia] is attempted,' a Japanese Imperial General Staff document said in March 1942, 'the Australians, in view of their national character, would resist to the end.'[1] Working in lockstep with the British Army, the troops of the Second AIF spearheaded the initial action in sweeping the Italians out of Libya and liberating Syria from the Vichy French, and the 9th Division helped secure the British victory at El Alamein, but once Japan had entered the war, our focus was keeping the nearer enemy at bay. While the army 'mopped up' Japanese resistance in the islands to our north, over 3000 Australians participated in D-Day, mostly in Royal Navy and Royal Air Force units, and Australian ships and planes continued to play their part in the global Allied war effort.

§

Three weeks after Lyons' death, the United Australia Party elected the 44-year-old Victorian Robert Menzies as party leader and he was subsequently sworn in as prime minister on 26 April 1939. His intellectual reputation had been established by his advocacy as a junior barrister in the landmark 1920 Engineers Case, which held that federal laws could bind state instrumentalities, thus overturning the previous judicial doctrine of 'implied immunities'. After a brief stint in the Victorian Parliament, in 1934 Menzies entered the federal parliament and was immediately one of its dominant personalities. He was both a confidante and a rival to Lyons, serving as his attorney-general and deputy leader. Most assumed Menzies would be Lyons' successor.

Coming from the small town of Jeparit in far western Victoria, Menzies would deny that he was 'born to the purple' – in other words, into the upper echelons of society – but his self-confidence sometimes alienated colleagues, including the Country Party leader Earle Page. In March 1939, Menzies resigned from the cabinet in protest over the postponement of the government's national insurance scheme, 'the last but weighty straw' in what he believed to be a series of leadership failures.[2] Lyons was devastated. Standing in the hospital shortly after Lyons' passing, Page openly blamed Menzies for his leader's death. Taking his anger to parliament, Page attacked Menzies for disloyalty and for cowardice, in particular, for his failure to serve in the Great War. Menzies' wife, Pattie, was sitting in the public gallery and never forgave Page for the insult.

The charge of cowardice was unfair, and it came to hurt Page, just as it dogged Menzies. Menzies had not served in the war because his parents had beseeched him not to, after two older brothers had volunteered. A Menzies biographer has surmised that 'nothing else he did or failed to do in his first thirty years was to have more impact on his future'.[3] Menzies recognised this and was never fully reconciled to it. Perhaps a lifelong commitment to public service was his way of atoning for not serving in the military.

Menzies' politics was a blend of liberalism and conservatism. 'I would rather belong to the Labor Party than to a party which has sold its soul,' he had told his electors in 1929.[4] With his friend Wilfrid Kent Hughes, he established the Young Nationalists to promote liberal candidates of high calibre and philosophical conviction. Born into the 1890s depression, enduring the Great War and the Great Depression, and coming to grips with a fractious and unstable interwar political climate, Menzies aspired to a more high-minded politics. A world crisis gave him that opportunity.

* * *

On 3 September 1939, the new prime minister intoned that it was his 'melancholy duty' to report 'that, in consequence of a persistence by Germany in her invasion of Poland, Great Britain has declared war upon her, and that, as a result, Australia is also at war'.[5] As he later put it, great things were at stake:

> I do not believe that you can compromise about the vital things in civilisation, about peace and justice and freedom and the sane settlement of disputes. Either you have them or you do not have them. And there are no people more interested in securing them than the people of small and weak nations, and the small and weak people of every nation. Our cause is that there shall be justice and a quiet living for the weak as well as for the strong. It is a great and humane cause. It has been the dynamic force in our

> domestic political growth for centuries; from now on it
> must animate our international affairs and give direction to
> the policies of nations.[6]

Along with the rest of the English-speaking world, Australia could hardly bear to contemplate another world war, even though Nazi Germany and Imperial Japan had long been preparing for one. The Axis powers rejected the global order that had emerged after Versailles. They celebrated the military state and their right to expand and subordinate 'inferior' races. As late as 11 September 1939, just days after he'd announced Australia's entry into the war, Menzies could still write 'that Hitler has no desire for a first-class war'.[7] That was probably true, but a first-class war was the logical consequence of Hitler's intentions.

A similar story had been unfolding in the Pacific. In 1934, after returning from a goodwill mission in Japan, the former Nationalist leader John Latham had warily accepted the assurances of the Japanese government that their ambitions were limited to Manchuria and China.[8] But, by 1937, Japan was identifying areas to its south as 'indispensable for industrial development and defence', as Australia scrambled for guarantees from Britain that its imperial defence strategy would provide a protective buffer.[9]

That strategy could be distilled to just one word: Singapore. In the event of a Japanese attack, Britain's main fleet was to make haste to the Singapore naval base, especially constructed to deter or repel Japanese aggression. Still financially constrained from the Depression and reliant on great and powerful friends, Australia was content to rest on the Singapore strategy even though, in hindsight, it was clearly wishful thinking. It was never satisfactorily resolved what Britain would do in the event of being tied up in a European war as well as a Pacific one.

Australia could hardly blame others for its lack of preparedness. In 1929, Scullin ended compulsory military training for Australian men. Defence spending halved between 1929 and 1933 and militia numbers fell by almost 50,000 to under 30,000.[10] In 1931, no new students were admitted to the military and naval colleges, and even by 1939 the permanent army numbered only 4000 personnel, with the part-time militia numbering 80,000.[11] Although a measure of re-armament eventually got underway – with defence appropriations quadrupling over four years from 1935 – on the eve of war, spending on the armed forces was still barely 1.5 per cent of GDP.

* * *

Having declared war, Australians fretted over their country's role during the so-called Phoney War, which lasted between September 1939 and May 1940. What would Japan do? Would the United States be involved? Where would the Royal Navy – the core of imperial defence – be deployed? Political leaders argued over what was the worse menace to Australia: Nazi Germany, and its threat to Europe and Britain, or the direct Japanese threat. Menzies agonised over these questions. Australians themselves were puzzled. No strenuous demands were being made of them – yet.

There was still an unwavering commitment to Britain, for the British way of life – reduced in its simplest form to parliamentary democracy, the rule of law, freedom of speech and religion – was the Australian way of life. Britain was by far our biggest economic partner and the imperial defence system sustained our civilisational choice. Menzies' declaration of war had been uncontentious. In a sense, it reflected John Curtin's statement of 1937 that had characterised Australia as 'seven million British subjects, but also three million square miles [7,800,000 km²] of British territory, and one thousand million [pounds] of British investments'.[12]

Menzies was concerned about Britain's capacity to defend Australia. He did not want to send an expeditionary force to Europe until Japan's position was properly established.[13] In a radio broadcast made on 26 April 1939, he had laid out his thinking on the Pacific: 'What Great Britain calls the Far East is to us the near north ... I have become convinced that, in the Pacific, Australia must regard herself as a principal providing herself with her own information and maintaining her own diplomatic contacts with foreign powers.'[14]

The government's decision to send the bulk of the Second AIF – the 6th, 7th and 9th Divisions – to the Middle East by the end of 1940 was the result of considerable discussion and pressure. In January 1941, Menzies left for London to press for regional reinforcements. On the way, a visit to the Singapore base left him worried by its exposed state. The government sent much of the 8th Division to Malaya to strengthen British defences.

Australian soldiers saw their first action against European fascism in January 1941, in the small fishing village of Bardia, on the Mediterranean coast of Italy's Libyan colony. The 6th Division, led by former school headmaster General Iven Mackay, captured the town from the Italians and forced the surrender of 40,000 enemy troops at the cost of only 130 casualties. Italian heavy guns and tanks were captured and recommissioned by Australian soldiers.[15] The 6th Division took a further 25,000 Italian prisoners by capturing the Port of Tobruk on 22 January, and moved through to take the Italian stronghold at Benghazi in February. This campaign, Operation Compass, was the first significant Allied land victory, confirming to the public that the Second AIF were worthy successors to the Anzacs.[16]

Meanwhile, some 37,000 Australians went through the Empire Air Training Scheme, mostly in Canada, before serving in the air campaigns over Britain and Europe. Some 13,000 of them served in bomber command, either in Royal Air Force or Royal Australian Air Force squadrons, and suffered the highest casualty rates of any Australian personnel. Air Commodore Hughie Edwards VC, an RAF pilot, became the most highly decorated Australian serviceman of the war.

* * *

Federal Labor was divided over the extent of Australia's war involvement. Its leader, John Curtin, attacked the idea of sending troops overseas and was critical of the reintroduction of conscription for home defence. Partly, this was to calm the radical wing of his party. Curtin was embarrassed by the communist element in Labor politics, which ferociously opposed the war while the Molotov–Ribbentrop pact lasted, with its Soviet–German carve-up of Poland until Hitler's invasion of Russia. In May 1940, the NSW Labor branch declared the war to be 'pursued in the interests of big finance and the monopolists', a flagrant parroting of the communist line.[17] Curtin's rejection of Menzies' proposed joint national government (as had happened in Britain) in favour of a War Advisory Council was an implied admission of Labor's own political fragility.

Ultimately, it took Japan's entry into the conflict for Labor to lose the languid utopianism of the interwar period. Menzies, meanwhile, faced a series of political crises that also hindered the war effort. He had a rocky relationship with the Country Party, which had ended the Coalition upon Menzies' ascension to the prime ministership, only to re-enter it again in May 1940 after the departure of Page from the leadership. Then, on 13 August 1940, a plane crash killed three high-profile UAP ministers: the minister for the army, Geoffrey Street; the minister for information, Sir Henry Gullet; and the minister for air, James Fairbairn; plus Sir Brudenell White, the chief of the general staff. Last but not least, the 1940 general election resulted in a hung parliament, so Menzies relied on two independent MPs for survival.

The news in London was worse. Menzies failed to get Churchill, who'd become prime minister after the botched British attempt to resist the German takeover of Norway, to commit to reinforcements in Southeast Asia. A subsequent visit to Washington yielded only a private assurance from President Roosevelt that America would stand with Australia in the event of Japanese aggression. On his return to Australia, Menzies declared that '[h]ere, and in Britain, we look to the great democracy of the United States, and believe we will not look in vain'.[18] This pronouncement came some seven months before John Curtin's more famous 'Look to America' declaration of December 1941.

Meanwhile, Australian forces were central to the North African, Greek, Crete and Syrian campaigns. The military historian David Horner has argued that 'without the presence of the AIF it is doubtful whether Britain could have conducted any of these campaigns successfully'.[19] The fall of France in June 1940 had shocked Australians and boosted recruitment. Those who ended up in the 9th Division and fought at Tobruk and El Alamein were, in historian Peter Stanley's words, 'some of the war's most determined fighters'.[20]

The defence of Greece proved both contentious and disastrous. As Britain's only ally on the continent, Churchill was adamant that Greece should be protected from a German invasion. A show of support was seen as crucial in winning help from the United States. Despite his doubts about the mission and its objectives, the Australian commander of the AIF, General Thomas Blamey, helped to lead the Greek campaign, commanding the Australian 6th Division, the New

Zealand Division and British units against eight armoured and mechanised German Divisions backed by the Luftwaffe's superior airpower.[21] Two weeks after the initial German attack, on 6 April 1941, Field Marshal Wavell ordered the withdrawal of all British and dominion troops. By 25 April, 50,000 troops had been evacuated, with thousands more unable to escape and taken as prisoners of war, including 2000 Australians.

Of the successfully evacuated troops, 30,000 were sent to Crete, where they met a similar fate. Facing a German paratroop assault, the Allied troops could only hold out for six days before being again ordered to evacuate on 26 May. Another 3000 Australian soldiers were taken prisoner.[22] Some 8000 of the 17,000 Australian soldiers involved in the Greece and Crete campaigns were killed, wounded or captured. At home, Menzies was attacked by the press for agreeing to it. Though he'd always been anxious about its chances of success, he stood by the decision, saying that failure to come to the aid of Greece would have been 'one of the infamies of history'.[23]

Despite these setbacks, major elements of the Australian 7th Division formed the bulk of the British force that attacked the Vichy French regime in Syria in June 1941 (to forestall the territory's use by German forces). In a campaign lasting just over a month, Damascus and Beirut were captured at the cost of some 1500 Australian casualties, including a future governor of New South Wales, Sir Roden Cutler, who lost a leg and won the Victoria Cross during the Battle of Damour.

The German Afrika Korps meanwhile swept into North Africa. Under the leadership of General Erwin Rommel, the Axis powers regained lost territory and surrounded Allied forces at Tobruk. As one of only two ports in the region, Tobruk was vital. Rommel could use it to re-equip the Korps and advance towards Alexandria, Cairo and then on to the Suez Canal. For six months, Tobruk withstood an epic siege.

Commanding a garrison two-thirds Australian and one-third British, Australian General Leslie Morshead lacked the heavy weaponry and anti-tank guns needed to defeat the Afrika Korps in open warfare so relied instead on innovative tactics to 'besiege the besiegers', including using night patrols to find and attack enemy camps.[24] After the Nazi propagandist William Joyce, also known as Lord Haw Haw, labelled the Australians the 'rats of Tobruk', the pejorative description quickly became a term of pride, celebrating the gritty and elusive heroics of the Australians.

* * *

On his return from London, Menzies confronted a deteriorating political situation. The UAP has been described as 'a coalition of pieces rather than parties, rest[ing] on a mass of shifting discontents'.[25] It was, after all, not only the creation of Joseph Lyons, now gone, but a semi-spontaneous answer to the economic problems of the early 1930s. Without a firm governing structure or philosophy, it lacked the ballast needed to endure.

As well, Menzies was tired, increasingly aloof and, as a result of his extended overseas trip, out of touch with certain elements in his own party. Sydney's media was vicious and colleagues were spooked by the persistent criticism. Internally, some believed that Menzies was not communicating the government's strategy clearly enough. Others thought him too slow to make decisions. Menzies' further offer to Curtin to form a national government was again rejected. At a cabinet meeting on 26 August, Menzies asked his team for a show of confidence. Of the 13 present, nine called for him to resign.[26]

On 28 August 1941, Menzies announced his resignation. His successor was the Country Party leader Arthur Fadden, who lasted a month before two independents, Arthur Coles and Alex Wilson, crossed the floor to bring down the government, whereupon the governor-general commissioned Curtin to form a new one.

Despite his political downfall, Menzies had much to his credit. Expenditure on defence had risen from £55 million in 1939–40 to almost £171 million in 1940–41, with further substantial increases to come. Four divisions were in the field, supported by a completely reshaped Commonwealth bureaucracy. Work traditionally undertaken by the Defence Department alone was spread across ten departments. The expansion of munitions production and other war-related endeavours, despite some blunders and hurdles along the way, still 'amazed even the experts brought out to supervise the expansion'.[27] There was a 20-fold increase in men and women serving in the Air Force in the first two years.[28] The effort was enough for the then permanent head of the Defence Department, Frederick Shedden, to remark that Curtin's achievements 'could not have been immediately effective, but for the foundations laid by the Defence Programme of the preceding United Australia Party Governments'.[29]

* * *

John Curtin was 56 when he took office, of genial but nervous temperament, democratic in his outlook and unquestionably patriotic. Because he led the country through its period of greatest danger, he is sometimes ranked among the best of Australian prime ministers, even the 'saviour of Australia'. Perhaps his most significant achievement was getting his own party – many of whom were psychologically and ideologically against it – wholeheartedly to prosecute the war. This came at a great cost to his own health.

Two months into his prime ministership, on 7 December 1941, Japan attacked the US naval bases at Pearl Harbor and in the Philippines, the 'day of infamy' that forced America into the war. Curtin subsequently declared war on Japan – the first Australian declaration of war made independently of Britain.

With the start of Japan's lightning conquests, and despite British assurances that Australia was not threatened, Curtin was desperate for US help. In a New Year message, published in the Melbourne *Herald*, Curtin declared that 'without any inhibitions of any kind, I make it quite clear, Australia looks to America, free of any pangs as to our traditional links or kinship with the United Kingdom'.[30]

The 'Look to America' statement, though celebrated by history, was not well received at the time. President Roosevelt thought the plea embarrassing and wrong-headed, as America's first commitment was to defeat Hitler.[31] What it did reveal, though, was a degree of official panic at the precariousness of Australia's already fragile position.

On 8 December 1941, Japanese forces attacked the Malay Peninsula. By Christmas, Penang had fallen. Kuala Lumpur fell in early January. By the end of the month, all Allied forces had withdrawn to Singapore. On 15 February, in Britain's worst ever military defeat, that 'impregnable citadel' fell, too. With a sense of foreboding, Curtin told the nation that it 'opens the Battle for Australia'.[32]

The 80,000 Allied troops left in Singapore became prisoners of war, including the 15,000 Australian soldiers of the 8th Division as well as the 18th Division of the British Army and the 9th and 11th Divisions of the British Indian Army.[33] A few Australians managed to escape, including their commander, Major-General Gordon Bennett, whose action in abandoning his troops was later found to be unjustified. In these first disastrous months of 1942, some 22,000 Australian POWs were taken from Malaya, Singapore and the Dutch East Indies, of whom 13,000 were sent to work on the Thai–Burma railway as Japan prepared for an invasion of India.[34] Clearing the thick jungle, drilling rocks and building bridges without any modern machinery, 2800 Australians died during its construction. About 8000 Australian POWs died in captivity, close to half of all Australian casualties in the war against Japan.[35]

On 19 February 1942, 240 Japanese aircraft bombed Darwin – the same fighter planes, launched from the same aircraft carriers and led by the same leader, Mitsuo Fuchida, that had attacked Pearl Harbor. This was the first air-raid on Australian soil and remains the largest ever attack on Australian territory. The official death count was 243, though the figure remains disputed. Two weeks later, Broome was bombed, killing about 70. From 19 February 1942 to 12 November 1943, Darwin endured 64 of the 97 air attacks on Australian soil, which also hit towns including Wyndham, Port Hedland, Katherine, Derby and Townsville.[36]

By the end of February, Curtin and the War Cabinet were informed by Australian chiefs of staff that Japan was 'now at liberty' to attack Australia. Curtin told the nation that the country was 'fighting for her very survival'.[37] Japanese propaganda fed the fear as Australians anxiously dug trenches in their backyards.

Although ambitious Japanese naval staff were contemplating invading Australia, the project was always opposed by the Army General Staff. By mid-April 1942, Allied intelligence intercepts had confirmed that there was no serious invasion plan. This, however, did not nullify the existential threat to Australia posed by a Japanese victory.[38] By March, Hong Kong, the Philippines, Malaya, Singapore, the Dutch East Indies and islands in the southwest Pacific had fallen. With the prospect of US supply lines to Australia being cut, no invasion was necessary to make Australia's position impossible.

Coming out of the Parliament House lobby bar to buy cigarettes one evening in February 1942, Curtin appeared to one journalist as 'the picture of a complete physical wreck'.[39] These were the darkest days of the war.

After the fall of Singapore, he was advised by the Australian chiefs of staff to bring the AIF back to Australia. Instead, Churchill and Roosevelt wanted Australian reinforcements for Burma. The Americans were desperate to open a Burma road that could supply materials of war to China – an objective with obvious benefits to Australia's defence. Against intense pressure, Curtin insisted on bringing the troops home, a victory that came with some delay: the 9th Division remained in the Middle East for some months, while the 6th and 7th Divisions started to return in early 1942, just in time for the arrival of General MacArthur.

It was in October 1942, in the midst of the 9th Division's decisive participation in the pivotal Battle of El Alamein, that Curtin cabled Churchill demanding that our last major formation be brought back 'in view of the situation' in the Pacific theatre (which, by this time – after Milne Bay and after the Japanese withdrawal from Imita Ridge behind Port Moresby – was starting to improve). Most historians have backed Curtin's decision and his sense of Australia's priorities, but this further withdrawal of Australian forces from the Middle East might have been a strategic mistake and was at odds with New Zealand's decision to leave the bulk of its army to fight in North Africa and then Italy.

* * *

To meet the peril, the whole nation fully mobilised. Public sector expenditure rose from 28 per cent to 42 per cent of GDP.[40] Civilian industries were converted to defence production and workers were limited in their choice of occupations. All citizens over 18 were required to register with the Manpower Directorate and carry identity cards.

Private investment outside the necessities of war virtually stopped and private consumption was restricted by rationing and regulation. Invoking national security regulations, the federal treasurer, Ben Chifley, expanded the powers of the Commonwealth Bank and imposed licensing requirements on private banks. The federal government monopolised the levying of income tax, a decision that has since reshaped Australian federalism by restricting the states' ability to finance themselves, thus making them more dependent on the federal government. As part of an austerity pledge, Curtin asked Australians to 'cut from our lives every luxury, every relaxation, every temptation to slack'.[41]

Much of the war effort fell on the private sector. No business leader did more than Essington Lewis, managing director of the Broken Hill Proprietary Company, who was plucked from private life to lead Australia's wartime industrial mobilisation. Lewis had visited Japan in 1934 and was so concerned by what he observed that he quickly began pushing for the stockpiling of raw materials and the manufacturing of munitions. In May 1940, he was appointed director of munitions, and in 1942 director-general of aircraft production. These powerful roles gave him control over much of Australia's war production. Commanding a workforce of several hundreds of thousands, Lewis worked long hours and took no salary. In his first six months alone, munitions output almost quadrupled.[42]

* * *

The arrival in Australia of the US general Douglas MacArthur, in March 1942, was accompanied by a vast collective sigh of relief.[43] At 62, tall, commanding and charismatic, he was already considered a war hero for leading a stand against Japanese forces in the Philippines. MacArthur told the Advisory War Council that invasion was unlikely but pledged to Australia's defence 'all the resources of all the mighty power of my country and all the blood of my countrymen'.[44] Over the next three years, nearly a million American personnel rotated through Australia and were mostly welcomed. There was occasional resentment against troops who were 'overpaid, over-sexed, and over here', which extended to a riot – involving hundreds of Australian and US troops over two nights – that became known as the 'Battle of Brisbane'.

From the moment he set foot on Australian soil, MacArthur was the driving force in the nation's war effort. The Australian government made it clear that MacArthur's orders were to be 'considered ... as emanating from the Commonwealth Government', and Curtin remained steadfast in backing him against opposition from other military officials and his own Labor Party. 'You take care of the rear and I will handle the front,' is how the American general proposed the relationship to Curtin.[45] One result was a sidelining of the Australian chiefs of staff and the inability of the Australian War Cabinet to deal with critical issues of strategy.

Public panic never again reached the peak of early 1942 but did not dissipate entirely. In May, three Japanese submarines crept into Sydney Harbour, eluding harbour defences, and sank a ferry, killing 21 sailors. The Battle of the Coral Sea, fought off the northeast coast, was the first serious loss for Japan. A Japanese fleet on its way to take Port Moresby was met by US aircraft carriers supported by the Australian ships *Hobart* and *Australia*. The ships were never within sight of each other – this was the first ever naval battle where victory was determined in the air. Through long-range bombing, Allied aircraft inflicted serious damage on the Japanese fleet, enough to deter their attack. On 8 May, Curtin informed the nation of the victory in a stirring parliamentary address. A month later at the Battle of Midway, the core of the Japanese Navy – including the four aircraft carriers used to bomb Darwin and Pearl Harbor – were sunk, turning the tide towards the Allies.[46]

Japan still sought Port Moresby, whose airfields provided a base from which its conquered territory could be defended and which would also expose Australia to future attacks. The Battles of Coral Sea and Midway made a Japanese naval assault impractical, so an overland offensive was Japan's next best option. On 21 July, 13,000 Japanese soldiers landed in northwest Papua. They met the heavily outnumbered Australian 39th Battalion, a militia unit comprised of soldiers who'd been called up for compulsory service but only within Australian territory – the so-called chocko soldiers (because, like chocolate, they were thought to melt in the heat). Brave but exhausted, hungry and undersupplied, outnumbered and battling malaria, they stalled the Japanese advance along the Kokoda Track long enough to allow for reinforcements. By the time the battalion was relieved on 5 September, its unit strength was down from about 1000 to 185. The Japanese advanced over 75 miles (120 km) through unforgiving jungle terrain towards Imita Ridge, approximately 25 miles (40 km) from Port Moresby. By then, the Japanese were themselves exhausted and depleted – their supplies had to be trekked from the northern coast – and the reinforced Allies gained the upper hand. The Japanese were pushed back along the Kokoda Track to establish a defensive position in the north of the island.[47]

Just prior to the conclusion of the Kokoda campaign, in September 1942, Australian forces had defeated a Japanese landing at Milne Bay on the eastern tip of Papua. This was a major morale boost as the Allies' first significant win on land.

The Papuan campaign again raised the issue of conscription for military service beyond Australian territory. Earlier in the war, Menzies and Curtin had rejected the idea: it was 'not required to invoke the patriotism of Australian men', Curtin had argued in 1941, knowing full well his own party's antipathy to conscription.[48] Yet a conscript militia, fighting in Papua but unable to be sent beyond Australian territory, made little sense strategically or morally. Conscripted Americans were dying for Australia, a fact which harmed MacArthur's own campaign for further supplies and reinforcements from the United States. Under intense pressure from MacArthur, Curtin argued for a change of policy in terms that Labor could accept. He tactically suggested a mere reinterpretation of existing policy, expanding the area where the Citizen Military Forces could be sent, this time to Japanese-occupied islands south of the equator. A federal Labor conference approved the change, despite vocal opposition.

During the Papuan campaign, malaria plagued both sides. The symptoms of fever, intense sweating and anaemia sometimes incapacitated more soldiers than enemy sanction. In 1943, Brigadier Neil Fairley, an Australian field doctor from the Great War, began experimenting with treatments. He found that higher doses of the drug mepacrine increased a soldier's immunity to the disease. The treatment was adopted by the Allied troops to dramatic effect. Earlier in the war, South Australian Howard Florey had achieved an even more remarkable scientific feat. Following the discovery of penicillin in 1928, Florey and his team at the University of Oxford developed the techniques to grow, purify and manufacture penicillin, which became the world's first effective antibiotic in 1941.

By 1944, penicillin was being used to treat infected wounds. Historian Brett Mason argues that Florey, alongside fellow South Australian scientist Mark Oliphant, who made microwave radar possible and convinced Oppenheimer of the feasibility of building an atomic bomb in 1941, 'changed history' and 'are the two most consequential Australians of the war'.[49] In 1945, Florey, Sir Alexander Fleming and Ernst Chain received the Nobel Prize for Medicine 'for the discovery of penicillin and its curative effect in various infectious diseases'. On Lord Florey's death in 1968, Menzies declared that 'in terms of world well-being, Florey was the most important man ever born in Australia'.[50]

* * *

By his own admission, Curtin was uncomfortable in the role of war leader. It required of him a mindset that he had rejected in his youth. His heroes were English socialists; his mentors radical trade unionists. He was repelled by militarism and, as a young man, yearned for the revolution that never came. He was a youthful pacifist, arrested and imprisoned for not registering for compulsory military training.

He hated the thought of Australians dying. His November 1941 announcement of the loss, with all hands, of the cruiser HMAS *Sydney* (which had earlier fought with distinction in the Mediterranean, sinking an Italian cruiser) was a particularly difficult experience. His own austere life, itself a series of personal sacrifices, was thought to mirror the national sacrifice. Labor's smashing win in the 1943 election was the nation's political tribute to the man who had led it through its darkest hour.

Curtin was probably a finer man than he was a great war leader. He over-relied on General MacArthur, quoting him in cables to Roosevelt, and allowing him to dictate lines in his addresses to the Australian public. Curtin never visited a battlefield and rarely thought about the war in any deep strategic sense. He tended to downplay the European theatre as 'anybody's war' with its 'far-flung battlefields'. He did not like the idea of the D-Day invasion, and turned down an invitation to visit the planning headquarters for it. Even at the time, this drew criticism. 'We must abandon the view that it is only our skins that matter,' said Earle Page, adding that the freedom of the world was at stake.[51]

In June 1943, Curtin declared Australia largely safe from invasion. Thereafter, the strategic role of Australia shifted away from defence to assisting the Allied thrust against Japan. Still a pacifist at heart, the prime minister saw Australia more as the chief supplier of the war effort, a food bowl for the Allied cause, than a principal combatant. In reorganising for this new task, the government struggled against competing vested interests on the one hand and an all-powerful General MacArthur on the other. Paul Hasluck was probably correct in concluding that Curtin's ministers 'were not in full command of their own policy'.[52] Likewise, the historian David Horner has described this period as a 'time of frustration rather than mastery'.[53]

As the battlefront shifted north from 1944, the highly capable Australian forces were largely engaged in 'mopping up' the remaining Japanese forces in New Guinea, New Britain, Bougainville and Borneo.[54] This is not to understate the intensity of the fighting, the courage displayed by the Australians and the scale of particular engagements, such as the largely Australian amphibious assault on Balikpapan in Borneo in July 1945. Nonetheless, it was a contrast to the central role that the AIF had played in the Great War. Officers and troops were frustrated at being sidelined; so were the public.

The British military historian Sir Max Hastings has associated what he called Australia's comparatively minor role in 1944–45 with the country's internal dissensions.[55] An outbreak of looting in Darwin following the Japanese strike was a symptom of indifferent morale. As was the plethora of industrial strikes. In 1944, with most conscripts languishing in camps and barracks, there was a feeling that the government simply lacked vigour; unsurprising, some felt, considering the Curtin ministry only included one former veteran of the Great War, John Dedman, while other ministers had spent their younger years as anti-war radicals. 'For a people whose soldiers, sailors and airmen won such admiration in other theatres,' said Hastings, by the war's end, Australia was punching below its weight.[56] A key factor in the Australian Army's marginalisation, said historian Karl James, was that MacArthur 'deliberately excluded the AIF from the Philippines', preferring to use only US troops.

Although Curtin had 'looked to America' at the end of 1941, as the war progressed, he was looking back to the Mother Country. In 1943, he proposed the King's brother, the Duke of Gloucester, as the next governor-general. In a 1944 Empire Day broadcast, he described Australians as 'trustees for the British way of life ... corresponding in outlook and purpose with that of the United Kingdom'.[57]

On a 1944 trip to London, his only overseas trip as prime minister, he proposed a new phase of co-operation within the British Commonwealth, underpinned by a new permanent secretariat to enable continuous consultation between the dominions and Britain. London made no commitments but Curtin continued to champion closer relations. He was 'as British as Churchill', journalists told the British high commissioner in Canberra.[58] His proposals were largely the same as the urgings of Alfred Deakin and Edmund Barton half a century earlier.

Curtin's health was near breaking point by the second half of 1944. Struck by a heart attack in November, he did not resume full duties until January. By this stage, far more attention was being given to post-war reconstruction. Curtin could not conceive of how post-war prosperity could be achieved without retaining large elements of wartime controls and state involvement. The war had, after all, made the government the largest manufacturer in the country.

Germany surrendered in May 1945. With Japan on its last legs, Curtin hoped to hang on until the Pacific War concluded. But his health was deteriorating and on 5 July, with his wife Elsie by his side, he died peacefully. '[A] war casualty if there ever was one,' the historian Geoffrey Serle wrote; plus, said historian John Hirst, 'the burden of being John Curtin'.[59] In his parliamentary eulogy, the interim prime minister Frank Forde declared, 'the captain has been stricken in sight of the shore'. MPs on both sides wept.

Troy Bramston, the contemporary biographer of several more recent prime ministers, regards Curtin as our greatest ever. People would stop to clap him in the streets, said Bramston, seeing in him:

> the dedication, determination, resilience, humanity and vision that are essential qualities in great leaders. They understood Curtin was a melancholy man, prone to self doubt, tortured by inner demons, and sometimes bed-ridden with depression ... This 'black dog', which also afflicted Churchill, gave Curtin an empathy and compassion to which Australians responded. Perhaps they could see elements of themselves in him.[60]

Ben Chifley was elected leader of the federal Labor Party and took office as prime minister. In a brief statement, he promised 'to follow in the footsteps of John Curtin', and to 'carry out the ideals and policies for which he stood'.[61]

13

The Liberal Revival

By the war's end, we'd built up our strength as a nation and were eager to make the most of the opportunities of peace. For a time, the Chifley government seemed successfully to be building a land fit for heroes to live in. Eventually, despite the spirit of shared sacrifice that the war had engendered, people started to tire of ongoing rationing and restrictions. As well, even inside the Labor Party, concern was growing about the communist influence in the union movement. Bank nationalisation gave a revitalised Menzies, leading a rebuilt Liberal Party, the political opportunity he was seeking to liberate Australia from the mindset of wartime control.

§

Wartime life had been dominated by government in ways unprecedented since the early convict era. At the height of the conflict, defence accounted for more than two-thirds of government expenditure, and more than one-third of gross domestic product. To fund the war effort, tax revenue doubled as a percentage of the economy, from 11 per cent to 22 per cent.[1]

Even more impactful were the restrictions on daily life. Basic items like clothing, tea and sugar were subject to coupon rationing. Interstate travel was limited and the use of petrol restricted. To divert labour and capital towards the war effort, the production of certain manufactures was simply outlawed. To build a dishwasher in either Victoria or South Australia was to break the law. Wool was stockpiled, meat was exported to feed Allied troops and wheat was bought up by the government as stock feed.[2] Workers in essential industries could not leave their employment. Advertising was heavily restricted. An infamous ban on Christmas ads at the end of 1942 forced the government to clarify that 'no action would be taken to prevent the appearance of "Father Christmas" at shops to hand toys to children'.[3]

Australians generally took these measures in their stride and, for the most part, dutifully abided by them. In a show of patriotic sacrifice, citizens often voluntarily gave up purchases and activities that weren't forbidden.

But the public sector was never going to revert quickly to its pre-war size. Too much had changed; too much power had been centralised. State governments had been stripped of their income-tax base. War mobilisation had rid the country of its unemployment – officials would even raid hotels and other public places to pressure able-bodied men into enlistment or wartime work in 'essential industries' – and a new fear arose, that too quick a transition back to a civilian economy would throw men and women out of work and lead to another depression. Still, a 1944 referendum to extend the Commonwealth's wartime powers for another five years was a step too far for most Australians.

Because its wartime planning had largely worked, reasoned the Labor government, systematic planning should extend to peace. The director-general of post-war reconstruction, H.C. (Nugget) Coombs, championed this new orthodoxy. Full employment became a permanent objective of government policy. State-sponsored development became the key to nation

Like most Australians, Menzies was thinking about the future. After losing office, he had briefly considered leaving public life altogether – until Pearl Harbor was attacked. From early 1942, he delivered weekly radio broadcasts every Friday on politics and on national issues. His most influential talk, on 22 May, was his appeal to 'the forgotten class – the middle class – whose people are constantly in danger of being ground between the upper and nether millstones of the false class war'.[4]

By the forgotten class, or *The Forgotten People*, as his 1943 book of collected talks was titled, Menzies meant both a political constituency and an ideal, typically embodied in mid-range salary earners, who were independent and values-driven, patriotic and civic-minded. Politicians might take them for granted but they were the ones that made democracy work. They volunteered for their communities, helped their neighbours, supported their friends and raised and educated their families. Menzies said:

> I do not believe that the real life of this nation is to be
> found either in great luxury hotels and petty gossip of
> so-called fashionable suburbs, or in the officialdom of the
> organised masses. It is to be found in the homes of people
> who are nameless and unadvertised, and who, whatever
> their individual religious conviction or dogma, see in their
> children their greatest contribution to the immortality of
> their race.[5]

These Australians had been let down, he said, by a 'political tradition of pandering and promises'.[6] The effect was to corrode the moral self-reliance and individualism that made Australia thrive.[7] Menzies' 'Forgotten People' theme was an attack on class-based politics that, in his view, had fundamentally misread Australian life and democracy. Talk of 'labour' and 'capital' (like today's identity preoccupations) missed something essential and shared about the national experience.

After regaining the federal leadership of the UAP after the 1943 election, Menzies called a unity conference for October 1944 to bring together all the liberal-leaning groups under a single banner, with an inclusive set of values and a more enduring organisational structure. The organisations in attendance included the Australian Women's National League, the newly formed Institute of Public Affairs, constitutional leagues, the UAP and Country Party organisations, federal MPs and state parliamentary leaders. In his address to the conference, Menzies called for 'a revival of liberal thought'.[8] The conference resolved to form the Liberal Party of Australia. It was to be a proper federal party, with state divisions backed by a federal constitution, with a federal council and executive – as distinct from the old UAP that had none of these features.

One of Menzies' best expositions of political philosophy was his main election speech of 1946. He began by asking Australians to consider the election as a contest over fundamental principles, of how the nation should be reconstructed in the wake of the war. He declared 'that the war was fought to overthrow the authoritarian state; that there can be no national progress except through the efforts of the individual; that life should be free and its horizons wide; and that, in a famous phrase "the ship exists for the sake of the passengers"'.[9] He promised a 20 per cent income tax cut and a revived contributory scheme for social insurance. He called for greater home ownership, large-scale migration, a closer integration of Commonwealth countries within the British Empire and a closer relationship with the United States. It was 'one of the greatest speeches of his career', *The Argus* reported.[10]

In 1946, Australians mostly knew Menzies as the man who had quit the prime ministership during the war. He returned to the federal leadership by qualification and intellect, but still had to prove his worth. 'You can't win with Menzies' was a critical refrain from his detractors. The early years of the Liberal Party's existence were precarious. State branches were slow to develop – in the case of Queensland, the centre-right Queensland People's Party retained its name until 1948.[11] The 1946 federal election, fought in the afterglow of a victorious war, was a huge disappointment to Menzies, whose party gained a 4 per cent swing but secured just 29 seats to Labor's 43 in the House of Representatives.

* * *

The 1946 election was the first time Labor had won two national elections in a row. Australians had faith in Ben Chifley; 'the plain man', *The Age* called him, an image the prime minister enjoyed and cultivated.[12] He was tall and slightly stooped, walked casually and spoke with a flat, gravelly voice. His suits were described by the *Woman's Weekly* as 'blue, single-breasted, usually a bit shabby', and his habits were frugal.[13] When in Canberra he stayed at the Hotel Kurrajong rather than The Lodge, and would happily walk around the corridors in his pyjamas, sometimes with a cardigan if the weather required it.[14] He had never left Australia before becoming prime minister and had little interest in doing so. 'No Prime Minister in my experience lived as simply as Ben Chifley,' said his driver, Ray Tracy.[15]

Chifley was a committed Labor man, but no class-war warrior. He could be calculating and shrewd when he needed to be. He was a disciplined treasurer under Curtin, graciously hearing out demands for more spending before declining with effusive charm. Although he believed in an interventionist government, he detested communism and radicalism of the more disruptive kind. He was prepared to listen as more excitable members fulminated over post-war international finance ('a world dictatorship of private finance more complete and terrible than any Hitlerite dream,' his fanatical colleague Eddie Ward said of the Bretton Woods Agreement, which was to peg national currencies to the US dollar that was convertible to gold at USD35 an ounce), but had the authority to convince caucus to make sensible decisions and to submit Australia to the emerging post-war consensus.[16]

The government's 1945 White Paper on Full Employment was its most important economic statement. Following Keynes, it recommended that private spending had to be stimulated by government spending if total demand in the economy was less than the level needed to keep unemployment sustainably low.

The new Keynesian consensus had the leading government 'mandarins' persuaded that they could successfully manage the whole economy with better data, modelling and the right policy levers. At least as important for Australia's post-war prosperity was the absence of big global shocks for the first time since the 1890s, plus rapid technological advancement. Peace was the best stimulant of all. That was the gift of the Allied victory, the revival of freedom and democracy thanks to the leadership of Churchill and Roosevelt.

* * *

Federal and state governments had to reconcile ambitious post-war agendas with the constraints of an economy bursting at the seams. Australians were itching to enjoy the improved standard of living that peace and opportunity promised. Employers wanted staff, unions wanted higher wages, and consumers wanted the goods and services they had been deprived of during two wars and the Great Depression.

building. The most ambitious project was the Snowy Mountains Hydro-Electric Scheme, which would take a quarter of a century to complete. National development needed workers, so Australia embarked on its great post-war migration boom.

* * *

Liberalism eventually revived in Australia as a reaction against the regimentation and socialisation of everyday life. The interwar years had been a comparatively bleak period. Some Australians yearned for the older world that had been destroyed by the Great War; others yearned for something quite different but were unsure of exactly what. The Allied victory engendered a sense that, whatever came, it would be an improvement on the past.

Naturally, intellectuals argued over what it all meant. John Maynard Keynes claimed that a more managed economy would save liberalism. Friedrich Hayek warned that too managed an economy might lead down the *Road to Serfdom* – the title of his most influential work. The war had already given Australians a taste of what a 'road to serfdom' might look like, if wartime regulation and bureaucracy were to continue.

The United Australia Party, although only officially dissolved in 1945, had really died with Joseph Lyons. By 1943, it retained only 12 seats in the federal parliament. The trend was similar in the two largest states. In 1941, in New South Wales, the number of UAP seats plunged from 37 to 14 following a period of internal strife; in Victoria, the UAP declined to third-party status against a Country Party buttressed by favourable electoral distribution rules. Labor dominated Queensland and had held office in Western Australia from 1933 and in Tasmania from 1937. Only in South Australia were the liberal forces strong under Thomas Playford's Liberal and Country League government.

Labour shortages across the country invited trade unions to exploit their increased bargaining power. The Australian Council of Trade Unions wanted an end to wage-pegging, an increase in the basic wage (which had eventually flowed from the Harvester judgment) and a 40-hour week. In total, 5.5 million working days were lost to strikes between 1945 and 1947, the most since the end of the Great War.

Australia's 'industrial anarchy' during the war years was an international embarrassment. On the waterfront, strikes had compelled troops to do the work of stevedores. Sometimes it was just shirking, as when labourers refused to work in the rain or handle refrigerated food and many other types of cargo. Sometimes, it was political, as many of these strikes were led by communist controlled unions. The Nazi invasion of the Soviet Union boosted Communist Party membership, which peaked at about 23,000 in 1944.[17] As well, by 1945, unions with some 480,000 members were broadly supportive of the CPA cause.[18] As a source of industrial strife, the CPA's role was obvious – more nefarious were the rumours, later to be confirmed by intercepted Soviet cables, that some individuals were involved in espionage and treason on behalf of the Soviets.

It was in this febrile environment that a group of Catholic anti-communists in Labor circles started the Catholic Social Studies Movement, later described simply as The Movement, initially to promote Catholic social action, but in practice largely to combat the communist infiltration of trade unions. The goal was to match the effectiveness of communist organisation and to beat them at their own game. The fight, said its moving spirit, B.A. Santamaria, 'should be essentially one of cadre against cadre, cell against cell, fraction against fraction'.[19] Santamaria had first come to prominence during the famous Spanish Civil War debate at Melbourne University in 1937, when he'd thunderously carried the Catholics in the thousand-strong crowd, declaring: 'when the bullets of the atheists struck the statue of Christ outside the cathedral in Madrid, for some that was just lead striking brass, but for me those bullets were piercing the heart of Christ the King'.[20] The Movement fed committed individuals into the so-called Industrial Groups that were sanctioned by the Labor Party – combinations of Labor members and unionists opposed to communist influence, starting first in New South Wales in 1945 – to run candidates in union elections.

* * *

An obvious cure for labour shortages was simply to bring more people to Australia. Another benefit of high immigration was greater national security. '[W]e cannot expect to hold Australia indefinitely with such a small population' was how the Department of the Interior described it.[21] 'Populate or perish' was the mantra of the 1940s and early 1950s.

The newly established Department of Immigration, led by Australia's first immigration minister, Arthur Calwell, had done the calculations: Australia would need about 70,000 migrants per year for industry to develop and the country to thrive. Calwell promised that nine in ten of these migrants would be British, the famous 'ten-pound Poms'. An early agreement with Britain provided free passage to ex-service families and partly subsidised passage for others. By late 1947, the government had received immigration applications from about 400,000 Britons.[22]

But to meet its population targets, Australia began to look beyond Britain. In 1947, Calwell left for Europe on a 12-week tour across almost two dozen countries in search of prospective Australians. He found many of them in refugee camps, displaced and scattered by the war, and agreed to take in some

4000 in 1947, and 12,000 in 1948. The first of them arrived in Fremantle on 28 November 1947. Aboard the *General Heintzelman* were 844 persons from Estonia, Latvia and Lithuania – mainly single men (who were normally both anti-Nazi and anti-communist) selected from camps in Germany to represent 'the pick of the bunch', blonde-haired and 'Australian-looking' people whom locals could comfortably welcome.

Calwell asked the Labor movement to set aside its traditional hostility to migrant competitors in the job market and requested that these arrivals be referred to as 'New Australians'. 'These people – let me put it bluntly – are coming to help us as well as coming to share our good fortune,' he said.[23] In loosening one policy valve, he tightened another: few ministers were as single-minded in enforcing the White Australia Policy. 'Two Wongs don't make a white,' he once quipped. By stressing that the Australian identity was secure, Calwell gained public acceptance for a migration program of unprecedented size. After 1949, this was enthusiastically continued by Menzies. By 1953 around 170,700 displaced persons had arrived. No other nation outside Europe, except the United States, took as many.

Today, Australians take for granted living in a multi-ethnic society, something that would have been unthinkable almost everywhere a century ago and that is still strange in many countries. Pre-war, except for a Britain that could hardly exclude the subjects of its global empire, almost every country practised racially exclusionary or discriminatory immigration policies. Post-war, the liberal democracies (especially the English-speaking ones) started successfully to integrate people of different backgrounds and cultures, reasoning that a free society that prioritises human dignity, protects free speech and freedom of religion, and supports the rule of law gives fewer grounds for immigrants to feel resentful and for existing citizens to feel insecure.

* * *

After its successful participation in two global wars, Australians felt that their country had well and truly earned its place on the world's councils. Curtin had despatched his deputy prime minister, Frank Forde, and the minister for external affairs, H.V. Evatt, to attend the formation conference of the United Nations in San Francisco. Curtin asked Forde to lead the delegation in preference to Evatt, a man he did not trust and hoped to keep in check. Evatt, for his part – a minister of notable intellect with grand ideas of his own – had no intention of playing second fiddle.

Herbert Vere 'Doc' Evatt is one of the more mercurial characters in the Australian story. He had an almost manic ambition, which was obvious to everyone but himself. Yet he was also an accomplished scholar, barrister, judge and politician. He was educated and intellectual; a combination that would have worked better for him as a Labor man some decades later. He had an 'amazing flair for doing very good work in the very worst possible way', the journalist Harold Cox remembered.[24] He belittled colleagues, interfered in their work and conspired against them.

Yet his forceful nature worked well at the United Nations, an environment full of egos. He was a tough negotiator, championing the status of smaller nations and widening the authority of the General Assembly to make small nations' voices better heard. He was an active participant in shaping the UN Charter and his energy did much to enhance the status of Australia. In 1948, he was elected president of the General Assembly, presiding in May 1949 over the admission of the State of Israel. Evatt supported Israel's creation, against US and British doubts. To Evatt, this was a progressive cause that he regarded as his greatest achievement as president.

* * *

In August 1947, Australian politics was upended by Chifley's decision to nationalise Australia's banking system. The Labor government had already restructured the Commonwealth Bank to take on the central bank responsibility of maintaining a stable currency and full employment. When the requirement that municipal authorities transact exclusively with the Commonwealth Bank was struck down by the High Court, Chifley resolved to fight back. For all his genial moderation, like so many Labor men who'd lived through the foreclosures and the hardships of the Depression, Chifley harboured an almost visceral animus against the banks.

Although bank nationalisation had been a Labor aspiration for decades, the immediate public reaction to Chifley's brief announcement, delivered in a 42-word press statement, was overwhelmingly hostile. A Gallup poll taken a month later found almost two-thirds of Australians opposed to it.[25] The banks mobilised quickly. Advertisements appeared in newspapers, thousands of doors were knocked by anxious bank clerks, while their wives and mothers joined the Australian Women's Movement Against Socialisation.

Here was the contest of principles that Menzies had wanted in 1946. It energised the new Liberal Party, bringing in members and funds on a scale that dwarfed its first two years. Menzies gave some of his most impressive and impassioned speeches, attacking the proposal as 'the most spectacular move towards complete socialisation ever made in any English-speaking country'.[26] The campaign quashed any doubts over Menzies' leadership credentials. 'I have heard the giants of the past,' said Billy Hughes – who, at 85, was old enough to have heard Henry Parkes, Alfred Deakin and George Reid in the 1890s – 'but Mr Menzies has out-topped them all.'[27]

Controlling both houses of parliament, the Chifley government hurried the nationalisation legislation through, and the Bill became law on 27 November 1947. Inevitably, the *Banking Act* was challenged in the High Court. Evatt insisted on being lead counsel for the government but performed poorly as he'd been out of the law since 1940. A majority of the bench found against the government. An appeal to the Privy Council, again led by an increasingly exhausted and distracted Evatt (who was simultaneously engaged in his UN work), also failed.

* * *

On 26 January 1949, following the creation of a separate Canadian citizenship in 1946 as part of a post-war loosening of imperial bonds, the *Australian Citizenship Act* came into force. Arthur Calwell said that a distinct Australian citizenship would symbolise 'our own pride in Australia' and that the new migrants he was seeking would be taught that 'they are fortunate to be British and even more fortunate to be Australian'. Menzies' Liberals opposed the legislation as a 'sinister plot to liquidate the Empire'. Prior to this, everyone born in Australia or granted residency rights here was simply a 'British subject', even though, under the White Australia policy, some British subjects could be excluded from Australia.

Without much fanfare, on Australia Day 1949, every British subject who had been born, naturalised or resident in Australia for five years acquired Australian citizenship. Until the *Passports Amendment Act 1984*, Australian passport-holders were described as 'British subject, Australian citizen'. British subjects resident in Australia could still go on the electoral roll regardless of whether they were also Australian citizens. Australians remained formally British subjects until the *Australian Citizenship Amendment Act* came into force in 1984. From this time, only Australian citizens could go on the roll and Britons coming after 1984 had to be naturalised in order to vote. Even now, there are some lingering vestiges of Australians' former status as British subjects, such as the entitlement of Australians resident in the UK to vote in British elections.

* * *

On 17 June 1949, the communist-led Miners' Federation agreed to a general strike on the coalfields. Because Australia ran on coal, households and businesses, especially in Sydney, found themselves subject to extreme rationing. Railways were shut down, gas was restricted to an hour's daily use and food shortages re-emerged. The government responded with an iron fist. Strike funds were frozen and union leaders arrested. Troops were sent to work the open-cut mines as strike breakers.

Chifley was deeply unnerved by the communist influence over this strike. A social democrat, he did not want the government hostage to outside forces, be it banks or unions. Speaking to a Labor gathering in October 1949, he declared that the fate of 'democracy itself' was on the line.[28]

The reintroduction of petrol rationing, late in 1949, to safeguard the pound and protect the sterling bloc, infuriated Australians, who had taken to the road like never before. The number of motor vehicles had increased from 800,000 to 1.25 million in just three years.[29] A new generation of Liberal activists capitalised on this sentiment and offered an energetic alternative. With the House of Representatives expanding from 74 to 121 seats to reflect a growing population, the Liberal and Country Party coalition were victorious in the 1949 election, securing 74 to Labor's 47 seats.

* * *

For the best part of a decade until the mid-1950s, the biggest issue in Australian politics was 'how to deal with communism'. Since those years, as more security intelligence has come to light, it is clear that Menzies had good reason to take the threat seriously. It certainly helps to explain his bid to ban the Communist Party in Australia.

As decrypted Soviet cables (the Venona decrypts, revealed in 1995) have shown, a small number of Australian citizens were spying for Russia, including some employed by the Department of External Affairs. The so-called Venona material, which includes more than 200 Moscow–Canberra cables, shows that a Soviet spy ring had been established in Australia from the early 1940s. Alarm at this penetration meant that between 1948 and 1950 Australia was cut off from receiving British and American signal intelligence.

By this time, the Cold War had divided much of the world into hostile blocs. The Truman Doctrine had emerged in March 1947 as a pledge to stop communist expansion. A few months later, the Communist Information Bureau (or Cominform) was established to co-ordinate the European communist parties. After Stalin unsuccessfully sought to expel the Allies from Berlin in 1948, the USA, Britain and their European partners formed the North Atlantic Treaty Organisation, declaring that an attack on one NATO country would be treated as an attack on all. As the Soviet grip on Eastern Europe tightened, the Australian Communist Party, following the Cominform, ratcheted up its hostility to liberal democracy.

Out of fear of splitting his party, Chifley was initially cautious in taking up the fight against communism; but in March 1949, the government established the Australian Security Intelligence Organisation (ASIO) to identify and monitor domestic security threats. It 'mark[ed] a change in government attitude that would have been inconceivable three years ago,' said Australia's high commissioner in London.[30]

Although the Country Party had long advocated a ban on the Communist Party of Australia, Menzies had argued as recently as 1946 that communism should be 'met by strength of argument ... by educating the people against its false doctrines'.[31] In March 1948, after another successful communist coup in Eastern Europe, Menzies changed his position on the grounds that the Communist Party could act as a fifth column in the event of war. 'We have seen the wheel turn in the past two years,' he told a party rally. 'We have seen disappear into the Soviet maw the Baltic provinces, the eastern half of Poland, the eastern section of Germany and a slab of the Danubian provinces.'[32]

Once in government, Menzies introduced the Communist Party Dissolution Bill in April 1950, 'for the safety and defence of Australia'. The proposed law would outlaw and dissolve the Communist Party, outlaw affiliated organisations and prohibit declared communists from holding office in government or trade unions. Controversially, the onus of proof was reversed on anyone declared to be a communist. 'We are not at peace today, except in the technical sense,' Menzies said.[33] A Gallup poll conducted the following month found 82 per cent supported the ban.[34]

Parliamentary debate spread across 39 days. Labor's deep internal divisions were only resolved when WA MP Tom Burke persuaded his state's branch to 'flip' its position on the federal executive, providing a majority in favour of the Bill.

Yet when ten communist-led unions challenged the legality of the *Dissolution Act*, Evatt agreed to represent one of them, the Waterside Workers' Federation, and successfully convinced the High Court, on 6 March 1951, to declare the legislation invalid because it relied on the defence power outside of wartime. With public opinion still in favour of a ban, Menzies triggered a double dissolution. On 28 April 1951, the government picked up six Senate seats to hold a majority in both houses. In July, Menzies announced that the issue would go to a referendum.

* * *

The invasion of South Korea by communist North Korea on 25 June 1950 raised global tensions. Menzies told the British high commissioner in Canberra that '[If] the United Nations does not make a stand on Korea the damage to the prestige of the democracies would be incalculable.'[35] The government quickly committed two naval vessels and a fighter squadron to support US forces operating under a United Nations mandate. Although Australian forces ultimately fought as part of the British Commonwealth Division under British command, along with Canadian, New Zealand and some Indian troops, this was the first time that Australia had not waited for Britain's lead before committing armed forces.

The moral struggle of the Cold War pitted democratic freedom against communist authoritarianism. For the young Catholic intellectual B.A. Santamaria, the Cold War had a spiritual dimension, too, after the Spanish Civil War's leftist violence against the Church. Similarly, Melbourne's Archbishop Daniel Mannix was disturbed by the implications of atheistic communism. Like Santamaria, he pondered the persecutions, first in Spain and later in eastern Europe, and what they could mean for Australia's future. Should communism prevail, Mannix feared for the survival of Christianity; nor could he understand 'the soft peddling upon anti-religion' by Australia's intellectual class.[36]

Nonetheless, both Santamaria and Mannix cautioned Menzies against an outright ban on the Communist Party.

Santamaria thought it could harm the ongoing effort of electing 'Groupers' to union leadership. Some of the biggest unions in the country had already voted out their communist leadership: the Ironworkers Federation, the Clerks Union and the Amalgamated Engineering Union. A new law providing for secret ballots had accelerated these gains. Writing to Mannix at the end of 1952, hinting at a wider ambition, Santamaria envisioned that within five to six years, the Groupers should 'be able to completely transform the leadership of the Labor Government'.[37]

* * *

Six weeks after the 1951 federal election, while staying at the Hotel Kurrajong on the evening of a parliamentary jubilee ball, Ben Chifley died from a heart attack. A distressed Menzies announced the news to the revellers and the evening ended abruptly. Chifley was, as Menzies said that evening, 'a fine Australian'. He was a straightforward politician, a democrat and a patriot. His successor was more complicated. Without much enthusiasm, the federal Labor caucus elected H.V. Evatt to be their leader.

At first, the political climate suited Evatt. Having successfully fought the communist ban in the courts, he revelled in leading the No campaign in the referendum and welcomed the debate as a matter of principle. Indeed, the Opposition leader's appeals to 'British justice', his declarations in favour of 'democracy and freedom', his warnings against the totalitarian implications of the ban and 'the gradual elimination of all forms of opposition' uncannily tracked the arguments Menzies had earlier marshalled against bank nationalisation.

What had started as a referendum that four in five voters intended to support turned into a cliff-hanger. The referendum ultimately failed by just 50,000 votes, with 2,317,000 supporting the ban and 2,370,000 against.

* * *

This early referendum success turned out to be the high point of Evatt's leadership. At that stage, everything was in his favour: an economy burdened by an inflationary surge, 22.5 per cent in 1952, due to the Korean War wool boom; a 'horror budget' to clamp down on prices with across-the-board tax increases; and two embarrassing by-election defeats for the government later that year.

By the end of 1953, though, inflationary pressures began to ease, strong employment growth resumed and the government was able to deliver a favourable budget, with tax cuts and optimistic economic forecasts. The political landscape changed again when, on 13 April 1954, Menzies informed a stunned parliament that the third secretary of the Soviet Embassy, Vladimir Petrov, had defected to Australia, providing incriminating secret documents of Soviet activities that a Royal Commission was subsequently established to investigate. Evatt was not present for the announcement, having left Canberra in the afternoon for Sydney to attend a dinner for his former school. This awkward timing planted seeds of conspiracy in Evatt's mind, which would eventually grow to consume him.

Unaware of her husband's decision, Petrov's wife, Evdokia, had been kept in a single room in the Soviet Embassy for 13 days to prevent her from also defecting. Now Moscow wanted her back. Taken to the airport in Sydney, she was gripped by two burly Soviet escorts and walked across the tarmac amid a hysterical crowd of onlookers who had broken through police barriers. A photograph of the moment has since become legendary: Evdokia – obviously distressed – sandwiched between two grim-looking Soviet agents. When the plane landed at Darwin to refuel, Australian security officials, on Menzies' instructions, intervened to take her off the plane and she was granted asylum.

The timing of the Petrov Affair so close to an election hurt Labor. Evatt believed that the whole episode was a stitch-up, although the evidence strongly suggests otherwise. By then, the government had much in its favour: a recovering economy, a savvy and strong leader in Menzies, and an increasingly erratic Opposition leader in Evatt, whose extravagant election promises had the sniff of desperation. Labor won the popular vote but not a lower house majority, with the Liberals securing 64 seats to Labor's 57.

The Petrov Affair had not yet played itself out. After the election, the Royal Commission revealed that two secret documents implicated some of Evatt's own staff as Soviet Embassy sources. Evatt was convinced they were forgeries. He obtained the right to appear before the Commission to defend those loyal to him. His party, meanwhile, was fracturing. Some thought Evatt communism's 'greatest asset'. The Opposition leader had barely consulted anyone before agreeing to appear before the Commission, and more and more of his time was spent combing through the mountains of evidence in search of conspiracy. The press began to speculate about his mental health.[38]

There were other causes for his paranoia. He'd had enough of the so-called Groupers, convinced that they had undermined his election campaign in Victoria. He decided to bring the conflict out in the open, speaking of 'disloyal and subversive actions' of a minority. He named Santamaria's *News Weekly* magazine as complicit. 'I am bringing this matter before the next meeting of the Federal executive with a view to take appropriate action,' he said.[39] It was a statement 'widely considered to be the match that triggered the explosion' of a Labor split, in the words of his biographer, John Murphy.[40]

At its next meeting, federal caucus was in uproar. An investigation into the Victorian Labor Party by the Federal Executive resolved to appoint a new state executive, effectively splitting Victorian Labor firmly in two, pitting the anti-communists against the Evatt forces. At Labor's Federal Conference in March 1955, the old executive was barred from entering the hall. In April, the new Victorian executive expelled over a hundred members from the party, including federal and state parliamentarians. Days later, the Grouper members of state parliament switched their support to the Opposition leader, Henry Bolte, in a vote of no confidence, bringing down the Cain Labor government. With no hope of winning the state election, the MPs of the newly established Labor Party (Anti-Communist), which was soon to become the Democratic Labor Party, called on their supporters to preference Liberals ahead of Labor. Bolte's Liberals secured a 13-seat majority, the first of six consecutive election victories over the next 17 years.

In September 1955, Menzies tabled the final report of the Royal Commission. Its conclusions were largely the same as those of the interim report: that the documents, and the Petrovs, were reliable. Nonetheless, no prosecutions were recommended. Evatt rose in parliament to speak. His speech was long, rambling and angry. He continued to claim conspiracy. Incredibly, he revealed that he had personally written to Molotov, the foreign minister of the Soviet Union, to confirm whether the documents were forgeries. Molotov's representative confirmed that they were. 'I attach great importance to this letter,' Evatt said, 'which shows clearly that the Soviet Government denies the authenticity of the Petrov documents.'[41] The government benches broke into laughter.

According to one journalist present, Menzies turned to his colleagues and said, 'The Lord has delivered him into my hands.'[42] This was the end of Evatt, who staggered on ghostlike until February 1960, when he left parliament to become chief justice of New South Wales. Menzies called a snap election for December 1955. The Coalition's majority rose from seven to 28. Fourteen years after his first term as prime minister was brought to a humiliating end, Menzies stood as 'unmistakably and unchallengeably the most powerful figure on the non-Labor side of politics'.[43]

14

The Age of Menzies

Far from being a time of stagnation, the Menzies era was one of vast change. By its close, our principal military partner was the United States of America, our principal trading partner was Japan and the White Australia policy was all but dead. The Commonwealth's role grew, universities expanded and Aboriginal people began to enter the mainstream of Australian life by securing for themselves greater political rights. In 1954, the first ever royal tour by a reigning monarch was a spectacle that arrested the nation for weeks. By the late 1960s, royal visits had become almost routine events. Although much had changed, Menzies made it seem like nothing that really mattered had. That was his unique political skill. For all the economic, political and social transformations of the two post-war decades, Australia remained a tranquil and prosperous society where more people than ever had a 'fair go' and, in turn, were encouraged to 'have a go'. By and large, Australians had never had it so good.

§

The Menzies era is often dismissed as a 'simpler time': a period of stability and continuity when Australians could get on with life without the turmoil of the previous decades. The suburb, the family home, the white picket fence – all have become emblematic

281

of a 1950s in which family members would enjoy their domestic rituals: sitting around the radio, tending to the garden, visiting the local picture theatre on a Saturday afternoon or evening, then a church service the following day. In his *Unreliable Memoirs*, Clive James gives a sense of this life. His mother was a war widow who lived on a pension and earned a little extra by knitting babies' dresses. The Jameses lived in a modest weatherboard house in the Sydney suburb of Kogarah. For young Clive, days were spent mostly outside: running, swimming or on expeditions to the Sydney Domain. The impression is of an uncomplicated and innocent existence, sometimes dull, but absent the turmoil of the years before and since.

While beguiling in its way, this misrepresents what was a time of immense change. When Menzies took office in 1949, the imperial connection remained strong. White Australia was bipartisan and popular. Indigenous Australians still endured legal and political discrimination. Australia's demography was overwhelmingly British. Our economic ties with Asia were minimal. When Menzies retired in 1966, the imperial project was over – the United States was Australia's most important ally; White Australia was ending – Australia was undergoing a very large non-British migration program; its prosperity was tied to the fortunes of East Asia; and Indigenous Australians were on the verge of achieving full legal and political equality.

This was not a social revolution from above. There was no wave of a legislative wand, although there were significant legislative moves. Mostly these changes came about because Australians' own attitudes were changing and governments were responding to them. Menzies himself well appreciated that governments and countries had to change and adapt. His practice was less to institute change than to manage it carefully with a liberal heart and a conservative disposition. This required a faith in people to act in accordance with their own judgment of what was best for them, which Menzies managed at least as successfully as any other prime minister.

Australians, Menzies once said, inherited the British mind. The British way, he said, is practical – its reasoning is inductive as it learns through observation and experience – and is less inclined to the political romanticism seen in the countries of continental Europe.[1] It was Menzies' ability to give the impression of enormous stability through a period of sweeping change that enabled him to become our longest serving national leader.

Although Menzies largely supported the Deakinite policies of protection and arbitration, he did not trust the state to solve all of Australia's problems. He did not grow up in the same political environment as the colonial liberals, where the great divide was between big state and small state 'liberalism'. Instead, he reflected a fusion of both, tempered by an instinctive personal conservatism and a deep aversion to anything verging towards communism. His mind was shaped by the 20th-century contest between socialism and individual liberty. In this sense he was more in tune with George Reid's 1906 'anti-socialist' sentiments. Similarly, his support for the 'Australian Settlement' was more pragmatic than ideological, and more open to revision if common sense required it. Menzies' generation of liberals was keen for Australia to emerge from the shadow of past crises, to be its former and best self.

* * *

White Australia was breaking down by the late 1950s. Menzies' first minister for immigration, Harold Holt, tried to avoid the term: 'We don't call it that,' he said to a Singapore reporter.[2] He preferred 'restricted immigration policy', an acknowledgment of the growing sensitivity towards a policy that discriminated against Australia's neighbours. After the war, many non-European refugees and servicemen were desperate to remain in Australia. One of the more widely publicised cases was of a Filipino ex-serviceman, Lorenzo Gamboa, who had served with the US military, been evacuated to Australia during the war, become an orderly at MacArthur's Brisbane headquarters, married an Australian woman and fathered two Australian-born children. Nonetheless, in 1945 he was one of many 'Asiatics' asked to leave by the Department of Immigration.

Holt thought the breaking up of families a step too far. In Opposition, he met with Calwell to discuss Gamboa's predicament.[3] Gamboa had fought on Australia's side and had proved that he would make a good citizen. When Holt took office at the end of 1949, he approved Gamboa's residency within weeks. He allowed more than 800 non-European wartime refugees to stay when their deportation had been all but underway. Though reluctant to spell it out, the 'merciless rigidity' of White Australia was changing.[4]

In 1956, the Menzies government approved changes to allow the naturalisation of permanently settled non-Europeans and to allow – at least in principle – the entry of highly qualified non-Europeans. Also in 1956, non-European war brides were granted citizenship rights; and, in 1958, the dictation test was finally abandoned, replaced with a permit system to be used at the discretion of the minister. These changes, though modest in scale, marked the beginning of the end of an immigration system on strictly racial lines.

As late as 1949, Calwell was arguing in the strongest of terms: '[W]e can have a white Australia, we can have a black Australia, but a mongrel Australia is impossible.'[5] Yet Australians were proving themselves bigger than that. In January 1957, Mrs Cherry Parker was the first non-European war bride to receive her naturalisation certificate. At the ceremony she was greeted with a 'particularly loud burst of applause'. The Melbourne *Age*, once an unapologetic proponent of White Australia, wrote simply, 'She's Australian now.'[6]

* * *

Post-war migration is one of Australia's great success stories. Almost two million migrants arrived between 1945 and 1965. Hundreds of thousands came from non-English-speaking countries. Even though this transformed Australia, it's now hard to imagine an Australia without them. It revealed that the vast majority of migrants came here not to change us, but to join us. Regardless of background, nearly all of them embraced what's been the Australian project since convict times: to enable people to better themselves and to leave their children with a better future than they had. As it's turned out, ours is a civic rather than an ethnic patriotism built on what are at least potentially universal values: personal freedom, the rule of law, democracy and a sense of the fair go.

At least for the first post-war decades, under Labor and Liberal governments, there was a clear expectation that migrants would embrace the Australian way of life. The character of Giovanni 'Nino' Culotta, an Italian immigrant in John O'Grady's comic novel *They're a Weird Mob* (1957), exemplified the ideal migrant's cheerful acceptance of Australian habits: the flat speech, the attitudes to work ('A bludger is the worst thing you can be in Australia') and the dry humour.[7] 'Mix with Australians, listen to them, work with them, and practise in secret the sentences you hear,' Nino advises. 'Until then, you will just be a "bloody New Australian".'[8]

Government policy enshrined 'assimilation', the notion that migrants would blend in to the point of becoming indistinguishable from the rest of the population. In practice, what this meant was an official insistence that migrants learn the language and adopt Australian values without necessarily losing their own culture. With less than 0.1 per cent of the immigration budget during the 1950s going to 'assimilation activities', this was hardly an exercise in social engineering or enforced conformity.[9] While British migrants mostly dispersed into the general community, many from continental Europe, particularly the large numbers of Italians and Greeks, tended to congregate together, often speaking their own languages at home and forming their own social clubs. It didn't stop them from participating in work and sport, and they were readily welcomed into the wider Australian community.

The real assimilation came from migrants' own desire to be part of Australia: to be accepted by their workmates, neighbours, community organisations and churches. Most importantly, their children – the dynamic link between past and future – received an Australian schooling and, over time, attended Australian universities. In inner cities, Greek and Italian communities could be found mingling with Irish-Catholic working-class and sometimes with Aboriginal families, too. Work, sport and fraternisation did more to aid integration than ministerial statements and government edicts.

Australia's greatest engineering project was also its greatest multi-ethnic project. The Snowy Hydro scheme, in its 25 years of construction, employed more than 100,000 people from across 32 countries. Some two-thirds of Snowy workers came from overseas, many recruited from Europe's refugee resettlement camps. The 'Snowy' was an enormous undertaking, featuring seven power stations, 16 dams and hundreds of miles of roads, train tracks, tunnels and aqueducts. It would not have been possible to complete such a complex engineering project – among the most complex in the world – without a migrant labour force. As the chief engineer, Sir William Hudson, told his workers: 'You aren't any longer Czechs or Germans, you are men of the Snowy.'[10]

Still, it was not always easy-going. In 1952, facing a lack of work and poor prospects, migrant workers rioted at the Bonegilla Migrant Camp, in northeast Victoria. A migrant family moving to the suburbs could face a range of reactions, from wariness to indifference to friendliness. Sometimes, old-world conflicts were brought into the country. This was hardly unique to Australia but it was still regarded as an unwelcome novelty, even in a country that had earlier felt the animosity between Irish and English. Eventually, the Commonwealth responded with a range of measures aimed at securing community support. An Adult Migration Education Scheme was established to break the language barrier; Australian Citizen Conventions brought together officials with new and old citizens to discuss immigration policy; and a Good Neighbour Movement co-ordinated hundreds of community organisations that assisted and welcomed migrants. Central to all of these was traditional Australian egalitarianism.

* * *

Not since the time of Governor Gipps and John Plunkett in the 1830s had the executive government given so much emphasis to Aboriginal equality as under the administration of Paul Hasluck, one of Menzies' best ministers. In a sharp break from past practice, Hasluck, as minister for territories, wanted to expunge the idea of race from the statute books. His general aim was to encourage Aboriginal Australians gradually to integrate and, if they so chose, to blend themselves into mainstream society. The actual practice varied between states and territories; Hasluck thought that labelling policy as 'assimilation' or 'integration' often hid the complexities and nuance of what he was trying to do.

Hasluck was not a typical politician. Unlike his colleague Harold Holt, he hated publicity and talking to the press. He had already published two works of major scholarship: first, his master's thesis, a lauded history of Aboriginal policy in Western Australia, which argued against 'protection and segregation', and in 1951 – the year he joined the ministry – the first of his two-volume contributions to the official history of Australia's involvement in the Second World War, *The Government and the People 1939–1941*.

Hasluck grew up in the small town of Collie in southwest Western Australia. His parents were Salvation Army officers and he extended this Christian sensibility to his own consideration of Australia's Indigenous history. From listening to old bush-workers' yarns, he'd developed a respect for Australia's ancient practices and an aversion to contemporary prejudice.[11] He joined the Australian Aborigines Amelioration Association and often wrote and lectured on Aboriginal issues.

As minister, Hasluck demanded 'a complete break from past approaches'.[12] 'I do not want a further report or statement of hopes, theories or principles,' he once wrote to his secretary.[13] 'I want proposals ... in the form of submissions which can be approved, rejected or amended without delay.' His most implacable hurdle was the federal Constitution: Aboriginal policy was the preserve of state governments. What he did control was the policy of the Northern Territory, which became his laboratory. He brought in money on a scale that dwarfed all previous efforts. From 1954–55 to 1962–63, Commonwealth Territory funding for Indigenous affairs rose from £166,000 to £1,200,000.[14] Old settlements and missions were renovated or rebuilt, schools expanded and health services improved. The number of Aboriginal children attending schools in the

Northern Territory rose from 900 to 2300 between 1951 and 1961.[15] For the first time, Aboriginal communities could receive the royalties from mining on their reserves.

Because Hasluck believed that race should not be a legal category, the Northern Territory's new welfare laws no longer referred to 'Aborigines'. The Native Affairs Branch became the Welfare Branch because, he held, language helped to drive thinking. Individuals deemed to be 'half-castes' were no longer required to carry identification to prove their legal status. 'Under the new system,' as Hasluck envisaged it, 'it is assumed that every British subject has citizenship as a birthright.'[16]

By the 1950s, most Australians believed in the fundamental equality of every person. A Gallup poll in 1954 found 90 per cent agreeing with the proposition that if 'an aborigine had the same kind of upbringing as you ... he could have learnt to do your work'.[17] In 1959, social security benefits were extended to most Aboriginal persons. They no longer required a certificate of exemption to receive pensions or maternity allowances. All specific references to Aboriginal people in the *Social Security Act* were finally removed in 1966. In 1962, the Menzies government passed the *Commonwealth Electoral Act*, granting all Aboriginal and Torres Strait Islanders the clear right to enrol and vote in federal elections, after a parliamentary select committee had travelled more than 30,000 miles (48,300 km) from city capitals to remote Australia, collecting submissions from hundreds of witnesses.[18]

The Aboriginal-Australian Fellowship was founded in 1956 by Pearl Gibbs and Faith Bandler. Gibbs had been the first Aboriginal woman to give a prepared radio address, in 1941, exposing the severe disadvantages faced by Aboriginal communities. In 1958, a number of Aboriginal rights groups formed the Federal Council for the Advancement of Aborigines and Torres Strait Islanders. Many of Hasluck's welfare changes reflected the recommendations of the Northern Territory's Half-Caste Association.

The most contentious aspect of Aboriginal welfare had long been the practice of child removal. Under Hasluck's reforms, 'partly coloured' children could only be taken if the child was neglected and the mother willingly consented.[19] Still, 'neglect' could be a highly subjective concept between two very different cultures. In some cases, the child's life might be in danger.[20] In other cases, a traditional way of living, with little of the material comforts associated with Western life, might be mistaken for neglect.

Not every official understood this; Warren Mundine – who chaired my Indigenous advisory council when I was PM – can remember his grandfather chasing a welfare officer away with a gun.[21] Even in official reports at the time, 'distressing scenes' of removals were widely reported.[22] In the Northern Territory, Hasluck wanted such decisions taken on purely welfare grounds, regardless of the child's ethnicity, and by the mid-1950s child removals in the Territory had notably declined.[23]

* * *

Meanwhile, Menzian liberalism was changing Australian foreign policy. Australia's engagement with Asia began long before 1972, when the People's Republic of China was formally recognised. Under Chifley, Australia was among the first to recognise Indonesian independence from the Dutch. Evatt launched the South Pacific Commission in February 1947, a regional forum to promote development. In a mere 17 months, between 1950 and 1951, Menzies' first external affairs minister, Percy Spender, established the three key pillars for Australia's post-war foreign policy: the Colombo Plan, the ANZUS Treaty and support for the Japanese Peace Treaty.

Evatt attacked the Japanese Peace Treaty as exposing Australia to the danger of being a Japanese colony within ten years.[24] Calwell called it obnoxious. Spender was indeed anxious that Japan might re-arm, but he was even more anxious for the post-war world to avoid the mistakes of Versailles in 1919. After the First World War, Billy Hughes had told his country that the German people must pay a heavy penalty for their crime. In a 1942 radio address on the topic, Menzies argued that if rank prejudice 'breeds into us a deep-seated and enduring spirit of hatred, then the peace when it comes will be merely the prelude to disaster and not an end of it'.[25] This was a fundamental shift in mindset that set apart the second half of the 20th century from the first.

Another big change was the gradual transformation of the British Empire that had nurtured and protected Australia for so long. Although Menzies hardly welcomed this transformation, he and his ministry adapted to it. The advent of the Cold War might have made the adjustment easier because it enabled us to be 'Western' rather than simply 'British'. In the new world of 'communist East' and 'anti-communist West', Australia was on the side of freedom. This explains the American and Australian conviction that Japan had to be brought into the Western fold. It also explains, in part, the Menzies government's cautious scepticism about the capacity of multilateral organisations, such as the United Nations, to resolve the big conflicts. Australia respected and supported these institutions but would not be directed by them.

Together with the Ceylon finance minister and the New Zealand external affairs minister, Spender proposed an aid program to help non-communist countries develop future leaders and to improve their economic infrastructure. While Papua New Guinea continued to receive the bulk of Australia's aid, most of the rest was distributed under the Colombo Plan.

Its most publicly recognised feature was accepting a sizeable number of Asian students into Australian universities. By the end of 1959, 2650 Asian students had arrived, contributing to the incremental opening-up of Australia to non-Europeans. Because many of them subsequently became leaders in their home countries, it was also an important aspect of Australia's 'soft power' in the region. Spender's successor, Richard Casey, thought it would do much 'to break down prejudices and misunderstandings on both sides'.[26]

Spender formalised the Australia–America alliance that had been at least 50 years in the making – since the advent of the Great White Fleet in 1908, and Americans first going into action in the Great War on 4 July 1918 at the Battle of Le Hamel under Monash's overall command. Curtin had famously 'looked to America' after Japan entered the Second World War. Yet it took the Menzies government to turn a growing strategic partnership into the formal alliance that has been the bedrock of our security ever since.

When the Korean War broke out, Spender told Menzies that Australia 'must scrape the bucket to see what we can give' as a way of proving to the Americans Australia's value as an ally.[27] He soon had his eyes on a formal defence agreement, arguing that Australia would not be satisfied with any peace treaty with Japan without assurances for its own security. In September 1951, the Australia, New Zealand and United States (ANZUS) Treaty was formally signed. Its operative article provides that in the event of 'an armed attack in the Pacific Area on any of the Parties' each 'would act to meet the common danger' in accordance with its constitutional processes.

Australia's regional engagement continued under Richard Casey. His first tour as external affairs minister was to Indonesia, Singapore, Vietnam, Thailand, the Philippines, Hong Kong and South Korea. Casey was personable and a good diplomat, who built up cordial relationships in the region and significantly increased Australia's diplomatic representation. The secretary of external affairs, Alan Watt, felt Casey knew the personalities and background of Southeast Asia 'probably ... better than any other Foreign Minister in the world'.[28]

This was the background to Australia's most important post-war trade agreement – the 1957 Australia–Japan Commerce Agreement. Three years earlier, Casey had argued before cabinet that Australia needed to adopt a more 'civilised' attitude to Japan, notwithstanding the hangover of fierce antagonism from the war, with RSL clubs as late as the 1960s seeking to ban Japanese vehicles from their car parks. The trade agreement itself was spearheaded by Menzies' trade minister and Country Party deputy leader, John McEwen. McEwen might have been a protectionist towards Australian manufacturing industries but his landmark trade agreement meant that, within a decade, Japan had overtaken the United Kingdom as Australia's biggest export market.

Further trade agreements were signed: with Malaya in 1958 and Indonesia in 1959. The Menzies government also quietly cultivated a growing bilateral trade relationship with the People's Republic of China, often against US advice. By 1963, about 40 per cent of Australia's wheat exports were to China.[29] Eleven new embassies or high commissions were established in Asia, and the Southeast Asia Treaty Organisation (SEATO), for a time, helped to shape Australia's defence priorities.[30]

* * *

In his 1964 book *The Lucky Country*, the writer Donald Horne bemoaned the propensity of Australians to find spiritual value in material things. This was a common complaint among intellectuals, who found little to admire in a culture that was, to them, provincial and humdrum; even though the post-material social and moral liberation they championed rested on an explosion of material progress.

Between 1949 and 1966, real GDP per capita rose by 2 per cent every year, all the more remarkable given the population increase of almost four million to nearly 11 million by 1966. Real average weekly earnings rose from a little more than $14 a week in 1949 to almost $21 in 1966, and real consumption expenditure doubled. Life expectancy increased from 66 to 71 years and infectious disease mortality rates declined from 45 per 100,000 to 10 per 100,000. The number of privately owned vehicles more than quadrupled and civil air travel boomed. Home ownership rose from 53 per cent to 71 per cent and Australia became the home-owning capital of the world.[31]

During the war, building materials and labour had been diverted away from construction towards military production. Rent controls had only reduced supply further.[32] In any event, Labor's focus was on social housing. '[We are] not concerned with making workers into little capitalists,' Labor's minister for postwar reconstruction, John Dedman, had said in parliament, a turn of phrase leapt on by Menzies.[33] The private home was central to the Menzian ideal of civic and democratic life. Homeowners not only had a stake in society but a private space unobstructed by the state. To own a home, Menzies said, is 'one of the best instincts in us'; it 'induces us to have one little piece of earth with a house and a garden which is ours; to which we can withdraw, in which we can be among our friends, into which no stranger may come against our will'.[34]

The 1950s turned out to be the decade of 'little capitalists'. Almost a third of housing construction that decade was owner-built and total housing stock almost doubled in the two decades after 1945. The most effective government policy was to not get in the way, to gradually remove most wartime restrictions and to encourage aspiration.

* * *

Since the founding of the Commonwealth in 1901, federal government power had slowly increased at the expense of the states. Australia's founding fathers had not anticipated this, yet as early as 1902, Deakin had said in parliament that the Constitution had left the states 'legally free but financially bound to the chariot wheels of the central government. Their need will be its opportunity.'

Menzies was a pragmatic federalist, comfortable with expanding Commonwealth power if circumstances required it. To the frustration of doctrinaire states' righters, Australians are rarely sentimental about their states and tend to support Commonwealth action whenever they feel that state governments are letting them down. Labor – though initially an opponent of federation – has turned out to be the more centralist party. Of the 13 constitutional changes that Labor governments put to the people prior to 1949, all involved the expansion of Commonwealth power and all but one failed.

Labor's one successful change was a 1946 proposal to expand Commonwealth power across a range of social services – a proposal that the Liberals supported and that turned out to enable Menzies' expansion of tertiary education through the Commonwealth Scholarship Scheme. For university buildings alone, £44 million was allocated across 1967–69, compared with less than £7 million in 1958–60.[35] In 1949, 32,453 students were enrolled in seven universities; by 1966, student numbers had increased to 83,320 in 12 universities, with more than 34,000 receiving some form of government assistance.

In 1962, Goulburn's Catholic bishop, John Cullinane, made the startling decision to close six schools in his diocese after the refusal of repeated requests for the NSW Education Department to fund the additional school lavatories that were required by law but that parish finances were in no position to meet. Across the country, population increases were straining Catholic school resources, especially as many Catholic schools were catering for the new migrant communities.

Previous governments had trodden carefully over 'state aid' to church schools to avoid arousing sectarian prejudice. Menzies had already allowed tax deductions for private school fees and donations. Even this incrementalism was enough for one Protestant minister to accuse the resolutely non-sectarian Menzies of 'flirting with the dictates of Rome'.[36] With state and federal Labor divided and population pressures making school funding a national issue heading into the 1963 federal election, Menzies promised 10,000 Commonwealth merit-based scholarships for secondary school students, plus an annual £5 million grant for science buildings and facilities for secondary schools, irrespective of the type of school, and an additional £5 million grant to state governments for building and equipping technical schools. This began a lasting change to the way the federation worked and represented a big funding boost for private schools.

* * *

Much of the change that Menzies presided over, he neither liked nor even tried to understand. He lamented the fading notion of 'duty' and was suspicious of the assertive demand for 'rights'. As a champion of middle-class morality, he did not like seeing those values trashed as the 'permissive' 1960s wore on.[37] The world had become more secular and less civic-minded.

Largely gone were the mutual associations and citizen groups once so central to the liberal identity in the first half of the century – although, as the 20th century became the 21st, civic-mindedness lingered on in organisations such as surf life-saving and the volunteer bush fire brigades. At the time of writing they have, respectively, some 20,000 and 70,000 trained and accredited volunteers in New South Wales alone. Fading, too, was the appreciation that modern Australia's deepest traditions, parliamentary democracy and freedom, were, after all, British traditions, embodied by the belief in the Crown as an enduring symbol of unity.

In his final election policy speech, Menzies spoke of 'a revolutionary change in the economic climate, in production, in the growth of trade with the world, in living standards, in social services, in the provisions for health, in the free choice of employment'.[38]

Yet 'there is no government department which can create these things,' he told a London audience in 1964.[39] In the same speech, he also said, 'We have learned that true rising standards of living are the product of progressive enterprise, the acceptance of risks, the encouragement of adventure, the prospect of rewards.'[40] Private citizens, he added:

> are under great temptations today, in the era of what has been called 'the welfare State'. It will be fatal if they come to regard the government as the only creator of all good things, as the perennially solvent guarantor of personal prosperity for all. For governments, and government departments, are administrative rather than creative, nor can any government guarantee or financial provision be any more effective than the sum capacity of the people, as producers and earners and taxpayers, to provide.[41]

Menzies was really the first and last prime minister to retire –
he did so in 1966 – at a time of his own choosing. To his
supporters, he had become the great constant of Australian
public life. To his critics, his deference to the monarchy and
imperial nostalgia were at odds with the emerging educated
class, impatient to forge an independent Australian identity.
Still, under his leadership, incrementally and without fuss,
Australia had become closer to America, closer to Asia, and
had diversified its trade and its sources of immigrants while
honouring its heritage.

15

Talkers and Doers

Rising levels of immigration and education are among the most powerful drivers of social change. For all the seeming stability of the Menzies era, the rapid increase in tertiary education and unprecedented levels of non-British migration were transforming Australian society. We were more white collar and less blue collar; more diverse and less traditional. A more 'progressive' Labor Party under Gough Whitlam better suited this new Australia than a Liberal government that was running out of puff after 23 years in office. Whitlam highlighted and revelled in the changes that Menzies had downplayed and often regretted: like multiculturalism replacing assimilation for migrants, self-determination replacing integration for Aboriginal people, and globalism replacing reliance on 'great and powerful friends'.[1] Whether Whitlam was a breath of much-needed fresh air or a deplorable aberration was a matter of perspective, but the progressive messiah ultimately fell victim to hubris and an electorate that thought his reach had well and truly exceeded his grasp.

§

In the 1950s, the expectation of most young Australians was that they would leave school at 15 and enter the workforce full-time. By the early 1970s, this had changed: Australians were staying longer at school and far more were going to universities. Of Australians aged 16 to 18, 16 per cent were at school in 1961; and 31 per cent were by 1974.[2] As well, education had become a national issue, not just the preserve of state governments. By the 1970s, white-collar jobs were growing as a proportion of the labour market and were increasingly being filled by university graduates, who were generally more cosmopolitan, more socially liberal, more internationalist in outlook and more sceptical of tradition than their less formally educated peers. An ANU survey of political attitudes, taken in 1967, found 62 per cent of tertiary-educated respondents thought the British Royal Family's relationship to Australia 'not very' important, compared with just 40 per cent of primary-educated respondents.[3] A positive impact of this new class was to make Australia less censorious, more tolerant and more open. A downside was to make life more technocratic and bureaucratic, and to make good jobs harder to get for people without degrees.

This did not go unnoticed at the time, although its social and political consequences were under-appreciated. Kim Beazley Snr famously remarked in 1970 that 'when I joined the Labor Party, it contained the cream of the working class. But as I look about me now, all I see are the dregs of the middle class.'[4] This may not have been an altogether fair comment but it identified a trend. That same year, the political scientist L.F. Crisp wondered whether the sons and daughters of the old working class, now living in the suburbs, might 'lose something of the old identity and neighbourly solidarity of the inner suburbs which so often expressed itself in a solid A.L.P. vote'.[5] No longer was income a reliable indicator of values or voting behaviour. Education was increasingly the key.

* * *

Arthur Calwell, the federal Labor leader from 1960 to 1967, was a man of high intelligence, with the ability to attend university but not the capacity to finance it. His mother died when he was young and his father, earning £3 a week as a policeman, had seven children to support. So, Calwell sat and passed the state public service examinations and began working as a clerk at the age of 16. When he entered federal politics, much of his vast knowledge was self-taught. In his private time, he studied Mandarin Chinese and read extensively in American history. To improve his vocabulary, he read the classics and studied Nesfield's *Manual of English Grammar and Composition*. He sometimes observed that most university students had never heard of Nesfield.[6]

Calwell was old Labor: working-class, socialist, fiercely anti-conscription and racially conscious. His attitudes had been shaped in countless party meetings as he moved through the ranks. He did not like those in the new Labor mould – more educated and progressive – 'long-hairs' and 'intellectuals' he called them, 'telling us we should re-think our philosophy, revise our ideas and alter our platform'.[7] He survived an assassination attempt in 1966 and generously forgave the young assailant, whose mother he met. His renowned empathy was the result of lived experience. His only son, Art, had died from leukaemia at the age of 11 and Calwell wore only black ties for the rest of his life.

Calwell's problem was that he wasn't winning. By the mid-1960s, 15 years out of office, his colleagues began to call themselves 'Her Majesty's Permanent Opposition'. A new approach was needed and it was delivered by Calwell's deputy, Gough Whitlam, who could not have been a greater contrast.

Whitlam was a representative of the 'talking' class rather than the 'working' one. He was one of the 'men and women with professional training', as he called them, who marked a growing constituency for Labor.[8] He was born in the leafy streets of Kew, Melbourne; his father, Fred, was a senior public servant. Gough studied law and classics at the University of Sydney and entered the RAAF in 1942. He became a barrister in 1947. He wasn't in any strict sense a tribal Labor man, a point Calwell would make in private. His father-in-law, who had once sought Liberal preselection, said of Gough that he had picked his party and his seat as 'the best bet'.[9] But Whitlam and Calwell were both equally embarrassed by the '36 faceless men' fiasco of 1963 – encapsulated in a photograph of Labor's parliamentary party leaders standing outside the Hotel Kingston waiting to be told by the federal conference whether they could support a new joint US–Australian communications facility in Western Australia.

After the November 1966 federal election delivered a landslide victory to Harold Holt and the Coalition, 82 seats to 41, Whitlam replaced Calwell as leader and set about giving the parliamentary leadership more say over Labor's official policy. In 1968, after the federal executive had refused to let the strongly anti-communist Tasmanian delegate Brian Harradine take the executive seat he'd been elected to, Whitlam abruptly spilled his leadership position. Recontesting, he defeated his opponent Jim Cairns by just six votes. This was Whitlam's crash or crash through style at work. The party began to reflect his more liberal views on immigration, education and Aboriginal policy.

* * *

As Lenin is reputed to have said, nothing happens for decades and then decades happen in weeks. The Vietnam War radicalised a large portion of young Australians, students especially, and became a defining generational moment. Whitlam's speechwriter Graham Freudenberg called Vietnam 'the name for an epoch'.[10] The war in Vietnam was a Menzies legacy that Australia's new prime minister, Harold Holt, intended to champion with vigour. Menzies had committed the first units in 1962 – a group of about 30 experts in jungle warfare and counter-insurgency, called the Australian Army Training Team. Then, in April 1965, Menzies sent an infantry battalion. By this stage the situation in the south was dire. What had started as a gradual infiltration of the south by the communist north had become a covert invasion that accelerated following the assassination of President Diem in November 1963.

There was nothing out of national character in committing troops to Vietnam. 'Forward defence' was the guiding principle of Australia's military commitments during the Menzies era, so that any enemy could be met 'as far away from our own soil as possible'.[11] After Korea, Australian troops had been sent to pre-independence Malaya to counter a communist insurgency. This was Australia's first battalion-sized combat force sent abroad in peacetime, forming part of what was known as the British Commonwealth Far East Strategic Reserve. In 1964, Australia made a small and cautious troop commitment towards combatting 'Confrontation' – Indonesia's armed infiltration into Borneo after the creation of the federation of Malaysia the previous year – which aroused the fury of Indonesia's President Sukarno.

Compulsory military service for home defence, first introduced in 1911, and suspended in 1929, was reactivated at the start of the Second World War; only to be suspended again at the end of the war, reactivated in 1951, and yet again suspended in 1959.

In November 1964, the government introduced a form of selective national service, or conscription by ballot – only this time for overseas service, too. Unless they could get a deferral – through going to university, for instance – all men whose

20th birthday fell on certain dates were called up for two years of full-time service in the regular army and then three years part-time service in the reserves. This preceded Australia's major commitment to Vietnam at a time when Indonesia was thought to be the main potential theatre of operations. Nineteen sixty-five was the year of Sukarno's self-proclaimed 'Year of Living Dangerously', with communist insurgencies in Malaysia, Thailand, Burma and the Philippines, as well as in Vietnam. Indonesia had the third largest communist party in the world and was lurching towards an alliance with China. If Saigon had fallen in 1965, it was not unreasonable to think, as the 'domino theory' held, that the regional consequences would have been dire.[12]

The Vietnam conflict helped to cement the Australia–US alliance, as the Australian government wanted it to. In the early 1960s, the circumstances under which Australia could rely on US support remained unclear. Holt wanted the USA in the region as a stabilising force and as a signal to Australia's neighbours that we did not stand alone. When Holt told Lyndon B. Johnson, the first serving US president to visit Australia, that he was 'All the way with LBJ', it carried greater political weight than Curtin's 'look to America' plea because it was a conscious policy decision rather than a cry from a nation in distress.

The situation in Vietnam certainly helped to radicalise Labor. The fiercest opponent of Australia's involvement in the war was Labor frontbencher Jim Cairns, a former lecturer in economic history at the University of Melbourne. Cairns led the largest protest in Australia up to that point, a 100,000-strong sit-down demonstration in Melbourne. The anti-Vietnam protest movement helped to fire up the educated progressive left as the creative energy inside Labor.

* * *

With far more university graduates, social norms came under more routine questioning. Popular culture became something to be studied and critiqued. Intellectual culture became increasingly anti-institutional. Under the influence of anti-war protests, a competing set of national myths developed, in which Australia had much to be ashamed of; a juxtaposition that historian Geoffrey Blainey later characterised as the 'three cheers' versus the 'black armband' versions of our history. The anti-war sit-ins of 1970 were seen as totemic, rather than the much larger mass gatherings that same year for the Queen's latest visit.

As in America, a characteristically rebellious 'counter-culture' developed among middle-class students. It was a movement predicated on affluence. Its adherents had known only relatively good times. They had no personal memories or experience of the Great Depression or the Second World War but saw themselves as expressing a generational frustration (even though they were not a majority). Most young people in the United States – those Richard Nixon called 'the silent majority' – were not tertiary educated. In Australia, Gallup polling found most were inclined to vote conservative.[13]

Nonetheless, public opinion *did* become less conservative. Television began to expose Australians to new and sometimes challenging ideas. Sexual norms loosened after the contraceptive pill came onto the market in 1960. By 1964, almost a third of married women were practising some form of birth control.[14] A 'liberated' era demanded access to abortion, then illegal. In 1969, in *R v. Davidson*, the Victorian Supreme Court ruled that abortion was not actually unlawful if the health and safety of the mother-to-be required it.

The Liberal government began to falter under Menzies' successors. The first of them, Harold Holt, was friendly and accessible to the media. He presented a new face to the world, strengthening Australia's engagement with the region through visits to Malaysia, Singapore and the Philippines in his first year. On moving into The Lodge, his wife, Zara, painted a bright white over the dark wood panelling and had the bedrooms coated in a distinct pink. Menzies was bemused. 'The psychedelic hand of Zara is heavy on the house,' he wrote. 'The guest rooms are painted in what I am told is shocking pink, and the colour certainly shocked me.'[15]

Holt gave his immigration minister, Hubert Opperman, the green light to undertake the largest reform to immigration laws since federation. Non-European residents could qualify for permanency and citizenship after five years of residence – the same rule as for Europeans. In 1967, some 5000 non-Europeans and 'mixed-descent' migrants entered Australia; there were almost 10,000 annually by 1971. Opperman's reforms marked the most significant legislative step to dismantling the White Australia policy. It effectively ended its functional operation by making clear, in the words of Peter Heydon, the secretary of the Department of Immigration, that 'for the first time' the law 'says positively that Asians can be admitted in a straightforward way and not merely as carefully defined exceptions in very limited areas'.[16]

* * *

The 1960s was the decade in which equality for Indigenous Australians became unquestioned. Although public policy and its administration remained far from perfect, the equal treatment of all Australians regardless of race or colour became a universal goal. The Australian Aboriginal Fellowship had petitioned as early as 1957 for a constitutional change that would allow the Commonwealth parliament to legislate on Indigenous policy. In 1965, the Student Action for Aborigines movement launched its 'Freedom Ride', a 15-day bus trip through regional New South

Wales led by Charlie Perkins, soon to become the first university graduate to identify as Aboriginal. This episode generated a national media spotlight on the gap between the fine promise and the then-very-imperfect practice of racial equality.

That year, the Menzies government first flagged repealing Section 127 of the Constitution, which excluded 'aboriginal natives' from being included in the Commonwealth population for constitutional purposes (chiefly the determination of electoral distributions). The proposal reflected Menzies' approach 'to treat the Aboriginal as on the same footing as all the rest, with similar duties and rights'.[17] Holt later added a proposal to amend Section 51 (xxvii), enabling the Commonwealth to legislate on Aboriginal policy, largely in response to advocacy by the Advancement Council, later renamed the Federal Council for the Advancement of Aborigines and Torres Strait Islanders (FCAATSI).

The 1967 referendum was the most successful referendum in our history because it embodied the principle of equal treatment and asked Australians to embrace their own. The Yes campaign was driven primarily by community movements, particularly FCAATSI. Advocates emphasised liberal principles, appealing to individual rights and legal equality with other Australians. Campaign materials asked Australians 'to give Aborigines a fair go'. Slogans such as 'Towards an Australia Free and Equal: Vote Yes' and 'Let's Be Counted – Vote Yes' sent a clear message that the referendum was about creating a unified Australia, free of discrimination.[18] Gallup polling at the time suggested most voters believed the changes would have real practical benefits for Indigenous Australians.

Four years earlier, at a meeting of the Ipswich Coloured Welfare Council in 1963, an articulate Aboriginal labourer named Neville Bonner had made an impassioned case for 'integration' over 'assimilation', a concept more acceptable to those wanting to preserve their identity, languages and culture. Bonner was then in his 40s and had worked a variety of manual jobs before being noticed by the Aboriginal community leader, Les Davidson, and encouraged to attend Welfare Council meetings. Bonner was a sharp thinker and a gifted communicator. Soon he was travelling around Queensland giving talks on Aboriginal issues. 'It had taken nearly 180 years since the first shot was fired over the heads of a tribe of Aborigines in Botany Bay,' Bonner put it. '[B]ut now the Aborigines began to fight back.'[19]

Neville Bonner was one of many volunteers handing out how-to-vote cards on polling day in 1967. Previously a casual Labor voter, he had struck up a friendship with a Liberal activist on Indigenous policy, Heather Ryan, in the course of their work at the One People of Australia League (OPAL), which advocated for integration and then assimilation for Aboriginal people. Bonner would later maintain that it was an incident on polling day that prompted his decision to become a Liberal Party member. In the afternoon, a black car pulled up at the booth, carrying a Labor MP. Stepping out, the Labor figure noticed Bonner standing with the Liberal volunteers and approached him. 'You should be giving out cards for us,' Bonner recalled him saying. 'Aren't you working for the wrong team?' Bonner deeply resented the implication: 'It browned me off,' he later said, 'the assumption that Aborigines should automatically belong to that party.'[20] Shortly after, he signed up to the Liberals. The minutes of the One Mile branch meeting on 22 August 1967 record the welcome of Bonner as 'the first coloured member of the Party'.[21]

Prior to 1967, only four out of 24 constitutional amendments had carried. On this occasion, though, just fewer than 91 per cent of formal votes were Yes, with a majority in every state. 'There was screaming when I heard it on the radio,' said the Yes campaigner Evelyn Scott. 'You just couldn't believe the percentage of the national vote.'[22] The next morning, the Brisbane writer Rodney Hall saw 'black people on the streets in a way that we had never seen them ... It was so touching. People were up, had washed their children, combed their hair and got themselves up in their very best gear and walked out in the streets of Brisbane, down Queen Street where they never went.'[23] By contrast, a proposal to break the 'nexus' requiring Senate numbers to be roughly half those of the House of Representatives, put on the very same day, received just 40.25 per cent and carried a majority in just one state.

* * *

On the morning of Saturday, 17 December 1967, Holt swam into the rough sea off Cheviot Beach, Portsea in Victoria, and never returned. Those with him did not recall any signs of distress. They watched Holt swim further into deeper waters until he was just dragged out – 'like a leaf', one recalled.[24] One of the largest search operations in Australia's history failed to find Holt's body. Late in the following evening, the governor-general, Richard Casey, terminated his friend's commission as prime minister.

The years 1968 to 1972 were a time of political transition, with two brief and turbulent prime ministerships.

John Gorton was a war veteran with a maverick streak. Despite an education at the Shore School, Geelong Grammar and Oxford University, he was egalitarian and unconventional, with a cool contempt for intellectuals that extended to some of the senior public servants working with him. When the situation in Vietnam deteriorated in early 1968 after the Viet Cong's Tet Offensive, Gorton impulsively declared that Australia would not increase its commitments.

One of his achievements was to give substantial funding to the Australian Council for the Arts – previously established by Holt – to promote ballet, opera and live theatre, which had rarely before received public funding. In 1969, the Commonwealth government laid the foundations of the Australian film revival of the 1970s by establishing the Australian Film Development Corporation (AFDC). Gorton helped foster cultural sophistication, despite admitting that he was, himself, 'not a cultured pearl', preferring westerns and detective movies.

After a poor showing at the 1969 federal election, he was replaced mid-term by William McMahon, whose government was beset by problems from the beginning. In under two years, ministerial sackings and resignations lent an air of chaos and decline. Nonetheless, McMahon liberalised Australia's censorship laws and passed the first *Child Care Act* in 1972, which funded centres, trained staff and subsidised fees for low-income families.[25] Under the leadership of Andrew Peacock as minister for external territories, preparation for transitioning Papua New Guinea to self-government had accelerated to the point where independence for PNG became accepted bipartisan policy.[26]

On 18 August 1971, McMahon announced that the Australian task force in South Vietnam would be withdrawn by the end of the year, after almost a decade of combat in which Australian numbers peaked at about 8000 in early 1968.

At the Battle of Long Tan, in August 1966, a company of Australians had fought off a much larger North Vietnamese force, establishing military dominance in Phuoc Tuy province. Normally, the Australians' battle tactics relied much less on firepower than the Americans'. A Viet Cong source later said that 'the Australians were more patient than the Americans, better guerilla fighters, better at ambushes. They liked to stay with us instead of calling in the planes. We were more afraid of their style.'[27] Still, while always capable of defeating their opponents in battle, America and its allies lacked the staying power to win over the population. By December 1972, fewer than 130 of the training team remained. Over 50,000 Australian personnel had served, with 519 killed and 2400 wounded.

* * *

On 2 December 1972, the Australian Labor Party – campaigning under the slogan 'It's Time' – defeated the 23-year-old Liberal government. It was a big historical moment secured on a relatively small swing of just 2.5 per cent, giving Whitlam a nine-seat majority. The modest margin was an early hint of the inherent conservatism of the Australian electorate, a message that went unheeded by an energetic and impatient new government.

The Whitlam era was a tumultuous experiment, elements of which remain embedded in Australian life. The size of government never returned to pre-Whitlam levels. Medibank, the precursor to Medicare, was established and free-of-charge health care became an accepted part of government service delivery. Legal aid was established at the Commonwealth level and quickly expanded. Tertiary fees were abolished (although reintroduced with a loans scheme by a later Labor government). Above all, progressive politics found a hero in Whitlam who remains an icon to people on the left.

With caucus not meeting until 18 December, Whitlam arranged with the governor-general, Sir Paul Hasluck – the former minister, by then retired from politics – to be sworn in as prime minister and to govern with his deputy, Lance Barnard, as a ministry of two in a duumvirate. Whitlam liked to compare himself to the Duke of Wellington, whose caretaker ministry in 1834 was the last small ministry with jurisdiction over

Australia.[28] But Whitlam was no caretaker; across 14 days he and Barnard made 40 policy decisions, many of them significant.

The first policy overturned was conscription. Seven men serving 18-month gaol sentences for refusing enlistment were released, over 300 cases of draft resistance were dropped, and the selective ballot was effectively abolished. Whitlam re-opened the equal pay for women case before the Arbitration Commission; began negotiations for formally recognising China; changed Australia's position on issues before the United Nations, including supporting sanctions against minority-ruled Rhodesia; added prescribed contraceptives to the Pharmaceutical Benefits Scheme; and began the process of abolishing the British honours system.

The speed with which these changes were rushed through was itself a policy statement: that Whitlam was determined to shake things up in a political version of shock and awe. Under the Coalition, the changes of the previous two decades had been downplayed; Whitlam played them up, with a language and a narrative that was self-consciously modern, ambitious and 'progressive'. He did not want to be perceived as reacting to events so much as leading them. In substance, though, there was more continuity than either he or the media cared to admit. The government's role in health care provision had already expanded as a result of the 1953 *Health Act* and the PBS. Participation in higher education was substantially increased under Menzies – more so than under Whitlam – yet the symbolism of free university remains powerful.

After 23 years of Coalition rule, there was a backlog of changes to be made. The death penalty was abolished for federal crimes, 'Advance Australia Fair' replaced 'God Save the Queen' as the national anthem, and the Australian National Gallery spent a third of its budget on Jackson Pollock's *Blue Poles*, a mid-century abstract painting that enamoured art critics and confused mass audiences. The remaining legal apparatus of White Australia was swept away, the *Racial Discrimination Act 1975* was passed and the *Family Law Act 1975* introduced no-fault divorce.

The pace of reform came with risks. For Whitlam, so long as his ministers made policy on evidence and reason, all would be well. But that implied that problems always had rational answers and could be solved technically. Whitlam was sceptical of the classical liberal argument that a nation might best progress by the voluntary decision-making of individuals acting in their own best interest.

He massively increased government spending, confident that continued growth would largely cover it. In 1973–74 and 1974–75, real budget outlays increased by 3.6 per cent and 14.5 per cent respectively.[29] But since the late 1960s, inflation had been gathering pace, driven by a commodity price boom and then the first oil-price shock in October 1973, when Middle Eastern countries raised prices and restricted supply in retaliation for the West's support for Israel. Whitlam and his team had a difficult choice, either to retreat from spending commitments or risk letting the inflation genie out of the bottle.

As it happened, interest rates were raised to dampen inflation, while government spending remained high to honour policy commitments. Government support for real wage increases led to big rises in labour costs. The success of the equal pay case added to these pressures. Contrary to the post-war Keynesian consensus, by the mid-'70s, inflation was in double-digits and unemployment was nearing 5 per cent – more than double the average of the 1960s. Stagflation had arrived.

The government's most controversial economic measure was an across-the-board tariff cut of 25 per cent.[30] Union leaders, manufacturers and some within Whitlam's own cabinet hated the decision. Whitlam was not a socialist of the old school; if anything, he was closer to a 19th-century 'new' liberal. His tariff cut foreshadowed the economic liberalisation to come in the 1980s, itself partly a product of the globalising instinct of the professional classes increasingly influential in policymaking.

Health policy was a key focus for the Whitlam government. A 1969 inquiry had found that 17 per cent of Australians were without health insurance. In December 1972, Whitlam appointed Bill Hayden as minister responsible for creating 'Medibank'. It was to provide 'free public hospital treatment' plus medical benefits totalling at least 85 per cent of out-of-hospital costs, 'with the maximum gap between scheduled fee and the benefit for any single service set at $5'.[31] But the legislation was twice rejected by the Senate, forming two of the six Bills that were the basis for a double-dissolution election, held on 18 May 1974.

Led by Billy Snedden, the Opposition attacked Labor's 'inflationary socialism'; but voters were inclined to give the new government the benefit of the doubt. It was the first election in which 18-year-olds were eligible to vote – and the first time a Labor prime minister claimed two consecutive election wins. Whitlam secured an additional three Senate seats, still not enough for a government majority but a joint-sitting of parliament – the first in the Commonwealth's history – provided Whitlam with the numbers to pass the six previously stalled Bills, including the Medibank legislation.

On Christmas Eve 1974, Cyclone Tracy slammed into Darwin, killing 66 people, rendering some 90 per cent of homes uninhabitable and prompting a partial evacuation until services could be restored and the city ultimately rebuilt to 'cyclone standard'. Whitlam was criticised for being overseas at the time – he was neither the first nor the last PM to prefer international diplomacy to the exigencies of domestic politics – but, for such a fraught and complex operation, the evacuation and rebuild was well handled by all arms of government. Although some 50 per cent of former residents never returned, within three years the population was back to pre-cyclone levels.

In early January 1975, disaster struck again when the ore carrier *Lake Illawarra* hit and brought down the Tasman Bridge connecting the two sides of Hobart, with 12 fatalities. For more than a year, many thousands of Tasmanians endured long ferry queues with reasonable equanimity, before the army built the temporary Bailey Bridge and the original bridge finally reopened almost three years later.

* * *

In March 1975, Malcolm Fraser defeated Snedden for the Liberal leadership. At 45, he was the Liberals' most formidable leader since Robert Menzies. He was a strong parliamentary performer, smart – another Oxford graduate – and intensely wilful. Hasluck wrote that he divided people into 'those who acted "according to principle", and those who did not'.[32] This characteristic made him a divisive figure even within his own party. Yet within nine months, Fraser had willed the Liberals back into government, making him one of the most brutally effective Opposition leaders in Australia's history.

Whitlam's downfall had been in the making for a year. On the evening of 14 December 1974, four men, including the prime minister, had signed what the journalist Alan Reid called 'the death warrant of the Whitlam ALP Government': authorisation for the minerals and energy minister, Rex Connor, to borrow $4 billion from sources in the Middle East to fund a monumental energy and infrastructure agenda.[33] Whitlam hoped that the loan could bypass Loan Council approval by justifying it as for 'temporary purposes' – a ridiculous argument considering its real objective. Supposedly making it happen for the government was a Pakistani commodities broker, Tirath Khemlani, a middleman of dubious reputation who promised Connor funds that never came.

The plan would have quadrupled Australia's overseas debt. When news of it first broke, in May, Whitlam revoked authorisation for the loan. In July, Jim Cairns was sacked for misleading parliament over his role in the scandal.

In June 1975, the government suffered a large swing against it at a Tasmanian by-election. Its Senate numbers had shrunk as a result of two appointments made by non-Labor premiers, who broke convention by appointing senators hostile to the government. In October, documents brought to Australia by Khemlani revealed that Connor had continued to pursue so-called petro dollars (the footloose capital available, even then, in the Middle East), without authorisation. For Fraser and the shadow cabinet, this was enough to suggest that Whitlam had lost control of his government. At a meeting on 15 October 1975, the shadow cabinet unanimously agreed to block the government's supply Bills in the Senate. In response, Whitlam declared there was 'no obligation, by law, by precedent or by convention ... which sets out that a Prime Minister must go to the Governor-General and ask him to dissolve the House of Representatives if an Upper House refuses Supply'.[34] How a government could continue without supply (the parliamentary appropriation to cover the ordinary business of government), he would not say.

Whitlam's plan was to exert pressure on Fraser to relent. 'If neither side backs down,' one journalist asked him, 'would chaos be inevitable?' 'In many respects, it would,' Whitlam responded. 'Well, Sir, then why don't you give in?' The PM replied: 'I shan't. It's not just my government. It is the future of parliamentary democracy in Australia as we know it.'[35]

To Fraser, the question was whether Whitlam would go voluntarily or involuntarily to the people. Fraser foresaw this endgame with a clarity that Whitlam lacked. Wanting to avoid yet another early election and likely defeat, Whitlam retreated from his earlier position that Senate obstruction could bring down a government – a view he had articulated as Opposition leader in Gorton's time.

As the crisis developed, the prime minister turned his mind to how the government might continue without supply. '[I]t is probable that the Government can govern without the Budget,' he said publicly.[36] A cabinet committee put together a plan to temporarily rely on bank credit to fund government employees, obviating the need for parliamentary approval. The plan unnerved Whitlam's colleagues, including his new treasurer, Bill Hayden, who had 'large doubts' and couldn't see the scheme lasting beyond the new year.[37] On 3 November, Fraser released a public statement condemning the move. 'Australia is a democracy,' the statement read. 'The great – the final – safeguard of democracy is parliament's control over money.'[38]

The crisis came to a head on Tuesday, 11 November 1975. It was the final date when an election could be called before the new year. At 9 am, the Liberal and Labor leaderships had met again to seek a resolution to the deadlock. None was forthcoming. Whitlam indicated he was going to advise the governor-general, Sir John Kerr, to hold a half-Senate election before the new year. He would not seek supply in the interim. He wanted Fraser to back down. Fraser, for his part, remembers warning Whitlam, '[Y]ou can't necessarily assume [Kerr] will do as you advise.' Whitlam responded, 'Nonsense.'[39]

By this time, Kerr had already made up his mind. He would withdraw Whitlam's commission as prime minister. He did not believe the half-Senate election was viable without supply guaranteed. At 9.55 am, Kerr called Fraser to seek assurance on several conditions necessary before he could be commissioned as prime minister, including passing supply and seeking a double-dissolution election. Fraser agreed to every condition and arranged to visit Government House at lunch break.

Whitlam arrived at Government House around 1 pm. In Kerr's account, Whitlam entered the governor-general's study and 'put his hand into his inside coat pocket'.

'Before you say anything, Prime Minister,' Kerr started, 'I want to say something to you.'[40] He summarised an earlier conversation – from the morning – confirming that the deadlock remained unresolved and that Whitlam intended to govern without parliamentary supply. That being the case, Kerr said, given Whitlam was unwilling to go to the people, he had decided to withdraw his commission as prime minister. 'Mr Whitlam jumped up, looked urgently around the room, looked at the telephones and said sharply, "I must get in touch with the Palace at once."'[41] In his own memoirs, Whitlam disputes this, though concedes he did later contact the Palace. After some brief words, the two men shook hands and Whitlam departed for The Lodge to have lunch alone.

Fraser, already waiting in Government House, was commissioned as the new prime minister. He was granted a double-dissolution election for 13 December and arranged for supply to be passed in the Senate. But lacking a majority in the House of Representatives, the caretaker prime minister that afternoon lost a no-confidence motion. When the speaker, Gordon Scholes, attempted to communicate the results to Kerr, in the hope that Whitlam might be reinstated, he was left waiting at the gates of Government House as parliament was dissolved and the election date confirmed.

Meanwhile, on the steps of Parliament House, a large crowd had heckled the governor-general's official secretary, David Smith, as he read the dissolution proclamation; Whitlam, standing behind him, then declared: 'Well may we say God save the Queen for nothing will save the governor-general.'

The events of 11 November 1975 created political uproar unlike anything Australia had experienced since federation. Perhaps only Victoria's constitutional deadlocks of the 1860s and 1870s are comparable. While these earlier crises can now be studied with a sense of distance, the memories of 1975 remain a matter of hurt and contention. There are allegations of conspiracy, involving the Palace or the US Central Intelligence Agency, but no strong evidence for either. The release of the 'Palace Letters' in 2020 confirmed that the Queen and the Palace did not interfere with the dismissal. In an irony of history, the only side urging royal interference was Labor. On 12 November, the day after Whitlam contacted the Palace to express his disbelief, Gordon Scholes wrote to the Queen demanding that Whitlam be restored as prime minister. 'We were trying very clearly to reverse the decision,' he told the journalist Troy Bramston in 2015. 'We wanted her to act.'42

The election, on 13 December 1975, was an unprecedented landslide to the Coalition. For the first time, the Coalition had a higher two-party-preferred vote in every state and territory except the ACT; it won every seat in Tasmania, every seat in Western Australia except Fremantle, and every seat in Queensland except Oxley.

In the end, the constitutional crisis of 1975 was resolved by democracy, the same means that Australia has used to solve all its political crises since self-government. Even if Whitlam's most die-hard supporters continue to 'maintain the rage', most Australians were comfortable settling the impasse this way. The loaded language still used about this episode, such as a 'coup' or 'authoritarianism', has never held much currency.

16

Opening the Doors

In important respects, the Australia of the late 1980s resembled the Australia of a century earlier, prior to the dashed hopes and rising fears of the anxious 1890s. Key elements of what Paul Kelly has called the post-federation Australian Settlement had been ditched: White Australia had started to go after the war; imperial benevolence had become a thing of the past by the 1960s; industry protection had begun to erode under Whitlam and was further dismantled under Bob Hawke, our greatest Labor prime minister; state paternalism didn't quite vanish, but under Hawke and Keating the state was as solicitous of success as of failure; even wage arbitration morphed into enterprise bargaining. The national mood was buoyant, too, fuelled by a resources boom that amounted to a second gold rush. Briefly, the political divide also resembled those 19th-century days, pitting Hawke's bigger government 'liberals' against Howard's smaller government Liberals.

§

Did the Dismissal-induced taint of illegitimacy handicap Malcolm Fraser's government? Originally, this was the claim of those who could never forgive Fraser for blocking supply and thwarting their hero. Later, it was those Liberals who were frustrated by his government's economic timidity who sought an explanation in the events of 1975.

Clearly, Fraser himself never felt inhibited by the manner of his accession to office, vindicated as it was by the overwhelming mandate he won in 1975 and again in 1977. Fraser was naturally economically cautious: a pragmatist who disliked utopian thinking of any kind. We have to accept, he once said, 'that while we strive for perfection, we will not reach it in this world, nor our sons after us. Recognition of this truth,' he continued, 'should soften the radical, bring tolerance to the fanatic, temper the extremes of love and hate.'[1] This bent of mind (perhaps best encapsulated in his wry observation that 'life wasn't meant to be easy') made him a formidable foe to the utopianism of social democrats, but also – to the consternation of some of his colleagues – sceptical of small-government enthusiasm on his own side.

Fraser liked to prod and scrutinise. The free-market economists Milton Friedman and F.A. Hayek met with him, in 1975 and 1976 respectively, but were left somewhat disheartened by the prime minister's robust questioning. Both urged significant monetary reform; not without reason. By 1976, inflation was running at almost 14 per cent and beating it became the core economic task of the Fraser government.[2]

As a Menzian Liberal, Fraser instinctively turned to the Keynesian tools of macroeconomic management. He'd slogged through Keynes' *General Theory of Employment, Interest and Money* when he was a student at Oxford and had absorbed the mid-century view that Keynes had saved liberalism and perhaps democracy itself from the crosswinds of fascism and socialism. In persuading policymakers that demand management was a viable economic alternative to central planning, Keynes had provided a fundamental starting point from which the post-war liberal revival could advance.[3]

But as Friedman and Hayek had argued was inevitable, Keynesian economic management was starting to fail by the 1970s, with both high unemployment and high inflation. The inverse relationship between the two, which Keynesian economists had postulated, no longer applied in practice, if it ever had. Together with skyrocketing oil prices and the growing complexity of trade and finance, government spending alone was not improving Australia's comparatively poor productivity.

An increasingly globalised economy was exposing Australia's comparative economic stagnation. Under longstanding and highly prescriptive regulation, banks had limited their supply of loans, refusing to lend to women without a male guarantor, for instance, or to people with no record of saving at the bank, let alone anyone with only modest security. Heavy regulation kept the banks sound but restricted competition and did little to foster entrepreneurial drive.[4] By some measures, Australia's financial system was among the most unsophisticated in the developed world.[5]

This was the background against which Australia started major economic reform. First, McMahon had provided banks with greater autonomy in foreign exchange transactions and suspended certain lending controls. Fraser moved the Australian dollar towards a 'managed float', allowing the currency to be monitored and managed daily. Significantly, he initiated a committee of inquiry into the financial system (the Campbell Committee), which recommended, among other liberalising reforms, a floating exchange range.

Fraser had a good economic record in his first term. Under Whitlam, government spending as a percentage of GDP had risen from 18.8 per cent in 1972–73 to 24.3 per cent in 1975–76.[6] Fraser stabilised it at 24.1 per cent in his first budget. Spending growth was reduced by almost a billion dollars (around 4.5 per cent of revenue), with staff ceilings on the federal bureaucracy, meaning 17,480 fewer public servants by the end of June 1976 than would have been the case under previous policy.[7] Personal income tax was temporarily subject to indexation, intended to eliminate future bracket creep and to reduce the need for larger wage claims. In 1978, income tax brackets were reduced from seven to three. By December 1977, inflation had dipped below 10 per cent, almost half the peak of mid-1975, and industrial disputes had fallen.

The most Menzian of Fraser's policy achievements was a generous family allowance scheme. Described by *The Age* as 'one of the most important advances in social welfare since federation', it replaced the regressive child tax rebate and was paid to mothers, not the family breadwinner. Around 300,000 low-income families benefited from this policy.

* * *

After leaving office, Fraser's public statements reflected a commitment to a 'more just society', including considerable criticism of the Liberal Party. Over time, his former critics became his admirers, and vice versa. Was it Fraser or was it the Liberal Party that changed? Most likely, critics on the left misread him when he was in government, while critics on the right misread him after government.

One of Fraser's landmark decisions was admitting large numbers of South Vietnamese refugees into the country. The fall of Saigon to the communists and the triumph of the Khmer Rouge in Cambodia caused millions to flee Vietnam, Cambodia and Laos over the next two decades. In 1975, Whitlam had had little appetite to respond to this developing humanitarian crisis. RAAF aircraft providing emergency assistance in the south were ordered not to take refugees.[8] 'I'm not having hundreds of fucking Vietnamese Balts coming into this country with their political and religious hatreds against us,'[9] Whitlam was reported as saying, mindful that the escapees were likely to be fervent anti-communists. Bob Hawke, president of the ACTU, was also opposed to bringing in more refugee labour in a time of high unemployment.[10]

Fraser felt that Australia could not simply abandon the South Vietnamese: 'We were fighting alongside these people,' he argued.[11] Equally, the government had to respond to the growing perception that Australia was losing control of its borders. The first Vietnamese refugee boat arrived in Darwin Harbour in 1976. By 1981, there'd been some 53 boats carrying more than 2000 people.

Rather than tolerate unauthorised arrivals by boat, the government placed immigration officials in refugee camps, with the aim of settling a limited number of refugees in Australia, arriving by air. Following a Geneva conference in December 1978, Australia agreed to significantly increase its resettlement places, achieving an important humanitarian objective while reducing spontaneous boat arrivals and restoring confidence in its borders. In total, Fraser accepted almost 70,000 Indochinese refugees, the largest intake of any country on a per capita basis. In Fraser's first four years of office, about a third of Australia's immigrants were of Asian descent.

Fraser embraced the multiculturalism that had first been articulated by Whitlam-era immigration minister Al Grassby. The theory of multiculturalism (at least to Fraser) was that it would 'promote intercultural understanding' and thus social harmony by fostering 'the retention of cultural heritage of different ethnic groups'.[12] His government commissioned the Special Broadcasting Service in 1978 and established the Australian Institute of Multicultural Affairs in 1979.[13] SBS catered for a 'multicultural' audience by presenting news from across the globe in a variety of migrant languages. Fraser saw

SBS as a unifying project, 'not something that divides, that sets apart, as just a foreign language broadcast would tend to do', but rather to unify, and to 'have people understand what this Australia is all about'.[14]

Fraser emerged as a champion against apartheid at the 1977 Commonwealth Heads of Government meeting, leading the debates on sporting and economic sanctions against the white minority regime. Outraged by the Soviet Union's invasion of Afghanistan, he opposed Australia's participation in the Moscow Summer Olympics of 1980. He exemplified a particular strand within the broad liberal and conservative tradition: a dedication to service founded on the gospel injunction 'To whom much is given, much is expected'. He was a liberal interventionist at home and a liberal internationalist abroad.

* * *

Fraser consolidated the new Whitlamite consensus on Indigenous policy. The conservative radicalism of Paul Hasluck was displaced by the progressive radicalism of the left. Assimilation and integration gave way to self-determination as the aim of policy. 'Assimilation' was said to be destructive to Indigenous culture; even though, for Hasluck, it had always meant giving full rights to Aboriginal people.[15] In later life, Hasluck rejected what he saw as the new separatism and despaired of 'the reawakening and at times active promotion of racial divisions and antipathies'; he was damning of 'salaried white advisers who had more good intentions than practical experience'. He deplored 'elaborate structures for consultation with Aborigines' that 'were more clearly evident than any clear expression by the Aborigines of their own ideas'.[16]

Fifty years on, the results have been disappointing, to put it mildly. As shown by the annual Close the Gap statements, instituted under Prime Minister Kevin Rudd, on life expectancy, employment and educational attainments, the 'gap' between Indigenous people living in remote areas and the rest of the Australian community – and, indeed, Indigenous people not living remotely – remains wide and stubbornly hard to close, despite vast social spending. To officialdom and much of the commentariat, this is due to 'institutionalised racism', 'intergenerational trauma' and 'settler colonialism', rather than any issue inherent in the notion of collective self-determination. The sad truth is that encouraging people to live in remote places with no real economy and few meaningful jobs, other than servicing disadvantage, is never going to give people First World outcomes. Yet it's supposedly necessary to preserve 'culture'. Half a century on, the result of 'self-determination' is an activist class largely publicly funded to bemoan the victim status of most remote Aboriginal people. This is perhaps our biggest national failure, but it's a failure of perverse policy rather than lack of popular goodwill.

To their credit, both Whitlam and Fraser detested racial discrimination. They were part of a new generation that welcomed the presence of Indigenous voices in public affairs and wanted to make amends for the dispossession of Aboriginal people after 1788. Under McMahon, negotiations had begun for the transfer of part of the Wave Hill cattle station lease to the Gurindji people, which was eventually formalised by Whitlam and immortalised by the photo of the prime minister pouring the red earth of Wattie Creek into the hands of the Gurindji elder Vincent Lingiari. Following the Aboriginal Land Rights Commission reports of 1973 and 1974, one of Malcolm Fraser's first legislative acts was passing the *Aboriginal Land Rights (Northern Territory) Act 1976*. This established four land councils to take control of former Aboriginal reserves and vacant Crown land. Today, roughly half of the Northern

Territory is held under native title, including 80 per cent of the coastline.

In 1980, Fraser appointed Charlie Perkins as the first director of the new Aboriginal Development Commission, tasked with helping Indigenous Australians finance homes and businesses. The Community Development Employment Projects (CDEP), established in 1977, was essentially a 'work for the dole' scheme: participants were expected to work part-time and be paid wages (in lieu of welfare) distributed via a local Indigenous entity as their employer. Because much of the work in remote communities was menial (sometimes characterised as 'painting rocks white'), and because the wage was usually paid whether the worker turned up or not, it came to be known as 'sit-down money', and was hardly distinguishable from welfare. At its worst, the CDEP discouraged mainstream employment and became emblematic of the welfare dependency that later Indigenous leaders, most notably Noel Pearson, would call 'the poison that's killing our people'.

There was an obvious tension between preserving traditional ways of life and encouraging economic development. Looming over this whole era was the figure of Herbert Cole 'Nugget' Coombs, appointed as co-chair of the Council for Aboriginal Affairs in 1967. Coombs sought to empower Indigenous communities through more government funding, 'land rights' and incorporating Aboriginal custom into local power structures. In practice, this left a vacuum of authority in many remote communities and allowed a breakdown of social order. In many cases, self-determination translated into unwieldy bureaucratic structures that often better served the managerial class than the communities themselves.

* * *

Even while Malcolm Fraser was prime minister, the Liberal Party was leaving 'Fraser-ism' behind. A 'vanguard' of free market liberals offering an alternative vision for Australia formed on the backbench. One of them, the Western Australian John Hyde, likened Fraser's approach to economic reform to St Augustine's prayer: 'Lord, give me chastity but not just yet.'[17]

Car industry protection particularly riled Hyde. He reckoned that every Australian was paying $3000 a year in direct subsidies and higher prices to fortify the nation's five motor-car manufacturers. Not even the United States had as many car makers. Meanwhile, tax reform and financial reform lagged, industrial relations laws continued to institutionalise conflict, and budget outlays spiked to record levels in 1982–83.

The rise of the 'free market lobby' inside the Liberal Party was – according to the former Fraser advisor, Howard government minister and historian of liberalism David Kemp – the consequence of 'something akin to a broad, though not unified, liberal movement', consisting of 'political and intellectual leaders, publicists and pamphleteers, journalists and commentators, [with] policy support in the public bureaucracy, and in private think tanks, (plus) interest group mobilisation and an ... expanding base of mass support'.[18] By the mid-1980s a rejuvenated Institute of Public Affairs championed significant economic liberalisation of the economy. The Centre for Independent Studies, founded in 1976 by young mathematics teacher Greg Lindsay, was also pushing the libertarian ideas of thinkers like Hayek and Friedman.

Few books captured the moment better than *Australia at the Crossroads*, published in 1980 and written by four economists: Wolfgang Kasper, Richard Blandy, John Freebairn and Douglas Hocking, plus the international relations expert Robert O'Neill. *Crossroads* modelled two versions of Australia's future: the 'mercantalist' path and the 'libertarian alternative', the former protecting 'established power positions' and relying on 'short-run tactical activism and interventionism', the latter 'welcoming and fostering innovation and ... opening the Australian society and economy to renewed competition'. The authors argued for free trade, deregulated markets, open international capital flows, strong competition laws and smarter welfare that did not disincentivise work.

Hyde studied *Crossroads* closely, as did his parliamentary colleague Jim Carlton from New South Wales. 'We essentially saw both Fraser and Labor as espousing collectivist solutions,' Carlton said.[19] Together they established the 'Crossroads Group', a collection of like-minded parliamentarians that coalesced with young academics and business figures to crystallise a reform agenda for Australia. This became what the journalist Paul Kelly would call 'the nucleus of the "free market" counter-establishment of the 1980s'.[20]

The parliamentary 'Dries', as the reform-minded backbenchers became known (a term popularised by the UK conservative leader Margaret Thatcher), were a nuisance to the prime minister but their influence grew steadily. A proposed government measure for continued tariff protection was met by a petition with 33 Liberal signatures opposing it. A 'Society of Modest Members' – a reference to the former free trade South Australian backbencher Bert Kelly (who penned a long-running newspaper column under that title) – was set up for state and federal Liberal MPs. The Dries' favourite minister was Fraser's ambitious young treasurer from 1977, John Howard. Hyde was impressed with Howard's understanding of economic issues.

* * *

A 20th-century constant was managing the endemic industrial conflict between employers and unions. The promise of arbitration as a cure to this conflict had long since faded; but with powerful interests still behind it, Fraser was unwilling to dismantle it, especially as few if any 'experts' recommended this path. Nonetheless, a series of wage hikes, which lifted inflation and unemployment even higher, demanded policy reform in an area that John Howard called a 'political, as well as economic, nightmare'.[21] Fraser soon found himself personally involved in negotiating compromises with union leaders. In 1979, the government was exactly where Stanley Bruce was more than half a century earlier – considering a referendum to refer industrial powers and wage-setting policy to the Commonwealth.[22]

Part of the problem, said commentator Gerard Henderson, was bad incentives: lavish benefits that accrued to members of the 'industrial relations club' – employer and union representatives who earned their keep as cogs in a complex administrative machine. The system had a life of its own regardless of the public interest. In 1982, wages increased several percentage points above inflation at the very moment the world plunged into recession.[23]

At the apex of this clubby arbitration system was the president of the Australian Council of Trade Unions: a national figure with significant power over the macroeconomy. In 1975, this was Bob Hawke, better known than anyone on the left other than Whitlam. Hawke revelled in this celebrity. To many, he was the quintessential Australian man, a beer-drinking larrikin who loved a laugh, but he was also a Rhodes Scholar who worked hard and had ideas.

In the lead-up to the 1980 federal election, Hawke nominated for the Victorian seat of Wills. At times, he appeared to be Labor's primary spokesman.[24] He featured in election material and attracted eager crowds. Polling suggested Australians wanted Hawke over Fraser.[25] The actual Labor leader was Bill Hayden: intelligent, moderate and a voice of common sense during the Whitlam years. He was understandably frustrated by the spectre of Hawke looming over him. In the end, Fraser proved the tougher campaigner and retained government with a reduced majority. Hawke won his seat and Labor leadership speculation began.

As a leftist firebrand who'd mellowed in his time as ACTU president and become more associated with ending strikes than starting them, Hawke was seen by many as a different type of politician. Yet again, there was a perception that the political class had failed the country. The recession of 1982–83 was compounded by a bad drought, while the Arbitration Commission's return to collective bargaining locked in high real wage growth, with inflation reaching 10.5 per cent and unemployment 9 per cent by the end of 1982.[26]

In the 1930s, at a time of great hardship, Australians had turned to Joseph Lyons; in the 1980s, they turned to another healer and patriot. In February 1983, Hawke attacked the 'Fraserian emphasis upon a punitive approach' to industrial matters and committed Labor to 'putting back into the forefront of the conciliation and arbitration system the emphasis on conciliation'.[27] In 1979, he had delivered a talk titled 'The Resolution of Conflict', championing consensus. Almost as Fraser was driving to Government House to advise the 1983 election, the Labor caucus replaced Hayden with Hawke, who went on to win the 5 March 1983 contest under the campaign slogan 'Bringing Australia Together'.

* * *

There had been nothing in the campaign speeches or comments of Hawke, or from his shadow treasurer, Paul Keating, to suggest a policy of market reform. They emphasised moderation and caution. Once in office, though, the pair embraced a more radical agenda because their economic advisors – especially Treasury secretary John Stone – persuaded them that it was essential in order to maintain the high living standards that Australians were used to.

The floating of the Australian dollar, in December 1983, was the first big reform of the Hawke government. For some time, the management of the exchange rate had been complicated by the activities of currency speculators.[28] In adjusting the exchange rate, authorities had to balance internal policy objectives against the likely response of speculators. Greater volatility in domestic interest rates was the price of keeping the dollar relatively stable. Financial deregulation took the pressure off interest-rate management by letting the dollar float. It let the value of the dollar and the cost of capital find their natural 'market' level.

Floating the currency, and the abolition of other financial controls, was less about connecting Australia to the world than recognising that existing arrangements were cutting it off. An overvalued dollar was hurting Australia's trade and an inward-looking financial system was hurting Australians' ability to do business. By 1980, more than 50 per cent of total exports were with Asia.[29] In Hong Kong and Singapore, foreign exchange dealers looking at Australia saw a sclerotic system ripe for speculation. Far from being 'market ideologues', by green-lighting more flexible financial markets, Hawke and Keating thought they were giving practical help to individual businesses.

Hawke strove for 'consensus' around a Prices and Incomes Accord between the Labor government and the ACTU, trading off wage restraint for legislated social benefits. Universal health insurance under Medicare (essentially Medibank mark 2, to restore what Fraser had dismantled) was one. The 'Accord' reflected the hard lessons of the Whitlam years and sought to reshape the relationship between labour and capital from the tug-of-war between profits and wages to a collaboration that gave primacy to economic growth.

Hawke's first grand symbol of unity, the National Economic Summit, held in Parliament House in April 1983, was highly corporatist. Bringing together leaders in business, finance, politics and the labour movement was in John Hyde's words 'a highly theatrical muster of the elites'. Although its participants were mostly unelected, the Summit took place in the people's house, the House of Representatives: a sign of how centralised institutions had placed enormous economic power in the hands of vested interests.[30]

* * *

Hawke and Keating complemented each other: Hawke's mission was to build a new consensus, while Keating's was to destroy the old one. Keating's late mentor was the old Labor warrior Jack Lang; and he emulated Lang's combination of charisma, conviction and hatred. Keating was attracted to big-picture thinking, with an appetite for questioning current orthodoxy.[31] Like Lang, Keating typically framed every argument as 'us versus them'.

Keating enabled Labor to make an unaccustomed leap on economic reform by connecting a more liberal economic policy to a grand narrative underpinned by traditional Labor values. In opening Australia's banks to foreign competition, he drew on the folk memory of earlier generations let down by the languid and monopolistic banking industry. 'It means that Australians will no longer feel like mendicants as they approach the banks for financial assistance,' he said.[32] Conjuring the spirit of Lang, he railed against the old established money power. 'It really surprises me that people in this party think we owe Westpac something, or ANZ Bank, or the National,' he told a Labor NSW conference.[33]

'Bob brought a big bank of public goodwill to the table,' Keating would later recall, 'which we could draw down and use politically for good policy ...'[34] It would be fair to say that Keating never fully explored the source of this 'public goodwill'. Certainly, he never tried to emulate it. The contrast between the two men was evident at the Tax Summit of July 1985 – a summit Hawke proposed without consulting Keating. 'I couldn't imagine a worse way of making good tax policy than by doing it in public,' Keating said, but it was very much in keeping with Hawke's 'consensus' model.[35] The most ambitious proposal to come out of a preceding government White Paper had been a combination of a 12.5 per cent broad-based consumption tax, the introduction of capital gains tax and fringe benefits tax, plus substantial cuts to personal income tax. While intense union pressure led the government to drop the idea of a consumption tax, leaving Keating dumbfounded and disappointed, big changes to other elements of the tax system continued.

Unlike Hawke, Keating's instincts were intellectual rather than democratic. Eventually, the relationship broke down because Keating felt that he was the taken-for-granted and under-appreciated creative energy behind the government's achievements. To justify his claim on the prime ministership, he revealed the Kirribilli House deal under which Hawke, supposedly, had agreed eventually to step aside in Keating's favour. When Keating resigned as treasurer in 1991, the government lost its policy drive. But after Keating became prime minister in 1992, the government was always at risk of losing its popular touch.

The two men thought about Australia in very different terms. Hawke loved Australia as it was. Keating loved the idea of the 'independent' Australia that might come to be in the future. Where Hawke credited our Anglo inheritance for 'the institutions of parliamentary democracy and freedom under the law', Keating saw the British stamp on Australian institutions as an anachronism.[36] In his autobiography, Hawke wrote of 'the surge of excitement I always experience when flying back to Australia feeling that I am returning to the best country on earth'.[37] But as Hawke once said of him, Keating was more inclined to see Australia as the 'arse end' of the Earth, far distant in every sense from the great centres of culture and learning.

* * *

In 1983, there was an explosion of national exuberance triggered by victory at the America's Cup, the world's oldest international sporting competition. Up until Monday, 26 September 1983, at 5.20 pm, it was also the most lopsided one. For 132 years, dating back to before the American Civil War, the New York Yacht Club had been undefeated. Then, concluding a seventh race off Newport, Rhode Island, *Australia II* surged past the American *Liberty* to cross the finish line with a 41-second lead. Skippered by John Bertrand, designed by Ben Lexcen and funded by the combative Perth businessman Alan Bond, *Australia II* had made history and stirred the nation into a patriotic frenzy.

The architects of that victory were themselves representative of a new Australia. Entrepreneur Alan Bond, the son of an English migrant, had left school at 14 to become an apprentice sign writer. He quickly established his own business, Nu Signs, undercutting competitors and branching out into real estate speculation and property development. Nu Signs became Lesmurdie Heights, which became the Bond Corporation. He had made a multimillion-dollar empire seemingly out of nothing.

Bond rode the wave of rising land values to attract capital as the mineral boom was transforming Perth. No other state capital had a higher rate of population growth between the mid-1960s and early 1990s. Along with Queensland, Western Australia had a mining boom that could only be compared to the gold rush in the previous century. Between 1960 and 1975, the contribution of mining to gross national product rose from under 2 to over 4 per cent as West Australian iron ore and Queensland coal powered the rising economies of East Asia.

The development of Australian mining over this period is a story of persistence and experimentation, often in the face of obstructive government policy. Continued export embargoes and regulatory barriers discouraged mineral exploration. The Pilbara pastoralist Lang Hancock, who had stumbled upon extensive walls of iron ore, experienced this first-hand in 1952 when he found himself unable to secure a licence to exploit it. Successive governments had concluded that iron ore was too scarce for export. Only once the embargoes and barriers were lifted could Hancock act.[38]

The resources boom also helped to wake up Australia's sleepy financial system. Non-bank financial institutions sprang up to co-ordinate the new markets, bypassing the heavily regulated traditional banks.[39] This 'second rush' primed Australia for the policy changes of the 1980s.

* * *

'Never before in Australian history had so much money been channelled by so many people incompetent to lend it into the hands of so many people incompetent to manage it,' Trevor Sykes wrote in his corporate history of the period.[40] There was a downside to the economic exuberance of the mid-80s. Inevitably, some went too far in this time of widening economic freedom. Highly publicised failures and scandals featured colourful and shady characters, among them Bond himself, who went from hero to zero after his business collapsed with massive debts.

It was the era of the high-rolling entrepreneurs and business tycoons, of huge mansions, private jets and art collections. It was a decade of confidence, and of new international icons, such as Kylie Minogue and *Neighbours*, Paul Hogan and *Crocodile Dundee*.

Less talked about were the Australians who'd had few opportunities but who were at last getting a fair go. Women were among the new breed of Australians in business. Since the end of the Menzies era, the employment-to-population ratio for women had risen from just 40 to 60 per cent.[41] The then wealthiest woman in Australia was said to be Millie Phillips, a mining magnate and Holocaust survivor who'd arrived in Australia penniless and had 'saved the hard way' with her former husband, 'sharing cigarettes, eating lunch in the park, and not going anywhere'.[42] The marriage was an abusive one and she left with her three children, the youngest 18 months. In 1960, she purchased a property with the intention of taking in boarders to earn an income. As a woman, Phillips required a male guarantor just to get a foot in the door. Scrounging funds, including borrowing from family, she purchased one property and then more. After amassing a hotel empire, in 1969, she became the first Australian woman to launch an initial public offering, before earning a greater fortune in nickel mining. Much more recently, Gina Rinehart, daughter of Lang Hancock, was for some years not just Australia's 'richest woman' but richest person.

Also making the most of new opportunities was a growing middle class of Indigenous Australians living in cities and larger centres. Even in remote Australia, there was some material progress as traditional owners formed joint ventures in mining, with those communities benefiting from negotiated royalties.[43] By the mid-1980s, Sotheby's ran annual auctions for Indigenous Australian art, which was now being acclaimed internationally for its evocation of country. In 2007, a Clifford Possum Tjapaltjarri work sold for $2.4 million. Emily Kngwarreye's iconic *Earth's Creation* has now been sold twice for over $1 million.

This was the new Australia, finally proud of its Aboriginal heritage, becoming less convinced about its British foundation and increasingly celebrating its immigrant character.

17

Consolidation

Whatever one thinks of their politics, Hawke and Howard were two of our very best prime ministers, and together they gave Australia close to a quarter-century of economic reform plus social harmony. There was one important difference, though, in their respective circumstances. Hawke's reforms were carried largely with Opposition support; Howard's in the teeth of a fierce antagonism.

The Australia of 2000 was comfortable with its past and confident about its future. Over the course of two centuries, a convict colony had become one of the world's great democracies and arguably the world's most successful immigrant society.

§

The bicentenary celebration of the First Fleet's arrival, held on 26 January 1988, was the largest public gathering in the nation's history. Spread across Sydney's foreshore and headlands were young and old of every background; on the harbour was a veritable sea of life, from small boats to tall ships and everything in between. Meanwhile, a large Aboriginal banner proclaiming, 'We Have Survived!' had been draped across North Head and a tent embassy was erected at Mrs Macquarie's Chair. In the city, thousands of protestors marched to Hyde

Park to demonstrate against Indigenous dispossession. For most, it was a day of celebration and reflection; for some, a reminder of the work still ahead. It was a day befitting one of the world's most successful democracies: alive with debate but suffused with goodwill, and with all committed to their own version of a better future.

Prince Charles, representing the Queen that day, well summed up the national mood:

> Even within the astonishingly brief span which covers the whole history of modern Australia, the process of making liberty an institution took time. For the original people of this land it must have all seemed very different, and if they should say that their predicament has not yet ended, it would be hard to know how to answer beyond suggesting that a country free enough to examine its own conscience is a land worth living in, a nation to be envied. Anyway, most people who live here, now, seem to think that Australia is the best place in the world, and the rest of the world finds it difficult to argue ...[1]

He went on: '[O]ne of Australia's oldest ties with the oldest of its old countries is the rule of law. They were harsh judges who sent the first Australians out here, but they were wisely framed laws that turned convicts into free men and women. And free men and women helped make a democracy which has become a model for the world.'[2]

The closing years of the 20th century were a golden time, when Australia was finally reaping the benefits of sustained reform. It was more prosperous, productive, tolerant and confident than at any time since the 1880s. Notwithstanding a sharp recession in the early 1990s, Australia had reforming governments determined to free up businesses from excessive red tape and bureaucracy. By 2000, Australia could boast nine years of continuous growth at historically high rates. As a nation, we had begun the century closed off and anxious but ended it open and assured.

The political story of the Hawke–Howard era is of governments relinquishing control of the economy back into the hands of individuals and businesses. This 'reform era' arguably reached its apogee in 1993, in the contest between the progressive political correctness of Prime Minister Paul Keating's vision for an independent Australia and the economic radicalism of then Opposition leader John Hewson. Not before or since has our politics been such a laboratory for big ideas.

The success of Hawke, and the later ascendency of John Howard, improved upon enduring elements of the Australian character. A century earlier, Sydney newspapers wrote of the 'broad cosmopolitan Liberalism' of Australia. 'It is the boast of this colony that we ask no man what country he comes from, provided he is willing to settle here and conform to the true obligations of Australian citizenship,' *The Australian Star* had declared in 1889.[3]

In his bicentenary address, Hawke asked, 'What is an Australian?' and answered that it's centred on a commitment to 'freedom, fairness, justice and peace'. In Australia, he said, 'there is no hierarchy of descent' and 'there must be no privilege of origin ... The commitment to Australia is the one thing needful to be a true Australian.'[4] The inference, though, was that without a near universal commitment to freedom, fairness and an egalitarian readiness for all to pull their weight, without a civic patriotism to replace a vanishing ethnic one, there could hardly be an enduring Australian nation.

* * *

A key government document of the 1980s was the FitzGerald Report, *Immigration – A Commitment to Australia*, commissioned by the Hawke government to advise on the integration of migrants into the wider Australian community. Its chair, Dr Stephen FitzGerald, was a diplomat and China expert. The report turned out to be the most comprehensive examination of immigration policy since the 1940s. Unlike most government reports, it steered between alarmism and complacency, and it took seriously the dangers of drastic change in a community whose success and harmony relied on social trust. The report forensically examined community views, finding 'confusion and mistrust of multiculturalism', which threatened 'community support of immigration'.[5]

Its frankness made the government uncomfortable. The report found 'many Australians are not convinced that immigrants are making a commitment to their new country'.[6] It blamed this failure on government policy that was too often dictated by sectional interest groups. It was a prophetic anticipation of subsequent recurring backlashes, yet it was not anti-immigration: it recommended, in fact, an increase in migrant numbers. Rather, it focused on what had to be done to win community support by encouraging migrants to integrate. In doing so, it broke a number of progressive shibboleths, reaffirming the need for a positive Australian identity based on a common commitment to: 'parliamentary democracy, the rule of law and equality before the law, freedom of the individual, freedom of speech, freedom of religion, equality of women, universal education'. It recommended 'linking the grant of citizenship with a declaration to respect the fundamental institutions and principles in Australian society'.[7]

The FitzGerald Report demonstrated that concern over migration was not limited to a handful of conservative commentators. In August 1988, Newspoll research found

77 per cent of respondents believed that Asian migration should be slowed.[8] Even Charlie Perkins, by then the head of the Federal Department of Aboriginal Affairs, suggested a curb on Asian migration and a rebalancing of immigration policy.[9] So, this was hardly the expression of racist grievance that some progressives made it out to be.

By 1988, the Australian population included people from some 130 nationalities. Already, about a third of Australia's annual migrants were of Asian origin.[10] It was also true that much was changing very quickly – too quickly for some. The FitzGerald Report's premise was that governments had a duty to justify these changes and to persuade people, in the democratic language of the country, why they were beneficial.

In quite a candid open letter, published in the wake of the report, Hawke declared that 'absorbing almost 5 million migrants from over 120 countries' had changed Australia 'from an insular economic and cultural outpost of Britain to being an accepted, respected partner of the most dynamic region of the world'. He praised his predecessors from both sides of politics for this achievement, noting that none of them had 'enjoyed majority community support for what they did'. It was, he said, 'a triumph of principle over populism, of reason over fear, of statesmanship over politics'. Hawke observed in 1988 that, based on 'current' projections, 40 years hence Asian-born Australians would reach 7 per cent of our population; actually, the figure is now about 13 per cent. He attacked Howard, who'd just previously said there was a 'case' for slowing down Asian immigration in order to foster social cohesion, for unleashing 'the darker forces that inhabit our body politic'.[11] But not even all Hawke's own ministers were supportive of such a large and diverse immigration intake or of silencing debate with accusations of racism. One of them, Peter Walsh, said that immigration policy had been driven by 'a sequence of blow outs and cave ins' to the ethnic lobby.[12]

* * *

The 1980s were not kind to the Liberal Party of Australia. At the federal level, it suffered successive election defeats. There was disunity with the National Party, division driven by philosophical differences, and leadership tension between John Howard and Andrew Peacock. The coalition agreement with the Nationals collapsed in early 1987 during an egotistical lunge at federal politics by the charismatic Queensland premier Joh Bjelke-Petersen. Under Howard, the Liberals took a bold program of reform to the 1987 election – large personal income tax cuts, deregulation of the labour market, privatisation of government assets and the dismantling of protective tariffs – but lacked the internal unity needed to make it credible. Hawke won comfortably.

The election confirmed the conventional wisdom that there's only a small constituency for economic purism. The Liberals were offering radical change to reorient Australia's economic future. Learning from this, Howard then tried synthesising his economic liberalism with his instinctual social conservatism. Out of this came the most substantial Liberal Party policy document since the party's founding in 1944: *Future Directions*, a 109-page manifesto released in December 1988. Five principles underpinned it: strengthening the family, restoring Australians' control over their own lives, providing more incentive and choice, ensuring a fair go for all, and building one Australia. Promising to 'restore hope and certainty to an Australian community which had grown anxious about the future', the document was an attempt to articulate an agenda of economic liberalisation within a Menzian framework of social cohesion and stability.[13]

As it turned out, *Future Directions'* time would come, but not yet. Hawke also had a knack for sensing the pulse of Australia, knew its ethos and respected its myths. At the 75th anniversary of the Gallipoli landing, he spoke of the 'special meaning of Australian mateship', paid tribute to Australia's fallen 'heroes' and again reiterated that 'more than ever it is that commitment to Australia, which defines, and alone defines, what it is to be Australian'.[14]

Hawke was a product of Australia's mid-century values and he, too, could draw on this history to justify change when change was required. Australians could celebrate their country while accepting the need for reform, such as a significant reduction in protective tariffs or the re-introduction of university fees via income-contingent loans.

Hawke was the consummate balancer. In foreign policy, he balanced party ideology against the pressures of realpolitik. He visited the United States five times as prime minister; he kept the former Liberal cabinet minister Sir Robert Cotton as Australian ambassador in Washington; he reinforced the bipartisan commitment to ANZUS. 'To me, the overriding importance of Australia's alliance with the United States was clear,' Hawke wrote. 'The Left of the Party had a different perspective; it was the United States that was suspect.'[15] Hawke saw the joint facilities at Pine Gap, Northwest Cape and Nurrungar – symbols of American imperialism to the radical left – as essential to world security. He felt comfortable in Washington and found his personal diplomacy an asset, most notably in withdrawing Australia from participating in the testing of American MX missiles without any obvious damage to the alliance relationship.

* * *

The late 1980s were characterised by a rare consensus on the importance of market mechanisms in driving prosperity.

Despite the replacement as leader of the market-enthusiast Howard with the more economically cautious Peacock, the 1990 federal election was notable for the recent accomplishments in economic reform that both parties were willing to accept. Yet while this new orthodoxy meant less government interference in business decision-making, it didn't mean less government involvement in people's lives. Governments took in more tax, the quantum of legislation continued its inexorable rise and technology-driven innovation invited, as always, the creation of regulation. What characterised the 'reform era' was better government rather than less.

As well, this new orthodoxy was as much empirical as ideological, a product of the hard-won lessons of economic trial and error. Hawke's corporatist model of managing different 'interests' in the economy through the Accord process could not completely defeat inflation. A threatened wage breakout had to be negotiated away by another Accord; it was unsuccessful. Policymakers and advisors were scrambling for answers and muddling through. In a revealing aside, in response to unpredictable movements in the dollar and the current account, Reserve Bank governor Bob Johnston reportedly confessed: 'Frankly, Treasurer, I don't know what to do!'[16]

Not for the first or last time, the technocratic experts were found wanting. A ballooning current account deficit had spooked Treasury into recommending sharp rises in interest rates. Between March 1988 and November 1989, the cash rate rose from 10 to 18 per cent. The subsequent 1990s recession was deep and long. From August 1990 to September 1991, GDP fell by 1.7 per cent, employment fell 3.4 per cent and unemployment rose to 10.8 per cent.[17] There was a trebling of long-term unemployment. In one of the more infamous statements of the decade, Treasurer Keating announced that this was the recession 'that Australia had to have'. He added, by way of explanation, 'We couldn't go on spending and consuming at the rate we were.'[18]

Even as jobs evaporated, the government continued with its reduction in tariffs. Not unreasonably, Keating was obsessed with microeconomic reform. Telecommunications policy was another bone of contention within the government. Keating pushed for a fully competitive model. Hawke wanted to subject Telecom, the government monopoly, to a competitive duopoly – the preference of telecommunications unions and executives. Keating abhorred this style of 'consensus' politics. In cabinet, he threw his pen down in a rage and walked out of the room. 'This is a f—ing second-rate decision from a second-rate government,' he reportedly spat.[19]

The Hawke–Keating partnership had by then broken down. Early in 1991, the prime minister informed his treasurer that he intended to fight another election, contrary to a previous understanding struck between the two. Invigorated by Australia's participation in the liberation of Kuwait in the First Gulf War, Hawke felt that his diplomatic powers and popular appeal made him indispensable. Keating's party-room leadership challenge in June 1991 was unsuccessful: 44 votes to 66. But it was enough, Keating calculated as he moved to the backbench, to keep 'alive' his prospects of deposing Hawke.

* * *

The eclipse of socialism changed the vernacular of politics. One of the terms that arose was 'economic rationalism' – a pejorative description for rigorous adherence to market forces.[20] Not since the late 19th-century hegemony of Gladstonian liberalism ('We're all liberals now,' the great English statesman William Gladstone declared) had free market economics boasted so many advocates. The appetite for policy boldness only grew among Liberals. They elected as their leader John Hewson, a former Treasury economist and academic, who represented a break from the Menzian political tradition. Hewson was less interested in the art of politics than the science of policy. His intellectual framework was pure economics.[21] He had served as an advisor to the Fraser government and entered parliament in 1987. To the public, he was a clean break from the Howard–Peacock years and quickly took the Liberals in a new direction.

The result was what Paul Kelly regards as 'the most audacious experiment in Liberal Party history'.[22] On 21 November 1991, Hewson launched *Fightback!*, a 600-page policy program that offered a transformation of the Australian state. Its centrepiece was a 15 per cent goods and services tax (GST) that, together with substantial cuts in spending, would fund big income-tax cuts as well as the abolition of several less efficient taxes. *Fightback!* advocated an extensive privatisation program, negligible tariffs by the year 2000, the abolition of compulsory arbitration and the establishment of voluntary workplace agreements (fully spelled out in *Jobsback!*, released the following year), the abolition of Medicare bulk-billing except for the neediest, a range of incentives for private health insurance, demand-driven places at university with the creation of a voucher system for higher education, and an independent Reserve Bank targeting inflation at between 0 and 2 per cent.

Significantly, it cast the Liberal Party as the agent of radical reform. Even Paul Keating's primary speech writer later admitted to 'admiring it', mentioning 'the energy in it, the conviction'.[23] Hawke did not know what to make of it. In a panicked cabinet reshuffle, he replaced the treasurer, John Kerin, with Ralph Willis. Observing how flummoxed this had made the prime minister, Keating made another leadership bid and this time just managed to defeat Hawke: 56 votes to 51. The outgoing prime minister was publicly gracious. Calling for unity, he asked to be remembered as 'a bloke who loved his country, still does, and loves Australians'.[24]

* * *

From his first moment as prime minister, Keating was a hunter in pursuit of Hewson. I'd earlier had a personal taste of just how effective Keating could be as a parliamentary warrior. Budget Day 1990 was my first time in the parliamentary chamber advisors' box: I was a new Hewson staffer. With the treasurer away in the budget lock-up, the Opposition enjoyed themselves. It was very different the next day, with Keating back. The Coalition backbench almost visibly quailed under the ferocity of his verbal assault. It was not until John Howard seconded then shadow treasurer Peter Reith in the post-Question Time Matter of Public Importance debate that a bit of fight returned to the Coalition.

Although Hewson initially flourished as Opposition leader, he was essentially an economist rather than a politician. When asked how the GST – which had been watered down in a 1992 re-release – would apply to a birthday cake, he answered like a professor. As Keating put it, Hewson was the 'feral abacus' and *Fightback!* was an attempt to fit up life to match theory. It was Menzies who had said, in his response to the Vernon Report of 1965, that 'policy in a democratic community does not depend upon purely economic considerations'.[25] *Fightback!* asked Australians to 'trust the professor' – something that, in the end, they weren't prepared to do. Still, to Hewson's credit, it remains the most comprehensive and far-reaching policy document that any Australian political party has ever produced. Much of it was eventually implemented; some of it, ironically, by Keating himself, when he part-privatised the Commonwealth Bank.

What should have been the 'unloseable' 1993 election turned out to be a disaster for the Liberals. A victorious Keating credited the 'true believers' in a tribute to the Labor faithful. In fact, by this time, Labor was changing fast from a traditional union-based workers' party to a rainbow coalition of environmentalists, ethnic lobbyists, Indigenous activists and progressive critics of the 'old' Australia. Keating's next term of government would reflect the preoccupations of these elites more than any previous government.

* * *

With Hawke gone, the narrative of consensus disappeared. Keating's rhetoric was more divisive and less grounded in Australian opinion. To Labor's credit, its economic program was not abandoned. Compulsory superannuation was legislated in 1992, enterprise bargaining in 1993 and competition reform in 1995. But as prime minister, Keating seemed less energised by an economic story than by a cultural one.

As prime minister, Keating became a radical nationalist, combining the history of Manning Clark with the rhetorical brutality of Jack Lang. He conjured up a new story of Australia – pitting an alleged cultural cringe of dependency on all things British against his own self-declared assertion of independence. He disliked the Australian flag, or at least the top left corner of it. In April 1992, he called for it to change, a move rejected by a clear majority of Australians. He went from economic reformer to culture war warrior, an odd transition, especially as the country was crawling slowly out of a recession.

It wasn't just Keating chafing against key aspects of the old Australian settlement. Even the High Court was discerning 'signs of the times' and, in the Mabo case, overturned the established doctrine of *terra nullius* – that unoccupied land belonged to the Crown. Eddie Mabo was an activist and visionary, whose ten-year crusade for land rights culminated in the landmark legal victory. On 3 June 1992 – five months after he himself had died of cancer – the High Court voted six to one in favour of the Mabo native title claim for Mer Island in the Torres Strait. The Court found that the native title had not been extinguished by British sovereignty over Australia because of the Meriam people's ongoing and unbroken cultural connection to the land in question. Subsequently, the *Native Title Act 1993* was passed, providing formal recognition and protection of native title and establishing a policy framework for native title claims.

In the wake of *Mabo*, Keating used an address at Redfern Park, on 10 December 1992, to offer a caustic opinion of British colonisation: 'We took the lands and smashed the traditional way of life. We brought the diseases and the alcohol. We committed the murders. We took the children from their mothers. We practised discrimination and exclusion. It was our ignorance and our prejudice.'[26] It was an eloquent but one-sided denunciation of Australia, and came strangely from a national leader. Expunged from this story were the evangelical humanitarians and Whig liberals and the success of Indigenous Australians themselves in achieving legal and political equality over the previous half-century. Such examples, which hint at a more complex story, held no place in Keating's imagination.

Keating wanted to reboot Australian nationalism. The convict stain was long gone but, for him, the British stain had taken its place. He tried to tell a different national story: it was the ground of the Kokoda Track that Keating kissed, not Gallipoli or the Western Front. The redirection of foreign policy towards Asia was another aspect of his nationalism. A new engagement with the region, he believed, required Australia to 'go to Asia as we are. Not with the ghost of Empire about us. Not as a vicar of Europe or as a US deputy.'[27] He signed a formal security pact with Indonesia, drafted in language partly borrowed from the ANZUS Treaty.

By early 1995, the Liberals had settled on giving John Howard another go. Keating had a particular antipathy to Howard. This spoke to their fundamentally different thinking and style. They were 'rivals who came from the same nursery – Sydney's south-west suburbs', yet the two leaders could not have been more different.[28] There was much about Howard that Keating disliked: the conservatism, the mistrust of elites, the idealisation of Menzies. Howard respected the views of his fellow Australians; Keating felt constrained by them. This temperamental gap only widened over time.

After Keating's 1995 statement on becoming a republic – replacing the Queen of Australia, represented by a governor-general appointed like a judge, with a president selected like a politician – Liberal research 'showed the biggest single lift in measures of being arrogant and out-of-touch'.[29] Howard capitalised on the government's misstep with a resonant election campaign of his own: 'For All of Us' was the Liberal slogan. The 1996 election was a landslide victory to the Coalition, 94 seats to 49.

* * *

There was, though, one key similarity between Paul Keating and John Howard. Both understood the importance of symbolism. From the commencement of his time as PM, Howard restored the Australian flag to the bonnet of the prime ministerial car. There was to be no more ambivalence over the Australian project.

Howard turned out to be much better than Keating at reconciling his vision with Australian opinion. He had learned the lessons of both *Future Directions* and *Fightback!* – namely that a leader's duty to lead couldn't outstrip the public's willingness to be led. Howard's ambitions for our country were hardly less vaulting than Keating's but he always gave credit to the good sense and judgment of the average voter. Howard never placed as much faith in the 'knowledge elite' as Keating or Hewson did.

In giving the control of policy development to a new Cabinet Policy Unit, led by his advisor Michael L'Estrange, he transferred the management of cabinet business from the public service to his own office and declared that the government's agenda and priorities were not going to be generated from within the bureaucracy.

The government's first budget cut real spending and delivered a clear path to a future surplus. Reducing interest payments and the cost of borrowing provided room to sustainably spend on better services and give the tax cuts that would be a central pillar of future tax reform. This was the aspirational logic behind the budget.

Waterfront reform was the epic battle of Howard's first term. As a nation inhabiting an entire continent with no land borders, Australians relied overwhelmingly on sea trade: by dollar value, 70 per cent of imports (50 million tonnes of cargo) and 78 per cent of exports (370 million tonnes of cargo) were transported by sea in 1995–96.[30] Yet Australia's waterfront productivity was abysmal.[31] The Maritime Union of Australia (MUA) was a hyper-militant union, politically aware and prepared to fight against any erosion of its privileges.

Chris Corrigan, the managing director of the seaport operator business Patrick Corporation, made plans for a substantial restructuring of Patrick in an effort to boost productivity. His methods were ruthless but probably necessary. On the evening of 7 April 1998, accompanied by black-clad guards, management asserted control of 17 Patrick terminals,

stood down the night shift and changed the locks. Corrigan
sacked his entire workforce of 1400 in favour of non-unionised
labour. Peter Reith, the minister for industrial relations, had
agreed to fund the cost of the redundancies, totalling around
$150 million. The labour dispute that followed exacted a
heavy toll on both sides. At the Newcastle wharf, four people
were injured when unionists attacked a bus carrying non-
union workers, smashing windows and throwing paint. More
distressing were scenes of screaming children brought to the
picket line, frightened by the fiery clashes with police, who
dragged away angry protestors.

Another battle was taking place in the courtroom. The MUA
succeeded in obtaining a stay of the dismissals on the grounds
that they breached the freedom-of-association provisions in the
Workplace Relations Act. Eventually, the case clawed its way
up to the High Court, which found in favour of the MUA, but
with the critical condition of a new agreement with Patrick
for a more efficient workforce. It was a classic compromise.
The MUA retained a closed-shop but conceded there was to
be a smaller, incentive-driven workforce. Within a few years,
productivity rose to world best practice. The waterfront – that
had been a source of power conflict from the Rum Corps to the
Cold War – receded from the centre stage of controversy.

* * *

Six weeks after the 1996 federal election, on 28 April, a lone
gunman armed with an Armalite semi-automatic rifle, opened
fire on men, women and children at the historic site of Port
Arthur, Tasmania, killing 35 and wounding 23. It was the
worst mass shooting since federation.

In Australia, unlike in America, there is no entrenched gun
culture; in part, because of our relatively peaceful settlement

and easy transition from colony to democracy. Although gun regulation was a state issue, the scale of the Port Arthur tragedy prompted a national response. Howard understood the importance of leadership to drive policy change under such dire circumstances. It helped that he was more pragmatist than dogmatist on states' rights. Working with state and territory ministers, the result was a National Firearms Agreement, settled just 12 days after the massacre, that banned the ownership of automatic and semi-automatic weapons, established a gun buy-back scheme, created a firearm registry and tightened restrictions on gun licences.

It was a tough sell for country voters but senior ministers didn't shirk it. The National Party leader and deputy prime minister, Tim Fischer, bore the brunt of the backlash. Protestors burned his effigy, hanging by a noose on a tree, during one meeting. At a gun rally in Sale, Victoria, Howard even wore a bulletproof vest. These early demonstrations of courage from both leaders were instrumental in securing community acceptance. There have been no comparable gun incidents since.

Still, change was either too slow or too fast for some voters. Conservatives wanting restoration rather than reform found a champion in the new member for Oxley, in Queensland, Pauline Hanson. A small business owner, Hanson had courted controversy by attacking the allegedly excessive benefits received by Aboriginal Australians.[32] These comments led to her disendorsement by the Liberal Party but did not prevent her winning Oxley with an extraordinary swing of 19.3 per cent – the largest anti-Labor vote in the country. In her maiden speech to parliament, Hanson denounced the 'reverse racism' of multiculturalism, excessive Asian migration and the so-called 'Aboriginal industry'.[33] Hanson's arguments proved especially popular in Queensland, where her party secured 11 seats at the 1998 state election.

Howard recognised that a substantial number of voters found some aspects of Hanson's criticisms appealing. She represented the conservatism that mistrusts change and instinctively resists it; while Howard represented the conservatism that respects what is and wants the future to reflect the best aspects of the past.[34] His small-c conservative strategy was to push back against One Nation's policies while assuring Australians sympathetic to her arguments that the government was taking their anger seriously. As Howard grew more ascendant, One Nation lost its appeal, although its initial rise (and subsequent comeback) testified to the 1988 FitzGerald Report judgment that political vacuums will be filled.

* * *

Howard led a remarkably united cabinet. Paul Kelly has argued that it was the most unified cabinet since Menzies, which invites a comparison between the two leaders. Neither were especially well regarded prior to proving their leadership credentials with successive election wins. While Menzies was more inclined to display his intellectual credentials, both took ideas seriously: Menzies had to reconcile his liberalism with the challenges of war and depression; Howard had to apply his liberalism to the reform of post-war big government and the breakdown of the 'Keynesian' consensus. Both were values driven. In Howard's case, that made the argument for tax reform – his most important second-term project – a product of his conviction that in order to drive productivity, the tax system should focus more on spending and less on earning.

The government launched its tax policy on 13 August 1998. Titled *A New Tax System*, it proposed a broad-based consumption tax – the GST – set at 10 per cent with the revenue to fund the abolition of less efficient indirect taxes and a reduction in personal income tax. From the beginning, Howard judged that, to succeed, it could not be an exercise in revenue raising and must be seen to be fair. Family payments were restructured accordingly so the benefits of reform did not simply accrue to high-income earners. It addressed the continuing issue of Commonwealth–state relations by ring-fencing all the GST revenue for state governments. Introduced on 1 July 2000, it was a complex change with three billion price points affected.[35] Three million businesses had to master new paperwork. By coming into effect at the end of the decade, it had the feel of the last piece of the economic reform puzzle.

The Asian Financial Crisis was the first big test of the Howard government's reform program. After a period of fast growth, a series of currency crises rocked the region.[36] There was a real fear of financial contagion; and yet, by 1999, Australia was one of the fastest growing economies of the OECD. It showed that a more flexible economy could absorb the blows from abroad. Australia's sound monetary and fiscal policy had further embedded an environment of low interest rates and institutional stability. Australia's offer of $1 billion to the most affected countries was indicative of its economic strength and standing in the region.

* * *

In May 1998, the Indonesian President Suharto resigned in favour of B.J. Habibie. An intellectual and an idealist, Habibie felt the time had arrived to lead Indonesia down the path towards a more open society. After he proposed a rethink of East Timor's status, long the 'pebble in the shoe' for Australian–Indonesian relations, Howard's foreign minister, Alexander Downer, sensed that East Timor could be moving towards independence, however uncertain the speed or method. Howard and Downer drafted a letter, sent to Habibie in December 1998, cautiously suggesting that the president engage directly with the East Timorese to work towards a model of autonomy, with a mechanism for future self-determination via a referendum.

Whether motivated by the letter or not, Habibie surprised everyone by accelerating the process to the earliest practicable moment. Not wanting to leave a 'time bomb' for his successor, he proposed an immediate referendum on independence. The situation in East Timor quickly began to unravel. Pro-integrationist militia forces, aided by the Indonesian Army, intimidated and attacked pro-independence supporters. A UN Mission in East Timor (UNAMET) was established to oversee the vote, with Australia providing considerable financial support. The voting turnout was remarkable – almost 99 per cent of registered voters. A super-majority of 78.5 per cent rejected autonomy under Indonesian sovereignty, preferring independence.

Widespread violence subsequently erupted. Howard informed the UN of Australia's willingness to lead a peacekeeping mission. Critical US diplomatic support enabled an Australian-led multinational force to restore peace and security. The Australian–Indonesian relationship was placed under massive strain; Keating's 1995 security agreement was abrogated. Nonetheless, Indonesia relinquished its claim to East Timor, and the UN Security Council established the United Nations Transitional Administration in East Timor.

Not since Borneo in 1945 had Australia organised and led a successful regional military operation. It marked Australia as a power in its own right, no longer wholly dependent on 'great and powerful friends', yet still committed to the values of freedom and democracy that had always underpinned Australia as a Western society in the Indo-Pacific. Tim Fischer said of the prime minister's letter to Habibie: 'There were two letters written last century that led to nations being created ... the Balfour letter and the Howard letter.'[37]

* * *

Australian 'independence' was the pet project of the 'progressive' elite, especially for Paul Keating, who had formally launched the Australian Republican Movement (ARM) in 1991. Few Australians were much moved by this argument, especially the inference that Australia was somehow a dependency, even if they liked the principle of a republic. As well, the Crown in Australia had become quite different to the Crown in Britain. All the Crown's powers were exercised by the governor-general, who for a generation had always been a distinguished Australian appointed by the monarch on the recommendation of the prime minister. This evolution had been driven by Australians themselves, since the appointment of the first Australian as governor-general, Sir Isaac Isaacs, back in 1931, mostly with the support of the British establishment. Regular polling gave volatile results, ranging as low as 39 per cent support for a republic, in September 1993, to almost two-thirds supportive, depending on the wording of the question and the proposed model.[38] The variability of public opinion indicated soft support, at most, for an issue that few wanted to prioritise.

Australians for Constitutional Monarchy (ACM) was formed on 4 June 1992 and, early the following year, I became its first national director. ACM encouraged Australians to be proud of Australia's history, culture and traditions. Australia's Constitution, designed by Australians for Australians, and endorsed by Australians, had worked very well. The nation had yet to face a crisis that our system could not resolve, nor had our model of constitutional monarchy caused any major problems of its own. The 1975 Dismissal had demonstrated clearly that the actions of the Crown in Australia were determined by the governor-general.

While always a convinced monarchist himself, Howard kept a previous policy commitment of a constitutional convention to propose a republican model to be put to a referendum. The convention was held at Old Parliament House from 2 to 13 February 1998. Half of the 152 delegates were elected, the other half appointed by the government. Although some doubted its value, the convention was a very Australian answer to a political problem. For supporters of the monarchy, the standout speech was delivered by Neville Bonner. 'How dare you!' he told the convention. 'You told my people that your system was best. We have come to accept that. We have come to believe that. The dispossessed and despised adapted to your system. Now you say that you were wrong and that we were wrong to believe you.' Then there was George Mye, then leader of the Torres Strait Islanders, who told the convention that his people regarded the arrival of Christian civilisation as no less than 'the coming of the light'.

The republicans were divided over whether a president should be directly elected by the people or appointed by the parliament. The direct election model was popular with the public but constitutionally riskier and likely to turn off more conservative voters. The convention ultimately resolved on a president nominated by the prime minister and endorsed by two-thirds of the parliament. The split in the republican movement hurt the referendum's chance of success. On 6 November 1999, it was narrowly defeated; almost 55 per cent voted 'No'. Only in the ACT was there majority support.

On the day of the referendum, Australia beat France at the Millennium Stadium in Wales to win the Rugby World Cup. A cartoon in *The Times* humorously depicted the Queen telling our captain John Eales that 'We've both beaten a republic on the same day.'[39] Earlier, in June, we'd beaten Pakistan at Lords to win the Cricket World Cup in what was a golden era for Australian sport.

* * *

Australians had rejected the republic but not our independence, nor confidence in a proud and successful nation. Between 15 September and 1 October the following year, Sydney hosted the 2000 Summer Olympics. It was an opportunity for Australia to showcase itself to the world as a diverse yet united community.

By any measure, the Games were a stunning success. Australia had the organisation, the facilities and, most importantly, the volunteers – some 45,000 of them – who won rave reviews from overseas visitors for their willingness to 'go the extra mile' to help. One of them, Laurie Smith, subsequently wrote a fine book about the experience, titled *Living is Giving*.

One athlete stood especially tall and proud. Cathy Freeman was a 27-year-old sprinter, born in Slade Point, Mackay, Queensland. At 16 years of age, in 1990, she was the first Aboriginal Australian to win gold at the Commonwealth Games, running in the 4 x 100-metre relay. Freeman was named the Young Australian of the Year, then went on to set further Australian records. She had placed second in the 400-metre dash in the 1996 Atlanta Olympics, and first in the 1999 World Championships. She was the 1998 Australian of the Year. The anticipation for the 400-metre race at Sydney was unlike anything that had come before.

Freeman lit the Olympic flame at Sydney's Opening Ceremony. Never before had a competing athlete been given that honour. Indigenous reconciliation was one of the Sydney Olympics' themes. Every Australian knew it was unfinished business. In May, 250,000 people had marched across the

Sydney Harbour Bridge in support of reconciliation. In the lighting of the flame, Freeman symbolised both progress achieved and progress hoped for. Her victory in the 400-metre final remains one of the most iconic moments in our sporting history. It was Australia's 100th gold medal since 1896. In her victory lap, she carried both the Aboriginal and the national flag. 'Everybody was just so at one together,' she recalled. 'It's like we were the only people who existed in the world.'[40]

18
Drifting Backwards

By comparison with the Hawke–Howard years, the subsequent decade and a half has been a time of some frustration and disappointment. As this book is being finalised, in Australia, scarcely less than elsewhere in the Anglosphere, there's a sense of economic and strategic risk compounded by cultural confusion.

To the extent that we're drifting as a nation, our leaders have let us down. In launching Paul Kelly's book *Triumph and Demise* back in 2014, I said that it was the historic mission of the Abbott government to show that the era of reform had merely been interrupted, not ended; and that the revolving-door prime ministership was an aberration, not the new normal. As it happened, that was not to be the case. Still, for nations, like people, better times are usually only a few good decisions and the emergence of a couple of key leaders away. If, as this book tries to show, we have a history to be proud of, that's because good people have made it so. Perhaps this account will encourage more of them to join our public life, to shape our future and to make our history.

§

At some point, history stops and current affairs begin. There's no hard and fast rule for how to judge it but, for me, that point was the Sydney Olympics. It was a high-water mark in the life of our nation; and shortly after that, in January 2001, I became a cabinet minister in the Howard government and thus more of a player in subsequent events that many readers would personally recall. But just because these are 'current affairs' doesn't mean that nothing happened. Forgive me if this account becomes rather more of a political stocktake but the main reason I sought public office was my conviction that politics matters: it changes the country and makes history, for better or for worse, even if most people, most of the time, go about their lives largely oblivious to it.

In late 2000, the Howard government had arguably 'hit its straps'. Bravely, it had fought the 1998 election seeking a mandate for the tax reform that Bob Hawke had contemplated in 1986, that John Hewson had unsuccessfully advocated at the 1993 election and that, before winning office in 1996, John Howard himself had said would never, ever happen. The only good grounds for breaking a major election commitment is a genuine belief that key circumstances and, therefore, important governmental priorities have changed. When that happens, political integrity requires putting the new position to the people at an election. To his credit, that's exactly what Howard did. And despite losing the popular vote, he emerged from the 1998 GST election with a working majority and a mandate that the centrist Democrats, who held the Senate balance of power, mostly respected; hence, the government was able to institute a reasonably broad-based GST in place of a range of less efficient taxes, plus big personal income tax cuts.

Perhaps it was the Olympics euphoria or perhaps it was the cumulative impact of the Hawke–Howard economic reforms, but there was more economic optimism than had been seen in many years and Australia began to be described as the world's 'miracle economy', notwithstanding the impact of the

Asian financial crisis and the 'tech wreck' of the late 1990s. Over the life of the Howard government, from 1996 to 2007, real wages increased by 21 per cent and per capita GDP grew by almost 2.5 per cent a year.[1] After being reduced to well below 100,000 a year at first, annual immigration picked up, especially towards the end of the Howard era, but still averaged only about 110,000 over the period.[2] In 2007, to strengthen popular support for immigration and to remind migrants of their responsibilities to Australia, the Howard government introduced a citizenship test that all intending new citizens had to pass, which included mandatory questions on Australian values. Popular support for immigration was also helped by the government's successful management of a wave of illegal migration by small boat.

It was in the Keating era that people from poor and troubled countries had once more begun to seek a better life by coming to Australia on small boats and then claiming refugee status. The Labor government had responded by putting illegal arrivals into immigration detention but activist lawyers and sympathetic tribunals meant that most of them ended up gaining refugee status and becoming permanent residents of Australia after a period in custody where they'd at least been well fed, adequately housed and given good health care. Unsurprisingly, the number of arrivals by boat steadily increased. The majority were flying from the Middle East and Central Asia into Malaysia and Indonesia, which had visa-free arrivals for the citizens of Muslim nations, making their way to southern Java and finding a fishing boat that would take them to Australian territory – usually Christmas Island, scarcely 300 kilometres away. Eventually, there was a thriving people-smuggling trade that was bringing 'asylum seekers', as a largely sympathetic media called them, to Australia at the rate of nearly 4000 a year by the late 1990s.[3] Coached by people smugglers, these 'boat people' mostly destroyed their documentation and usually had an unverifiable story of persecution in their homeland.

As the number of people in immigration detention grew, detainees mounted protests, including by staging sit-ins on roofs and sometimes even sewing their mouths closed. Notwithstanding a vocal refugee lobby, it seemed to many Australians that, however unfortunate their previous lives, boat people were exploiting our goodwill and gaming the system to 'jump the queue' ahead of the less 'pushy', and perhaps more deserving, displaced people waiting in camps overseas.

In countries such as Iraq, Afghanistan and Iran, arbitrary and sometimes cruel government was a fact of life for everyone; but did that, alone, give people a right to permanent residency in Australia as refugees? Besides, these asylum seekers had invariably passed through several safe countries, drawn by the gravitational pull of the Australian way of life. The introduction of 'privative clauses' to stop tribunals over-ruling officials' initial findings that people were would-be economic migrants, not genuine refugees, plus attempts to have failed asylum claimants returned to their home countries, were largely ineffective because countries of origin often wouldn't accept that boat people were their citizens. Meanwhile, many rickety and overcrowded boats were lost at sea, including one tragic incident in which more than 300 would-be migrants were drowned off Java.

The issue came to a head in August 2001 when a Norwegian freighter, the MV *Tampa*, picked up some 400 boat people whose vessel was in distress. As required by international law, the captain then proceeded to the nearest port, in Indonesia, to deliver his human cargo to safety – only to be effectively hijacked by those he'd rescued, demanding they be taken to Christmas Island. Given that no one aboard the *Tampa* was in any danger, the Howard government refused permission to dock, and when the captain refused to depart Australian waters, special forces soldiers were deployed to take control of the ship. Meanwhile, the government negotiated a deal with Nauru under which boat people would be housed there, in an Australian-run camp, while their refugee claims were assessed. Thus, offshore processing was born. That, plus subsequent boat turn-backs (in which the navy intercepted people-smuggling boats, secured them and sailed them to the edge of Indonesia's territorial waters with just enough fuel to return) effectively ended this wave of illegal migration by boat. No one was going to hand over several thousand dollars for what could turn out to be a return trip to Java or a long time in limbo. During the subsequent 2001 election campaign launch, Howard memorably declared, 'We shall decide who comes to this country and the circumstances under which they come.'

On 11 September 2001, Howard happened to be in Washington on an official visit when three hijacked jets slammed into the Twin Towers and the Pentagon; a fourth crashed into a field near Pittsburgh after passengers realised what was happening and brought the plane down. Ten Australians were among the nearly 3000 innocent people killed that day. In a sign of solidarity with the United States, Australia invoked the ANZUS Treaty and fully supported the US campaign that swiftly dislodged Afghanistan's Taliban government, which had been harbouring the terrorist mastermind Osama bin Laden. A strongish economy, Howard's success in dealing with people smuggling and a sense of rally-round-the-flag-in-a-time-of-crisis saw the government returned with an increased majority despite some early poll wobbles.

While the Howard government pushed on with economic reform (such as expanding work-for-the-dole to beat the 'something for nothing' mindset, a policy that I had responsibility for as employment minister), dealing with the challenge of apocalyptic 'death to the infidel' Islamism dominated its third term. In October 2002, at the Sari Club in Bali, an Islamist bombing killed 202 innocent people, including 88 Australians. It seems that the club was targeted because the extremist Jemma Islamiyya movement regarded drinking and dancing as especially decadent and wanted to punish all involved, including the numerous Hindu and Muslim Balinese working at the club. This atrocity ended up strengthening the relationship between Australia and our giant Muslim neighbour, thanks to the sustained police co-operation in tracking down the perpetrators and subsequent intelligence co-operation against extremism. This was further reinforced by the swift and extensive Australian response to the Indian Ocean tsunami at the end of 2004, largely put together by the acting prime minister at the time, John Anderson, under the rubric of 'regional mateship'.

There were further 'anti-Australian' terror attacks at our embassy in Jakarta in 2004 and, again, in Bali in 2005. I happened to be holidaying there at the time and spent the aftermath trying to ensure that the Australian survivors were medevaced to Darwin or to Singapore. Also at about this time, about two dozen Australian residents, mostly of Middle Eastern background and sometimes former Taliban volunteers, were convicted of plotting serious Islamist terrorist attacks in Australia.

In March 2003, despite widespread street protests against a war the UN had not authorised, the United States, the United Kingdom and Australia formed a 'coalition of the willing' to invade and overthrow the Iraqi regime of Saddam Hussein. Australia's role was to provide special forces to enter Iraq to capture swiftly the western desert airbases thought to hold weapons of mass destruction plus Scud missiles that could be used against Israel; also, to give naval support to a British amphibious assault to capture Basra. Overall, the invasion and conquest of Iraq was a remarkably swift and casualty-light operation as Saddam's forces largely melted away.

Regrettably, there was a much better plan for the war than for the subsequent peace. The immediate disbandment of the Iraqi Army left half a million unemployed men with guns, and the sacking of the Baathist civil service meant that the administration collapsed. It turned out that Saddam had largely been bluffing about his WMD and the Westernised exiles that formed the early interim administrations under a US pro-consul turned out to lack credibility and competence. It was a fertile recruiting ground for a vicious Islamist insurgency that took several years to bring under control and cost thousands of US, hundreds of British and tens of thousands of Iraqi lives, and that ultimately left a weak Iraqi government, heavily influenced by the ayatollahs in Tehran.

Meanwhile, after deploying a small special forces contingent in 2002 to help track down remaining Al Qaeda operatives, Australia returned in some strength to Afghanistan in 2005 to help stabilise a country that was lapsing back into a Taliban-inspired insurgency. While Iraq, by that time, was the 'bad war', given the continuing mayhem and the absence of the WMD that had been its justification, Afghanistan was the 'good' one, with NATO allies helping to build a civil society where women could get an education and farmers were encouraged to grow crops other than opium.

Between 2007 and 2013, there were usually about 1500 Australian soldiers based at Tarin Kot in Uruzgan province, about a quarter in the SAS and commando special operations task group, about a quarter in the mentoring task force and the rest in support roles, mostly 'behind the wire'. The special forces did sterling work hunting down Taliban leaders and bomb-makers, the infantry helped to improve the effectiveness of the Afghan Army and the reconstruction element facilitated the construction of schools, clinics and roads. In important respects, Afghanistan was changed and improved by this 'nation-building' exercise but not enough to turn a feudalistic, clan-based society into a modern liberal one in under two decades.

Although the 41 Australians killed in Afghanistan hardly died in vain, our forces did not have the legacy hoped for, as the ultimate return of the Taliban in 2021 shows. It's telling that the Americans peremptorily rejected the immediate post-Taliban call by the Loya Jirga (the country's tribal quasi-parliament) for the restoration of the king, even though limited monarchy is well suited to tribal and clan-based societies. Perhaps the key long-term outcome from our military role in Afghanistan (plus the wider Middle East) was further to reinforce our standing with our US and British allies.

Meanwhile, after churning through two leaders – Simon Crean, who'd been a creditable minister in the Keating government, and Kim Beazley, who, alongside the Liberals' Peter Costello, is one of the very best PMs we never had – in 2004, Labor pitched the brash and volatile Mark Latham against a PM entering statesman mode. Incidentally, the 'trail of human wreckage' speech I made as leader of the house in response to Latham on his first day as Opposition leader earned me a prime ministerial rebuke; yet was (in my view) one of my best. After initially troubling Howard, including forcing him prospectively to scrap the defined benefit parliamentary pension scheme, the Liberals' campaign against 'L-plate Latham' plus his late-campaign 'assault handshake' on Howard, produced a further increase in the government's majority at that year's election.

By then, though, the government was running out of steam. After successfully 'fixing' workplace relations in its first term, a PM looking for ideas went back to the old well with *Work Choices*. By abolishing the 'no disadvantage test', it made entry-level workers fearful for their pay and conditions, thus alienating the 'Howard battlers'. Earlier successful economic reforms plus historically high terms of trade produced a revenue boost that the government baked into out-of-character spending increases rather than tax cuts. In Kevin Rudd, Labor produced a shiny new leader claiming to be a 'fiscal conservative'.

After staring down a 24-hour challenge from Treasurer Peter Costello in late 2006, Howard agreed that the following term would be his last, meaning that voters were asked to elect Howard but get Costello. In the end, the government ebbed out of office. I was thought to have contributed to the rout by turning up late to a National Press Club debate with my Labor counterpart (because of an earlier interstate campaign commitment) and saying of a dying workers-rights' campaigner, who'd been protesting outside my office, that 'just because you're sick doesn't mean you're pure of heart'.

At that time, I was resolutely against Howard's retirement, figuring that a government without him would always be weaker than one with him. In retrospect, I underestimated the burn-out factor in a long-serving leader, plus the public's desire for a fresh face. The government probably would have lost the 2007 election regardless, but a handover would have allowed Howard to retire unbeaten and full of honour, as well as given Costello his chance at the top. In the end, these are the 'might have beens' arising from the human factor in history, usually the most important of all, because of the agency key individuals have in handling particular circumstances.

Leaving aside partisan barracking, Howard has a strong claim to be regarded as our best-ever PM. As well as fiscal repair, tax and welfare reform, gun control, strong alliances and the liberation of East Timor, he presided over a period of business dynamism, general prosperity and substantial societal content. He was mistaken when he'd said, in his first stint as Opposition leader, that 'the times will suit me', but eventually they did.

He had the luck of being the last Liberal standing when the 'it's time' factor accounted for a Labor government and of having potential successors who wouldn't wreck the place to succeed. But he also made the most of his luck, generally fought culture wars to a draw and succeeded in creating the 'relaxed and comfortable' country he'd once been mocked for aiming at. It was an honour to have been one of his lieutenants.

Some Howard government measures, though they seemed like good ideas at the time, became problematic later. There was the ban on civil nuclear power, inserted in a deal to win Senate support for the refurbishment of the medical nuclear reactor at Lucas Heights in Sydney. There was the renewable energy target, initially just 2 per cent, in a sop to the beginnings of climate activism. There was environmental legislation that gave green busy-bodies legal standing to challenge developments they didn't like because of alleged threats to supposedly endangered species. And there was the late-in-the-day commitment to acknowledging Indigenous people in the Constitution, as a political alternative to a formal apology; something that was easy to support in principle but turned out to be exceedingly difficult to agree in practice, as more recent events have shown. It's hard to call these mistakes, given that they made sense in the circumstances of the time, but they illustrate the unintended and often unforeseeable consequences that can bedevil any change; and also the modern reality that the detail of government is often crafted by officials who don't necessarily share the convictions of government ministers.

It was in Howard's time, for instance, that the concept of the national school curriculum was developed, including what became the three 'cross-curricula' priorities of Indigeneity, sustainability and Asia, that are supposed to inform the teaching of every subject from maths and science to French and Latin. To the extent ministers were specifically made aware of this, because it would have largely been handled through the education ministers' council, whereby elected and accountable state and federal ministers typically rubber-stamped the work of unelected and unaccountable officials, there would have been an assurance that this was no more than a respectful nod to unavoidable realities. And changing it, as with everything that's a joint federal–state initiative, would have required ministerial unanimity, which is almost never forthcoming.

Even though Labor's Kevin Rudd 'hit the ground reviewing', upon his election in late 2007, for the best part of two years his poll numbers defied gravity. He was acclaimed for his formal parliamentary apology to Indigenous Australians, despite it being much easier to apologise for past wrongs than to fix present ones. Then Opposition leader Brendan Nelson was panned for saying, in response to the prime minister: 'Spare a thought for the real, immediate, seemingly intractable and disgraceful circumstances in which many Indigenous Australians find themselves today' in what was arguably the finer speech. Rudd's 2008 'ideas summit' came up with a thousand (often impractical) proposals to improve the country, ranging from becoming a republic, to what became the Ken Henry tax review, and an emissions trading scheme (ETS) to impose a levy on businesses emitting carbon dioxide as a by-product of their operations.

Not long after I became Opposition leader in December 2009 and started campaigning against 'Labor's great big new tax on everything', Rudd dropped the ETS, which had become his signature policy. When, in May 2010, the Henry review came up with a mining tax that the big miners said was confiscatory, the uproar led to a successful caucus lightning strike against Rudd and his replacement by Julia Gillard, Australia's first female prime minister, who justified the coup by claiming that 'a good government had lost its way'. After scaling back the mining tax, she fatefully promised during the 2010 election campaign, 'There will be no carbon tax under a government I lead.'[4] The era of the revolving-door prime ministership had begun.

Prior to this, however, a government whose first budget had flagged years of surpluses had been panicked into a $10 billion stimulus package and then a further $40 billion stimulus package in response to the Global Financial Crisis of late 2008. This was a genuine banking meltdown triggered by US banks' 'ninja' (no income, no job, no asset) housing loans. Even though none of our banks had made anything like the same mistakes (indeed, at the time, they were rated among the world's strongest), it was necessary for the Australian government to stand behind them to maintain confidence. What certainly was not necessary, though, was a giant spending spree that owed more to Labor's big government instinct than any need to stimulate the economy. In the end, the government spent some $16 billion on a program called 'Building the Education Revolution', which typically provided massively overpriced covered outdoor learning areas and new halls to schools that often already had them. As well, there was a program to put insulation, or batts, into roofs, not just to stimulate the economy but to reduce power consumption and combat the climate change that Rudd had called the 'greatest scientific, economic and moral challenge of our time'.[5] It ultimately cost as much removing the batts as installing them, after poor workmanship led to hundreds of fires and four deaths.

Campaigning against Labor's emissions obsession and general incompetence, the Opposition took seven seats off

Labor at the 2010 election to reduce a first-term government to minority status. Then Gillard sabotaged her own government by agreeing to the Greens' demand, in return for support on the floor of parliament, for a fixed-price carbon levy that she agreed in a subsequent interview was the tax she'd promised never to have. She had a rhetorical triumph with her 'misogyny' speech directed at me, in the parliament, in October 2012, which went 'viral' even though it was clearly an attempt to deflect an attack on her handpicked parliamentary speaker's sexual harassment of a staffer. The establishment of the National Disability Insurance Scheme in July 2013 was a genuine attempt to help people with life-altering disabilities. Unfortunately, elastic 'who is eligible?' and 'for what are they eligible?' criteria soon led to massive cost blow-outs. And a governance structure that required near unanimity between federal and state ministers along with the politics of 'attacking the vulnerable' have made the fiscal pressures all but impossible for subsequent governments to bring under control.

Labor abolished the Howard government's border protection system and closed down offshore processing, and at the end of 2008, the people-smuggling boats had started up again, first as a trickle but eventually almost a flood. In the single month of July 2013, there were 5000 illegal arrivals by boat. All up, some 50,000 people arrived in almost 1000 boats during the Rudd–Gillard period; at least a thousand people are thought to have perished at sea. Meanwhile, a government that had inherited some $50 billion in fiscal assets and only nominal debt had run up close to $250 billion in cumulative deficits. Staring at defeat, within three months of the 2013 election, a panicked Labor caucus opted for a notionally more popular Rudd to replace Gillard – who went on to a notably dignified post-prime ministerial life, chairing the mental health body Beyond Blue and a major UK charity.

Campaigning to 'stop the boats, axe the tax, fix the budget and build the roads', the Opposition won a thumping majority on 7 September 2013, making me Australia's 28th prime minister. Over the next two years, the boats were indeed stopped, the carbon and mining taxes were repealed, the biggest federal infrastructure spend in history commenced and a start was made on budget repair. As well, negotiations that had been languishing for a decade were finalised within 12 months, producing trade deals with our three biggest partners: China, Japan and South Korea.

Under border protection ministers Scott Morrison and later Peter Dutton, Operation Sovereign Borders added a unified command structure to Howard-era policies. To combat people smugglers scuttling their boats, would-be illegal migrants were held on a mother ship before being put into unsinkable orange life-rafts with just enough fuel to return to Java. For nearly a decade after early 2014, almost no illegal boats made it to Australia – a unique achievement.

The 2014 budget delivered by Treasurer Joe Hockey was the first since 1996 (and actually the last till now) to involve a cut in real government outlays. As well, by seeking to raise the age pension age, introduce a co-payment for otherwise bulk-billed GP consultations on Medicare, standardise the indexation on all social security benefits to the Consumer Price Index rather than Male Total Average Weekly Earnings, reduce subsidies for domestic university students and insist that school leavers 'earn or learn' but not go on the dole, it was the last attempt at significant economic reform. Previously, the Rudd–Gillard government had sought to 'Abbott-proof' the budget by moving most government spending from the appropriations Bills (which, by convention, are not blocked) to legislation, which can be blocked in the Senate. Although most of the 2014 budget's specific reforms were thwarted by Labor and a populist crossbench, it laid the foundations for a return to budget balance by the end of the decade.

After Malcolm Turnbull lost the Opposition leadership in 2009 through trying to get the Coalition to back Rudd's emissions trading scheme, John Howard had helped to dissuade him from leaving the parliament. But Turnbull hadn't stayed on with the intention of being someone else's minister. In September 2015, harnessing backbench anxiety about poor polls, claiming that there'd been too many 'captain's calls', playing on concerns about 'climate denial' and offering several junior ministers promotion to cabinet, he persuaded a majority of the Liberal party room to inflict on itself the same destructive political cannibalism it had earlier witnessed on the other side.

With his support for climate action, becoming a republic and gay marriage, Turnbull was an initially popular PM, but after he walked away from mooted tax reform, failed to counter a Labor scare campaign that he'd privatise Medicare or to stress any big differences with Labor, the man my former chief of staff turned media commentator Peta Credlin called 'Mr Harbourside Mansion' managed to lose a big majority and scraped back into office by just one seat.

In 2017, utilising the plebiscite that he'd previously opposed, he welcomed the public approval of same-sex marriage. It turned out to be a respectful campaign with 60 per cent of voters supporting 'marriage equality' and opponents almost universally accepting the result. In 2018, Turnbull again lost the leadership of the Liberal Party while trying to get the Coalition to support further emissions reduction, this time the National Energy Guarantee, which was backed by the Labor states.

His successor, Scott Morrison, won a 'miracle victory' in 2019, campaigning strongly against Labor's proposed new taxes on retirees and investors, and the proposed 45 per cent emissions reduction by 2030 that Labor wouldn't cost but that the Coalition estimated would cost some $500 billion in new generating infrastructure with consequent higher power prices.

But Morrison's government was knocked off course by the Black Summer bushfires of 2019–20 and then flattened by the Covid-19 pandemic. Rather than producing a unified national response, the formation of a 'national cabinet' with the premiers and chief ministers made the PM look more like the chairman of a committee than a national leader. As well, the massive spending needed to support the states' repeated lockdowns (in a futile attempt to eliminate the Covid virus) damaged the Coalition's standing as the party of smaller government and greater freedom. The Coalition's adoption of Labor's net zero emissions target by 2050 removed what had been another key difference between the parties.

As a consequence of 262 days of pandemic lockdown in 2020 and 2021, 'rings of steel' around the city, restrictions on congregating in parks, many businesses and most schools largely closed and peacetime curfews, Melbourne became the most repressed city in the world outside of China. For the first time in two centuries, Australia was once more a prison island, with almost no one allowed to leave. For the first time in a century, we were more a collection of states than a united nation: Western Australia was shut off from the rest of the country for much of two years; and people were dying in New South Wales because, in the then Queensland premier's words, 'In Queensland, we have Queensland hospitals for our people.'[6] Old people died unvisited by loved ones in hospitals and nursing homes because the top priority was keeping such places Covid-free. Overseas observers marvelled at the passivity of a country they'd supposed was populated by rugged individualists. Eighteen months in, when freedom protests began, they were fiercely repressed. On one occasion, Victoria Police fired tear gas and rubber bullets at protestors around the Shrine of Remembrance in Melbourne.

Strangely, in a country accustomed to holding royal commissions into almost all disasters, there was no comprehensive inquiry into why Australia had implemented a version of the Wuhan plan rather than the pandemic plan carefully prepared and revised over two decades. Both sides of politics were complicit, hence neither side wanted to be held accountable for the policies of a dispiriting time that everyone would rather forget.

A feature of the pandemic was the complete cessation of immigration for over a year. Far from exposing skill shortages, the absence of overseas workers meant a dearth of cleaners, waiters, carers, drivers and pickers. Then, from 2022, migration surged, with net overseas migration (the balance of those coming against those going for 12 months or more) approaching half a million annually – an all-time record. Migration averaging over 220,000 a year in the decade up to 2020 had already put upward pressure on housing costs, downward pressure on wages and sustained pressure on infrastructure. Treasury officials had long supported high immigration because it kept the economy growing in the absence of politically difficult economic reforms. While record migration in 2023 and 2024 kept headline economic growth positive, GDP per person actually declined for two successive years, presumably because migration was lowering overall productivity.

The notable presence of recent migrants from the Middle East in the pro-Hamas demonstrations that erupted in Sydney and Melbourne after the 2023 October 7 atrocity, with a mob chanting, 'F—k the Jews' and what sounded very much like 'Gas the Jews' outside the Sydney Opera House on 9 October 2023 – Australia's own Day of Infamy – suggested problems with integration as well. It seemed that at least some of our recent migrants were living in 'hotel Australia' rather than joining 'team Australia'. It's our broadly Anglo-Celtic culture and fundamentally Judeo-Christian ethic that's made our country attractive to migrants from all over the world. Yet it is record migration, without any effective discrimination on values, that could put this at risk.

Like its Labor predecessor, the Coalition government that ebbed out of office in 2022 had never lived up to its promise. Morrison did have one key achievement to his credit though: the AUKUS agreement for Australia to obtain nuclear-powered submarines; it put aside decades of strategic caution in what was, for us, the most significant defence move since the original ANZUS Treaty. To have persuaded British prime minister Boris Johnson and US president Joe Biden that the US should make available nuclear technology previously only shared with Britain as a pay-off for its wartime participation in the Manhattan Project was an extraordinary breakthrough. I'd informally explored this option back in 2014, only to be told that Britain couldn't do it without US consent and that the US nuclear navy would simply never agree. Hence, my attempt to buy a new conventional submarine fleet from Japan, utilising a strong relationship with Prime Minister Shinzo Abe and our shared anxieties over China's increasing assertiveness. This was eventually scuttled by the cargo-cult politics of Adelaide, a city long encouraged to see domestic shipbuilding as an economic saviour.

Another key achievement was the Quadrilateral Security Dialogue linking India with the US, Japan and Australia. Like AUKUS, the main impetus was the mutual anxiety generated by China's declared objective to be the global hegemon by mid-century. The Quad was Abe's original proposal back in 2007, which Kevin Rudd had then unwisely scuttled, I had strongly supported, Malcolm Turnbull had largely ignored and Scott Morrison then helped to revive with the enthusiastic involvement of India's prime minister Narendra Modi.

It took a determined and far-sighted Asian instigator in Abe, and a self-confident Indian patriot in Modi, free of independence-era anti-Western instincts, to make the Quad a reality. That said, like the Five Eyes intelligence-sharing partnership, it's an entirely informal arrangement. Given the extent to which India has assimilated democracy and the rule of law, plus substantially adopted the English language, the Quad should be sustainable on the basis of largely shared values and mutual self-interest. Provided, of course, the US can accept that India is their equal partner. If the world is to remain safe for democracy, India needs to be onside.

A late achievement of the Morrison government was the 2022 trade deal with India, which I'd styled the economic arm of the Quad; I'd also had a hand in finalising it as Australian special trade representative. This was India's most liberal trade deal ever, and its first in over a decade.

As Opposition leader, Anthony Albanese campaigned for the 2022 election as 'safe change'. Labor denied that it planned to bring in industry-wide industrial bargaining, to increase taxes on retirees or to reduce the Morrison government's legislated tax cuts. Labor did, though, commit to a 43 per cent legislated emissions reduction target. Further, it insisted that producing much more renewable energy would cut electricity prices by $275 per household per year, even though that would require gargantuan extra spending on new wind and solar power and extra transmission lines, plus back-up for when the wind wasn't blowing and the sun wasn't shining. In the event, Labor won a bare majority, with just 32 per cent of the primary vote, and the election of record numbers of minor party and green-tinged 'Teal' independent MPs.

On claiming victory, the new prime minister's very first public remarks were to commit to implementing 'in full' what had become known as the Uluru Statement. This was the poetically crafted one-page document that had emerged from a 2017 meeting of Indigenous leaders, in turn building on 13 earlier meetings and backed up by a 25-page narrative of historical wrongs and present grievances. In essence, the Uluru agenda was 'Voice, Treaty, Truth': a constitutionally entrenched Indigenous Voice to the parliament and to the executive government; a series of treaties between governments and particular Indigenous groups focused on land management and possible reparations; and a recasting of Australian history to focus on Indigenous dispossession and mistreatment.

While constitutional recognition had been bipartisan policy since 2007, it meant different things to different people: to activists it meant giving Indigenous people more power over government; to constitutional conservatives, it meant merely acknowledging that Aboriginal people were the first Australians. A Gillard-era proposal to insert in the Constitution a clause specifying that legislation had to be for Indigenous people's 'benefit' was deemed unsuitable as a 'one-line Indigenous bill of rights' that would invite litigation over all Indigenous policy. As PM, I'd jointly hosted a round table with the Opposition leader and key Indigenous leaders, which I'd hoped would kick off a series of consultations involving the whole community. Under my successor, though, these became the largely Indigenous-only consultations that culminated in the Uluru Statement.

The Uluru demand for a constitutionally entrenched Indigenous Voice was initially rejected by both sides of politics: when he was prime minister, Malcolm Turnbull had considered it akin to a 'third chamber of the parliament', while the then Labor leader, Bill Shorten, had said that it would never command support in the electorate. That should have meant starting again with a different proposal, such as amending the preamble to the Constitution to declare that our 'one indissoluble federal Commonwealth under the Crown' had an 'Indigenous heritage, a British foundation and an immigrant character'. But influential and articulate Indigenous leaders, such as professors Marcia Langton and Megan Davis, and in particular the redoubtable Noel Pearson, were very invested in the Uluru agenda, causing the Morrison government to dither over whether to legislate for local and regional 'voices', but not a national one.

The proposal ultimately put to the people in the referendum of October 2023 would have given the Voice power to 'make representations' to the parliament and to the executive government on 'matters relating' to Indigenous people. The government's case was that this was a reasonable response to a 'gracious invitation' by the Indigenous leadership for all of us to walk together into a united future. The counter-argument was that it would inject ancestry into the Constitution, make the processes of government even more gummed up and entrench the separatism that was at the heart of Indigenous disadvantage.

The whole of the Labor Party and quite a few senior Liberals urged a Yes vote. Sporting, big business and cultural bodies were all but unanimous in favour of the Voice. But first the National Party, persuaded by the Alice Springs-based Indigenous Senator Jacinta Price (who subsequently became the Coalition's Indigenous affairs shadow minister), and then the wider Liberal–National Coalition opted to campaign against it. Half a century on from the Indigenous referendum in which 90 per cent had voted *for equality*, this time, just over 60 per cent ultimately voted *against inequality*. Despite the Yes campaign outspending No by a margin of at least three to one, the Voice was rejected in every jurisdiction except the ACT. Yet this resounding loss of the popular vote wasn't immediately reflected in any state government rethink of their own voice and treaty processes or in any less official enthusiasm for acknowledging 'country' on every official occasion – as if it belongs more to some of us than to all of us; and flying the Indigenous flag co-equally with the national one – as if the flag of some of us has the same status as the flag of all of us. There's still the near-ubiquitous official use of the term 'First Nations', even though it's fundamentally misleading about the state of Aboriginal societies in 1788.

This was merely the latest sign of the gulf that's been opening up for at least a couple of decades between 'official' and 'mainstream' thinking; between a governmental, media and corporate class that's climate and identity 'aware' and a more down-to-earth Australia that's generally sceptical about 'luxury' beliefs. For many Voice supporters, the electoral rebuff confirmed their ambivalence towards Australia and Australians; for Voice opponents, it reinforced their faith in the Australian people, if only they're given a say.

Combatting climate change has been an Albanese government crusade. Ministers typically portrayed extreme weather events as evidence of potentially catastrophic man-made climate change, requiring ever-more-urgent 'climate action'. Yet the Federation Drought was more severe than any subsequent one, the 1851 Victorian bushfires were probably our worst ever and 1974's Cyclone Tracy was certainly our most destructive storm.

From late 2022, there were three successive Hawkesbury River floods in scarcely a year. Yet none of these exceeded 14 metres at Windsor, where the flood records went back to 1799. In fact, on ten prior occasions, including three after the completion of Warragamba Dam in 1960, Hawkesbury floods had exceeded 14 metres at Windsor, with the record – a whopping 19.7 metres – set in largely pre-industrial 1867, well before there could have been any human-induced climate change.[7] Still, despite the fact that the Earth's climate has changed dramatically without any human factors (the ice ages, for instance), the government's view was that 'the science is settled' and that human-produced carbon dioxide's threat to the planet justifies an end to the use of fossil fuels, however impractical, and less flying, less meat-eating and much less heavy industry – in Western countries but not, somehow, in China, whose emissions are driving a continued global increase.

* * *

Despite presiding over two successive years of declining GDP per person and despite an 8 per cent fall in Australians' real disposable incomes over its term, the Albanese government won re-election in May 2025 with an unexpectedly large majority. The government's promise to cut 20 per cent of students' debt was very popular with young voters. By contrast, the Coalition jeopardised its low tax credentials by promising to reverse an already legislated tax cut and failed to campaign for its pro-nuclear power policy and against Labor's promised tax on the unrealised capital gains of superannuation balances over $3 million. On a primary vote of just 35 per cent, up two points since 2022, Albanese secured a bigger majority than all his predecessors since Curtin in 1943, thanks to a strong preference flow, especially from the Greens. At just 32 per cent, the Coalition's primary vote was down four points since 2022 and a massive 14 points since 2013.

Post election, the government announced a Productivity Summit to help craft a second-term policy agenda, while the Coalition, under its first female federal leader, Sussan Ley, announced a sweeping policy review in an attempt to square the circle of reducing emissions without damaging the economy.

* * *

In mid-2025, Australia remains relatively prosperous and untroubled. Yet as much as ever before in our history, there is a nagging sense that the country has been marking time or even drifting backwards, influenced by the politics of climate and identity.

In common with much of the Anglosphere, we're materially rich but spiritually poor. The explosion of mental ill-health is one symptom of people's widespread loss of a sense of life's deeper meaning and purpose. It's worth noting that Australians telling the census that they adhered to a religious faith has dropped from over 90 per cent in the 1960s to just over 50 per cent in 2021. An early chronicler of this growing malaise was (my one-time mentor) B.A. Santamaria, of whom Cardinal George Pell said: 'He could not remove or much deflect the mighty forces damaging faith and morals in the Western world but ... managed to alert an increasing number of us to the folly of embracing the forces seeking our destruction.'[8] Religious faith, it should be said, is not the only source of meaning and purpose but it's long been our main one.

From its beginning, modern Australia has been a place where only the very unlucky have missed out on a decent life. As the early convicts, then migrants from all over the world, and eventually even the descendants of the original inhabitants have largely found, people prepared to 'have a fair go' have normally been abundantly blessed with 'getting a fair go' in return. As a society, we are still less stratified than Britain and less individualistic than the United States, although perhaps no longer quite so sure we have the best life on Earth.

Housing is a case in point. With the price of the average dwelling increasing from four times median earnings in 1975 to eight times median earnings today (even in Hobart where price growth has been slowest), young Australians are finding it much harder to achieve their dream of home ownership. Not all our migrants seem as ready to fit in as before. It's far from clear that our efforts to save the planet or to make amends for past discrimination are working or are even much appreciated. In order to reduce emissions, we're phasing out the extraction and local use of the fossil fuels that once gave us among the world's lowest energy prices, were a key comparative economic advantage and have lately been two of our three biggest exports. And in order to atone for past injustices, we're giving special consideration to people on the basis of race and gender. Instead of being regarded as the genesis of modern Australia, the British settlement of Australia from 1788 now has the taint of illegitimacy due to the disruption of Aboriginal society. For at least a generation, the tenor of education has been that modern Australia is the result of invasion, environmental despoliation and disrespect for minorities, even though that's only a very small part of the overall Australian story.

Still, as this account has also endeavoured to show, individuals do make a difference. For better or worse, the world changes person by person. Australia is a land built by heroes, both known and unknown. Each generation's challenge is to be worthy of them and to build on their mighty legacy so that our best days as a nation might still be ahead.

Acknowledgments

If you've read to this point, you've probably grasped how much research goes into writing a credible history. It would be remiss not to thank John Roskam, who urged me to take on this project, and the team that's helped with countless hours of research – supported by the Institute of Public Affairs: the writers and historians Andrew Kemp and Alex McDermott; plus my researchers Paddy and Dom O'Leary. Thanks to them, I'm much better informed and trust I've done justice to their work. I am further indebted to the team at HarperCollins, led by Mary Rennie, whose queries and suggestions have improved my work.

Notes

Author's Note

1 Charles Moore, 'What Ladybird books taught me about history', *The Spectator Australia*, 17 December 2022.

2 Ben Chifley, 'The Light on the Hill – speech by Ben Chifley', 12 June 1949, australianpolitics.com/1949/06/12/chifley-light-on-the-hill-speech.html

3 Bella d'Abrera, 'Captain of the Enlightenment', *IPA Review*, Autumn 2020.

4 Kate Fullager, *Bennelong and Phillip: A History Unravelled*, Scribner, Sydney, 2023, p.165.

Introduction

1 Peter Hiscock, Sue O'Connor, Jane Balme and Tim Maloney, 'World's earliest ground-edge axe production coincides with human colonisation of Australia', *Australian Archaeology*, 2016, vol.82, no.1.

2 Billy Griffiths, *Deep Time Dreaming: Uncovering Ancient Australia*, Black Inc., Melbourne, 2018, p.214.

3 W.E.H. Stanner, *The Dreaming & Other Essays*, Black Inc., Melbourne, 2009.

4 Tim Flannery, *The Future Eaters: An Ecological History of the Australasian Lands and People*, Grove Press, New York, 2002.

5 Robert Hughes, *The Fatal Shore: A History of the Transportation of Convicts to Australia, 1787–1868*, Vintage Books, London, 2003, pp.14–15.

6 William Dampier, *A New Voyage Round the World*, 1697, gutenberg.net.au/ebooks05/0500461h.html

7 James Cook, *Captain Cook's Journal During the First Voyage Round the World Made in H.M. Bark 'Endeavour'*, Captain W.J.L. Wharton (ed.), Elliot Stock, London, 1839, 'August 1770', p.323, gutenberg.net.au/ebooks/e00043.html

8 Geoffrey Blainey, *The Tyranny of Distance*, Sun Books, Melbourne, 1982, p.23.

9 See Alan Frost, *Botany Bay and the First Fleet: The Real Story*, Black Inc., Melbourne, 2011, chap.7.

10 Ibid., p.130.

11 Queen Elizabeth I, 'Tilbury Speech', elizabethi.org/contents/armada/speech.html

12 Queen Elizabeth II, 'A speech by the Queen on her 21st birthday, 1947', royal.uk/21st-birthday-speech-21-april-1947

13 The modern phrasing is attributable to Thomas Fuller in *Gnomologia: Adagies and Proverbs; wise sentences and witty saying, ancient and modern, foreign and British*, Barker and Bettesworth Hitch, London, 1732. The principle was championed by Lord Coke, most notably in The Case of Prohibitions [1607] EWHC J23 (KB).

14 Alfred Lord Tennyson, 'You Ask Me, Why, Tho' Ill at Ease', poetry.com/poem/1129/you-ask-me,-why,-tho'-ill-at-ease

1: An Enlightened Beginning

1 Psalm 116:12.

2 Alan Frost, *Arthur Phillip: His Voyaging*, Oxford University Press, Melbourne, 1987, p.145.

3 D. Southwell to Mrs J. Southwell, 'Journal and Letters of Daniel Southwell', F.M. Bladen (ed.), *Historical Records of New South Wales, Volume II – Grose and Paterson*, Appendix D, 19 May 1787.

4   On Phillip's physical characteristics, see George Landmann, *Adventures and Recollections of Colonel Landmann*, Vol. 1, Colburn & Co. Publishers, London, 1852, p.123, archive.org/details/adventuresrecoll01land/page/122/mode/2up

5   D. Southwell to Mrs J. Southwell, 'Journal and Letters of Daniel Southwell'.

6   Alan Atkinson, *The Europeans in Australia: Volume One – The Beginning*, UNSW Press, Sydney, 2016, p.83.

7   See Anthony Vaver, *Bound with an Iron Chain: The Untold Story of How the British Transported 50,000 Convicts to Colonial America*, Pickpocket Publishing, Westborough, MA, 2011, pp.167, 172.

8   Grace Karskens, *The Colony: A History of Early Sydney*, Allen & Unwin, Sydney, 2009, p.11.

9   See, for example, John Howard, *The State of the Prisons in England and Wales, 1777*, Cambridge University Press, Cambridge, 2013; or Jeremy Bentham's 1812 writings in *Panopticon versus New South Wales and other writings on Australia: The Collected Works of Jeremy Bentham*, UCL Press, London, 2022.

10 Quoted in Michael Pembroke, *Arthur Phillip: Sailor, Mercenary, Governor, Spy*, Hardie Grant, Melbourne, 2013, p.160.

11 Alan Atkinson, 'Conquest' in Deryck Schreuder, Stuart Ward and William Roger Louis (eds), *Australia's Empire: Oxford History of the British Empire Companion Series*, Oxford University Press, UK, 2008, p.41.

12 Watkin Tench, *Watkin Tench's 1788*, Tim Flannery (ed.), Text Publishing, Melbourne, 2009, pp.19–20.

13 Pembroke, *Arthur Phillip*, p.70.

14 Frost, *Arthur Phillip*, p.142.

15 Thomas Keneally, *Australians: A Short History*, Allen & Unwin, Sydney, 2016, p.53.

16 Adam Wakeling, *A House of Commons for a Den of Thieves: Australia's Journey from Penal Colony to Democracy*, Australian Scholarly Publishing, North Melbourne, 2020, p.41.

17 Margaret Cameron-Ash, *Beating France to Botany Bay: The Race to Found Australia*, Quadrant Books, Sydney, 2022, p.376.

18 Edward Gibbon, *The History of the Decline and Fall of the Roman Empire*, Vol. I, 1776, p.93; Robert Dixon, *The Course of Empire: Neo-Classical Culture in New South Wales, 1788–1860*, Oxford University Press, Melbourne, 1986.

19 John Hirst, *Australian History in 7 Questions*, Black Inc., Melbourne, 2014, p.32.

20 Evan Nepean to Thomas Townshend, Lord Sydney, 9 November 1786, MLMSS 7656.

21 Ibid.

22 John Hirst, *Sense & Nonsense in Australian History*, Black Inc., Melbourne, 2005, p.108.

23 Robert Hughes, *The Fatal Shore*, Collins Harvill, London, 1987, p.74.

24 Cameron-Ash, *Beating France to Botany Bay*, pp.355–56.

25 Ibid., p.381.

26 David Hill, *1788: The Brutal Truth of the First Fleet*, William Heinemann, North Sydney, 2008, pp.185–86.

27 Josephine Flood, *The Original Australians: The Story of the Aboriginal People*, Allen & Unwin, Sydney, 2019, p.35.

28 Commonwealth Bureau of Census and Statistics (Australia), *Official Year Book of the Commonwealth of Australia*, 1930.

29 Lisa Ford and David Andrew Roberts, 'Expansion, 1820–50', in Alison Bashford and Stuart Macintyre (eds), *The Cambridge History of Australia, Volume 1: Indigenous and Colonial Australia*, Cambridge University Press, Melbourne, 2013, p.143; Bain Attwood, *Empire and the Making of Native Title*, Cambridge University Press, Melbourne, 2020, chap.1.

30 David Kemp, *The Land of Dreams: How Australians Won Their Freedom*, The Miegunyah Press, Melbourne, 2018, p.67.

31 Governor Phillip's instructions in Atkinson, 'Conquest', p.42.

32 Michael Cathcart, *The Water Dreamers: The Remarkable History of Our Dry Continent*, Text Publishing, Melbourne, 2009, pp.19–20.

33 Grace Karskens, 'Phillip and the Eora: Governing race relations in the colony of New South Wales', *Sydney Journal*, 2016, vol.5, no.1, p.43.

34   Karskens, *The Colony*, p.323.
35   David Collins, *An Account of the English Colony in New South Wales, 1798*, London, p.88, gutenberg.org, ebook 12565, 2004.
36   David Hill, *Convict Colony*, Allen & Unwin, Sydney, 2019, p.104.
37   Karskens, *The Colony*, p.323.
38   Quoted in Gary L. Sturgess, George Argyrous and Sara Rahman, 'Commissioning human services: Lessons from Australian convict contracting', *Australian Journal of Public Administration*, vol.76, no.4.
39   Quoted in Thomas Keneally, *Australians: Origins to Eureka*, Allen & Unwin, Sydney, 2009, p.207.
40   John Hirst, *Freedom on the Fatal Shore: Australia's First Colony*, Black Inc., Melbourne, 2008, p.viii.
41   Tench, *Watkin Tench's 1788*, p.117.
42   Quoted in Rachel Perkins, *First Australians*, Melbourne University Press, Melbourne, 2010, p.11.
43   Kate Fullager, *Bennelong and Phillip: A History Unravelled*, Scribner, Sydney, 2023, p.166.
44   Quoted in Karskens, *The Colony*, p.387.
45   J.L. Kohen, 'Pemulwuy (1750–1802)', *Australian Dictionary of Biography*, National Centre of Biography, Australian National University, Canberra.
46   Frost, *Arthur Phillip*, p.217.
47   Alan Frost, *Botany Bay and the First Fleet*, Black Inc., Melbourne, 2019, p.193.
48   Atkinson, *The Europeans in Australia: Volume One – The Beginning*; Grace Karskens, 'The Early Colonial Presence, 1788–1822', in Bashford and Macintyre (eds), *The Cambridge History of Australia, Volume 1*; D.R. Hainsworth, *The Sydney Traders: Simeon Lord and His Contemporaries 1788–1821*, Cassell Australia, Melbourne, 1972.
49   Hirst, *Australian History in 7 Questions*, p.62.
50   Hainsworth, *The Sydney Traders*; D.R. Hainsworth, *Builders and Adventurers: The Traders and the Emergence of the Colony 1788–1821*, Cassell Australia, Melbourne, 1968.
51   Karskens, 'The Early Colonial Presence, 1788–1822', p.97.
52   Ibid., p.101.
53   Atkinson, *The Europeans in Australia: Volume One – The Beginning*, p.171.
54   Quoted in Hainsworth, *Builders and Adventurers*, p.13.
55   A.G.L. Shaw, *The Economic Development of Australia*, Longmans Green and Co, London, 1955, p.19.
56   Quoted in Andrew Tink, 'John Hunter', in Bashford and Macintyre (eds), *The Governors of New South Wales 1788–2010*, Federation Press, Sydney, 2009, p.57.
57   Atkinson, 'Conquest', p.36.
58   Judith Iltis, 'John Boston (?–1804), *Australian Dictionary of Biography*, National Centre of Biography, Australian National University, Canberra.
59   Alex McDermott, *Australian History for Dummies*, John Wiley & Sons, Melbourne, 2022, p.70.

2: Rebellion and Restoration

1   Quoted in Grace Karskens, '"This spirit of emigration": The nature and meanings of escape in early New South Wales', *Journal of Australian Colonial History*, 2005, vol.7, p.14.
2   Russell Earls Davis, *Bligh in Australia: A New Appraisal of William Bligh and the Rum Rebellion*, Woodslane Press, Sydney, 2010, p.10.
3   Kemp, *The Land of Dreams*, p.48.
4   Jane Elliot, 'Was there a convict dandy? Convict consumer interest in Sydney, 1788 to 1815', *Australian Historical Studies*, April 1995, vol.26, issue 104.
5   Hainsworth, *The Sydney Traders*, p.24.
6   Hainsworth, *Builders and Adventurers*, p.76.
7   Karskens, *The Colony*, p.88.
8   Davis, *Bligh in Australia*, p.29.
9   Bligh to Windham, 5 November 1806, *Historical Records of Australia*, ser.1, vol.6, p.26.

10   Davis, *Bligh in Australia*, p.31; A.G.L. Shaw, 'Bligh, William (1754–1817)', *Australian Dictionary of Biography*, National Centre of Biography, Australian National University, Canberra.

11   Matthew Allen, 'Alcohol and authority in early New South Wales: The symbolic significance of the spirit trade', *History Australia*, 2012, vol.9, issue 3, p.12.

12   Hainsworth, *Builders and Adventurers*, p.22.

13   Hainsworth, *The Sydney Traders*, p.56.

14   Karskens, 'The Early Colonial Presence, 1788–1822', pp.114–15.

15   Atkinson, *The Europeans in Australia: Volume One – The Beginning*, p.279.

16   Ibid., p.282.

17   Hainsworth, *Builders and Adventurers*, p.38.

18   Alan Atkinson, *Elizabeth and John: The Macarthurs of Elizabeth Farm*, NewSouth Books, Sydney, 2022, p.228.

19   Atkinson, *The Europeans in Australia: Volume One – The Beginning*, p.424.

20   Grantlee Kieza, *Macquarie*, HarperCollins, Sydney, 2019, p.264.

21   Ibid.

22   Malcolm Ellis, *Lachlan Macquarie: His Life, Adventures and Times*, Angus & Robertson, Sydney, 1958, p.166.

23   Hirst, *Freedom on the Fatal Shore*, p.143.

24   Quoted in Hughes, *The Fatal Shore*, Random House, London, 2010, p.295.

25   John Ritchie, *Lachlan Macquarie: A Biography*, Melbourne University Press, Melbourne, 1986, p.133.

26   Stuart Macintyre, *A Concise History of Australia*, Cambridge University Press, Melbourne, 2020, p.56.

27   Hirst, *Freedom on the Fatal Shore*, p.143.

28   Ellis, *Lachlan Macquarie*, p.330.

29   Atkinson, *The Europeans in Australia: Volume One – The Beginning*, p.445.

30   Russell Ward, *Finding Australia: The History of Australia to 1821*, Heinemann Educational Australia, 1987, p.345.

31   Hughes, *The Fatal Shore*, 2010, p.359.

32   Hainsworth, *Builders and Adventurers*, pp.32–33.

33   Karskens, 'The Early Colonial Presence, 1788–1822', p.112.

34   Stephen Gapps, *The Sydney Wars: Conflict in the Early Colony 1788–1817*, NewSouth Books, Sydney, 2017, pp.116, 204.

35   Grace Karskens and Richard Waterhouse, '"Too sacred to be taken away": Property, liberty, tyranny and the "rum rebellion"', *Journal of Australian Colonial History*, 2010, vol.12, p.483.

36   Quoted in Kieza, *Macquarie*, p.370.

37   *Sydney Gazette*, 18 June 1814.

38   Gapps, *The Sydney Wars*, p.190.

39   Flood, *The Original Australians*, p.71.

40   *Daily Telegraph* (NSW), 23 January 1888, p.6.

41   See Lynette Russell, *Roving Mariners: Australian Aboriginal Whalers and Sealers in the Southern Oceans, 1790–1870*, State University of New York Press, Albany, 2012.

42   Jack Brook and James Kohen, *The Parramatta Native Institution*, UNSW Press, Sydney, 1991, p.88.

43   Luke Slattery, *The First Dismissal: How Governor Macquarie Invented an Idea of Australia, a Convict Built It and Britain Tried to Tear It Down*, Penguin, Sydney, 2015, p.152.

44   Marion Phillips, *A Colonial Autocracy: New South Wales Under Governor Macquarie, 1810–1821*, P.S. King & Son, London, 1909, pp.125–26.

45   Wakeling, *A House of Commons for a Den of Thieves*, p.47.

46   Ian McLean, *Why Australia Prospered*, Princeton University Press, New Jersey, 2013, pp.54–56.

47   Karskens, *The Colony*, p.172.

3: 'Not all the armies in England'

1   Lisa Ford, *The King's Peace: Law and Order in the British Empire*, Harvard University Press, Cambridge, MA, 2021, p.179.

2   T.M. Perry, *Australia's First Frontier: The Spread of Settlement in New South Wales 1788–1829*, Melbourne University Press, Melbourne, 1963, p.43.
3   Quoted in Barry Stone, *The Squatters: The Story of Australia's Pastoral Pioneers*, Allen & Unwin, Sydney, 2019, p.33.
4   Alan Atkinson, *The Europeans in Australia: Volume Two – A Democracy*, UNSW Press, Sydney, 2016, p.10.
5   Portia Robinson, *The Hatch and the Brood of Time: A Study of the First Generation of Native-born White Australians, 1788–1829*, Oxford University Press, Melbourne, 1985, p.185.
6   Michael Persse, 'William Charles Wentworth (1790–1872)', *Australian Dictionary of Biography*, National Centre of Biography, Australian National University, Canberra.
7   William C. Wentworth, *A Statistical Description of New South Wales*, G. & W.B. Whittaker, 1820, p.377.
8   John Manning Ward, *Colonial Self-government: The British Experience 1759–1856*, University of Toronto Press, Toronto and Buffalo, 1976, p.134.
9   Quoted in Andrew Tink, *William Charles Wentworth: Australia's Greatest Native Son*, Allen & Unwin, Sydney, 2009, p.49.
10 Grantlee Kieza, *The Remarkable Mrs Reibey*, HarperCollins, Sydney, 2023.
11 Quoted in A.C.V. Melbourne, *Early Constitutional Development in Australia: New South Wales, 1788 to 1856*, University of Queensland Press, St Lucia, 1963, p.125.
12 J.D. Heydon, 'Brisbane, Sir Thomas Makdougall (1773–1860)', *Australian Dictionary of Biography*, National Centre of Biography, Australian National University, Canberra.
13 Ibid.
14 James Boyce, *Van Diemen's Land*, Black Inc., Melbourne, 2018, p.121.
15 Richard Broome, *Aboriginal Australians: A History Since 1788*, 5th edn, Allen & Unwin, Sydney, 2019, p.42.
16 Lyndall Ryan, 'List of multiple killings of Aborigines in Tasmania: 1804–1835', *SciencesPo*, 5 March 2008.
17 Ibid.
18 John Connor, *The Australian Frontier Wars: 1788–1838*, UNSW Press, Sydney, 2002, p.93.
19 Ibid.
20 Quoted in Attwood, *Empire and the Making of Native Title*, p.5.
21 Quoted in Tink, *William Charles Wentworth*, p.67.
22 Ibid., p.72.
23 Hirst, *Freedom on the Fatal Shore*.
24 Macintyre, *A Concise History of Australia*, Cambridge University Press, Melbourne, 2000, p.79.
25 Quoted in John Ramsden, *An Appetite for Power: A History of the Conservative Party Since 1830*, HarperCollins, Sydney, 1998, p.40.
26 *Sydney Monitor*, 21 September 1983, p.2.
27 Mark Tedeschi, *Murder at Myall Creek: The Trial That Defined a Nation*, Simon & Schuster, Sydney, 2016, chap.1.
28 Quoted in Frank Bongiorno, 'Sir Richard Bourke', in David Clune and Ken Turner (eds), *The New South Wales Governors, 1788–2010*, The Federation Press, Sydney, 2009, p.178.
29 Stephen H. Roberts, *The Squatting Age in Australia 1835–1847*, Melbourne University Press, Melbourne, 1935, p.136.
30 Margaret Kiddle, *Men of Yesterday: A Social History of the Western District of Victoria, 1834–1890*, Melbourne University Press, Melbourne, 1962, p.42.
31 Roberts, *The Squatting Age in Australia 1835–1847*, chap.6; Macintyre, *A Concise History of Australia*, pp.59–60.
32 Marjory Harper and Stephen Constantine, *Migration and Empire, The Oxford History of the British Empire Companion Series*, Oxford University Press, London, 2010, p.50.
33 Rosalind Stirling, 'John Batman: Aspirations of a currency lad', *Australian Heritage*, Spring 2007, p.41.

34 Attwood, *Empire and the Making of Native Title*, chap.2.
35 James Boyce, *1835: The Founding of Melbourne & The Conquest of Australia*, Black Inc., Melbourne, 2012, p.115.
36 Glenelg to Bourke, 13 April 1836, *Historical Records of Australia*, vol.18, p.379.
37 Quoted in Hazel King, 'Bourke, Sir Richard (1777–1855)', *Australian Dictionary of Biography*, National Centre of Biography, Australian National University, Canberra.
38 James Murtagh, *Australia: The Catholic Chapter*, Sheed & Ward, New York, 1946, p.72.
39 Quoted in Duncan Bell, *Reordering the World: Essays on Liberalism and Empire*, Princeton University Press, New Jersey, 2016, p.216.
40 Geoffery Blainey, *A Shorter History of Australia*, Vintage Books, Sydney, 2014, p.55.

4: Towards Self-government
1 Diary of Elizabeth Macquarie, 3 August 1809, Lachlan and Elizabeth Macquarie Archive online, Macquarie University, www.mq.edu.au/macquarie-archive/ lema/1809em/1809em.html
2 Report from the Select Committee on Aborigines (British Settlements), Parliamentary Papers, 1837 (425), p.3.
3 *Sydney Morning Herald*, 21 June 1844, p.2.
4 Alexander Harris, *Settler and Convicts: Recollections of Sixteen Years' Labour in the Australian Backwoods by an Immigrant Mechanic*, W. Clowes & Sons, London, 1847, pp.382–85.
5 Quoted in Atkinson, *Elizabeth and John*, p.312.
6 John Hirst, *Convict Society and Its Enemies: An Early History of New South Wales*, Allen & Unwin, Sydney, 1983.
7 Hirst, *Australian History in 7 Questions*, p.33.
8 Ibid.
9 R.J. Shultz, *The assisted immigrations, 1837–1850: A study of some aspects of the characteristics and origins of the immigrants assisted to New South Wales and the Port Phillip District, 1837–1850*, PhD thesis, Australian National University, 1971, p.69.
10 Quoted in Michael Roe, '1830–50', in Frank Crowley (ed.), *A New History of Australia*, William Heinemann, Melbourne, 1974, p.122.
11 Edwyna Harris and S. La Croix, 'South Australia's employment relief program for assisted immigrants: Promises and reality, 1838–1843', *Labour History*, 2020, vol.61, issue 5–6, pp.586–607.
12 W.K. Hancock, *Australia*, Ernest Benn, 1930, p.72.
13 Quoted in A.W. Martin, *Henry Parkes: A Biography*, Melbourne University Press, Melbourne, 1980, p.21.
14 A term used in the Durham Report (1839), quoted in Kemp, *The Land of Dreams*, p.189.
15 Flood, *The Original Australians*, p.124.
16 Richard Broome, *Aboriginal Australians: A History Since 1788*, 5th edn, Allen & Unwin, Sydney, 2019, p.46.
17 'Colonial Frontier Massacres in Australia, 1788–1930', The Centre for 21st Century Humanities, University of Newcastle, c21ch.newcastle.edu.au/ colonialmassacres
18 Broome, *Aboriginal Australians*, p.60.
19 Flood, *The Original Australians*, p.254.
20 Anne Fairbairn, *Shadows of Our Dreaming: A Celebration of Early Australia*, Angus & Robertson Publishers, Sydney, 1983, p.3.
21 Glenelg to Gipps, 38 January 1838, *Historical Records of Australia*, vol.XIX, p.254.
22 Ian D. Rae, 'William Thomas (Bill) Williams (1913–1995)', *Australian Dictionary of Biography*, National Centre of Biography, Australian National University, Canberra.
23 Flood, *The Original Australians*, p.246.
24 See Attwood, *Empire and the Making of Native Title*.

25 Gregory Pemberton, 'Why New Zealand's Maori got a treaty, and Australia's Indigenous people didn't', *Sydney Morning Herald*, 2 June 2017.
26 James Belich, *Replenishing the Earth: The Settler Revolution and the Rise of the Angloworld*, Oxford University Press, Oxford, 2009, pp. 361, 553.
27 *Sydney Herald*, 22 February 1839, p.2.
28 Ibid., 21 June 1838, p.2.
29 Tedeschi, *Murder at Myall Creek*, p.145.
30 Quoted in Jane Lydon, '"No moral doubt ...": Aboriginal evidence and the Kangaroo Creek poisoning, 1847–1849', *Aboriginal History*, 1996, vol.20, p.153.
31 Ibid., p.158.
32 Ibid.
33 Stephen H. Roberts, *History of Australian Land Settlement (1788–1920)*, Melbourne University Press, Melbourne, 1924, chap.15.
34 Andrew Tink, *William Charles Wentworth: Australia's Greatest Native Son*, Allen & Unwin, Sydney, 2009, p.157.
35 *Sydney Morning Herald*, 6 February 1841, p.2.
36 Roberts, *The Squatting Age in Australia 1835 to 1847*, p.47.
37 Samuel Clyde McCulloch, 'Gipps, Sir George (1791–1847)', *Australian Dictionary of Biography*, National Centre of Biography, Australian National University, Canberra.
38 John Manning Ward, *Colonial Self-Government: The British Experience 1759–1856*, University of Toronto Press, 1976, pp.169–70.
39 Peter Cochrane, *Colonial Ambition: Foundations of Australian Democracy*, Melbourne University Press, Melbourne, 2006, p.208; Martin, *Henry Parkes*, p.57.
40 Geoffrey Blainey, *A History of Victoria*, Cambridge University Press, Port Melbourne, 2013, p.54.
41 Atkinson, *The Europeans in Australia: Volume Two – Democracy*, p.340.
42 Quoted in Martin, *Henry Parkes*, p.57.
43 Quoted in Kemp, *The Land of Dreams*, p.318.
44 Tink, *William Wentworth*, p.218.
45 Ibid., p.219.
46 Ibid., p.220.
47 Hirst, *Australian History in 7 Questions*, p.55.

5: Gold!

1 J.A. La Nauze, *Alfred Deakin: A Biography – Volume One*, Melbourne University Press, Melbourne, 1965, p.105.
2 Macintyre, *A Concise History of Australia*, 4th edn, Cambridge University Press, Melbourne, 2014, p.89.
3 McDermott, *Australian History for Dummies*, p.136.
4 Ibid.
5 Quoted in Geoff Hocking, *To the Diggings! A Celebration of the 150th Anniversary of the Discovery of Gold in Australia*, Lothian Books, Melbourne, 2001, p.99.
6 Ambrose Pratt, *David Syme: The Father of Protection in Australia*, Ward Lock & Co., London, 1908, p.29.
7 Geoffrey Serle, *The Golden Age*, Melbourne University Press, Melbourne, 1963, p.25.
8 Ibid., p.19.
9 Geoffrey Blainey, 'The gold rushes: The year of decision', *Historical Studies*, vol.10, issue 38, p.129.
10 William Howitt, *Land, Labour and Gold; or, Two Years in Victoria: with Visits to Sydney and Van Diemen's Land, Volume 1*, Ticknor & Fields, Boston, 1854, p.38.
11 *Statistics of the Colony of Victoria for the Year 1852*, Government Printer, Melbourne, 1853.
12 Engels to Marx, 23 September 1851, quoted in David Goodman, *Gold Seeking*, Stanford University Press, Redwood City, 1994, p.1.
13 Ben Wilson, *Heyday: The 1850s and the Dawn of the Global Age*, Basic Books, New York, 2016, p.55.

14   Ben Wilson, *Heyday*, p.xxiv; William Howitt, *Land, Labour and Gold*, p.365.
15   Andrew Roberts, *Salisbury: Victorian Titan*, Faber & Faber, London, 2010, p.38.
16   Serle, *The Golden Age*, p.20.
17   *Sydney Morning Herald*, 21 February 1852, p.4.
18   Ibid.
19   Hocking, *To the Diggings!*, p.167.
20   Ben Wilson, *Heyday*, p.42.
21   Howitt, *Land, Labour and Gold*, p.365; Mark Peel and Christina Twomey, *A History of Australia*, Palgrave Macmillan, New York, 2011, p.75.
22   Goodman, *Gold Seeking*, p.58.
23   Quoted in Andrew Markus, *Fear & Hatred: Purifying Australia & California 1850–1901*, Hale & Iremonger, Sydney, 1979, p.15.
24   Mae Ngai, *The Chinese Question: The Gold Rushes and Global Politics*, W.W. Norton & Company, New York, 2021, p.86.
25   Ibid.
26   Quoted in Ibid., p.230.
27   Goodman, *Gold Seeking*, p.186; Keneally, *Australians: Origins to Eureka*, p.495.
28   Wakeling, *A House of Commons for a Den of Thieves*, p.202.
29   Ibid., p.194.
30   Ibid., p.171.
31   Keneally, *Australians: A Short History*, p.329.
32   Kemp, *The Land of Dreams*, p.385.
33   Frank Welsh, *Great Southern Land: A New History of Australia*, Allen Lane, Sydney, 2004, p.197.
34   Wakeling, *A House of Commons for a Den of Thieves*, p.200.
35   Goodman, *Gold Seeking*, p.177.
36   David Hill, *The Making of Australia*, William Heinemann, North Sydney, 2015, p.208.
37   Ballarat Reform League Charter, Public Record Office Victoria, 1854, VPRS 4066/P0000/1, p.69.
38   *The Argus*, 3 December 1854, cited and described in Benjamin Jones, 'Eureka Britannia: civic republicanism and the politics of rebellion in the British world', in David Headon and John Uhr (eds), *Eureka: Australia's Greatest Story*, The Federation Press, Sydney, 2015; Wakeling, *A House of Commons for a Den of Thieves*, p.231.
39   Claire Wright, *The Forgotten Rebels of Eureka*, Text Publishing, Melbourne, 2013, p.437.
40   Keneally, *Australians: A Short History*, p.348.
41   Ibid.
42   The phrase 'Eureka Britannia' is drawn from Ben Jones's essay 'Eureka Britannia: civic republicanism and the politics of rebellion in the British world', in Headon and Uhr (eds), *Eureka: Australia's Greatest Story*.
43   Mark Twain, *Following the Equator: A Journey Around the World*, vol.I, 1897, p.215.
44   Benjamin Jones, *Republicanism and Responsible Government: The Shaping of Democracy in Australia and Canada*, McGill-Queen's University Press, Montreal, 2014, p.214.
45   Ibid., p.76.

6: Colonial Liberalism
1   Serle, *The Golden Age*, p.92.
2   John Shaw, *A Gallop to the Antipodes: Returning Overland Through India*, J.F. Hope, London, 1858, p.205.
3   John Hirst, *Sense and Nonsense in Australian History*, Black Inc., Melbourne, 2009, see chapter 'Australia's Absurd History'.
4   Shaw, *A Gallop to the Antipodes*, p.202.
5   Henry Parkes, *Fifty Years in the Making of Australian History*, vol.2, Longmans, Green & Co., London, 1892, p.21.
6   Ibid., p.247.
7   Quoted in Jones, *Republicanism and Responsible Government*, p.135.

8   Shaw, *A Gallop to the Antipodes*.
9   Judith Brett, *From Secret Ballot to Democracy Sausage: How Australia Got Compulsory Voting*, Text Publishing, Melbourne, 2019, p.16.
10 Ibid.
11 See John Hirst, *Looking for Australia: Historical Essays*, Black Inc., Melbourne, 2010, pp.99–124.
12 Brett, *From Secret Ballot to Democracy Sausage*, p.25.
13 T.H. Irving, '1850–70', in Frank Crowley (ed.), *A New History of Australia*, William Heinemann Australia, 1974, p.154.
14 Stuart Macintyre, *A Colonial Liberalism: The Lost World of Three Victorian Visionaries*, Oxford University Press, Melbourne, 1991, p.99.
15 *The Argus*, 29 August 1860, p.5.
16 Geoffrey Serle, 'The Victorian Legislative Council, 1856–1950', *Australian Historical Studies*, 6:22, 1954, p.194.
17 Charles Dilke, *Greater Britain: A Record of Travel in English-Speaking Countries During 1866 and 1867*, vol.II, Macmillan and Co., London, 1868, p.51.
18 Blainey, *A Shorter History of Australia*, p.98.
19 Ross Fitzgerald, *Made in Queensland: A New History*, University of Queensland Press, Brisbane, 2009, p.20.
20 Jonathan Richards, *The Secret War: A True History of Queensland's Native Police*, University of Queensland Press, Brisbane, 2008, p.17.
21 David Marr, *Killing for Country: A Family Story*, Black Inc., Melbourne, 2023, p.206.
22 Mark Finnane and Jonathan Richards, 'Speculating about genocide: The Queensland frontier 1859–1897', *Asia-Pacific Economic History Review*, 2024, vol.64, issue 1.
23 Richards, *The Secret War*, p.46.
24 *Queensland Figaro*, 22 November 1884, p.15.
25 *The Queenslander*, 1 May 1880, p.560.
26 C.D. Rowley, *The Destruction of Aboriginal Society*, Social Science Research Council of Australia, ANU Press, Canberra, 1970, p.166.
27 Heather Douglas and Mark Finnane, *Indigenous Crime and Settler Law: White Sovereignty after Empire*, Palgrave MacMillan, 2012.
28 Mark Finnane, '"Payback", customary law and criminal law in colonised Australia', *International Journal of the Sociology of Law*, 2001, 29, p.303.
29 Flood, *The Original Australians*, pp.138–39.
30 Marie Hansen Fels, *Good Men and True: The Aboriginal Police of the Port Phillip District, 1837–1853*, Melbourne University Press, Melbourne, 1988.
31 Raymond Evans, 'Samuel Griffith and Queensland's "War of Extermination"', published online, Griffith University, 2023, www.griffith.edu.au/__data/assets/pdf_file/0028/1890325/Samuel-Griffith-Essay-Dec2024.pdf
32 Paul Bugeja, *Outback Women: Tales of Outstanding 'Amazons' of the Australian Outback*, Brolga Publishing, Melbourne, 2013, p.53.
33 Paul Sendzuik and Robert Foster, *A History of South Australia*, Cambridge University Press, Melbourne, 2018, p.64.
34 Anthony Trollope, *Australia and New Zealand*, vol.2, Chapman & Hall, London, 1873, p.189.
35 David Hilliard and Arnold D. Hunt, 'Religion', in Eric Richards (ed.), *The Flinders History of South Australia*, vol.1, Wakefield Press, Cowandilla, 1986, p.212.
36 J.B. Polding, *The Pastoral Letter of John Bede Polding ... on the Subject of Public Education, 1859*, quoted in Frank Crowley (ed.), *Colonial Australia, 1841–1874: A Documentary History of Australia: Volume 2*, Thomas Nelson Australia, West Melbourne, 1980, p.401.
37 Robert McClory, *Faithful Dissenters: Stories of Men and Women Who Loved and Changed the Church*, Orbis Books, Maryknoll, 2000, p.154.
38 Macintyre, *A Colonial Liberalism*, pp.130–31.
39 Geoffrey Bolton, *Land of Vision and Mirage: Western Australia Since 1826*, University of Western Australia Press, Perth, 2008, p.25.
40 Russell Earls Davis, *A Concise History of Western Australia*, Woodslane Press, Sydney, 2018, pp.56–57.

41 Ibid., p.59.
42 Macintyre, *A Colonial Liberalism*, p.106.
43 Graeme Snooks, 'Manufacturing', in Wray Vamplew and Ian Mclean (eds), *Australians: Historical Statistics*, Fairfax, Syme & Weldon Associates, Sydney, 1987, p.288.
44 Sean Scalmer, *Democratic Adventurer: Graham Berry and the Making of Australian Politics*, Monash University Press, Melbourne, 2020, p.109.
45 Ibid., p.111.
46 Alfred Deakin, *The Crisis in Victorian Politics, 1879–1881*, Melbourne University Press, Melbourne, 1957, p.15.
47 *Empire* (Sydney), 12 December 1863, p.8.

7: Empire and Federation
1 A.W. Martin, 'Parkes, Sir Henry (1815–1896)', *Australian Dictionary of Biography*, National Centre of Biography, Australian National University, Canberra.
2 Parkes, *Fifty Years in the Making of Australian History*, p.81.
3 Henry Parkes, 'Our Growing Australian Empire', *Nineteenth Century*, January 1884, p.138.
4 Ibid., p.142.
5 Ibid., p.143.
6 John Seeley, *The Expansion of England*, MacMillan & Co, London, 1897.
7 Ibid., p.75.
8 Parkes, 'Our Growing Australian Empire', pp.146–47.
9 Ibid., p.138.
10 Ibid., p.145.
11 Quoted in Mark McKenna, *The Captive Republic: A History of Republicanism in Australia, 1788–1996*, Cambridge University Press, Melbourne, 1996, p.126.
12 *Sydney Morning Herald*, 23 August 1887, p.4.
13 Ibid.
14 *The Ballarat Star*, 6 July 1887, p.2.
15 Ibid.
16 *The Argus*, 5 July 1887, p.6.
17 *Sydney Morning Herald*, 13 December 1889, p.8.
18 Calculations made by dividing Australian population (ABS, *Australian Historical Population Statistics*, 2014, 3105.0.65.001) by post office data in Wray Vamplew and Ian Mclean (eds), *Australians: Historical Statistics*, Fairfax, Syme & Weldon Associates, Sydney, 1987, chap.10; for UK, population statistics derived from Office of National Statistics, post office data from *Thirty-Sixth Report of the PMG on the Post Office*, 1890, p.3.
19 *Sunday Times* (Perth, WA), 31 May 1925, p.9.
20 Geoffrey Blainey, *The Rush that Never Ended: A History of Australian Mining*, Melbourne University Press, Melbourne, 1993, p.240.
21 Department of Parliamentary Services, '"Gold! Gold to Australia! Gold!" Australian gold statistics', Parliamentary Library Research Note, no.22, 6 December 2005.
22 Earls Davis, *A Concise History of Western Australia*, p.62.
23 Francis Keble Crowley, *Big John Forrest, 1847–1918: A Founding Father of the Commonwealth of Australia*, University of Western Australia Press, Perth, 2000, p.38.
24 Herbert Hoover, *The Memoirs of Herbert Hoover*, Macmillan, 1951, p.30.
25 Parkes, *Fifty Years in the Making of Australian History*, p.264.
26 *The Express and Telegraph* (Adelaide), 23 July 1885, p.328.
27 Martin, *Henry Parkes*, p.383.
28 Ibid.
29 New South Wales, *Parliamentary Debates*, Legislative Assembly, 7 August 1889, p.3813.
30 Ibid.
31 Parkes to J.A. Froude, 16 August 1889, Parkes papers, A 916, ML.
32 *Sydney Morning Herald*, 25 October 1889, p.8.

33 *The Argus*, 7 February 1890, p.7.
34 Quoted in Cephas Daniel Allin, *A History of the Tariff Relations of the Australian Colonies*, University of Minnesota, Minneapolis, 1918, p.112.
35 Susan Priestly, *Echuca: A Centenary History*, Jacaranda Press, Echuca, 1965, p.134.
36 Ibid.
37 *The Argus*, 7 January 1896, p.5.
38 *Daily Telegraph*, 13 March 1897, p.5.
39 'Reminiscences of a Victorian journalist', *Corowa Free Press*, NSW, 6 December 1895, p.3.
40 Ray Markey, 'Explaining union mobilisation in the 1880s and early 1900s', *Labour History*, 2002, vol.83, p.21.
41 P.F. Donovan, 'Australia and the great London dock strike: 1889', *Labour History*, November 1972, no.23, pp.17–26.
42 *Sydney Morning Herald*, 29 January 1887, p.9.
43 *The Argus*, 3 March 1891, p.7.
44 John Williamson, 'Clark, Andrew Inglis', in Helen Irving (ed.), *The Centenary Companion to Australian Federation*, Cambridge University Press, Melbourne, 1999, p.345.
45 See Greg Taylor, 'Why were Aborigines originally excluded from the races power?', *The University of Queensland Law Journal*, 2018, vol.37, issue 2.
46 *Brisbane Courier*, 16 April 1885, p.5.
47 Official Report of the Australasian National Convention Debates, 3 April 1891, NSW Government Printer, 1891, p.703.
48 *Australian Star*, 21 January 1891, p.2.
49 Greg Taylor, 'A history of section 127 of the Commonwealth Constitution', *Monash University Law Review*, 42, 2016, p.206.
50 Quoted in Judith Brett, *The Enigmatic Mr Deakin*, Text Publishing, Melbourne, 2017, p.228.
51 Macintyre, *A Concise History of Australia*, Cambridge University Press, Melbourne, 2016, p.132.
52 Chay Fisher and Christoper Kent, 'Two depressions, one banking collapse', Reserve Bank of Australia, Research Discussion Paper, 1999–2006, p.11.
53 Macintyre, *A Concise History of Australia*, p.132.
54 *Australian Workman*, 13 July 1895, p.2.
55 *Sydney Morning Herald*, 17 March 1896, p.5.
56 Marilyn Lake and Henry Reynolds, *Drawing the Global Colour Line: White Men's Countries and the International Challenge of Racial Equality*, Cambridge University Press, Melbourne, 2008, pp.43–44.
57 Quoted in Stuart Ward, *United Kingdom: A Global History of the End of Britain*, Cambridge University Press, Melbourne, 2023, p.67.
58 Alfred Deakin, *The Federal Story: The Inner History of the Federal Cause*, Robertson and Mullens, Melbourne, 1944, p.77.
59 Quoted in Clare Wright, *You Daughters of Freedom: The Australians Who Won the Vote and Inspired the World*, Text Publishing, Melbourne, 2018, p.68.
60 Ibid.
61 Ibid., p.71.
62 Ibid.

8: A Bold Experiment

1 Marian Simms, '1901: Getting the job done', in Benjamin T. Jones, Frank Bongiorno and John Uhr (eds), *Elections Matter: Ten Federal Elections That Shaped Australia*, Monash University Publishing, Melbourne, 2018.
2 Michael Davitt, *Life and Progress in Australasia*, Methuen and Co., London, 1898, p.408.
3 Stuart Macintyre, *The Succeeding Age, 1901–1942: The Oxford History of Australia, Volume 4*, Oxford University Press, Melbourne, 1986, pp.42–43.
4 Quoted in A.G. Austin (ed.), *The Webbs' Australian Diary 1898*, Sir Issac Pitman & Sons, Melbourne, 1965, p.109.
5 Mark Twain, *Following the Equator*, American Publishing Company, Hartford, 1897, p.138.

6 Brad Delong, *Slouching Towards Utopia: An Economic History of the Twentieth Century*, Basic Books, 2022, p.9.
7 Ronald Norris, *The Emergent Commonwealth: Australian Federation, Expectations and Fulfilment 1889–1910*, Melbourne University Press, Melbourne, 1975, p.15.
8 Ibid.
9 *Daily Telegraph* (NSW), 6 March 1901, p.3.
10 *The Worker* (Wagga, NSW), 23 February 1901, p.4.
11 Quoted in Timothy Kendell, *Within China's Orbit? China Through the Eyes of the Australian Parliament*, Parliamentary Fellowship Monograph, 2008, chap.1.
12 Quoted in David Kemp, *A Democratic Nation 1901–1925*, The Miegunyah Press, Melbourne, 2019, p.50.
13 Ibid., pp.55–56.
14 Commonwealth Parliamentary Debates 1901–2, vol.4, pp.5157–58.
15 Geoffrey Bolton, *Edmund Barton: The One Man for the Job*, Allen & Unwin, Sydney, 2000, p.245.
16 Banjo Paterson, 'The Offer of Troops', in *The Story of South Africa, Volume II*, World Publishing Co., 1902.
17 Wright, *You Daughters of Freedom*, p.107.
18 Brett, *From Secret Ballot to Democracy Sausage*, p.57.
19 Commonwealth Parliament, *Hansard*, Senate, 10 April 1902.
20 Kemp, *A Democratic Nation 1901–1925*, p.161.
21 Peter Lloyd, 'The Links Between Tariff Protection and Wage Protection in the Early Federation', Austaxpolicy: Tax and Transfer Policy Blog, 15 February 2018.
22 Marian Sawer, *The Ethical State? Social Liberalism in Australia*, Melbourne University Press, Melbourne, 2003, p.73.
23 John Rickard, *Class and Politics: New South Wales, Victoria and the Early Commonwealth: 1890–1910*, ANU Press, Canberra, 1976, p.221.
24 Broome, *Aboriginal Australians*, p.98.
25 Hirst, *Australian Democracy*, pp.24, 113, 181–83.
26 Kemp, *A Democratic Nation 1901–1925*, p.200.
27 Ross McMullin, *The Light on the Hill: The Australian Labor Party 1891–1991*, Oxford University Press, Melbourne, 1991, p.56, quoted in John Hirst, 'Nation Building 1901–14', in Bashford and Macintyre, *Cambridge History of Australia, Volume 2: The Commonwealth of Australia*, Cambridge University Press, 2013, Melbourne, p.23.
28 Hirst, 'Nation Building 1901–14', in Bashford and Macintyre (eds), *Cambridge History of Australia, Volume 2*, chap.1.
29 Quoted in John Uhr, '1910: Fisher leads Labor to victory', in Ben Jones, Frank Bongiorno, John Uhr (eds), *Elections Matter*, p.55.
30 Quoted in Kemp, *A Democratic Nation 1901–1925*, p.272.
31 Ibid., p.268.
32 *The Argus*, 3 August 2014, p.14.

9: The Great War

1 C.E.W. Bean, *The Official History of Australia in the War of 1914–18, Volume VI*, Angus & Robertson, Sydney, 1942, p.1096.
2 Sir Irving Benson, *The Man with the Donkey: John Simpson Kirkpatrick, the Good Samaritan of Gallipoli*, Hodder & Stoughton, London, 1965, p.46.
3 *The Argus*, 8 May 1915, p.1.
4 C.E.W. Bean, *The Official History of Australia in the War of 1914–1918, Volume II*, Angus & Robertson, Sydney, 1924, p.910.
5 Winston Churchill, *The World Crisis 1911–1914*, Thornton Butterworth, London, 1923, p.195.
6 *Sydney Morning Herald*, 23 August 1887, p.4.
7 *Port Pirie Recorder and North Western Mail*, 10 August 1914, p.3.
8 'Caleb Shang', Australian War Memorial, www.awm.gov.au/learn/schools/resources/anzac-diversity/chinese-anzacs/caleb-shang

9   Jeffrey Grey, *A Military History of Australia*, Cambridge University Press, Melbourne, 2008, p.89.
10   Quoted in Jean Bou, 'Introduction', in Jean Bou (ed.), *The AIF in Battle, How the Australian Imperial Force Fought, 1914–1918*, Melbourne University Press, Melbourne, 2016, p.20.
11   Grey, *A Military History of Australia*, p.89.
12   C.E.W. Bean, *The Official History of Australia in the War of 1914–1918: Volume III*, Angus & Robertson, Sydney, 1929, p.600.
13   Grey, *A Military History of Australia*, p.92.
14   Quoted in A.B. 'Banjo' Paterson, *Song of the Pen: Complete Works, 1901–1941*, Lansdowne Press, Sydney, 1983, p.644.
15   Nicholas Lambert, *The War Lords and the Gallipoli Disaster: How Globalized Trade Led Britain to Its Worst Defeat of the First World War*, Oxford University Press USA, Cary, 2021.
16   Quoted in Hirst, *Sense and Nonsense in Australian History*.
17   *Sydney Morning Herald*, 8 May 1915, p.13.
18   C.E.W. Bean, *The Official History of Australia in the War of 1914–1918, Volume I*, Angus & Robertson, Sydney, 1941, p.607.
19   Quoted in James McWilliams and R James Steel, *Amiens 1918: The Last Great Battle*, Tempus Publishing, Stroud, 2007, p.24.
20   'Great War Nurses', Australian War Memorial online, www.awm.gov.au/visit/exhibitions/nurses/ww1
21   Geoffrey Blainey, *The Story of Australia's People: The Rise and Rise of a New Australia*, Penguin Random House, Sydney, 2020, p.236.
22   Grey, *A Military History of Australia*, p.117.
23   Peel and Twomey, *A History of Australia*, pp.163–64.
24   Grey, *A Military History of Australia*, p.102.
25   McDermott, *Australian History for Dummies*, p.249.
26   Grey, *A Military History of Australia*, p.103.
27   Quoted in Ian Turner, '1914–1919', in Frank Crowley (ed.), *A New History of Australia*, William Heinemann, Sydney, 1974, p.330.
28   L.F. Fitzhardinge, *The Little Digger: 1914–1952*, Angus & Robertson, Sydney, 1979, p.190; Bolton, *Edmund Barton*, p.324.
29   Fitzhardinge, *The Little Digger: 1914–1952*, p.227.
30   McDermott, *Australian History for Dummies*, p.261.
31   Joan Beaumont, *Broken Nation: Australians in the Great War*, Allen & Unwin, Sydney, 2013, p.385.
32   *The Age*, 4 November 1939, p.30.
33   Kemp, *A Democratic Nation 1901–1925*, p.354.
34   Quoted in Peel and Twomey, *A History of Australia*, p.164.
35   David Lloyd George, *War Memoirs of David Lloyd George, 1918*, Little, Brown, and Company, 1937, p.345.
36   A.J.P. Taylor, *Illustrated History of the First World War*, Hamish Hamilton, London, 1963, p.179.
37   Roland Perry, *Monash: The Outsider Who Won a War*, William Heinemann, North Sydney, 2007, p.134.
38   Ibid., p.306.
39   Ross McMullin, '"Never Forget Australia": Transformation at Villers-Bretonneux', Proceedings of the Conference held at the Pompey Elliot Memorial Hall, Camberwell RSL, Victoria, 14 April 2018, www.mhhv.org.au/wp-content/uploads/Never-Forget-Australia-Dr-Ross-McMullin.pdf
40   Peter Doyle, *Gallipoli 1915: The Fight for the Dardanelles Strait*, The History Press, Gloucestershire, 2011, p.96.
41   'Villers-Bretonneux: "France and Australia together forever …"', Sir John Monash Centre, Australian National Memorial, France, sjmc.gov.au/villers-bretonneux-france-and-australia-together-forever
42   John Monash, *The Australian Victories in France in 1918*, Hutchinson & Co., London, 1920, pp.75–76.
43   Blainey, *The Story of Australia's People*, p.245.
44   Keneally, *Australians: A Short History*, p.560.

45 Department of Veterans' Affairs, *A Guide to Australian Memorials on the Western Front in France and Belgium, April 1916–November 1918*, www.dva.gov.au/sites/default/files/files/publications/commemorations-war-graves/westernfront.pdf, accessed 17 February 2023.

10: A Funereal Decade

1   *Newcastle Morning Herald and Miners' Advocate*, 19 April 1917.
2   Stephen Garton, *The Cost of War*, Sydney University Press, 2020, chap.3.
3   John Rickard, *Australia: A Cultural History*, Monash University Publishing, Melbourne, 2017, p.114.
4   Quoted in Keneally, *Australians: A Short History*, p.566.
5   Blainey, *The Story of Australia's People*, p.247.
6   Quoted in David Lee, *Stanley Melbourne Bruce: Australian Internationalist*, Continuum International Publishing Group, London, 2010, p.20.
7   The Parliament of the Commonwealth of Australia, *Report of the Repatriation Commission for the year ending 30th June 1924*, Commonwealth Government of Australia, Canberra, 1924, p.5.
8   Stephen Garton and Peter Stanley, 'The Great War and its aftermath, 1914–22', in Bashford and Macintyre (eds), *The Cambridge History of Australia, Volume 2*, p.59.
9   Keneally, *Australians: A Short History*, p.620.
10 McDermott, *Australian History for Dummies*, p.277.
11 Frank Bongiorno, *Dreamers and Schemers: A Political History of Australia*, Black Inc., Melbourne, 2022, p.145.
12 Hirst, *Australian History in 7 Questions*, p.150.
13 Quoted in Geoffrey Serle, *John Monash: A Biography*, Melbourne University Press, Melbourne, 1982, p.423.
14 Ibid.
15 Frederic Eggleston, *State Socialism in Victoria*, P.S. King & Sons, London, 1932, p.168.
16 Perry, *Monash*, p.486.
17 Peel and Twomey, *A History of Australia*, p.171.
18 Macintyre, *The Succeeding Age*, p.183.
19 Quoted in John Rickard, *H.B. Higgins: The Rebel as Judge*, Allen & Unwin, Sydney, 1984, p.238.
20 Ibid.
21 F.C. Browne, *They Called Him Billy: A Biography of The Rt. Hon. W.M. Hughes*, Peter Huston, Sydney, 1946, p.137.
22 Marnie Haig-Muir, 'The Economy at War', in Joan Beaumont (ed.), *Australia's War, 1914–18*, Routledge, New York, 2020, p.138.
23 Carl Bridge, 'Page, Sir Earle Christmas (1880–1961)', *Australian Dictionary of Biography*, National Centre of Biography, Australian National University, Canberra.
24 Quoted in Frank Welsh, *Australia: A New History of the Great Southern Land*, Allen Lane, London, 2004, p.390.
25 Quoted in Stephen Wilks, *'Now is the Psychological Moment' – Earle Page and the Imagining of Australia*, ANU Press, Canberra, 2018, p.91.
26 Quoted in Blainey, *The Story of Australia's People*, p.262.
27 *The Argus*, 20 April 1923, p.9.
28 Alan McLean, *Why Australia Prospered*, Princeton University Press, New Jersey, 2013, p.147.
29 Ibid., p.148.
30 Ibid., p.149.
31 McDermott, *Australian History for Dummies*, p.289.
32 John K. Wilson, 'Government and the Evolution of Public Policy', in Simon Ville & Glenn Withers (eds), *The Cambridge Economic History of Australia*, Cambridge University Press, Port Melbourne, 2015, p.340.
33 Quoted in Macintyre, *The Succeeding Age*, p.208.
34 Ibid., p.209.
35 Peel and Twomey, *A History of Australia*, p.176.

36 National Museum of Australia online, 'Qantas established', www.nma.gov.au/
    defining-moments/resources/qantas-established
37 Bruce Mitchell, 'Booth, Edgar Harold (1893–1963), *Australian Dictionary of
    Biography*, National Centre of Biography, Australian National University; Harry
    G. Mond, J. Graeme Sloman and Rowland H. Edwards, 'The First Pacemaker',
    Pacing and Clinical Electrophysiology, March 1982, vol.5, issue 2, pp.278–82.
38 Larry Rhodes and Robert Campbell, 'History of cardiac pacing and defibrillation
    in the young', in Maully Shah, Larry Rhodes and Jonathan Kaltman (eds), *Cardiac
    Pacing and Defibrillation in Pediatric and Congenital Heart Disease*, Wiley
    Blackwell, Edinburgh, 2017, p.3.
39 Bess Nungarrayi Price, 'Foreword', in Gabriël Moens and Augusto Zimmermann
    (eds), *The Spirit Behind the Voice: The Religious Dimension of the 'Voice'
    Proposal*, Connor Court, Redlands, 2023.
40 *Macleay Chronicle*, 7 October 1925, p.8.
41 Brett, *From Secret Ballot to Democracy Sausage*, p.120.
42 See John Hirst, 'The Communist Threat', *Sense and Nonsense in Australian
    History*, Black Inc., Melbourne, 2009.
43 Quoted in Stuart Macintyre, *The Reds: The Communist Party of Australia From
    Origins to Illegality*, Allen & Unwin, Sydney, 1998, p.56.
44 Ibid. For examples, see Nick Dyrenfurth and Frank Bongiorno, *A Little History of
    the Australian Labor Party*, UNSW Press, Sydney, 2011, p.69; Stuart Macintyre's
    monumental two-volume history of the Australian Communists: *The Reds*, and
    The Party, Allen & Unwin, Sydney, 2022.
45 Hirst, 'The Communist Threat'.
46 Ibid.
47 Bede Nairn, *The 'Big Fella' – Jack Lang and the Australian Labor Party, 1891–
    1949*, Melbourne University Press, Melbourne, 1986, p.62.
48 Ross Fitzgerald, *'Red Ted': The Life of E.G. Theodore*, University of Queensland
    Press, Brisbane, 1994, p.178.
49 Quoted in Bede Nairn, 'Lang, John Thomas (Jack) (1876–1975)', *Australian
    Dictionary of Biography*, National Centre of Biography, Australian National
    University; Gough Whitlam, 'Socialism within the Australian Constitution', John
    Curtin Memorial Lecture, 1961, john.curtin.edu.au/jcmemlect/whitlam1961.html
50 Fitzgerald, *'Red Ted'*, p.165.
51 Nairn, *The 'Big Fella'*, p.71.
52 Gideon Haigh, *The Brilliant Boy: Doc Evatt and the Great Australian Dissent*,
    Simon & Schuster, Cammeray, 2021, p.70.
53 Quoted in Cecil Edwards, *Bruce of Melbourne: A Man of Two Worlds*,
    Heinemann, London, 1965, p.89.
54 Ibid.
55 Quoted in Judith Brett, *Australian Liberals and the Moral Middle Class: From
    Alfred Deakin to John Howard*, Cambridge University Press, Melbourne, 2003,
    p.80.
56 Quoted in Lee, *Stanley Melbourne Bruce: Australian Internationalist*, p.85.

11: The Economic Crisis

1   David Potts, *The Myth of the Great Depression*, Scribe Publications, Melbourne,
    2006, p.10.
2   Ibid., p.80.
3   Joan Beaumont, *Australia's Great Depression*, Allen & Unwin, Sydney, 2022,
    p.81.
4   Ibid., p.186.
5   Quoted in William Coleman, Selwyn Cornish and Alf Hagger, *Giblin's Platoon:
    The Trials and Triumphs of the Economist in Australian Public Life*, ANU
    E-Press, Canberra, 2006, p.109.
6   *Yass-Tribune Courier*, 17 October 1929, p.2.
7   Ibid., p.275.
8   Beaumont, *Australia's Great Depression*.
9   Keneally, *Australians: A Short History*, p.643.
10 Blainey, *The Story of Australia's People*, p.284.

11 Census of the Commonwealth of Australia, 1933, pp.2256–57; United States Census Bureau, Historical Census of Housing Tables: Homeownership, www.census.gov/data/tables/time-series/dec/coh-owner.html; Alex J. Pollock, 'Long-term Home Ownership Trends: The US, England, and Canada', American Enterprise Institute, March 2014, www.aei.org/articles/long-term-home-ownership-trends-the-us-england-and-canada

12 Macintyre, *The Reds*, p.205.

13 Potts, *The Myth of the Great Depression*, p.18.

14 Ibid.

15 Macintyre, *A Concise History of Australia*, 5th edn, Cambridge University Press, Melbourne, 2000, p.188.

16 Robert Cooksley, *Lang and Socialism: A Study in the Great Depression*, ANU Press, Canberra, 1971, p.10.

17 Ibid., p.22.

18 Quoted in Anne Henderson, 'Peace and War', in Zachary Gorman (ed.), *The Young Menzies: Success, Failure, Resilience 1894–1942*, Melbourne University Press, Melbourne, 2022, p.100.

19 Serle, *John Monash*, p.517.

20 Ibid., p.520.

21 *The Herald* (Melbourne), 1 June 1928, p.4.

22 Enid Lyons, *So We Take Comfort*, Heinemann, Melbourne, 1965.

23 Welsh, *Great Southern Land*, p.397.

24 Henderson, 'Peace and War', pp.235–36.

25 Ibid.

26 Judith Brett, *Australian Liberals and the Moral Middle Class*, Cambridge University Press, Melbourne, 2003, pp.99–100.

27 McLean, *Why Australia Prospered*, p.175; Beaumont, *Australia's Great Depression*, p.404; T.J. Valentine, 'The Battle of Plans: A Macroeconomic Model of the Interwar Economy', in R.G. Gregory and N.G. Butlin, *Recovery from the Depression: Australia and the World Economy in the 1930s*, Cambridge University Press, Melbourne, 1988, chap.7.

28 Quoted in Kate White, *Joseph Lyons, Prime Minister of Australia 1932–1939*, Black Inc., Melbourne, 2000, p.123.

29 Quoted in Henderson, 'Peace and War', p.256.

30 Quoted in Macintyre, *The Succeeding Age*, p.268.

31 Matthew Cunningham, *Mobilising the Masses: Populist Conservative Movements in Australia and New Zealand During the Great Depression*, ANU Press, Canberra, 2022, p.120.

32 Beaumont, *Australia's Great Depression*, p.389.

33 Anne Henderson, *Joseph Lyons: The People's Prime Minister*, NewSouth Books, Sydney, 2011, p.266.

34 Quoted in Donald J. Markwell, 'Keynes and Australia', Reserve Bank of Australia, Research Discussion Paper, June 2000, p.20.

35 Bongiorno, *Dreamers and Schemers*, p.169.

36 Ibid., p.170.

37 *Sydney Morning Herald*, 14 May 1932, p.13.

38 John Robertson, *J.H. Scullin – A political biography*, University of Western Australia Press, Nedlands, 1974, p.371; Rickard, *Australia: A Cultural History*, p.129.

39 Macintyre, *The Succeeding Age*, p.318.

40 Bain Attwood, *William Cooper: An Aboriginal Life Story*, The Miegunyah Press, Carlton, 2021, p.142.

41 McDermott, *Australian History for Dummies*, p.307.

42 Bongiorno, *Dreamers and Schemers*, p.158.

43 John Murphy, *A Decent Provision: Australian Welfare Policy, 1870 to 1949*, Ashgate Publishing, Farnham, 2011, p.187.

44 Quoted in A.W. Martin, *Robert Menzies: A Life, Vol. 1*, Melbourne University Press, Melbourne, 1993, p.257.

45 Lyons, *So We Take Comfort*, p.276.

12: Australian Threatened

1 Quoted in T.R. Frame, *Pacific Partners: A History of Australian–American Naval Relations*, Hodder & Stoughton, Rydalmere, 1992, p.49.
2 Martin, *Robert Menzies: A Life, Vol. 1*, p.261.
3 Cameron Hazlehurst, *Menzies Observed*, Allen & Unwin, Sydney, 1979, p.28.
4 *The Age*, 12 November 1929, p.9.
5 'War in Europe Again – "My Melancholy Duty"', National Library of Australia, www.nla.gov.au/digital-classroom/year-10/internment-world-war-ii-1939-45/themes/war-europe-again-my-melancholy
6 Quoted in Paul Hasluck, *The Government and the People, 1939–1941*, Halstead Press, Sydney, 1965, p.201.
7 Quoted in Troy Bramston, *Robert Menzies: The Art of Politics*, Scribe Publications, Melbourne, 2023, p.105.
8 Kosmas Tsokhas, '"Trouble must follow": Australia's ban on iron ore to Japan in 1939', *Modern Asian Studies*, 1995, vol.29, no.4, p.874.
9 Honae H. Cuffe, 'The limits of Empire: Australia, eastern appeasement and the drift to war in the Pacific, 1937–41', *History Australia*, 2018, vol.15, issue 4.
10 Jeffrey Grey, *A Military History of Australia*, Cambridge University Press, Melbourne, 2008, p.138.
11 Kate Darian-Smith, 'World War 2 and Post-War Reconstruction, 1939-49', in Bashford and Macintyre (ed.), *The Cambridge History of Australia, Volume 2*, p.89.
12 Quoted in James Curran, *Curtin's Empire*, Cambridge University Press, Melbourne, 2011, p.74.
13 David Horner, *The War Game: Australian war leadership from Gallipoli to Iraq*, Allen & Unwin, Sydney, 2022, p.118.
14 Broadcast speech by R.G. Menzies, 26 April 1939, Department of Foreign Affairs and Trade Historical Documents website, www.dfat.gov.au/about-us/publications/historical-documents/Pages/volume-02/73-broadcast-speech-by-mr-rg-menzies-prime-minister
15 McDermott, *Australian History for Dummies*, p.318; Keneally, *Australians: A Short History*, p.683.
16 A.W. Martin, *Robert Menzies: A Life, Vol. 2*, Melbourne University Press, Melbourne, 1999.
17 Quoted in Bongiorno, *Dreamers and Schemers*, p.263.
18 Quoted in John Hirst, *Looking for Australia: Historical Essays*, Black Inc., Melbourne, 2010, p.179.
19 David Horner, 'Strategy and Command in Australia's Campaigns of 1941', Remembering 1941 Conference, Australian War Memorial, 2001.
20 Peter Stanley, *Invading Australia: Japan and the Battle for Australia, 1942*, Penguin Books, Sydney, 2008.
21 Grey, *A Military History of Australia*, p.181.
22 Ibid., p.162.
23 Keneally, *Australians*, p.698.
24 Ibid., p.708.
25 Hasluck, *The Government and the People, 1939–1941*, p.280.
26 David Kemp, *A Liberal State: How Australians Chose Liberalism Over Socialism, 1926–1966*, The Miegunyah Press, Carlton, 2021, p.240.
27 Quoted in Hasluck, *The Government and the People, 1939–1941*, p.560.
28 Dr Alan Stephens, 'The Royal Australian Air Force in 1941', Remembering 1941 Conference, Australian War Memorial, Canberra, 2001.
29 Quoted in Anne Henderson, *Menzies at War*, NewSouth Books, Sydney, 2014, p.57.
30 *The Herald* (Melbourne), 27 December 1941, p.10.
31 Peter Edwards, 'From Curtin to Beazley: Labor leaders and the American alliance', Lecture, John Curtin Prime Ministerial Library, 2001, john.curtin.edu.au/events/speeches/edwardsp.html
32 *Sydney Morning Herald*, 17 February 1942, p.5.
33 Kate Darian-Smith, 'World War 2 and post-war reconstruction, 1939–1949', in Bashford and Macintyre (eds), *The Cambridge History of Australia, Volume 2*, p.95.

34 McDermott, *Australian History for Dummies*, pp.326–27.
35 Ibid.
36 'Bombing of Darwin', Australian War Memorial, Canberra, www.awm.gov.au/collection/E84294
37 *The Argus*, 12 February 1942, p.3.
38 McDermott, *Australian History for Dummies*, p.319.
39 Quoted in John Edwards, *John Curtin's War, Volume 1*, Penguin Random House, Melbourne, 2017, p.423.
40 S.J. Butlin and C.B. Schedvin, *War Economy, 1942–45*, Australian War Memorial, Canberra, 1977, p.340.
41 Hirst, *Looking for Australia*, p.194.
42 Geoffrey Blainey, *The Steel Master: The Life of Essington Lewis*, Sun Books, Melbourne, 1971, p.154.
43 Quoted in David Day, *John Curtin: A Life*, HarperCollins, Sydney, 1999, p.462.
44 David Horner, 'MacArthur: An Australian Perspective', in William M. Leary (ed.), *MacArthur and the American Century*, University of Nebraska Press, Lincoln, 2001, p.112.
45 Quoted in Peter Edwards, 'Curtin, Macarthur and the "Surrender of Sovereignty": A historiographical assessment', *Australian Journal of International Affairs*, 2001, vol.55, no.2, pp.175–85.
46 Geoffrey Blainey, *The Story of Australia's People: The Rise and Rise of a New Australia*, Penguin Random House, Sydney, 2020, p.317.
47 'Kokoda Trail campaign', Australian War Memorial, Canberra, www.awm.gov.au/collection/E84663
48 Quoted in Day, *John Curtin*, p.427.
49 Brett Mason, *Wizards of Oz: How Oliphant and Florey Helped Win the War and Shape the Modern World*, NewSouth Books, Sydney, 2022, prologue.
50 Quoted in Lennard Bickel, *Howard Florey*, Melbourne University Press, Melbourne, 1992.
51 Quoted in Hirst, *Looking for Australia*, p.188.
52 Paul Hasluck, 'Manpower limits on the Australian war effort', Address to the United Service Institution of Western Australia, Perth, 24 May 1990.
53 Horner, *The War Game*, p.251.
54 Darian-Smith, 'World War 2 and post-war reconstruction, 1939–49', in Bashford and Macintyre (eds), *The Cambridge History of Australia, Volume 2*, p.103.
55 Max Hasting, *Nemesis: The Battle for Japan, 1944–45*, William Collins, Sydney, 2009, see chapter 'Australians: "Bludging" and "Mopping Up"'.
56 Ibid., p.372.
57 John Curtin, speech, BBC, 26 May 1944.
58 Ibid.
59 Hirst, *Looking for Australia*, p.196.
60 *Weekend Australian*, 5 July 2025, p.24.
61 *The Age*, 14 July 1945, p.1.

13: The Liberal Revival
1 Sam Reinhardt and Lee Steel, 'A Brief History of Australia's Tax System', *Economic Roundup*, Commonwealth Treasury, Winter 2006.
2 Geoffrey Bolton, *The Oxford History of Australia: Volume 5 – The Middle Way, 1942–1988*, Oxford University Press, Melbourne, 1990, p.12.
3 *Sydney Morning Herald*, 13 November 1942, p.7.
4 Ibid., pp.401–02.
5 Robert Menzies, *The Forgotten People*, Connor Court Publishing, Redland Bay, 2006, see chapter 'The Forgotten People'.
6 Quoted in Kemp, *A Liberal State*, pp.256–57.
7 Judith Brett, *Robert Menzies' Forgotten People*, Melbourne University Press, Melbourne, 2007, Introduction.
8 Robert Menzies, 'Opening Speech to the Canberra Conference', 13 October 1944, NLA MS 4936/6/14.
9 Robert Menzies, 20 August 1946, available online at Museum of Australian Democracy website, electionspeeches.moadoph.gov.au/speeches/1946-robert-menzies

10 *The Argus*, 21 August 1946, p.16.
11 Ian Hancock, *Federal or Permanent? The Federal Organisation of the Liberal Party of Australia, 1944–1965*, Melbourne University Press, Melbourne, 2000, pp.42–43.
12 *The Age*, 13 July 1945, p.2.
13 Sue Martin, *Remembering Ben Chifley: Memories and Stories From His Family and Friends*, Inspiring Publisher, Calwell, 2015, p.221.
14 Chris Wallace, *Political Lives*, UNSW Press, Sydney, 2022, p.133.
15 Martin, *Remembering Ben Chifley*, p.298.
16 Welsh, *Great Southern Land*, p.446.
17 Tom Sheridan, *Division of Labour: Industrial Relations in the Chifley Years, 1945–49*, Oxford University Press, Melbourne, 1989, p.225.
18 David Horner, *The Spy Catchers: The Official History of ASIO: 1949–1963*, Allen & Unwin, Sydney, 2014, p.40.
19 B.A. Santamaria, *Santamaria: A Memoir*, Oxford University Press, Melbourne, 1997, p.66.
20 Ibid., p.30.
21 Gwenda Tavan, *The Long, Slow Death of White Australia*, Scribe Publications, Melbourne, 2005, p.33.
22 Stuart Macintyre, *Australia's Boldest Experiment: War and Reconstruction in the 1940s*, NewSouth Books, Sydney, 2015, p.467.
23 Quoted in Macintyre, *Australia's Boldest Experiment*.
24 Ibid.
25 *The Herald*, 27 September 1947, p.1.
26 *The Courier-Mail* (Qld), 18 August 1947, p.1.
27 Quoted in Martin, *Robert Menzies: A Life, Vol. 2*, p.79.
28 *Canberra Times*, 27 October 1949, p.2.
29 Bolton, *The Oxford History of Australia: Volume 5*, p.75.
30 Phillip Deery, 'Communism, security and the cold war', *Journal of Australian Studies*, 1997, vol.21, issue 54–55, p.169.
31 *Sydney Morning Herald*, 18 February 1946, p.4.
32 *Sun News-Pictorial*, 13 March 1948.
33 Robert Menzies, Second Reading Speech, Communist Dissolution Bill 1950, 27 April 1950, CPD, 1994.
34 *The Herald*, 18 May 1950, p.3.
35 Quoted in Martin, *Robert Menzies: A Life, Vol. 2*, p.154.
36 *The Argus*, 7 June 1943, p.5.
37 Keneally, *Australians: A Short History*, p.911.
38 *News* (Adelaide), 10 September 1954, p.1.
39 *Sydney Morning Herald*, 6 October 1954, p.1.
40 John Murphy, *Evatt, A Life*, NewSouth Books, Sydney, 2016, p.352.
41 Quoted in Martin, *Robert Menzies: A Life, Vol. 2*, p.310.
42 Frank Chamberlain interview with Mel Pratt, Mel Pratt Collection, National Library of Australia.
43 *The Argus*, 26 December 1955, p.4.

14: The Age of Menzies
1 Sir Robert Menzies, 'The Foundations of Australian Liberalism', Speech to the Liberal Party of Australia (Western Australian Division), Perth, 12 May 1970.
2 Quoted in T.R. Frame, *The Life and Death of Harold Holt*, Allen & Unwin, Sydney, 2005, p.66.
3 Ross Walker, *Harold Holt, Always One Step Further*, La Trobe University Press, Melbourne, 2022, p.106.
4 *Sydney Morning Herald*, 11 January 1950, p.2.
5 *Sydney Morning Herald*, 10 February 1949, p.1.
6 Tavan, *The Long, Slow Death of White Australia*, p.104.
7 Nino Culotta (pseudonym of John O'Grady), *They're A Weird Mob*, Ure Smith, Sydney, 1959, p.203.
8 Ibid., p.202.
9 Andrew Markus and Margaret Taft, 'Postwar immigration and assimilation: A reconceptualisation', *Australian Historical Studies*, 2015, vol.26, no.2, p.240.

10   Eric Sparke, 'Hudson, Sir William (1896 – 1978)', *Australian Dictionary of Biography, Volume 14*, Melbourne University Press, Melbourne, 1996.

11   Paul Hasluck, *Mucking About: An Autobiography*, University of Western Australia Press, Perth, 1994.

12   Quoted in Russell McGregor, 'Avoiding "Aborigines": Paul Hasluck and the Northern Territory welfare ordinance, 1953', *Australian Journal of Politics and History*, vol.51, no.4, pp.518–19.

13   Robert Porter, *Paul Hasluck: A Political Biography*, University of Western Australia Press, Perth, 1993, p.209.

14   Ibid., p.208.

15   Ibid., p.210.

16   Quoted in McGregor, 'Avoiding "Aborigines": Paul Hasluck and the Northern Territory welfare ordinance, 1953', p.516.

17   John Murphy, *Imagining the Fifties: Private Sentiment and Political Culture in Menzies' Australia*, UNSW Press, Sydney, 2000, p.172.

18   Ibid.

19   Geoffrey Bolton, *Paul Hasluck: A Life*, University of Western Australia Publishing, Perth, 2014, p.250.

20   Flood, *The Original Australians*, p.280.

21   Warren Mundine, *In Black & White: Race, Politics and Changing Australia*, Pantera Press, Sydney, 2018, p.28.

22   See Sitarani Kerin, *'Doctor Do-Good?' Charles Duguid and Aboriginal Politics, 1930s–1970s*, PhD thesis, Australian National University, 2004, Part III, chap.5.

23   Jeremy Long, *The Go-Betweens: Patrol Officers in Aboriginal Affairs Administration in the Northern Territory 1936–1974*, North Australia Research Unit, Australian National University, Canberra, 1992, p.84.

24   *The Age*, 3 September 1951, p.1.

25   Robert Menzies, *The Forgotten People: And Other Studies in Democracy*, Angus & Robertson, Sydney, 1943, see chap.10.

26   Ibid., p.79.

27   Martin, *Robert Menzies: A Life, Vol. 2*, p.157.

28   Quoted in Alan Watt, *The Evolution of Australian Foreign Policy, 1938–1965*, Cambridge University Press, Melbourne, 1968, p.301.

29   J. Wilcynski, 'The economics and politics of wheat exports to China', *The Australian Quarterly*, June 1965, vol.37, no.2, p.44.

30   David Kemp, *A Liberal State*, The Miegunyah Press, Melbourne, 2021, p.503.

31   Mikayla Novak, 'The Condition of the People', in John Nethercote (ed.), *Menzies: The Shaping of Modern Australia*, Connor Court Publishing, Redland Bay, 2016.

32   Mike Berry, 'Unravelling the "Australian housing solution": the post-war years', *Housing, Theory, and Society*, 1999, 16, pp.108–9.

33   Macintyre, *A Concise History of Australia*, Cambridge University Press, Melbourne, 2016, p.209.

34   Menzies, *The Forgotten People*, chap.1.

35   Bob Bessant, 'Robert Gordon Menzies and education in Australia', *Melbourne Studies in Education*, November 2006, vol.47, nos.1&2, p.180.

36   *Canberra Times*, 15 May 1962, p.3.

37   Robert Menzies, *The Measure of the Years*, Cassell Australia, North Melbourne, 1970, p.93.

38   Robert Menzies, Federal Election 1963, see pmtranscripts.pmc.gov.au/release/transcript-853

39   Robert Menzies, 'First Baillieu Lecture: The interdependence of political and industrial leadership in the modern state', 6 July 1964.

40   Ibid.

41   Ibid.

15: Talkers and Doers

1   A term coined by Robert Menzies. See Allan Gyngell, *Fear of Abandonment: Australia in the World Since 1942*, La Trobe University Press, Melbourne, 2017, chap.3.

2 David Kemp, *Society and Electoral Behaviour in Australia*, University of Queensland Press, Brisbane, 1978, p.313.
3 Donald Aitkin and Michael Kahan, Australian National Political Attitudes Survey, Australian National University, Research School of Social Science, 1967.
4 Paul Keating, *The End of Certainty: The Story of the 1980s*, Allen & Unwin, Sydney, 1992, p.32.
5 L.F. Crisp, *Australian National Government*, Longman, Croydon, 1970, p.187.
6 Arthur Calwell, *Be Just and Fear Not*, Lloyd O'Neil, Hawthorn, 1972, p.263.
7 Quoted in Jenny Hocking, *Gough Whitlam: A Moment in History*, The Miegunyah Press, Melbourne, 2008, p.198.
8 Ibid., p.199.
9 Paul Hasluck, *The Chance of Politics*, Text Publishing, Melbourne, 1997, p.199.
10 Graham Freudenberg, *A Certain Grandeur: Gough Whitlam's Life in Politics*, Viking, Melbourne, 2009, Introduction.
11 Judith Brett, 'The Menzies Era, 1950–66', in Bashford and Macintyre (eds), *The Cambridge History of Australia: Volume 2*, p.121.
12 Peter Edwards, 'Australia and the Vietnam War: 50 years on', *Australian Strategic Policy Institute*, 20 February 2020.
13 *Canberra Times*, 26 November 1968, p.2.
14 Geoffrey Bolton, *The Oxford History of Australia, Volume 5: The Middle Way, 1942–1988*, Oxford University Press, Melbourne, 1988, p.121.
15 Quoted in Ross Walker, *Harold Holt: Always One Step Further*, La Trobe University Press, Collingwood, 2022, p.160.
16 Quoted in Tavan, *The Long, Slow Death of White Australia*, p.166.
17 Quoted in Nicolas Peterson and Will Sanders, *Citizenship and Indigenous Australians: Changing Conceptions and Possibilities*, Cambridge University Press, Melbourne, 1998, p.123.
18 Bain Attwood and Andrew Marcus, *The 1967 Referendum: Race, Power and the Australian Constitution*, Aboriginal Studies Press, Canberra, 2007, p.49.
19 Angela Burger, *Neville Bonner, A Biography*, Macmillan, South Melbourne, 1979, p.45.
20 Burger, *Neville Bonner*, p.51.
21 Ibid.
22 Attwood and Marcus, *The 1967 Referendum*, p.56.
23 Ibid., p.57.
24 Tom Frame, *The Life and Death of Harold Holt*, Allen & Unwin, Sydney, 2005, p.250.
25 Patrick Mullins, *Tiberius with a Telephone: The Life and Stories of William McMahon*, Scribe, Melbourne, 2018, chap.46.
26 Hank Nelson, 'Liberation: The end of Australian rule in Papua New Guinea', *The Journal of Pacific History*, 2000, vol.35, no.3, pp.277–78.
27 David Chanoff and Doan Van Toai, *Vietnam: A Portrait of Its People at War*, J.B. Tauris & Co., London, 1996, p.108.
28 Ibid., p.25.
29 Michael Keating, 'Evolution of macroeconomic strategy since WW2', *The Cambridge Economic History of Australia*, Cambridge University Press, Melbourne, 2014, p.446.
30 Whitlam, *The Whitlam Government, 1972–1975*, p.191.
31 David Kemp, *Consent of the People 1966–2022: Human Dignity Through Freedom and Equality*, The Miegunyah Press, Melbourne, 2022, p.122.
32 Hasluck, *The Chance of Politics*, p.214.
33 Alan Reid, *The Whitlam Venture*, Hill of Content, Melbourne, 1976, p.1.
34 *Canberra Times*, 13 September 1975, p.1.
35 Quoted in *The Eleventh*, ep.5, 'Deadlock', ABC podcast, 2020.
36 *Canberra Times*, 4 November 1975, p.2.
37 Paul Kelly and Troy Bramston, *The Dismissal: In the Queen's Name*, Viking, Melbourne, 2015, p.174.
38 *Canberra Times*, 4 November 1975, p.7.
39 Ibid.

40 John Kerr, *Matters for Judgment: An Autobiography*, Aprolon, Melbourne, 1978, p.358.
41 Ibid.
42 Kelly and Bramston, *The Dismissal*, p.142.

16: Opening the Doors
1   Malcolm Fraser, 'Towards 2000: Challenge to Australia', Alfred Deakin Lecture, 20 July 1971, library.unimelb.edu.au/asc/collections/highlights/collections/malcolmfraser/resources/postparliamentspeeches/towards-2000-challenge-to-australia
2   *Canberra Times*, 25 October 1976, p.3.
3   Malcolm Fraser and Margaret Simons, *Malcolm Fraser: The Political Memoirs*, Melbourne University Press, Melbourne, 2010, p.51.
4   Ian Harper, 'Bank deregulation in Australia: choice and diversity, gainers and losers', Reserve Bank of Australia, RBA Annual Conference 1991.
5   Stephen Grenville, 'The evolution of financial deregulation', Reserve Bank of Australia, RBA Annual Conference 1991.
6   *Commonwealth Budget Papers 2023–24*, Budget Paper No.1, Statement 11: Historical Australian Government Data, p.412.
7   Philip Ayres, *Malcolm Fraser: A Biography*, William Heinemann Australia, Melbourne, 1987, pp.304–5.
8   Peter Edwards, *Australia and the Vietnam War*, NewSouth Books, Sydney, 2014, p.257.
9   Tavan, *The Long, Slow Death of White Australia*, p.205.
10 Geoffrey Blainey, *A Shorter History of Australia*, Vintage Books, Sydney, 2000, p.259.
11 Fraser and Simons, *Malcolm Fraser*, p.420.
12 Kemp, *Consent of the People 1966–2022*, p.198.
13 McDermott, *Australian History for Dummies*, p.392.
14 Ibid, p.393.
15 See Hasluck's comments in *Goulburn Evening Post*, 26 October 1954, p.2.
16 Paul Hasluck, *Shades of Darkness: Aboriginal Affairs, 1925–1965*, Melbourne University Press, Melbourne, 1988, p.149.
17 John Hyde, *Dry: In Defence of Economic Freedom*, Institute of Public Affairs, Melbourne, 2002, p.178.
18 David Kemp, 'Liberalism and Conservatism in Australia Since 1944', in Brian Head and James Walter (eds), *Intellectual Movements and Australian Society*, Oxford University Press, Melbourne, 1988, p.340.
19 Ibid.
20 Paul Kelly, *The End of Certainty: The Story of the 1980s*, Allen & Unwin, Sydney, 1992, p.41.
21 John Howard, *Lazarus Rising*, HarperCollins, Sydney, 2011, p.146.
22 Ibid., p.364.
23 Fraser and Simons, *Malcolm Fraser*, p.371.
24 *Canberra Times*, 24 September 1980, p.16.
25 *The Bulletin*, 15 April 1980, p.22.
26 Fraser and Simons, *Malcolm Fraser*, p.371.
27 *Canberra Times*, 9 February 1983, p.20.
28 John Phillips, 'Australia's Floating Dollar', Address to the Australian Institute of Bankers, 7 March 1984, published in *Collected Speeches of M.J. Phillips, Deputy Governor, Reserve Bank of Australia 1987–1992*, Reserve Bank of Australia, Sydney, 1993.
29 Wray Vamplew (ed.), *Australians: Historical Statistics*, Fairfax, Syme & Weldon Associates, 1987, p.201.
30 Hyde, *Dry*, p.141.
31 Ibid., p.31.
32 *The Age*, 11 September 1984, p.1.
33 *The Age*, 11 June 1984, p.1.
34 Kerry O'Brien, *Keating*, Allen & Unwin, Sydney, 2015, p.196.
35 Ibid., p.206.

36 Bob Hawke, *The Hawke Memoirs*, Heinemann, Melbourne, 1994, p.99.
37 Ibid.
38 Neil Lawrence, *The Stump Jumpers: A New Breed of Australians*, Hale & Iremonger, Melbourne, 1985, p.44.
39 Alexander Ballantyne, Jonathan Hambur, Ivan Roberts and Michelle Wright, 'Australia's Experience With Financial Reform', Reserve Bank of Australia, Research Discussion Paper 2014–10, 2014.
40 Trevor Sykes, *The Bold Riders: Behind Australia's Corporate Collapses*, Allen & Unwin, Sydney, 1994, p.2.
41 Australian Bureau of Statistics, 'Changing female employment over time', Labour Force, Australia, February 2021, www.abs.gov.au/articles/changing-female-employment-over-time
42 Lawrence, *Stump Jumpers*, p.224.
43 Richard Broome, *Aboriginal Australians*, Allen & Unwin, Sydney, 2019, p.256.

17: Consolidation
1 *Sydney Morning Herald*, 27 January 1988.
2 Ibid.
3 *Australian Star*, 8 August 1889, p.4.
4 *Sydney Morning Herald*, 27 January 1988.
5 Committee to Advise on Australia's Immigration Policies, *Immigration: A Commitment to Australia*, Australian Government Publishing Service, Canberra, 1988, p.1.
6 Ibid.
7 Ibid., p.2.
8 *The Australian*, 9 August 1988.
9 *Sydney Morning Herald*, 11 January 1988, p.1.
10 Australian Bureau of Statistics, *Australian Year Book: 1988*, 1300.0.
11 *Migration Action*, vol.X, no.3, pp.34–36.
12 Peter Walsh, 'Cabinet dynamics of immigration policy', *People and Place*, vol.2, no.2, Centre for Population and Urban Research, Monash University, Clayton, 1994, p.28.
13 *Future Directions: It's Time for Plain Thinking*, Liberal Party of Australia, 1988.
14 Bob Hawke, Speech at Lone Pine Ceremony, Gallipoli, 25 April 1990.
15 Hawke, *The Hawke Memoirs*, p.204.
16 O'Brien, *Keating*, p.255.
17 Kemp, *Consent of the People 1966–2022*, p.276.
18 Quoted in Troy Bramston, *Paul Keating: The Big Picture Leader*, Scribe Publications, Brunswick, p.348.
19 Paul Kelly, *The End of Certainty*, p.617.
20 Michael Pusey, *Economic Rationalism in Canberra*, Canberra University Press, Canberra, 1991.
21 Norman Abjorenson, *John Hewson: A Biography*, Lothian Books, Melbourne, 1993, p.38.
22 Paul Kelly, *The March of Patriots: The Struggle for Modern Australia*, Melbourne University Press, Carlton, 2009, p.43.
23 Don Watson, *Recollections of a Bleeding Heart: A Portrait of Paul Keating PM*, Random House, Sydney, 2002.
24 *The Age*, 20 December 1991, p.4.
25 Robert Menzies, House of Representatives, Commonwealth Parliament, 21 September 1965.
26 Paul Keating, Redfern Park address, 10 December 1992, in Pamela Robson (ed.), *Great Australian Speeches*, Murdoch Books, Sydney, 2009, p.174.
27 Allan Gyngell, *Fear of Abandonment: Australia in the World Since 1942*, La Trobe University Press, Melbourne, 2017, p.283.
28 Kelly, *The March of Patriots*, p.7.
29 Ibid., p.244.
30 Productivity Commission, *International Benchmarking of the Australian Waterfront*, Research Report, 1998, pp.13–14.
31 Peter Reith, *The Reith Papers*, Melbourne University Press, Melbourne, 2015, p.138.

32 Macintyre, *A Concise History of Australia*, Cambridge University Press, Melbourne, 2020, p.289.
33 Ibid.
34 Tony Abbott, *Battlelines*, Melbourne University Press, Melbourne, 2009, p.73.
35 David Alexander, '"Never ever": Introducing the GST', in Tom Frame (ed.), *The Howard Government, Volume II, Back from the Brink: 1997–2001*, UNSW Press, Sydney, 2018, p.142.
36 Glenn Stevens, 'The Asian Crisis: A retrospective', Reserve Bank of Australia, Address to The Anika Foundation Luncheon Supported by Australian Business Economists and Macquarie Bank, 18 July 2007.
37 Kelly, *The March of Patriots*, p.489.
38 See *The Australian*, 29 September 1993; *Sydney Morning Herald*, 8 February 1994.
39 Lawrence Dallaglio, *More Blood, Sweat and Beers: World Cup Rugby Tales*, Simon & Schuster, London, 2011, p.194.
40 Laurence Billiet (director) in collaboration with Stephen Page and Bangarra Dance Theatre, 2021, *Freeman*, General Strike and Matchbox Pictures, www.freemanthefilm.com

18: Drifting Backwards

1 The Hon. Peter Costello MP, 'National Accounts – March Quarter 2007', Press Release, 6 June 2007, ministers.treasury.gov.au/ministers/peter-costello-1996/media-releases/national-accounts-march-quarter-2007
2 Australian Bureau of Statistics, 'Migration: Permanent additions to Australia's population', in *Australian Social Trends*, 2007, 4102.0.
3 Janet Phillips and Harriet Spinks, 'Boat arrivals in Australia since 1976', *Parliament of Australia – Department of Parliamentary Services*, 26 May 2010.
4 Quoted in 'Gillard rules out imposing carbon tax', *Sydney Morning Herald*, 17 August 2010.
5 Kevin Rudd, 'Prime Minister's prizes for science', 28 October 2009, pmtranscripts.pmc.gov.au/release/transcript-16882
6 'Double-lung recipient misses critical check-up because of Queensland border closure', ABC News, 19 August 2020.
7 NSW Reconstruction Authority, 'Hawkesbury-Nepean River Flood Study', Overview, June 2024.
8 George Pell's obituary to B.A. Santamaria, *AD2000*, vol.11, no.3, April 1998, p.10.

Bibliography

General histories of Australia

Alan Atkinson, *The Europeans in Australia: A History,* Volumes 1 & 2, UNSW Press, Sydney, 2016 Press

Alison Bashford and Stuart Macintyre (eds), *The Cambridge History of Australia,* Volumes 1 & 2, Cambridge University Press, Melbourne, 2013

Geoffrey Blainey, *A Shorter History of Australia,* Vintage Books, Sydney, 2000

Frank Bongiorno, *Dreamers and Schemers: A Political History of Australia,* Black Inc., Melbourne, 2022

Frank Crowley (ed.), *A New History of Australia,* William Heinemann, Melbourne, 1974

W.K. Hancock, *Australia,* Ernest Benn, 1930

John Hirst, *Looking for Australia: Historical Essays,* Black Inc., Melbourne, 2010

——, *Australian History in 7 Questions,* Black Inc., Melbourne, 2014

Thomas Keneally, *Australians: A Short History,* Allen & Unwin, Sydney, 2016

Stuart Macintyre, *A Concise History of Australia,* Cambridge University Press, Melbourne, 2016

Alex McDermott, *Australian History for Dummies,* John Wiley & Sons, Melbourne, 2022

Alan McLean, *Why Australia Prospered,* Princeton University Press, New Jersey, 2013

Mark Peel and Christina Twomey, *A History of Australia,* Bloomsbury Publishing, Sydney, 2017

John Rickard, *A Cultural History of Australia,* Monash University Publishing, 2017

Frank Welsh, *Great Southern Land: A New History of Australia,* Allen Lane, Sydney, 2004

Aboriginal Australia

Geoffrey Blainey, *The Story of Australia's People: The Rise and Fall of Ancient Australia*, Penguin Random House, Sydney, 2015

Richard Broome, *Aboriginal Australians*, 5th edn, Allen & Unwin, Sydney, 2019

Josephine Flood, *The Original Australians: The Story of the Aboriginal People*, Allen & Unwin, Sydney, 2019

Billy Griffiths, *Deep Time Dreaming: Uncovering Ancient Australia*, Black Inc., Melbourne, 2018

W.E.H. Stanner, *The Dreaming & Other Essays*, Black Inc., Melbourne, 2009

Peter Sutton and Keryn Walshe, *Farmers or Hunter-Gatherers? The Dark Emu Debate*, Melbourne University Press, Carlton, 2021

Early Colonial Australia

Bain Attwood, *Empire and the Making of Native Title: Sovereignty, Property and Indigenous People*, Cambridge University Press, Melbourne, 2020

James Boyce, *1835: The Founding of Melbourne and the Conquest of Australia*, Black Inc., Melbourne, 2011

Margaret Cameron-Ash, *Beating France to Botany Bay: The Race to Found Australia*, Quadrant Books, Sydney, 2022

Alan Frost, *Botany Bay and the First Fleet: The Real Story*, Black Inc., Melbourne, 2011

D.R. Hainsworth, *Builders and Adventurers: The Traders and the Emergence of the Colony 1788–1821*, Cassell Australia, Melbourne, 1968

——, *The Sydney Traders: Simeon Lord and His Contemporaries 1788–1821*, Cassell Australia, Melbourne, 1972

David Hill, *1788*, William Heinemann, North Sydney, 2008

John Hirst, *Freedom on the Fatal Shore: Australia's First Colony*, Black Inc., Melbourne, 2008

Robert Hughes, *The Fatal Shore: A History of the Transportation of Convicts to Australia, 1787–1868*, Vintage Books, London, 2003

Grace Karskens, *The Colony: A History of Early Sydney*, Allen & Unwin, Sydney, 2009

David Kemp, *The Land of Dreams: How Australians Won Their Freedom, 1788–1860*, The Miegunyah Press, Carlton, 2018

Stephen H. Roberts, *The Squatting Age in Australia 1835–1847*, Melbourne University Press, Melbourne, 1935

Portia Robinson, *The Hatch and the Brood of Time: A Study of the First Generation of Native-born White Australians, 1788–1829*, Oxford University Press, Melbourne, 1985

Barry Stone, *The Squatters: The Story of Australia's Pastoral Pioneers*, Allen & Unwin, Sydney, 2019

Mark Tedeschi, *Murder at Myall Creek: The Trial That Defined a Nation*, Simon & Schuster, Sydney, 2016

Adam Wakeling, *A House of Commons for a Den of Thieves: Australia's Journey from Penal Colony to Democracy*, Australian Scholarly Publishing, North Melbourne, 2020

Russell Ward, *Finding Australia: The History of Australia to 1821*, Heinemann Educational Australia, 1987

Self-government to federation

Judith Brett, *From Secret Ballot to Democracy Sausage: How Australia Got Compulsory Voting*, Text Publishing, Melbourne, 2019

Peter Cochrane, *Colonial Ambition: Foundations of Australian Democracy*, Melbourne University Press, Melbourne, 2006

Margaret Kiddle, *Men of Yesterday: A Social History of the Western District of Victoria, 1834–1890*, Melbourne University Press, Melbourne, 1962

Stuart Macintyre, *A Colonial Liberalism: The Lost World of Three Victorian Visionaries*, Oxford University Press, Melbourne, 1991

Ronald Norris, *The Emergent Commonwealth – Australian Federation: Expectations and Fulfilment 1889–1910*, Melbourne University Press, Melbourne, 1975

John Rickard, *Class and Politics: New South Wales, Victoria and the Early Commonwealth: 1890–1910*, ANU Press, Canberra, 1976

Geoffrey Serle, *The Golden Age*, Melbourne University Press, Melbourne, 1963

Clare Wright, *You Daughters of Freedom: The Australians Who Won the Vote and Inspired the World*, Text Publishing, Melbourne, 2018

John Manning Ward, *Colonial Self-government: The British Experience 1759–1856*, University of Toronto Press, 1976

Australia in the 20th century

Joan Beaumont, *Australia's Great Depression*, Allen & Unwin, Sydney, 2022

——, *Broken Nation: Australians in the Great War*, Allen & Unwin, Sydney, 2013

Judith Brett, *Australian Liberals and the Moral Middle Class: From Alfred Deakin to John Howard*, Cambridge University Press, Melbourne, 2003

Matthew Cunningham, *Mobilising the Masses: Populist Conservative Movements in Australia and New Zealand During the Great Depression*, ANU Press, Canberra, 2022

Jeffrey Grey, *A Military History of Australia*, Cambridge University Press, Melbourne, 2008

Paul Hasluck, *The Government and the People, 1939–1941*, Halstead Press, Sydney, 1965

David Horner, *The Spy Catchers: The Official History of ASIO: 1949–1963*, Allen & Unwin, Sydney, 2014

——, *The War Game: Australian War Leadership from Gallipoli to Iraq*, Allen & Unwin, Sydney, 2022

John Hyde, *Dry: In Defence of Economic Freedom*, Institute of Public Affairs, Melbourne, 2002

Paul Kelly and Troy Bramston, *The Dismissal: In the Queen's Name*, Viking, Melbourne, 2015

David Kemp, *Consent of the People 1966–2022: Human Dignity Through Freedom and Equality*, The Miegunyah Press, Melbourne, 2022

——, *A Democratic Nation 1901–1925*, The Miegunyah Press, Melbourne, 2019

——, *A Liberal State*, The Miegunyah Press, Melbourne, 2021

Stuart Macintyre, *Australia's Boldest Experiment: War and Reconstruction in the 1940s*, NewSouth Books, Sydney, 2015

Robert Manne, *The Petrov Affair*, Text Publishing, Melbourne, 2004

Brett Mason, *Wizards of Oz: How Oliphant and Florey Helped Win the War and Shape the Modern World*, NewSouth Books, Sydney, 2022

Ross McMullin, *The Light on the Hill: The Australian Labor Party 1891–1991*, Oxford University Press, Melbourne, 1991

Robert Menzies, *The Forgotten People*, Connor Court Publishing, Redland Bay, 2006

David Potts, *The Myth of the Great Depression*, Scribe Publications, Melbourne, 2006

Alan Reid, *The Whitlam Venture*, Hill of Content, Melbourne, 1976

Peter Stanley, *Invading Australia: Japan and the Battle for Australia, 1942*, Penguin Books, Sydney, 2008

Gwenda Tavan, *The Long, Slow Death of White Australia*, Scribe Publications, Melbourne, 2005

Australian states

Geoffrey Blainey, *A History of Victoria*, Cambridge University Press, Melbourne, 2006

Geoffrey Bolton, *Land of Vision and Mirage: Western Australia Since 1826*, University of Western Australia Press, Perth, 2008

Ross Fitzgerald, *Made in Queensland: A New History*, University of Queensland Press, Brisbane, 2009

Beverley Kingston, *A History of New South Wales,* Cambridge University Press, Port Melbourne, 2006

Lloyd Robson, *A Short History of Tasmania*, Oxford University Press, Melbourne, 1985

Paul Sendzuik and Robert Foster, *A History of South Australia*, Cambridge University Press, Melbourne, 2018

Biographies

Alan Atkinson, *Elizabeth and John: The Macarthurs of Elizabeth Farm*, NewSouth Books, Sydney, 2022

Geoffrey Blainey, *The Steel Master: The Life of Essington Lewis*, Sun Books, Melbourne, 1971

Geoffrey Bolton, *Edmund Barton, The One Man for the Job*, Allen & Unwin, Sydney, 2000

——, *Paul Hasluck: A Life*, University of Western Australia Publishing, Perth, 2014

David Day, *John Curtin: A Life*, HarperCollins, Sydney, 1999

Cecil Edwards, *Bruce of Melbourne: A Man of Two Worlds*, Heinemann, London, 1965

Malcolm Ellis, *Lachlan Macquarie: His Life, Adventures and Times*, Angus & Robertson, Sydney, 1958

Graham Freudenberg, *A Certain Grandeur: Gough Whitlam's Life in Politics*, Viking, Melbourne, 2009

Alan Frost, *Arthur Phillip: His Voyaging*, Oxford University Press, Melbourne, 1987

J.A. La Nauze, *Alfred Deakin: A Biography*, two volumes, Melbourne University Press, Melbourne, 1965

A.W. Martin, *Henry Parkes: A Biography*, Melbourne University Press, Melbourne, 1964

——, *Robert Menzies: A Life, Vol. 1*, Melbourne University Press, Melbourne, 1993

Sean Scalmer, *Democratic Adventurer: Graham Berry and the Making of Australian Politics*, Monash University Press, Melbourne, 2020

Geoffrey Serle, *John Monash: A Biography*, Melbourne University Press, Melbourne, 1982

Andrew Tink, *William Charles Wentworth: Australia's Greatest Native Son*, Allen & Unwin, Sydney, 2009

Memoirs/Diaries

Tony Abbott, *Battlelines*, Melbourne University Press, Melbourne, 2009

A.G. Austin (ed.), *The Webbs' Australian Diary 1898*, Sir Issac Pitman & Sons, Melbourne, 1965

Arthur Calwell, *Be Just and Fear Not*, Lloyd O'Neil, Hawthorn, 1972

David Collins, *An Account of the English Colony in New South Wales, 1798*, London

James Cook, *Captain Cook's Journal During the First Voyage Round the World Made in H.M. Bark 'Endeavour'*, Captain W.J.L. Wharton (ed.), Elliot Stock, London, 1839

Malcolm Fraser and Margaret Simons, *Malcolm Fraser: The Political Memoirs*, Melbourne University Press, Melbourne, 2010

Alexander Harris, *Settler and Convicts: Recollections of Sixteen Years' Labour in the Australian Backwoods by an Immigrant Mechanic*, W. Clowes & Sons, London, 1847

Bob Hawke, *The Hawke Memoirs*, Heinemann, Melbourne, 1994

John Howard, *Lazarus Rising*, HarperCollins, Sydney, 2011

William Howitt, *Land, Labour and Gold; or, Two years in Victoria: with visits to Sydney and Van Diemen's Land*, Ticknor & Fields, Boston, 1854

Elizabeth Macquarie, *Diary of Elizabeth Macquarie*, Lachlan and Elizabeth Macquarie Archive online, Macquarie University

Henry Parkes, *Fifty Years in the Making of Australian History*, Longmans, Green and Co., London, 1892

B.A. Santamaria, *Santamaria: A Memoir*, Oxford University Press, Melbourne, 1997

Watkin Tench, *Watkin Tench's 1788*, Tim Flannery (ed.), Text Publishing, Melbourne, 2009

Don Watson, *Recollections of a Bleeding Heart: A Portrait of Paul Keating PM*, Random House, Sydney, 2002

Index

Note: Military ranks and titles are ignored in filing.

TERRA DOS PAPOS

NEW G

HOLLANDIA

TROPIC

NOVA

SOUTHERN CONTINENT

Stadt House at Amsterdam